Rolling Stoned

Rolling Stoned

Andrew Loog Oldham

Vancouver, British Columbia
Because Entertainment Inc., Canada
2013

Cataloguing-in-Publication:

Oldham, Andrew Loog, 1944-
    Rolling Stoned / Andrew Loog Oldham.
    p. : ill., ports. ; cm.
    ISBN 978-0-9920275-0-6
    1. Oldham, Andrew Loog, 1944- . 2. Rock musicians - Management - Great
Britain - Biography. 3. Rock groups - Management - Great Britain - Biography.
4. Artists' representatives - Great Britain - Biography. 5. Concert agents - Great
Britain - Biography. 6. Rolling Stones. 7. Beatles. 8. Faithfull, Marianne, 1946- . I. Title.
    ML429.O43 A3 2013
    781.66092 - dc22   AACR2

First Canadian print edition.

Published originally as a Gegensatz Press e-book in the U.S.A. in 2011.
ISBN 978-1-933237-30-5 (Amazon Kindle).
ISBN 978-1-933237-33-6 (Smashwords Epub).

Earlier versions of portions of this work appeared in *Stoned: A Memoir of London in the 1960s* (2000) and *2Stoned* (2002).

Andrew Loog Oldham asserts his moral and legal rights to be identified as the author of this book.

Front cover design by Sarah von der Luft.
Editing, layout, back cover, and interior design by Gegensatz Press.
Back cover photo by Betina La Plante.

All illustrations either from the public domain or used with gratitude from the private collections of Maureen Cleave, Dr. Neil Clifton, Bob Gruen, Richard Havers, Betina La Plante, Gered Mankowitz, the Monterey International Pop Festival Foundation, Not Fade Away Gallery <NFAgallery.com> (copyright ©2269 Productions, Inc.), Andrew Loog Oldham, Genya Ravan, Mick Rock, Chris Stamp (photo by Sally Burgess), Philip Townsend, the Trinifold Archive, and Allan Warren.

CONTENTS

PREFACE

I wrote *Stoned* and *2Stoned* between 1996 and 1999. Or more accurately, that's when I rewrote them. I had been writing them most of my life, if only in my mind - and is not writing thinking on paper?

As a tween growing up in postwar London I enjoyed a fantasy life that Walter Mitty might have envied. Saturday mornings at the "pictures" somewhat compensated for the rather thin gruel served up on TV at the time. This weekly ritual at the Odeon Swiss Cottage N.W.3 was more inspiring than educational. Flash Gordon and Superman made sure we'd be back the following week, because no sooner was one crisis bravely confronted than another arose in the last five minutes of every episode. Within a year I'd found a way to slip in the back door of this same and various other local cinemas as my tastes moved toward the not altogether wholesome, brought on by ambition of both mind and groin. My first female crushes were Jean Seberg and Dolores Hart; for lust I settled upon Rhonda Fleming and Arlene Dahl. Their 1956 U.S. attempt at film *noir*, *Slightly Scarlet*, with John Payne, showed me the side of town I wished to walk on. I found role models in the surliness of Tony Curtis, the assertiveness of Laurence Harvey, and the teenage angst of James Dean. For me these actors were not portraying fictional characters, but rather demonstrating life as it was meant to be lived.

A year or so later, the same cinemas would risk destruction at the hands of crazed teenagers who adopted *The Girl Can't Help It* as their own *Ten Commandments*, a rock 'n' roll epic in which Eddie Cochran, Gene Vincent, and Little Richard led the downtrodden youth of Britain out of the desert into a land of music, the mob, jukeboxes, and Jayne Mansfield.

The schools that I'd attended failed to appreciate my higher calling, and both schoolmasters and my mother kept impatiently urging me to settle down and get on with the business of "real life." However, the Rolling Stones and quite a few other artists benefited from my commitment to life in another dimension. I have always thought we become more interesting than we really are by pretending to be somebody who might interest us a little more than we do ourselves.

In 2006 I was invited back to my old public school, Wellingborough - the one that had asked me to leave - to open a new music wing. I realise more than ever how my mother had schemed and plotted the improvement of our lives, including my having been able to go to the school in the first place, and how she should be added to the list of divine hustlers I have known. She passed in 2002. Of course I wish she were still here but am glad at the same time that she is not. These several years later, in addition to my writing, I am a deejay on American satellite radio. I work from my Bogotá home for my pal, Steven Van Zandt, part-time Bruce Springsteen E Street Band guitarist and HBO *Sopranos* mob and cast member, and all-time rock 'n' roll maven. It's a wonderfully safe and productive way of staying in touch with music and its business. My mum would have been proud; it's almost a regular job.

The specific inspiration for *Stoned* and *2Stoned* was a biography of Warhol "superstar" Edie Sedgwick, written by Jean Stein and brilliantly edited by George Plimpton in the form of an oral history. Despite the fact that Edie and her scene held no particular appeal for me, I found the voices describing them to be arranged in something like a literary wall of sound. The interweaving of so many points of view raised a to-the-manor-born trailer-trashy B-list version of Jean Seberg to Joan of Arc heights. The heroine on heroin of *Edie* reminded me of a New York dollish version of Brian Jones and the way the book was put together made Edie/Brian more fascinating than they really were. I also saw it as a true forum, allowing others to tell their truth.

In my world, there are no accidents. A young man from England who was unsure if he was a musician or a journalist, but aspired to both, managed to track me to my adopted home in Bogotá, Colombia, claiming that he wanted to include me in a story about managers that he was writing for the trendy pop culture magazine, *The Face*.

When he turned up unannounced on my doorstep (which was not exactly a tube stop or two away from his home) I was a little put out. But my wife Esther and I opened the door and welcomed the young visitor, then known as Simon Dudfield, from England into my life. He published the magazine piece and hustled me to let him write my biography. I was flattered and intrigued, given that the subject of the proposed biography would be a different Andrew Oldham than the one currently living a day for night existence in an unmaterial world.

I put him off and hit the road, ending up in Seattle at a horrendously haughty bed and breakfast on Capitol Hill. I took myself to bed with a dozen plain white leather-bound folders and began to write. And write. And write. Sometime later, when the more drug soaked passages had been wrung out of the manuscript, what remained became the foundation of *Stoned* and *2Stoned*.

Once again my favourite little criminal, now calling himself Simon Spence, trailed me, this time to Buenos Aires, where I was producing an Argentine rock band, Los Ratones Paranoicos. Give him credit for finding another magazine to pay his way. He wouldn't let up about the fuckin' book that he wanted to write about me and, after I finally agreed, it dawned on me why he had been so insistent: He'd already received quite a handsome advance to deliver an *authorised* biography, which of course he was in no position to guarantee.

If anyone is going to play fast and loose with my reputation, it had better be me, and my would-be biographer's ethics or lack thereof pissed me off. But when I reached the publishers in London to discuss the situation with them and perhaps splash some cold water on their parade, I was told, "Look, Mr, Oldham, we operate on a much more good faith basis than your music business."

I was astonished to hear that in polite literary circles wide boys were welcomed as gentlemen.

"So, if I came in and said I'd been authorised by Mick Jagger or Henry Kissinger to write their autobiographies you'd just take me at my word?" I asked sarcastically. "No letter of consent from Mick or Henry needed? You'd just hand over the money?"

"Well, it is a question of degree. If it were Mr. Jagger or Mr. Kissinger ..."

I got it. They did not mind being taken for a quiet amount, one that could only yell so loud.

I attempted to negotiate a better deal on my own behalf, but the publisher whom my young friend had conned decided they'd rather eat the advance they'd given him than continue under the circumstances.

My bookshelf had swelled to include Graham Greene's autobiographies, George Melly, Nick Tosches, and Richard Price. Also Jim Carroll, Gay Talese, Gore Vidal, Robert Hewison, and Chet Baker.

Then finally I was ready to reread my original master in literature, Anthony Burgess. As influential as the gents mentioned have been on my thinking about biography, Burgess was most significant of all, because he was my *first*. Before I discovered Burgess I had not read much at all, because I was always being *told* to read. My education up to that time had been almost exclusively aural and visual rather than textual.

But in another one of those non-coincidences I had discovered *A Clockwork Orange*, just as the Stones and I were beginning to see ourselves as a tribe with a culture all its own. Keith came along for the ride, binding us more closely than ever together, and Mick kept his friendly aloofness, watching our revelry from a safe social distance, from where he observed and, with the other Glimmer Twin, wrote us all into song. If we were going to play the parts of outcasts from society, Alex and his droogs set us a very high standard. As a "phase" we went through, our immersion in Burgess's dark vision came to be as important as Buddy Holly had been at an earlier stage.

Stoned was published in 2000, followed two years later by *2Stoned*. A decade later, the music business is so dispirited that it no longer waits and wishes for a new Nirvana, let alone a new Beatles. Those of us who created "The Sixties" are now in our sixties and frankly, either the lives we led were not conducive to longevity or a few of us should have realised that it was time to leave the stage. The sixties are a shrinking violet and, as age defies reason and decorum, there has been a stampede of revisionism and unreasonableness about those smashing times. As so much since 2000 or thereabouts has changed, including the fellow travellers about whom I wrote, I thought it appropriate to take a look again and update both books for the times we live in today, when a book no longer needs paper or ink and a record no longer needs a stylus to play.

****

Four sets of hands have been an important part of this triography: Ron Ross, Dave Thompson, Simon Dudfield, and Simon Spence. I'd also like to thank a major fifth, Eric v.d. Luft, for breaching me into the e-world.

Playing in my first band: second row, second from right

INTRODUCTION

It was an English summer, a few years ago. Ex-Rolling Stones bass player Bill Wyman and his lovely Suzanne invited Esther, myself, and an old, old friend, interior decorator Nicky Haslam, out to his Essex mansion for Sunday lunch. Bill and I had been having dinner on occasion the past few of those years, something we had not managed to do the previous forty.

I had never been to this domain, although I did recall Bill buying it in 1968. We had a delightful meal, which was followed by a scrumptious stroll around Bill's grounds, munching on crab apples, and enjoying a perfect English day, the light, the company, and the view.

I had not seen Nicky since the mid-sixties, when he resided in New York and I wished I did. America had had its president slain, not an uncommon occurrence in historical fact, and had had its music industry assassinated the very next year by the British Invasion, led by the Beatles, Herman's Hermits, and the Dave Clark Five. We, the Stones and I, had taken a little longer to find our vinyl legs, arriving later and, save the very idea of the Beatles, staying longer. But, unlike the Beatles, it could be said that the Rolling Stones were merely born in England. They were made in America.

Bill explained to Nicky how he came upon the house and grounds, and how, had he more than a thousand pounds in his bank account in 1968, he could have bought more than twice the land he ended up with. What he ended up with is, of course, not bad at all for a boy from Penge; but a thousand pounds in the bank really does not seem enough for membership in the band that road manager Sam Cutler was already announcing as: "Ladies and Gentlemen, the greatest rock and roll band ever!" or whatever the phrase was. But, as Bill explained, "That's how little money we really had." He turned to me: "You remember how our money was tied up in loans with Allen Klein."

After nosh, I ask Bill, "Has Mick ever been here?"

Bill looks at me in the old way, "Naaa, he's never invited me to his place, why should I invite him to mine?" So ran the social motor of the world's greatest rock 'n' roll band ...

Bill was not a Stone anymore, and I have not seen the

Stones for some years either; the last time was in Seattle in 2005.
My younger son, Max, was attending college in Santa Monica, and
I was in Vancouver, where Esther and I had a second home. We
planned to drive down, see the Stones in Seattle, then drive him in
a fresh set of wheels to Los Angeles and back to school. My older
boy, Sean, could not make it, being at a Yoga retreat in Spain.

The Rolling Stones were playing the Key Arena on Sunday,
October 30. Paul McCartney would play there the following
Thursday, November 3.

We checked into the Hotel Andra on 4th and, after a snack,
strolled down toward the downtown area and the Four Seasons
Hotel, where the boys were. Compared to my first visit, a decade
earlier, I found I now liked Seattle. I liked the drizzle, the pace,
and the people - and it had, after all, been the place where, a dozen
years before, I began this triography.

We announced ourselves. Jagger's personal assistant, Tony
King, came down a few minutes later and joined us in the elevator. It was four o'clock and Charlie Watts had invited us to tea.

"Well, Andrew," said Tony in the elevator.

"Well, Tony," I replied.

"Well, they are ... I mean ... just like the royal family now,
aren't they? I mean, they just are ..."

"And you're the fuckin' lady-in-waiting," I thought, "the
sycophantic diaper changer to the stars, or one of them." I bit my
lip. How could I respond? One, Max was watching me for a reaction; after all, this was a comparison that neither of us had heard.
Two, Tony and I were supposed to be pals. I wasn't sure whether
to laugh or cry. They may be the biggest, longest lasting, very best,
incredibly invincible, pragmatic, truly real, and most profitable
rock 'n' roll band on earth, but royalty? I had hoped that Tony
had been pulling my leg, but the stretched, Bette Davis eyes and
the "I-have-said-the-right-thing" expression on his still very good
looking face did not say, "I was joking." Rather, they invited, "Well,
dear. I'm waiting for your reply."

I guess that's what ladies-in-waiting do, they wait. I must
ask Nicky Haslam the next time I'm in London, I thought, he would
surely know.

I cannot remember how I replied, save that it was a sensible cop-out. But I know I never mentioned Dorian Gray.

The last couple of times we had seen the Stones, they were mixed to magnificent. In Glasgow on the previous tour, they played an 8000-seater of a corrugated roof shed, the Scottish Exhibition and Conference Centre, appallingly set up, perhaps, for Mariah Carey, who would play the place the end of the next month. It was a stand-up audience, not meaning comedians, although in Glasgow there are always more than a few; but 7000 of the 8000 were standing as if in a ballroom, while the other grand were *very* grand, bummed into seats that clung and slinked around three of the four walls, priced between 150 quid and a lot more.

Watching the crowd from the rollerballed, five-deep, seating pad resembled a rock 'n' toll *Gladiator* with the Stones as Christians and lions and we, *hoi polloi*, watching. It should have been on ice, it would have made much more sense.

The sound was atrocious; well, perhaps that's a bit unfair ... let's just say cavernous. The Stones spent most of the show warming up. It was all very impersonal; there was not much, if any at all, of a connection between the Glimmer Twins, at least not for public show. Mick danced, pranced, oyed, yobbed, and souled his amazing self around the room. Keith enjoyed the fact that he was worshipped, and was much more choreographed - God help Pete Townshend if he tried the Keith movements now! Every few minutes or verses, he would spread himself in front of his fans; it seemed that on this nice, warm, Glasgow evening that Mick had a crowd and Keith had fans. Or, as Johnny Marr puts it, "The Rolling Stones are Keith Richards's band and Mick Jagger's business."

I had no time for their new bass player. Perhaps Keith remembers Cuddly Dudley Heslop on Jack Good's TV shows. That's who he reminds me of, except with the addition of "I've played with Sting" and all those little jazzified frills. Of course, it's not his fault; he could be great, but he cannot win me because, without Bill Wyman, the Stones are always a little less than a band.

Nor have I ever liked a Stones night much when Ronnie Wood overplays to the crowd. He's a second banana at best, and a slippery one at that. Whenever I notice the talented little git playing out and showing off, it usually means that Mick and Keith are doing less, and it shows. Or perhaps - and if I do it's my fault - I

see a ghost upon the stage, the ghost of Brian Jones when the playing was not enough for him, when Mick was too much for him,
and he just had to flash the falsest smile this side of Sharon Os-
bourne, play out, and show off, to make me cringe.

Ronnie played well in Glasgow, but Keith was no more
than good, which remains above the very best of the rest of the
anchors and guitarists in our world. Charlie was immaculate; he
has managed to maintain the incredible gift that he has always
displayed, coming under "I play as I go."

The keyboard player got on my nerves. He always has. I
realise that he's there to fill in the spaces which are bound to appear on a five-year tour, but does he have to prance around like
someone whom Journey or Heart let go? The horns are lucky the
Stones employ them, or else they'd be playing cruise ships, which
is exactly the way the night in Glasgow felt: one big fucking luxury
liner looking for a port. It did not find it that often, as shit doth
happen. It was less *Titanic* and more *The Poseidon Adventure* - all
really rather weird. The core Stones should really think about
getting rid of the peripheral band.

In front of me, there sat a forty-something, Simpsonesque,
short-sleeved, perfect child-molester look-alike: groomed and clean,
outdoor arms, checked button-down casual shirt, and those awful
beige trousers that people with awful bums insist on wearing
along with their battleship shoes. He could have been a schoolteacher or a surveyor, I thought, as a lack of obvious energy for a
song or two allowed me the time to study and criticise him.

I'm glad I did. He had remained quiet, pensive, his only
movement a self-fondling of the well-built arms. Then, all of a
sudden, my fair perv leapt up from his seat, grabbed the railing in
front of him, and yelled - louder than the Liza Minnelli take on
"You Can't Always Get What You Want" that was coming, well,
slogging, from the stage - "Mick, I love you; you know I always
have!"

I looked at Max and Esther, then at Sean, who had joined
us for this Glasgow brawl. I guess I was wrong; perhaps it's Keith
who has the crowd and Mick who has his fans.

Apart from all I've said, they, the Stones that is, are the
greatest show on earth. It does not matter whether the night is all
theirs, or if they're hardly there at all, shared with, or owned by

the crowd, it always, one piece or another, comes together and the
night ends up total. This is their job of work and the reason that
they are the greatest band in the world. But, if you have the opportunity to see the boys, I would recommend hopping down to
Buenos Aires and catching them there. They not only take over the
stadium, they take over the town, they take over the night. And
the audience takes over everything. The unsophisticated love of
a third-world audience is a heroin-ic, euphoric miracle, so the
band has no alternative but to respond in kind to a country that
beats just for them.

A couple of weeks later in Twickenham Stadium, London,
they were all that and more. That night, the 67,000 who crowded,
filled, and spilled into the rugby cathedral came to worship and
groove to the Stones. The Stones were a celebration of their lives,
the fact that the forty to sixty-plus-year-old audience did not, as
their folks had, only have a life of getting poorly to look forward
to, and could still have nights when they'd be forever young.

The first two songs, "Brown Sugar" and "Jumpin' Jack
Flash," as I recall, were downright amazing. I looked around at
the crowd, and thought that, if the Stones kept this up, the audience would implode. But in the event, they didn't, as the third
song was something new that would find its way onto *A Bigger
Bang*, for which Mick slung on a guitar and became a boy in the
band. I loved it, we loved it, and it allowed us to catch our breath
and celebrate our lives together.

Back at the Four Seasons Hotel in Seattle, we alighted the
elevator on what I will presume was a very high floor. Sitting
guard outside the bank of elevators were a bunch of Phil Silvers
and William Bendix security clowns, who did not even bother to
nod or acknowledge anyone lucky enough to be allowed on this
floor. Charlie opened the door to his suite, all sweetness and
smiles. We had a lovely tea, even if it was from a teabagged urn.
We caught up on the past, gave thanks for the present, and left
the future to the whatever of whatever we already had done.
Perhaps they were royalty. For all the politeness, kindness, and
memories shared, I could have been with Prince Michael of Kent,
as to how reserved and mannered the occasion was.

Charlie was neat, looking strong and rested after his recent
bout with cancer, but I did so want to drag him out, take him shop-

ping, see him out and about and one with the crowd, but I guess that's the night job. Finally, we were both pleased to see each other well.

We left Charlie to do whatever it is he does to get ready, which is probably no more than combing his hair and calling home. We went off for an hour and at 7.30 p.m., we were backstage, being ushered into Keith Richards's domain. What a pleasure it was to hear him call my name.

"Andrew."

"Keith."

A hug, a check-out, an okay we're okay grin.

Then to Max, a smile and, "Look what your dad started."

We talked about the new record; he knew which track I'd like. I studied him closely; after all the man was soon to fall off a shrub or a bush, would have either brain damage, brain surgery, an aneurysm, blood clots straight to the heart, some of that or all of that; and that night in Seattle, I promise you, his eyes had seen the coming of his Lord. He darted around the room like Jack the Lad; his hands conducted and conjured up the life, but, when I met him on that Sunday, his eyes stood still. The skin was a little grey, but that might just have been a reflection of the main colour of Seattle. We were getting along so well, so jovial, so then and now, that I might have made a mistake.

"Keith" I said, "You know you are going to South America?"

Why should I presume that Keith would know? This was, after all, the man who, on an occasion in the eighties had to leave New York on some visa renewal business, checked into an apartment in Paris, did the embassy bit for a couple of days, then got ready to fly back into America. As the story goes, he turned to his manager, Jane Rose, and said, "Jane, nice pad. Perhaps we could buy it."

Manager Jane replied, "You can't, Keith; it's already yours."

"Well, perhaps," I continued, glancing over at Max, "You could use someone there; the tour could use someone who I'd like to see the trenches, to tell you the difference between coffee and tea."

"You mean Max?" asked Keith, giving my lad the Keefover.

He studied the well turned out son of mine, English city beige overcoat with brown velvet collar, tennis shoes, and jeans, and reached the obvious conclusion.

"I guess he doesn't hump gear."

No, we smiled, he does not.

"Well, the problem of course is Madame," said Keith, heaving his look over an imaginary wall toward Brenda. "I mean," continued Keith, "I could ask, but couldn't you change his second name?"

I resisted equally taking umbrage and replying with my first response, "How about Max Klein?" That would have been below the belt and impolite.

I settled for, "Would Max Easton do?"

"Touché!" he smiled, and the subject, I thought, was closed. Keith went out to run the gauntlet of privileged fans, a fiasco wherein a crowd of honoured folk get to stand against the walls of a corridor whilst the Stones run through them giving five, slapping palms, and out the other door. For whatever they pay for this, these fans get a plastic bag full of Stones goodies. Once you are all out in the audience, you can see this flushed lot on their cell phones, calling all over the world, letting it be known that they have just pressed flesh with a Rolling Stone.

Yes, look what your dad started.

Tony King was furious. I suppose that Keith had passed on the trenches request, and Madame King had received it on behalf of Madame Jagger. He was overqueeny and rather rude. This was something that he would not condition to, regardless of how many times he has been fairy godmother to some unsuspecting little bairn. He got overqueeny and very rude in front of my son. I wanted to whack the stupid bitch, but I'm a pragmatic thug and often quite Zen; I knew that if I thumped the cunt, I'd be jumped and no doubt trampled by the inbred minders who would have to do so, Tony King being so close to the throne.

I didn't see Mick, nor did it look as if another Sir, Ian McKellen, did either. I'd seen Ian a week before, looking rather trim and well, at the marvellously talented Noam Gagnon's Pilates place in Vancouver, where a lot of us go to stay limbered up. Tonight Ian was in a positive huff, although I could not say, nor did I ask, whether that was because he had seen Mick or had not. Prince Rupert Lowenstein sat or folded into a chair in the green room and gave me the look reserved for someone from the Allen

xxvi   ROLLING STONED

Klein side of town. Or perhaps Mick and Keith had forgotten to tell him and Charlie didn't know.

    We had tickets to see the Stones the next week in L.A. at the Hollywood Bowl. I just could not face the idea of it again, and neither could Max. To him, they were old men that his dad liked and had worked with once upon a time. So I did something I never thought I'd have cause to do. We sold the tickets to a scalper and Max bought himself a spanking new computer. I'm typing on it now.

Laurence Harvey

CHAPTER 1

the little bastard is born, say hallo to yankee doodle andy / left and kept by polish jews / a single mum in a married world / single rooms of gloom in post world war ii london / hope from the american cinema and movement from its music / the gas oven abroad and a broad called lady joan / suburban jazz education and struttin' on ambition avenue / all poofs at the inn / the real prince of wails - johnnie ray / first job - the flower bum song

There are three sides to every story: yours, mine, and the truth.

I lost my father before I knew the meaning of loss; I lost him before I was born. World War II had kept my mother busy as a nurse by day and nightingale by night. But she found a moment for herself with one Andrew Loog, a Texan of Dutch origin, who served in the United States Army Air Corps from July 15, 1941, until the day of his separation by death, June 13, 1943. First Lieutenant Loog, assigned to the 332nd Bombardier Squadron, 94th Bombardier Group H, was shot down over the Channel. I shot out on January 29, 1944, when Celia was admitted to Paddington General Hospital having gone into labour prematurely; perhaps she was working there already. Thus Air Medaled and Purple Hearted, Louisianan Loog left a wife and a child dependent in Texas, and, perhaps, this happy, independent little barsted in London.

My birth was complicated, and I was born ill, weak and puny, a mere four pounds. I had a "soft skull": a "hard hat" was specially designed to protect me, and I wore it for the first year of my life, until my head became as hard as it has remained ever since. I was named Andrew Loog Oldham, in memory of Airman Andrew Loog, although on my birth certificate the space for daddy is blank.

The day I was born, Germany mounted its final offensive, the most vicious Blitzkrieg over England yet. My mother and I spent many a night getting acquainted in the Underground as the German "doodlebugs" rained down on the capital and drowned out the sound of Bow Bells, and along with them much of life, but not the spirit of our fellow Londoners.

My mother, Celia Oldham, got Alzheimer's, so I am telling

you her story with help from some who knew her back in the day. She was born in Paddington, New South Wales, on February 11, 1920. It has been pointed out to me that my first real employer, Mary Quant, was also born on February 11 some years later.

Celia's father was an Ashkenazi Jew named Militar Schatkowski, born in Plotaly, Kovno, Russia, who fled Poland in 1916. Militar had looked across the oceans of choice and ended up in New South Wales, where he met my grandmother, whose name I've never known.

Perhaps they were wed, and two years after my mother, Cecelia Olga, was born, a brother, whose name might have been Robert, joined her. In 1923, my mother's mother gathered her brood together and shipped off for England leaving a bemused and culture-baffled Militar horizontal with drink at the Sydney race track; for him the race was over.

My mother was four years old when she arrived in London. She was schooled to conceal her Australian and Jewish lineage, socially a double whammy at that time, and grew up to become a fiercely proud, aloof, and radiant redhead. I'm afraid that it is typical of my mother's reticence, shall we put it, that nothing is known of what happened to my maternal grandmother or how my mother was raised. I could presume she passed on before I was born, but I cannot commit to that as a fact. My mother never mentioned her so there was no reason for me to reason. Why should I? It's not just that she was the grandmother with no name or face; she simply never was.

Growing up in London, Celia cultivated a certain style which, along with "correct" behaviour, mattered to her above all else. She was nineteen when what would become World War II was declared with Germany, women of Britain playing an active part in the war effort. Many succumbed to recruitment posters that made service dress look smart and sophisticated.

My uncle was drafted or enlisted into the Royal Australian Navy, and Celia joined the Women's Voluntary Services, my fashion-conscious mother opting to become a nurse. Norman Hartnell, the prestigious dressmaker, designed the uniforms.

Once, when I was about nine, I asked my mother what had happened to her brother. She gave me a look that warned me not to cry "uncle" and went on to tell me that she had not got on with her brother very well before the war, so there hadn't been any point in finding out whether he had survived it. I was happy that she felt more for me: the only thing that was mine was my mother. Most other people's "my"s were in the plural. I knew already that my mother had taken some cold, hard decisions as a woman on her own with a young boy child and that perhaps warmth of heart had settled for second place as a consequence.

Celia, and ain't life genetic, had already developed an opiatic cotton lair around her that prevented one from entering as she went about the business of life. Detail was for the poor and unfortunate, and I would continue to cross over that line with Celia when, aged eleven, I worried (not for the last time) about the future prospects of my hairline and asked my mum for details on my father.

I started at the bottom. "Where was he buried?" I asked. My mother fetched from her desk some forbidding-looking papers and showed me one letter from an American Air Force Chaplain, who had written in answer to my mother's enquiries. In officialese, he informed her that 1st Lt. Andrew Loog was interred at the Ardennes American Cemetery and Memorial, Neurille-en-Condroz, Belgium.

"What did he look like?" I continued. She smiled and went back to the good place in her heart. Her face was radiant, then she frowned and looked around the room as if wary of eavesdroppers.

"He was tall, over six foot, handsome ... a good man," she said quietly.

"But don't you have any photos of him, mummy?" I persisted.

I could see from her eyes that her mind was flashing through the snaps of her life as she pursed her lips and replied, "Well, Andy, there was a war on, we really didn't have time for pictures."

Later, I often thanked God that my mother, when considering whether or not to abort me, had not displayed the characteristic coldness with which she allowed the rest of her family to slip away. I believe there was a real shyness beneath her seeming self-confidence.

After the war, we were continually on the move. Celia rented a series of horrific single rooms in houses and flats around northwest London. By winter 1947, the worst for over a hundred years, the British economy and morale were at an all-time low. There were queues for everything, the country was getting worse, not better (rationing of food and clothes continued until 1949). The black market burgeoned and spivs took control of the streets, the crackmen of their time. Familiar neighbourhoods still looked like lunar landscapes, abandoned airfields dotted the countryside, and all the spontaneity and joy had gone out of life. It was a deadly dull and demanding time, and all in all I'm quite glad to have been too young to remember much of it.

Celia was as devoted to me as she was to herself, determined that I should receive the very best upbringing. She installed me at a nursery school in Sussex, far away from the destitution and disease of London. I remember my mother's visits when more often than not a Doctor Jimmy, who'd reputedly made himself rich practising illegal abortions during the War, accompanied her. In the postwar austerity years, running one car was an extravagance few could afford; Jimmy had two - twin Sunbeam Talbots, grey and maroon.

My mother could have stayed kept but she opted for keeping busy, forging a career for herself as a freelance comptometer (a primitive tallying machine that was a predecessor to the modern computer) operator, keeping the books for several small companies. On this steady but small wage, the only luxury my mother could afford was the knowledge that her Andy was being kept at a decent school. The general postwar malaise of the British working classes horrified Celia. Despite her rather *outré* position as a single mother, she wanted her son to rise above the gloomy masses, just as she felt she had, though she never detailed from what to what she had risen.

By 1950 Celia was relatively settled in a one-room apartment at 18 Old Marylebone Road, close to Edgware Road. She shared this tiny space with an old wartime friend, Joan Bingham, or "Lady Joan" as she liked to be called, who had over-enjoyed the wartime party when each night's revelry held the possibility of the final snuff-out. Joan had no one to anchor her as Celia had me; the war had burnt her out like some tired old silent movie star. Joan got straight to the point, and during my first summer holiday in London we returned home to find Lady Joan dearly departed with her head in the oven, stone cold dead from gas poisoning. Not a very jolly experience for a six-year-old. We think the sixties were wild, but that decade's death we brought upon ourselves. Surviving World War II, greedy for life, with no choice about death, must have been the ultimate head trip. Despite the odds some managed to grasp a postwar existence, but some like Lady Joan couldn't handle the return to norm and moved on.

Celia moved out of the room in Marylebone Road shortly afterwards, finding accommodation on the other side of Edgware Road in Maida Vale at 6 Elgin Avenue. Here she rented a room in an apartment belonging to two Hungarian refugee sisters, both working as airline stewardesses to earn enough money to retire to Spain. I was growing up fast and very much enjoyed the double fun of listening to the radio in the room of the sister I fancied while silently ogling her.

In the summer of 1951, Celia first introduced me to her steady boyfriend, Alec Morris, a man who was to play a significant paternal role in my life. Twenty years older than Celia, Alec was a successful Jewish businessman. His company, Made By Morris, was one of the best known manufacturers of furniture in the country. By the late fifties he moved out of the furniture business and into private banking with his Alec Morris Investments Ltd.

Alec had grown up in the East End at the turn of the century, tired of it as a teenager, and in 1915 smuggled himself aboard a troop ship heading for the States. There he spent time in New York teaching the tango and foxtrot alongside George Raft, the alleged gangster, gigolo, and, later, movie star. The same George was drummed out of the U.K. years later for fronting the mob-connected Colony Club.

After a few years in the States up to everything, Alec returned to London to join the family furniture business. When World War II began, all furniture manufacturers had to go into war work, making ammunition boxes and wooden rifles for the home guard and the army. After the war, Made By Morris started to produce utility furniture and from then until 1950 the Morrises lived the good life, rolling in money - living on the right side of Hampstead and getting there in a Rolls-Royce.

My mother was Alec's long-term outside affair, but he had no intention of deserting his wife and two children, an arrangement that suited all. Unlike many wayward husbands, Alec showed genuine concern for his "second family," and lavished attention on me. He would pay for my education and for our holidays abroad, La Baule on the Normandy coast, and the Costa Brava.

By the time I met Alec, Made By Morris had been sold and he'd invested his time and money into becoming Alec Morris Investments Ltd. As well as driving a Rolls-Royce, Alec practically lived in The Ivy, London's most elite restaurant, the moneyed show biz haunt. His other favourite home away from home was Cunningham's on Park Lane.

Alec acted like a real father to me, and I liked to imagine he was. He rewarded me when I did well in school by taking me to dinner at The Ivy. This practice continued for many years. When I did less well, it was Lyon's Corner House, corner of Oxford Street and Tottenham Court Road.

My mother never gave up her day job or her independence and continued with her career as a comptometer operator. To me life seemed normal, the relationship between Celia and Alec did not bother me; it was all I knew and I felt truly loved by two people who had a great deal of apparent affection for each other. My education was her primary concern, and Alec paid for this agenda. I was enrolled at a new boarding school, the Aylesbury School for Boys.

In early September 1952, just a few weeks before the new school term started, my mother was informed that Aylesbury was "overcrowded" and I was to be relocated to an alternative school, the Cokethorpe School for Boys, situated in the leafy Oxfordshire hamlet of Witney, in blanket country. This school would leave a lasting impression on me.

Cokethorpe to me seemed like the Oxford of *Brideshead Revisited*. The school occupied a magnificent mansion with stables and many acres of lush green fields. I was particularly impressed with the clothes of our stylish headmaster - a three-piece tweed suit and hush puppies made him appear to be as comfortably aristocratic as the exiled Windsor. By his side, his glamorous wife, in her tartan skirt and Shetland wool sweaters, looked like nothing so much as a "royal." So this was the world Celia wanted us to live in!

Since I was acutely aware of my "illegitimacy" and dreaded

the subject being brought up by my classmates, I was grateful that the head treated all of us as if we were his own sons. I recall an occasion when one boy's parents forgot his birthday, since they were too busy separating for such sentiment, and the head took him into town to the toy store and bought him a present.

Then one day a new headmaster arrived to take over at Cokethorpe. Colonel Elston was a brooding bachelor with a handlebar mustache. Customarily attired in a double-breasted blazer, he wore crisp shirts set off by the navy and maroon striped regimental tie of the Royal Guards.

Colonel Elston aroused much curiosity amongst the pupils, particularly as at midday every Wednesday he left the school in his sleek black Rover, returning hours later in the early evening. Rumours abounded as to what the Colonel was up to. We fantasised that he was an advisor to the War Office or involved with the Secret Services. Seven years after VE Day, the War still provided the scripts for the comics that children devoured.

After my first year at Cokethorpe, I returned home to London for the summer holiday. Mother had moved again, now sharing a flat at 65 Eton Avenue in Swiss Cottage with an extravagant hairdresser, Harry Mizelas. Mizelas later became the "André" of the André Bernard chain and, beginning with the flagship salon in Mayfair, his empire eventually stretched to over twenty establishments. But he met with a brutal death: shot dead in Hyde Park in 1970. He drove from his schlock-Regency town house down High Street, Kensington, turned left into Hyde Park at Knightsbridge, steered his Roller to the right in the direction of Park Lane, and pulled over to the left, having noticed an acquaintance, who shot him in the head. I remember my mother being questioned by the police on many occasions, but to this day the case goes unsolved.

There was no fridge at Eton Avenue, so for most of the year we kept milk cold on the window ledge. There was no telephone, but Celia had bought her own radio set, which became my window on the world. I regularly listened to BBC melodramas like *The Archers*, *Riders of the Range* (whose hero Jeff Arnold also featured in an *Eagle* comic strip) and *Dick Barton, Special Agent*.

The BBC radio monopoly offered little in the way of musical entertainment that would appeal to the postwar generation.

Two-Way Family Favourites was a weekly two-hour music show that played the requests of British soldiers still serving abroad for their families and sweethearts at home and vice-versa. Dickie Valentine and Slim Whitman were popular favourites, but I preferred my dramas.

Every morning Alec arrived in his wildly exciting silver Rolls-Royce to chauffeur Celia to work and drop me off with Pamela Marshall, a wartime friend of Celia's who kept her home fires burning minding me whilst her Wing Commander husband still served his country overseas. I would walk the neighbourhood if Pamela was detained by some errand, and it was on one of these excursions that I encountered a way of life as far from Alec's Silver Cloud as could be, just over the next block. It made me shudder and set off in me both ambition and appreciation for the perhaps austere, but well-decorated womb with a view that Celia had made for us.

As I crafted my way down Crawford Street, a shell-shocked, withered-to-the-bone elderly lady in apron and carpet slippers stood, arms folded, eyes searching, in the doorway of her depressing one-up, two-down. She caught my eye and my attention, beckoned me toward her, held out a coin in her grimy, work-worn hand, and asked if I minded coming inside to feed her gas meter, which was too high for her to reach with her deformity. I was happy to return her to light and heat, but chilled by the poverty to which I was exposed for the first time, ashamed that my discomfort might be perceived by her as disdain.

Back on the sunny, well-heated side of Old Marylebone Road, Pamela kept me on a loose leash, thankfully, and I was able to explore her neighbourhood without fear of Celia's disapproval. I returned to the ABC Cinema off the Edgware Road any number of times to stare at the movie posters, and finally plucked up the courage to sneak in. Geography, psychology, and anatomy were on offer at the Academy of Motion Pictures, and so Pop became my favourite schoolmaster.

The first film I remember is John Huston's *Moulin Rouge* (1952), starring Zsa Zsa Gabor and José Ferrer, who played the crippled painter Toulouse-Lautrec. It was one of the first films to have been shot in CinemaScope, and I was reeling afterwards. Widescreen close-ups of chorines doing the can-can gave me my first glimpse of how art could get away with murder, as legs I might wait a lifetime to see in real life pummelled me in the stalls. I left the cinema shaken and stirred. The film experience put off any appreciation I might later have for women's legs, as in *Moulin Rouge* they just seemed like lethal weapons.

I had just returned home from Cokethorpe's spring term when Celia received a letter from the local vicar. There was "something awfully wrong" at the school. I didn't know what that something was, but I never returned to Cokethorpe. A year later, Celia and I were on a train taking us to the South Coast for our holidays. She got comfy and opened up the *Daily Express* to see a photograph of Cokethorpe School for Boys on the front page, beneath a headline that read "Four Jailed in School Swindle Ring." My beloved Cokethorpe had been the work of confidence tricksters! The "gang" had opened and closed seven private schools in total, including the supposedly overbooked Aylesbury School. After collecting up the tuition and boarding fees, the con men then ran up credit in a small town and then moved on without paying to open yet another "school" in another town. Cokethorpe was their final scam before they were caught. They'd been averaging out about £80,000. Colonel Elston's mysterious midweek sojourns were to a parole officer and not the Foreign Office. While my mother paced the corridor, ruing her bad luck, I devoured the larger-than-life newspaper with a great deal of interest and some delight. To me, it was an ingenious scheme, original and entertaining.

Celia next bought a five-room basement flat at 44 Belsize Park Gardens near Swiss Cottage with financial assistance from Alec. She quickly arranged for me to attend the local Swiss Cottage junior school. At first, I was happy to be staying at home, and thrilled to learn that at mum's new flat I would have my own bedroom at last. For Celia the Belsize Park flat was a rung up the ladder of respectability. She had a telephone installed and, best of all, a television delivered.

The Swiss Cottage state school was unremittingly grimy and depressing, all the more so after the glamor of Cokethorpe. I was frequently ill from fear and revulsion. I nevertheless enjoyed running credits for the film I hoped the day would become. The older boys ritually inducted new pupils, and on my very first day I was forced into the local sweet shop and ordered to steal something. I got caught, an early indication that I was about true romance, not true crime. I tried to make the most of our new accommodation; after school, between 7:00 and 10:00 p.m. every night, I tuned into Radio Luxembourg. The invariably bad reception annoyed my mother, who under any circumstances did not suffer imperfection gladly, but I was glad to have an alternative to the Beeb.

Television and film combined with radio to stimulate my hungry senses. Unlike most of my peers, I wanted a peek behind the scenes; I remembered the names of producers and directors as well as actors. While the major American studios such as MGM, United Artists, and Warner Brothers found a ready audience in Europe, I was always attracted for some reason to the independent producers of my homeland. Romulus films, a production company formed in 1949 by the brothers Woolf, James and John, sons of the veteran producer C.M. Woolf, specialised in Anglo-American co-productions. The films produced by the Woolfs and their Romulus atelier were most distinguished: *The African Queen* (starring, of course, Humphrey Bogart and Katharine Hepburn, 1951), *Cosh Boy* (1952), *Beat the Devil* (John Huston's wicked satire with an all-star cast, again including a "mature" Bogart, 1954), *The Bespoke Overcoat* (1956), *I Am a Camera* (Christopher Isherwood's memoir of decadent 'tween-wars Berlin, 1955, later turned into *Cabaret*), and best (and worst) of all, *The Good Die Young* (1954), which introduced me to the actor who would tower in my youthful imagination as a paragon of accomplishment and style: Laurence Harvey.

Both "above the line" and on the screen, *The Good Die Young* was my kind of deal. I found it fascinating that James Woolf managed Larry, and both brothers produced his movies. James also found time to touch Terence Stamp's life and died in 1966 at the age of 53. But Laurence Harvey was his crowning achievement.

Laurence was born Zvi Mosheh (or Laruschka Mischa) Skikne in 1928 in Lithuania and as a child moved with his Jewish parents to South Africa. He joined the Royal South African Navy at fourteen by lying about his age and was enlisted for the last two years of World War II. By 1946, he was in England studying at the Royal Academy of Dramatic Arts (RADA), and by eighteen he was playing lead roles in Rep. At twenty, in 1948, he had his first lead role in a film. My kind of guy, pace, and life!

The British character actress Hermione Baddeley, twenty years his senior, took him under her wing. Larry, too ambitious to be swayed by the glamor of youth, made this his pattern. He married the much older West End theatre star Margaret Leighton in 1953, and her introduction to the stages of the West End and Broadway provided complementary challenges to his suave roles in films like *Darling*. He did *As You Like It* in 1953, toured with the Old Vic as *Henry V* on its 1958-59 tour and starred in *Camelot* in the late sixties in the West End and on Broadway. He married Joan Cohn in 1968, she being the widow of Columbia Pictures mogul Harry Cohn and, again, some twenty years Mr. Harvey's senior. The last eleven months of his too-short life, he was married to the model Paulene Stone, a younger woman for a change and the mother of his only child, the bounty hunter Domino Harvey. He passed in 1973 from cancer.

Laurence Harvey signed with the Associated British Picture Corporation in 1948 and remained a "contract" actor until 1952. He was due a salary raise that year from £25 to £35. ABPC cried poverty and asked Harvey to re-sign for the same wage. That same week, ABPC announced profits for the year of £3,000,000. Mr. Harvey, understandably, left ABPC and was out of work for most of a year before signing with the Woolfs. Commuting between London and Los Angeles, rubbing noses with the likes of Jane Fonda and Kim Novak, Larry leapt off the screen into immortality as Joe Lampton in the 1959 Romulus-produced *Room At The Top* and the 1965 sequel, *Life At The Top*.

Messrs. Harvey and the Woolfs are together responsible for remarkable bodies of work and illuminating lives. Harvey's stardom and James Woolf's management of it would inspire me throughout the turbulence of my youth and show business career, and encourage the birth of my own Immediate Records by their example. As Immediate staggered between controlling its acts and trying to remember who they actually were, I, like Larry, would remain "happy to be part of the industry of human happiness." To this day I am indebted to their genius, which has lighted my life even in its darkest moments.

Back in the "real" life of mid-fifties London, Hollywood-on-the-Thames beckoned in the form of Harold Lang, a B-movie gangster in many Anglo-Amalgamated-produced films, who lived just round the corner from us. Although he was not in the same league as Laurence Harvey, I'd seen Harold on TV, so I went a-knockin' and the kindly actor let me in. His huge blonde peroxide quiff and exaggerated gestures fascinated me. Over tea and biscuits, I barraged him with questions: "Have you met ...? What's he like? Who's the best director? How do you do that?" Offscreen Harold was a nice man, not at all like a gangster. He did, however, radiate something different. The tension of an actor's life appealed to me even then, and Harold had that attractive aura of a man working in a field apart from the norm.

About this time, I made friends with a young Swiss Cottage boy, Jeremy Holt. Jeremy's father, Seth Holt, was the Ealing comedy editor who'd worked on *The Lavender Hill Mob*. For a short while I fell heavily under the influence of Mr. Holt, who was tickled that I could knowledgeably discuss the work of British producers like Sir Alexander Korda and the Boulting Brothers.

Holt went on to direct Britain's first teenage angst film, *Nowhere To Go* (written by Kenneth Tynan) in 1958. He told me that Swiss Cottage was home to many celebrities, including Stephen Spender, who in 1946 had been sent to de-Nazify German libraries, and Humphrey Lyttleton, the British jazzman who, with his partner Chris Barber, launched the 100 Club.

I myself became interested in jazz while visiting my immediate next-door neighbour, Bob Carroll. Bob taught me how to listen critically to a record, to listen for the part around which the music wrapped itself: the horns, the trombone, or the bass. He played me Miles Davis, Count Basie, Duke Ellington, Frank Sinatra, Nat King Cole, the Hi-Lo's, the Modern Jazz Quartet, Gerry Mulligan, Chet Baker. He showed me how Sinatra and Nat King Cole used their voices as instruments and were in fact an extension of the orchestra. I know I applied that one later on. Why Bob chose me I don't know, but he did, and I've never forgotten what he gave me. I don't remember what I was learning in school at the same time but I remember producers and arrangers like Frank DeVol, Billy May, Gordon Jenkins, and Nelson Riddle.

After one jazz session in Bob's top-floor apartment, I returned home to the basement flat, and glimpsed, through an open bedroom door, my mother and Alec making love. They didn't realise I was home until they dressed and came out into the hall. I was standing on top of a chair with one end of a rope around my neck and the other end attached to the pipes running along the ceiling, threatening to kill myself. "Come down, Andy," advised Alec, first of the many practical men who have remained unswayed by my flair for the dramatic, "you'll only break the string."

Celia rented out a spare room in the basement flat to Gladys Byrne, a no-nonsense Joan-Crawford-on-top type in her late fifties who worked at the BBC. When she learned of my addiction to television and film, she promised to introduce me to her brother, Gus Byrne. Should either of them ever have considered an operation they had only to look at each other to guess the outcome. Gus was personal assistant to one of TV's top personalities, commentator Gilbert Harding, celebrated as "Britain's Rudest Man." On the radio he hosted *Twenty Questions* and on TV compered *What's My Line?*, a celebrity panel quiz show that the whole of Britain gawked at throughout the fifties. Harding remains famous for saying "But I do wish that the future was over" and for breaking down in tears while talking about his mother on Britain's most provocative interview programme, John Freeman's *Face To Face*, in 1957. At the tail end of the fifties, Harding co-starred in *Expresso Bongo*.

After Gus and I met and I pumped him for everything he could tell me about life behind the scenes, Gus told Celia that I had "show business in my blood," which could hardly have come as good news to mum.

By this time, I was allowed to attend the cinema on my own. I had a new favourite every week. John Payne was for a short period one of them; his *Tennessee's Partner* starred future American President Ronald Reagan as the bad guy. I followed Payne's subsequent career, as he went on to co-write and produce his next big movie, *The Boss*. The dark *Slightly Scarlet* scored a double hit with me due to the resemblance between leading lady Arlene Dahl and the leading lady in my own life, my mother.

I loved bad boy Tony Curtis in *Six Bridges to Cross*, and fell for Audrey Hepburn after seeing her star in Billy Wilder's *Sabrina*. Miss Hepburn was the first of my androgynous icons, a fascination that would grow in intensity and refinement over time. Victor Mature's versatility impressed me since he was just as convincing as Samson or a gangster. And we happened to share birthdays.

As the up-and-down first year at Swiss Cottage was drawing to a close, with the summer holidays looming, I began to search in earnest for a suitable Saturday job. Even at ten I was keenly clothes-conscious and longed for a wardrobe worthy of my fantasies. Alec had given me a good start by passing down a stylish suede golf jacket and a pair of cufflinks for my tenth birthday, and I was grateful for his sartorial example since I knew most of my models only from the silver screen.

I landed a job at André's on Finchley Road, a refined Swiss Cottage hairdressing salon. For a month I swept up the dead hair and fetched cappuccinos from across the road for the clients. I enjoyed the responsibility and the opportunity to earn my money, play flash, and buy presents for my mother. Unfortunately, a valued customer sat on a plate of biscuits I'd left on a chair. She didn't take too kindly to me calling her a "silly bitch" and telling her that next time she ought to look where she was sitting. Here endeth the first job.

I tried to put out of my mind the looming prospect of another year at the squalid Swiss Cottage state school. Television was a handy escape route, and the advent of the commercial channel offered a welcome alternative to the BBC. I fell under the spell of Donald Gray's Mark Saber, the one-armed sometimes private, sometimes Scotland Yard, sometimes globetrotting, sometimes Selfridges store detective, and for a few television minutes I weighed the possibility of a regular store job, so suggestible was I to any scenario that was photographed and cleverly acted.

Mother's favourite programme was one of the few American shows going, *Liberace*, and we often watched together on a Sunday. Celia loved to hear the smiling queen croon "I'll Be Seeing You (in All the Old Familiar Places)," while I preferred the programme that followed, *Free Speech*, a political debate show with Michael Foot for the left and Lord Boothby for the right.

I went to call on Lord Boothby at home one Sunday morning, knowing he'd be in, and he opened the door himself, still attired in his dressing gown. He blinked twice at the package the Lord's day had deposited on his doorstep, and, thinking better of rearranging his plans for the day, gave me an autograph and sent me on my way.

ITV had hit the jackpot with *Sunday Night at the London Palladium*. This, and two quiz shows not dignified enough for the

Beeb - Michael Miles's *Take Your Pick* and Hughie Green's *Double Your Money* - firmly established the alternative channel. Britain's families worshipped at this shrine of show business in far greater numbers than had attended church in the preceding twelve hours.

Both mum and I really enjoyed our new "sideboard style" record player, stacked with 78s by Frank Sinatra, Nat King Cole, and Johnnie Ray. With a record player at home, music began to play an increasingly influential role in my life. I took to the fan magazines to learn all I could about Mr. Ray, whose chart-topping single, "Cry," had won him the devotion of British fans. His concerts at the London Palladium were noted for the mass female hysteria they inspired, which led to accusations that he was a hypnotist. Johnnie was an Oregon-born bar and club singer discovered by CBS and developed as the male equivalent of the four-hankie movie. After "Cry" came "The Little White Cloud that Cried," and "Such a Night."

Ray took music for me to a whole other level, for which my jazz sessions had not prepared me. With his sexual presence (and despite his sexual preference), Johnnie Ray was a *popular* star in the same way as Laurence Harvey, but with a legion of adoring, crazed female fans. From now on film, television, *and* music were equally to be my escape routes from the earthiness of school life. In April 1955 I bought my first record: a single by Perez Prado, called "Cherry Pink and Apple Blossom White." When I played it, I was transported for a few minutes to glamorous movie sets inhabited by *femmes fatales* and white-dinner-jacketed could-be villains.

Johnnie Ray was booked to appear at the London Palladium in spring 1955, and the event would be televised on the Sunday night show. I had bought his latest single, "Such a Night," and counted down the days until the "Cry Guy" arrived in town. I was amongst the hundreds of fans gathered outside the Palladium waiting for Ray when he arrived to rehearse his performance. I watched gobsmacked as Ray, flanked by ten soldiers he had befriended just that afternoon, was ushered into the venue. Then I hung around until Ray appeared later at the stage door to sign autographs. That evening found me at home watching Ray perform his brilliant short live set. I teased my mother by pointing out that even the country's protectors were in awe of his unique talent. I was fascinated with stars. They stopped traffic, made hearts beat a little faster, and had their pictures taken when they walked through airports. They had the best lighting on offer and lived a life that didn't end up on the cutting room floor. There was no doubt in my mind who was the real Prince of Wails.

The line had been crossed, and for the first time in Great Britain audiences were tearing themselves apart over the Nabob of Sob who, from '52 till '55, recorded nonstop emotional classics as sexual as any careless whisper heard on the airwaves the past twenty years. With "Such a Night" Ray was live sex, made safe and acceptable by the vulnerability he wore like a sheath dress. He came to Britain, saw, suffered, and conquered. Johnnie seared a lyric into your life, twisting the words into shameless tears, and then wrung them out over hot wax, scarred by every groove. On disc and stage he was as much a method actor as Montgomery Clift; he hurt from here to eternity and he was deaf to boot. After reading that Ray wore a hearing aid, I got hold of one and wore it the way earrings are worn by young men today.

The forties Paramount Theatre Sinatra and the fifties Prince of Wails Ray set the sexual mould of pop. Ray did not have a great voice, but he acted a great song, sucking you into his three-minute screenplays of shame and pain. He affected mothers and daughters alike and was able to rule in British households because he posed no threat in the master bedroom. The subliminal awareness of Ray's sexual calling made him no competition where it counted; he wouldn't hurt your missus or your daughter - a Johnnie Ray was too hurt himself.

By mid-1957 Ray had his last *bona fide* British hit, "Yes Tonight Josephine," and ended his U.K. run on a slight chart appearance with "Build Your Love." He didn't build anymore and disappeared under the wash of Dean, Presley, Eddie Cochran, Gene Vincent, Little Richard, and the after-skiffle arrival of Tommy Steele and the early Cliff Richard. I didn't think any more about him, paying the rent on the lounge circuit always miles away from the expressways of contemporary America.

During the mid-eighties in New York, I saw an ad in the *Village Voice* announcing a week of appearances by Mr. Ray at a club in Soho. By now I'd witnessed countless "popular" *artistes* who had had their five minutes or five years, and when it was over they had dried up, moneyed up, bottomed out, and disappeared, literally. The magic of those moments had been siphoned out of their bottle of life, faster than soda, no bubbles left, no bottle, only the sad reality of the moment gone.

The Nabob of Sob was still nervous, still hurt, but he'd grown into it; he was American pie around the waist but in the face the man was still the Prince of Wails. He took me there one more time, and I was glad to go. He talked about appearing with Judy Garland at the London Palladium in 1964. He sang a verse, then played on the piano the verse that Garland would sing. He had the ability and talent to take us back those twenty-odd years out of that New York club into the stalls of the London Palladium, and showed us how it had felt.

Back to the future, with my eleven-plus exam coming up, I studied unusually hard - the result would determine whether I'd be accepted by the local grammar school or sent to the dreaded secondary modern. Summer 1955 was one of mixed emotions. I was glad to have left behind my hateful infant school, yet full of trepidation over the eleven-plus result, and all shook up by the excitement that the American singer Bill Haley was generating in the U.K. His "Rock Around the Clock" single was causing a sensation amongst British teenagers, already hooked on the new rock 'n' roll craze emanating from America. I bought the record, played it endlessly, and teased my hair into a Haley-inspired kiss-curl.

The eleven-plus exam result proved positive, and Marylebone Grammar accepted me. It was a rough school, situated in an intimidating five-story Victorian building, surrounding a dark and dismal courtyard. Had it still been standing, Stanley Kubrick could have used it as a location in *Full Metal Jacket*, which was filmed in London. Mum told me I "just had to survive," or was it succeed? Didn't matter, I was in trouble from day one.

Over the summer I'd seen *Rebel Without a Cause* many times and James Dean was now my ultimate idol. *Blackboard Jungle*, which featured Bill Haley's "Rock Around the Clock," was another controversial smash. Angry parents attacked the film, claiming it was a threat to the decency of British adolescents. This only served as added publicity, as we were now even more desperate to see this "shocking" film.

At Marylebone I inadvertently estranged myself from my

new classmates. While they gossiped about the potential "bad influence" that *Blackboard Jungle* might be having on them, I pronounced the film "a bore," unable to admire any film where the lead character was a schoolteacher - this was not an escape from reality. I felt isolated and alienated at Marylebone Grammar, mostly for thinking for myself. Initially the only way I could survive was by imagining that I was starring in a film. Each day as I walked in through the gates I'd see the opening credits start to roll.

Walking to school one morning, they caught me singing the theme tune to *The Man From Laramie*, a James Stewart western I'd seen the previous Saturday afternoon. During the morning break, the lads trapped me in the school toilets and forced me to sing the song for the pleasure of forty braying boys. For a few weeks I toned down the effluence of my charisma.

Just after my twelfth birthday I yielded to yet another new obsession: Elvis Presley had broken onto the British charts like a teenager's spots. "Blue Suede Shoes," "Heartbreak Hotel," and the sexy ballad, "I Want You, I Need You, I Love You," sounded totally original to me, but more than anything I loved the "look" of Presley. However, this only served to increase my sense of alienation. Only a couple of other lads I knew could spend hours contemplating Elvis in a pink-striped jacket with black-velvet collar turned up, or understand that Elvis was indeed as attractive as Natalie Wood.

Meanwhile, my teachers frequently reprimanded me for my tendency to disrupt classes. My attitude toward what was being taught was *blasé* at best, and I was by way of grooming myself into a strident problem child. Apart from English and art, I had no interest in school lessons. What could they teach me at Marylebone Grammar? There was little attempt to teach anything the least bit useful, only to force memorisation in order to gain a satisfactory report and move on.

Marc Guebard (later the actor Marc Gebhard) lived on the same street as me and attended the local private school, St. Mary's Town and Country. Marc was thirteen to my eleven.

At Marylebone, I started blackmailing other pupils with the help of a mate I called "Big Elvis." He did the dirty work under my direction. We would sneak up on an unsuspecting boy after school, at a bus stop or train platform, and forcibly steal his wooden pencil box. This little box was compulsory at Marylebone, so the unfortunate victim always accepted our offer to sell it back for sixpence. This scam continued on regular basis for few weeks, until an aggrieved pupil complained to the headmaster. Celia was summoned to the school and informed that her son was to be punished by expulsion. A kindly prefect, George Lowenstein, tried to intervene on my behalf, but to no avail.

Forced to find another school anyway, I longed to return to the "refined" environment of public boarding school, where I had hopes that my distinctive style might be more appreciated. Another plus was that I could get away with more once removed from Celia's ever-watchful eye. I was in a funk. At both Swiss Cottage and Marylebone I'd stuck out the wrong way. The trouble I'd gotten into wasn't even fun. Probably due more to my mother's own sense of pride than any empathy for my individuality, I was soon placed at a private school in Hampstead which specialised in "problem kids." Here I studied to pass a Common Entrance exam, a qualification needed to gain entrance to public school.

Unfortunately for mum's peace of mind, I couldn't start until the beginning of the new school year in September 1956. That was almost five months away and Celia worried whether I could be trusted to stay out of trouble while she was out at work. I argued persuasively that I was old enough to look after myself, and she had few alternatives to leaving me alone.

I was allowed finally to spend these school-free days at home. I spent hours listening to the radio or records like "I'm in Love Again" by Fats Domino, watching television, and visiting the cinema. This was *my* idea of studying. I read about rock 'n' roll voraciously, intrigued by Gene Vincent, whose first U.K. EP ("extended play" 7-inch 45 rpm) had just been released. I bought the EP and wore it out spinning the lead track, "Say Mama," back-to-back with the latest Elvis single, "Hound Dog."

American rock 'n' roll was the real thing; Britain as yet had nothing to compete. Tommy Steele, trumpeted as "Britain's Answer to Elvis," was a poor imitation of his Yank counternumbers. Thousands of British teenage kids disagreed with me on this (as, I'm afraid, they have from time to time ever since) and made his debut single "Rock with the Caveman" an instant hit. Lionel Bart wrote the song.

Through reading about Tommy Steele, I understood that
the new British rock 'n' roll scene was all happening in the coffee
bars of Soho. Here, young hopefuls sang, sneered, and swivelled
their hips. Managers plucked them from obscurity and launched
them to fame in the charts. Business was conducted in Tin Pan
Alley, where agents, publishers, managers, producers, and songwriters all worked their magic.

So naturally, I decided to write a rock 'n' roll song and sell
it down Tin Pan Alley. I'd read an article which suggested that
songwriters were the real winners of the British rock 'n' roll boom
- a hit rock 'n' roll record earned the songwriter a small fortune.
My dream was to write a number one hit and never have to return to school at all.

After a week of singing and scribbling, I completed an
awful rip-off of whatever Tommy Steele ripped-off. I was sure
my very own - wait for it! - "Boomerang Rock!" could be a hit.

> *Boomerang Rock!*
> *Throw it here*
> *Throw it there*
> *It'll always*
> *Come back at'cha*
> *Through the air*
> *Boomerang Rock!*
> *Do the Boomerang Rock!*

Soho's Tin Pan Alley was not what I had pictured in my imagination. I had expected a glitzy Mecca for fantastic looking rock 'n'
rollers, and what I (and everybody else) got was short, shabby
Denmark Street, just off Charing Cross Road. Tin Pan Alley was
an inhospitable place, full of brutish men with none of the grace
of those I felt I had come to know from the world of film and television. I rang every buzzer on Denmark Street attempting to get
"Boomerang Rock!" heard and sold, and returned the next day to
try again. Eventually one small company, Box and Cox, let me up
to their offices, gave my song a hearing and some kind words which,
summed up, meant "not this month, mate." Close up, the rock 'n'
roll business was uninspiring at best. In fact, neither school nor
commerce seemed to be of the stuff that made life worth living.

Nevertheless, I returned to Soho as often as I could - its neon hustling crassness was like a drug before drugs. I was lying to my mother, of course, telling her I was visiting a friend in the evenings, then rushing off to Soho, to the coffee bar on Old Compton street where British rock 'n' roll was being put on the map. "The world famous 2 I's coffee bar, home of the stars," the neon sign above the door proclaimed.

The 2 I's had started playing host to "live" rock 'n' roll and skiffle acts in early 1956, when Australian wrestlers Ray Hunter and Paul Lincoln took over the lease. Tommy Steele had made his name there, and since signing to Decca Records his success had brought the 2 I's unlimited publicity. Downstairs, in the tiny basement that had been decorated by the already successful songwriter Lionel Bart, a regular crowd of two hundred teenage hipsters danced the night away.

The coffee bar was a haven for managers and agents on the hunt for fresh talent, eager to cash in quick on the current teenage thirst for rock 'n' roll. Larry Parnes, who became the most successful and notorious manager of the fifties rock 'n' roll scene, was a regular. Duffy Power, Georgie Fame, Sammy Samwell - all were trying their luck and, as yet, all were absolute beginners.

I was only twelve and hadn't a farthing, but I stood for hours outside the 2 I's, watching the customers slide downstairs to the "skiffle" bar. Skiffle, according to Lionel Bart, became popular because no one could get their hands on electric instruments or amps. I was on the outside looking in, checking the names on the shining jukebox placed strategically in the window, and chatting to the doorkeeper, Nora. After many such evenings of window shopping, the kindhearted Nora took pity on me and let me downstairs without paying the usual one shilling cover charge. Here I saw my first live rock 'n' roll shows, courtesy of Vince Taylor and the Playboys, and Paul Raven (Gary Glitter in the making). Eventually, I started lugging cases of Coke downstairs at the 2 I's for 2/6d a night.

In September I started back at my new private school in Hampstead. Headmasters Welland and Wilcox, used to dealing with "problem" children, took me under their wing. Encouraged by their concern, I worked studiously, knowing the result of my endeavours would determine whether I got a place as a boarder at a public school. I absolutely couldn't bear the prospect of having to return as a dayboy to a "normal" state school.

Another boy attending this "crammer" was Nicholas Mason, who lived over the other side of Spaniard's Inn, off the road that led down to Golder's Green. His first-floor bedroom was given over to what seemed, to my size and station, a massive drum kit. Nicholas's agenda was already set. A dozen years on he would be known as Nick Mason, the Pink Floyd drummer.

The 1956 Suez crisis was a political disaster and the final nail in the coffin for a no longer "Great" Britain. The crisis provided me with my second job, at a Swiss Cottage florist, Cater's. Miss Cater was a pleasure to work for: chic, tweedy, grey-haired, stern, but kindly. Her live-in companion and driver, a tough little lady named Billie, seemed less happy about the new shop assistant. I was brought in for the busy Christmas season when the country's petrol gave out, and Billie could no longer drive Miss Cater to work from their Hampstead Garden suburb. Despite the scarcity of public transport, I delivered holiday flowers to all points of Hampstead, its N.W.3 and 6, doing very well in the tip department from grateful homes surprised that someone had braved heavy winter snow to bring them cheer and dead flowers.

Miss Cater was kindness itself, Billie held her butch tongue - had there been no fuel crisis I'd have been jobless, and she'd have been off in the wood-panelled, powder-blue Morris Traveller herself, perhaps doing well enough off the tips to afford another pair of her manly brogues. I remember fondly the gratitude of my customers, but better yet, the smile of heartfelt pleasure on my mother's face that Christmas. A significant portion of my largesse went to buying her a handsome clock in sincere appreciation for her having had the time for me.

CHAPTER 2

*uncle bill brings rock 'n' roll to england / three celluloid saints
of rock - eddie cochran, little richard, and gene vincent / the
importance of being elvis / epiphonic moment number one -
"expresso bongo" on stage with paul scofield / suddenly, i knew
what i wanted to be / sent off to boarding school to make me forget /
the divine intervention of rock on tele - jack good, the patron saint of
pop / epiphonic moment number two "sweet smell of success" - first
whiff of the lovely gutter*

Billed as the "American rock 'n' roll originator," Bill Haley became
the first American rock 'n' roll act to tour Britain in February 1956.
Alec bought me a ticket (at ten shillings and sixpence) for Haley's
show at the Dominion Theatre on Tottenham Court Road. I went
by myself, which was just fine, since most others wouldn't have
understood my pre-show ritual in the men's room perfecting my
kiss-curl.

The northeast corner on which the Dominion Theatre stands
is hallowed ground, home to the longest running hits of the West
End such as *The Sound of Music*. Earlier, on the southeast corner,
the Astoria premiered impresario Mike Todd's scam 'n' star laden
Todd-AO extravaganza *Around the World in Eighty Days*. That
building later became the dance club of the eighties, Heaven.

Bang opposite the Dominion was Lyons Corner House,
where Mother and Alec took me on those occasions when my
grades did not warrant The Ivy or Wheeler's. I got to know the
Dominion's façade well, since I was at Lyons more often than
The Ivy. The Dominion is a magnificent theatre; its stalls slope
toward the object of the evening's awe like an audio-visual
wedding train. It is a feast for the eyes and ears that impresses
all who gather there, regardless of their taste in entertainment.
The two thousand Teds in that beautiful old theatre were ready
to rock. In their powder-grey drape jackets and brothel creepers,
they looked like royalty against the backdrop of the Dominion
dress circle. Their girls appeared to be bleached quiffed Pearly
Queens enjoying their own version of Covent Garden opening
night. Imagine how our modern British couple must have felt
when their first taste of genuine American rock 'n' roll turned

out to be so unsavoury.

Haley was a nightmare. There was an hour and a half by the spastic Vic Lewis and his Orchestra, then a paltry thirty-five minutes from this fat, kiss-curled housewife from the middle of America, the uncle you never wanted, Bill Haley. It gave me pause, I'll tell you, as at the end of Taylor Hackford's fabulous pop flick, *The Idolmaker*, when all seems to slip away whilst Ray Sharkey works out what to do next. That's what happened to me at the Dominion. Confronted by the mediocrity that was Haley, I thought for a moment that rock 'n' roll was over. But recalling the Then of Johnnie Ray and the Now of Buddy Holly and Little Richard saved the day, and my imagination roared on intact, faith returned replete with sound and texture.

Haley was also featured in two other rock flicks that summer of 1956: *Rock Around the Clock* and *Don't Knock the Rock*. Audiences on both sides of the Atlantic danced in the aisles, ripped up the seats, and gave rock 'n' roll a reputation for mayhem to live up to. I saw the movies in the primly sterile Haverstock Odeon with twenty or so uptight patrons who tutted and shifted in their seats, while I quietly tore a gash in mine. Had I dared myself to take the tube two stops south to Camden Town, I wouldn't have missed the party. A few years later I attempted, as a newly hatched independent publicist, to kindle the same reaction on behalf of Don Arden and Little Richard, with similarly controversial results. Perhaps I was making up for the lost opportunity.

Teds were magnificent specimens with an attitude way out above any station. They were the first teenagers to stand up, let it rip, and be counted. Beatniks didn't count; they sat around drinking coffee and smoking Gauloises, while the Teds draped and duck's-arsed themselves into a national outrage that made headlines. They spent their newly disposable incomes taking the piss. I loved the sight of a Ted on the high street a whole lot better than the first American rock 'n' roller I got to see live.

So what if Bill Haley looked like an Oklahoma City short-order cook; there was the thrilling sky-grey slub fabric that clothed the Crickets, and the silky mohair drape-suited vision of Little Richard in *The Girl Can't Help It*. For good measure, I also fell for Grace Kelly and got a huge lesson from her duet of "True Love" with Bing Crosby, which I applied years later when I met Marianne Faithfull. Some people like their sluts to be backstreet girls, but I prefer tramps that pass for pure, and that kind, the all-too-rare Kellys and Faithfulls, you can bring home and have a good laugh at Auntie's expense.

In June 1957 I took and passed the Common Entrance Exam and, while I waited to discover which boarding school would welcome the pleasure of my company, my mother offed me away to board for the summer with a farmer's family in Dulverton, near Taunton. There, I fell in love for the first time with a "real" girl: the beautiful eighteen-year-old redhead who tended the horses on a well-to-do farm at the other end of the manor. I became suddenly and suprisingly interested in all things equine and spent most of my time helping her in the stables. At the end of the summer I was rewarded with my first real kiss. The smile was still on my face when my mother met me off the train at St. Pancras with the good news that I'd been accepted as a boarder at Wellingborough, a public school in Northamptonshire.

Celia took me out to celebrate, an early supper at Lyon's Corner House and, for the special treat of my choice, I chose the musical, *Expresso Bongo*. Written by Wolf Mankowitz, this was the first ever British dramatisation of the fifties rock 'n' roll scene and the revolution in the streets it was fomenting. "Soho Johnny Never Had It So Good - Or Lost It So Fast," blared the billboard. Even more than the censored weekly TV shows that pandered to "Youth," or the increasing interest by promoters in cashing in on live rock, *Expresso Bongo*'s run in the West End signalled a coming of age for the new music, the new style, the new hustle. Even better, it owed very little to its Yank progenitors; it was Brit to the core. It would become my liturgy: a scenario where the manager was equally important as the artist. Johnny Jackson became my object of worship.

I sat in the stalls at the Shaftesbury Avenue Theatre mesmerised as Paul Scofield brought the street-smart manager Johnny Jackson alive before an audience that was no doubt both titillated and 'orrified. In the first run, Bongo Herbert, Johnny's wanna-be star from the coffee bar, was played by Jimmy Kenney, a young blond actor I'd noted in some of the Woolf brothers' Romulus films. I learned the basics of self-restraint that night (would that the lesson had stuck somewhat) so as not to let Celia know just how wholly I identified with this work of "fiction."

Just before intermission, Bongo, an overnight sensation in the classic sense, starts to sing a ballad, "The Shrine on the Second Floor." He allows us to think he's singing about his girlfriend, but by the bridge it's apparent he's singing about his mother! It's her flat that's "the shrine on the second floor." As we're absorbing this delicious irony, huge stained glass windows drop down, transforming the stage into a veritable shrine; and a church choir enters to take the song to its heavenly erotic climax. *Expresso Bongo* was at once so incredibly obvious and yet oh so subtle: sex, religion, and a whiff of incest (which I believe to be the rock coupling that dares not speak its name). I saw through those cheesy imitation stained glass windows to a future where Bongos would beg me to be their Johnny. Almost as important as the boost the play gave to my own aspirations was the reassurance that, despite the loneliness I often felt, I was not alone, and with like-minded fellows anything was possible.

This new feeling of well-being was short lived. When I boarded the train at St. Pancras bound for Wellingborough, smartly attired in my dark maroon blazer, and waved goodbye to Celia, I was leaving the streets of London I knew so well for a life of narrow-mindedness and sport that has tortured British thirteen-year-olds from time immemorial. I felt that all I was taking with me was Elvis's latest number one and a little suitcase that I packed by myself.

A two-hour journey by train from London, Wellingborough was a small, quiet town between Northampton and Market Harborough. When I arrived at the four-hundred-year-old all-boy public school, I was registered as A.L. Oldham and shown around the square mile of stately red brick buildings that was to be my home for the next three years, then dropped off at my single bed in a row of twenty. The floors were bare and the bathroom had just two tiny tubs for all twenty boys. Interesting how the British idea of aristocratic education resembles a poor and rather dirty imitation of ancient Sparta.

Competition with and for boys was the social order of the day for those at Wellingborough Public School who wished to "fit in." The five houses, Garne's (which housed me), Parker's, Platt's, Fryer's, and Weymouth, vied with each other at soccer from September till Christmas. Rugby and "Athletics" divided the spring term, and cricket and swimming the summer term. Marksmanship and other games of war were on for all three terms, as was the constant rivalry for the attentions of those lads one fancied. In an environment where the traditional, unofficial curriculum was romancing the boys, the school establishment merrily condoned this childish lovemaking amongst their charges with the understanding that not too long after one left school, one "settled down," and gave the girls the benefit of one's experience. Of course, films like Dirk Bogarde's *Victim* (1962) reveal the dreadful consequences of this hypocrisy rather more realistically.

Our uniforms were grey suits, sweaters, and shirts. A straw boater and white shirt with stiff detachable collars signified Sunday, the boaters a must for any walk into town. The wardrobe for Wednesday Cadet Corps afternoons was standard army gear, and in short order I managed to get myself into the Cadet marching band, playing drums, inside the middle of the sound, where I could either be on time or mime it.

That same first term I got myself into the Wellingborough School Film Society, due to my artistic talents coming to light. Films as old as Richard Widmark's *Halls of Montezuma* from 1950 were shown on Sunday nights.

The film society members were amazed at how close in likeness I managed to make my posters to the originals. I just couldn't tell them that during the school holidays, as I lived in London and knew the six films booked for the next term, I could whoop down Wardour Street in Soho, the epicentre of the British film industry, and pester the film companies to give me the original posters. If I got them I would trace them and they would be deemed original and brilliant, otherwise I was merely great.

My housemaster at Garne's was John Oughton, who only caught me out three times on an offence that warranted caning, but that was three times too many, thank you. I made every effort to stay out of Mr. Oughton's way. The first assistant housemaster was a young and pleasant science teacher, E.R. Marson, who was good enough to let a select five or six devotees into his quarters on a Saturday night to watch Jack Good's *Oh, Boy!*

In January 1957, two new rock 'n' roll shows for teenagers had made their television debuts. Although the BBC's *Six-Five Spe-*

cial and ITV's *Cool for Cats* were lackluster in comparison to what was really happening on the streets of Soho, I never missed the Jack Good-produced *Six-Five Special* every Saturday. For a while I was taken with the house band, the John Barry Seven, who would later perform the soundtrack for the Hammer flick, *Beat Girl*.

Cool for Cats, presented every Wednesday by Kent Walton, offered up aging acts and treated rock 'n' roll as just one more "teenage fad" that would quickly pass. It was evident that the British entertainment hierarchy was wop-bop-a-loo-bopped by rock 'n' roll and vastly underestimated its staying power. In time, Jack Good left the Beeb, moving over to the independent channel to create a show that defined the times, the earth-moving *Oh, Boy!* It went out in the same Saturday slot as Good's old show, which was soon axed. So too were the BBC's next couple of music shows, *Dig This* and *Drumbeat*, as *Oh Boy!* ruled during an incredible 38-week run.

On *Oh Boy!*'s first show, Good introduced a fresh-faced and very British seventeen-year-old Cliff Richard, making his debut with the Drifters. He performed "Move It" (written by Ian "Sammy" Samwell), and for me the earth stood still. The following week Maurice Kinn wrote in *New Musical Express* (*NME*): "His violent hip-swinging was revolting, hardly the kind of performance any parent could wish their children to see. He was wearing so much eyeliner he looked like Jayne Mansfield. If we are expected to believe that Cliff was acting naturally, then consideration for medical treatment may be advisable." Sounded like a rave to me.

Though Jack may have toned it down some from the pilot, *Oh Boy!* was a weekly communion of pure sex and energy, with words and rhythm proving to me that there was more to life than what was being dictated. The subversive music had sounds, melodies, and words that echoed exactly how I felt. Suddenly I was not alone.

Oh Boy! was the perfect showcase for the sublime Eddie Cochran. His U.K. appearances so far had been brief, with small parts in two big films, *The Girl Can't Help It* and Mamie Van Doren's *Untamed Youth*. He came to London to play "Summertime Blues" at the Hackney Empire, and the *Oh Boy!* spots made him a legend.

Oh Boy! also established Billy Fury. His debut Decca single, "Maybe Tomorrow," raised the stakes amongst the Brit rock boys. He was the only English solo star who was comfortable sharing a stage with Eddie.

Jack Good was soon promoting fantastically successful *Oh Boy!* package tours with Larry Parnes around the U.K. starring Cliff and the Drifters, Billy, Vince Taylor, Adam Faith, and Wee Willie Harris, who dyed his hair a different colour, pink or green, every time he appeared on *Oh Boy!*

Mr. Marson, our benefactor with the TV, would move on to head up another house and would be replaced by another science teacher, John Elwick. He was a cat of a different stripe altogether. I was besotted with the man and his style: thirtyish, slim, fair, with intense eyes and a hook nose that added to his haughty attitude. Plus, he was a bachelor, which meant that his wardrobe would be more extensive and expressive than any married teacher's could be.

John Elwick played Himself: he was simply "on" all the time, you never caught him offstage, he never left the lights as he strode around the school grounds. He even managed to make watching a school soccer match, sitting on his "horsie" saddle stick, an elegant affair. He presented himself to us each day with variations on the same sartorial theme: cavalry twill two-buttoned suits with gen-u-ine bone buttons, flaired at the waist, slanted "hacking" pockets, lapelled vest, and trousers not too tight to disturb his fellow teachers, but turned up and tight enough to impress me. White wing-collared shirt, striped tie, and suede chukka boots made up the length and breadth of the man. He roamed the grounds so well dressed that even the teachers' mandatory black gown did not diminish his elegance. He wore that most antiquated and unstylish of British academic garb with a "Blackglama: What Becomes a Legend Most?" insouciance, walking at a pace that allowed the breeze to part the gown and reveal the haberdashery beneath.

An equal admirer of Elwick was my best friend from the Wellingborough years, John Douglas. Fine featured and fine looking, John had the same priorities as I but came from a completely different background. John's Scottish father was a respected physician who, with his wife and John's sister Liz, lived in what seemed to me a huge mansion opposite a park on the outskirts of nearby Northampton.

We loved to the same degree of distraction Elvis lounging

poolside in *Jailhouse Rock*, his flappy black trews foreshadowing Armani, his black and white shoes, and his tight cable-knit dark sweater with upturned collar symbolising the triumph of rock 'n' roll in the world of show biz. We were sure that the way he had treated Dolores Hart in *Loving You* had caused her to take the vows that ended her screen career prematurely. We loved the choreography of the *Jailhouse Rock* production number, with its innumerable Elvis clones, and we just knew He had created the routines Himself. John and I shared Eddie Cochran, Buddy Holly and the Crickets, Gene Vincent, Jack Good's *Oh, Boy!* and the later (1959) *Boy Meets Girls*, Cliff Richard, Billy Fury, and Marty Wilde stalking his way through Bill Parsons's "All-American Boy," Jody Reynolds's classic "Endless Sleep," and Thomas Wayne's "Tragedy."

On camera, we appreciated Tony Curtis as a wide boy in *Sweet Smell of Success*. Curtis was hounded by co-star Burt Lancaster, and the film was co-produced by Curtis's Curtleigh Productions and Lancaster's Hill-Hecht-Lancaster Productions. *Success* was shot partly on location in New York, where the lobby of the Brill Building took a break from housing a hit factory to serve as J.J. Hunsecker's apartment block. *Elmer Gantry* and *Trapeze* were also hits from the Lancaster organisation. Another muscleman turned movie mogul whom I admired was Kirk Douglas. His Bryna Productions would deliver some of Kirk's biggest successes, among them *Paths of Glory* and *Spartacus*, inspiring young Michael Douglas along the way.

The other Douglas in my life shared my love of stars and style. I left Elvis to John, and expressed myself with a peroxide dip that I fancied combined Jet Harris's moodiness and Adam Faith's air of displacement with the Marlon Brando of *The Young Lions*. Anything James Dean was fair game for me to cop. Apart from John and our other pal David Miranda, I was the only one who knew in my head what film was playing at the cinema.

Miranda had a dark Jewish Tony Curtis look, which meant he was cool. Our friendship took some doing on all our parts, since fraternisation between houses was not encouraged, only competition, but David was always on the perimeter of whatever John and I were up to.

We were not allowed to mix with the local town girls. Consorting was generally *verboten* at Wellingborough, except for dance lessons and the Cat's Whiskers *fêtes* that we organised, at which we were allowed to exhibit our dancing prowess. But how can you learn to dance when your partner is dissatisfied with her very physical being? The girls were nervous whether they were wearing bras or not yet wearing them. If they made up their lips, they were embarrassed, as if make-up made them tarts. It was like partying on the Planet of the Apes.

After my first year at Wellingborough, I returned home to London for the summer vacation. Celia, ever with her eye on the main chance, stressed that success at Wellingborough was only the first step in my life trajectory: "O" then "A" levels, university, a "good" job. She had moved house again and our new home was much grander than the basement flat at Belsize Park Gardens. Close to the bohemian affluence of Hampstead, 19 Netherhall Gardens was an austere two-floor flat of which Celia was very proud.

Alec Morris had a son John and a daughter Pat. John, the elder of the two, was an ace at waterskiing, had been on the British team in the south of France, and was a flash all-rounder about town. On Saturdays, John took me to Chelsea football matches in his left-hand drive Lincoln Continental convertible. I was really knocked out. We'd come out of the football ground and sit in the King's Road, ostentatiously buzzing the canvas roof up and down. Everyone would be staring at us in this incredible car. I loved it.

Jimmy Greaves, Chelsea F.C., was it, and only eighteen, a wonder striker, idol to me and all blue-and-white scarved Stamford Bridge lads. I was there in August '58 when he woofed five goals past Wolves. Alec and John always took me to Chelsea during my school holidays, and I stayed Greaves-struck all the way to 1961 until he left for AC Milan. I think he put three away that last match. I cried. There were a lot of lumps in the throats of grown men as well as boys that day.

Among my continual run-ins with the authorities were tiffs over clothing. At the start of each new term, I would show up with unsatisfactory variations on the grey flannel school uniform. I turned the standard on its head with clothes of my own design bought with money I'd got from various school holiday jobs. When the masters would ask me just what I thought I was doing, my stock answer was, "But it is grey, sir ..."

My masterpieces were made at the Burton's tailoring chain

in the West End. Although I lived in one of the world's largest cities, it simply wasn't done to venture far out of one's proper neighbourhood. Had I been able, I might have discovered that real bespoke was readily available in the East End, and within my means, so long as I knew my manor, my wants, and my needs. I was on a strictly Hampstead to the West End run, however. It just wasn't done, and possibly a bit dangerous, to go wandering about.

Burton's had made a fortune providing suits for ten to twelve guineas to the lower and middle classes who had to be suited for work in imitation of their masters, normally just knocking off two or three-button suits from the same pattern. I drove them berserk by taking them up on their tailoring invitation in which you picked the details. I had a dove-grey mohair suit with nipped waist, covered buttons, inverted pleat in the back of the jacket, draped trousers, slanted pockets, and a paisley lining. As he took my suit away, Mr. Housemaster Oughton said, "I don't know why you bother, you only wore it for a day." "Yeah," I thought, "but what a day."

You needed a lot of pocket money to keep up with Buddy Holly. The man had so many hits in his head, he could sustain a solo career along with fronting the Crickets, who had just gone number one in America with "That'll Be the Day." Disc jockey Alan Freed had launched them at his Brooklyn Paramount showcase gig after which they'd broken out nationwide on a seventeen-act Freed-promoted U.S. package tour, "The Biggest Show of Stars" - and that it was. Our minds boggled: Buddy Holly and the Crickets, Chuck Berry, the Everly Brothers, and Jerry Lee Lewis all on one bill! Decca Records had the license to Coral Records (Holly's label as a solo artist) in the U.K. and they couldn't get his stuff out fast enough for us; the hits just kept comin' and comin'. You'd have wept; it was incredible: "Not Fade Away," "Oh, Boy!" "Peggy Sue," "That'll Be the Day," "Rave On," "Think It Over," "Fool's Paradise," "I'm Lookin' for Someone to Love." This man's B-sides were number ones! It was a wonderful time to be in your early teens. Music was life confirming, problem resolving, and everything that mattered started with a count-off and a look.

CHAPTER 3

*an interlude that passes itself off as education / sex and school -
whatever wets you thru the night / school daze; school plays; what a
drag it is being young / we gotta get out of this place ... and we do*

After *Oh, Boy!*, the Film Society, and the Cat's Whiskers, the next
move had to be a band. A local boy, Vic White, was Cliff Richard
and the Drifters crazy, owned a guitar he could actually play, so
we were off. I should have managed the band and let John sing,
but I insisted on doing "Tell Laura I Love Her" at a school concert.
The loudest sound in the room as I entered stage left was the
sound of my knees knocking. I couldn't hit the high notes without
breaking into a pig's squeal.

Every year the Wellingborough School Theatrical Society
would mount a dramatic or musical work, something light and
Gilbert-and-Sullivan-ish, wherein effort could hopefully be mistaken for entertainment. This particular year it was *H.M.S. Pina-
fore*. John and I got the gig of painting the sets and backdrops.

As the Theatrical Society rehearsals progressed from round
table readings to cues, blocking and run-throughs on stage, the
leading "ladies" started getting into costume. Up in the rafters,
painting the sets, John and I were beside ourselves at this bizarre
transformation of boys into girls.

Contact with girls, unless supervised, was an offence
punishable by expulsion. Our boyhood crushes were hardly
homosexual by deliberate, conscious choice, just "one of those
bells that now and then rings." This was a world of innocence,
before the terrorism of AIDS; we were working with what we
had at hand. Had we been on a desert island with hundreds of
young girls, we'd have gladly welcomed our fate.

At Wellingborough you'd be expelled if caught smoking a
cigarette, so there was little margin for more serious breaches of
conduct. Before the pill, a young girl who came up with child
ruined both her own and the young man's future. In view of the
fear and awkwardness that surrounded all things sexual, it was
safer to stay home and play. Anyway, the boys were prettier, and
available.

I made a pass at the "leading lady," a snotty but pretty little
farmboy, who belonged to the in-crowd prefect of another house.

For my troubles, I got cornered on a cricket pitch one Sunday, and well and truly decked. One punch and I decided to stay down. A stretcher was called. I acted knocked out, and was carried away to the school sanatorium.

What was amazing was that my mother took me back to London, got my mouth stitched back up and sent me straight back to school, never mentioning the fact that I had been accused of running a homosexual ring. She was told not to expect the school to discipline my attackers. I don't think she believed them for a moment, but she understood the rules. Celia could only hope that some day I would understand at least some of them, too.

There were more lies to come. A few concerned locals had seen me being taken off the school fields on a stretcher and wanted to know what had happened. In the local paper the following week, the school explained away the incident by claiming that, "the pupil was knocked unconscious by a cricket ball." Tail wagging the dog is nothing new, you see.

There was an upside to my end-of-term misadventure. The alluring wife of the headmaster took pity on me and invited me into the mansion for tea and sympathy. I was lucky that the stir this caused didn't result in another beating, and even luckier that the head didn't knock me down himself.

Summer and the comparative freedom of London couldn't have come at a better time. I'd read an article about Shirley Bassey, which mentioned that her manager (and later her husband), the producer Kenneth Hume, lived off Hyde Park. I wanted to meet Hume, because I appreciated the Svengalian effect he'd had on the development of substance and style in the Welsh singer's career. To me, Hume *was* Shirley Bassey. I looked up the show biz couple's address in the telephone directory and went to visit. Hume himself opened the door and engaged me in an inspiring chat over a cup of tea, the great British social lubricant. There was a marvelous paradox in those days between the national and even international celebrity of many British show business figures, and their openness to my "knock-knock" visits. Perhaps it helped that I was impossibly young and unbearably precocious. They couldn't believe their eyes and ears.

In the summer of 1959, my two major passions, rock 'n' roll and cinema, collided to sensational effect in the long-awaited film version of *Expresso Bongo*. No one could have pleased me more as manager Johnny Jackson than my own Larry Harvey, who was as at home in the coffee bars and strip joints of Soho as he had not been in the society drawing rooms of his immediately previous hit, *Room at the Top*. To indicate even further that my subconscious was beginning to control the audio and video of "real life," Bongo Herbert was played by Cliff Richard.

What really struck me was the upbeat conclusion after a music business tycoon and an over-the-hill floozy conspire to steal Bongo from Johnny. Just as he's decided to get his drums out of hock and go on the road, leaving the scrumptious Sylvia Syms behind in her pasties, a notorious show biz deadbeat repays a loan Johnny never thought he'd see again. The movie ends with Johnny dropping his drums in the street and strolling off in search of the next Bongo. Although I may not have articulated it at the time, that attitude became one of my mantras: "They always fuck you for the first one."

Johnny Jackson, *Expresso Bongo*:

> The picture in the fan mag showed this gangly kid in jeans and a sweatshirt, his face contorted, mouth wide open, beating with both hands on a bongo set round his shoulder, over it the headline "BONGO SCORES AT TOM TOM." The same terrible stuff, but this time it was good, because it was me who dropped the deadbeat drunk columnist a fiver to run it. Because this new boy, Bongo Herbert, playing nightly for the past week at the Tom Tom Express back of Frith Street, he's under contract to nobody but *me*. Half of the £10 he picks up this Friday comes to me. Half of everything he beats out of those little bongos for the next five years comes to me.
>
> I had wet-nursed this kid along, bought him cigarettes, coffee, and sandwiches, a couple of sweatshirts with bongos painted on them, a pair of tailored black jeans, and a fancy haircut. Turned him from Bert Rudge, snotty-nosed nobody, to Bongo Herbert, Britain's latest answer to America's latest solution of how to keep discs selling by the million.

Just before Christmas, John and I skived off school to see the Shadows share the bill with Emile Ford and the Checkmates at the Granada Cinema in nearby Kettering. Emile Ford had just become the first black Briton to have a number one, with "What Do You Want to Make Those Eyes at Me For?" Emile sat on the edge of the stage with his feet in the orchestra pit and managed to get the whole audience to sing "White Christmas." This was another pivotal realisation of the possibility of rock 'n' roll as total entertainment. The hairs on the back of my neck tingled. I was in love with show biz. The Shadows were more than show business, they were life.

It was 1960, I was sixteen, and I decided to lose my virginity. Regular dances were held at school, to which girls from the dancing classes of Mrs. Josie Marsh were invited. Naturally enough, I set my sights on the prize catch, Mrs. Marsh's daughter. She was two years older than I, and, as John said, "out of my league."

Alexis was soon confiding that she was most unhappy about her mother's plan for her to be married to a man of Mrs. Marsh's choosing. Alexis, though dutiful, was put out by the calculation of it all. I invited her to visit me at my mother's flat in Hampstead. She agreed, obviously keen on having an adventure before her mother had her way. I celebrated with John over a brandy and Havana cigar. We both vomited.

Over the Easter holiday, as promised, Miss Marsh rang me at my mother's: "Could you meet me at the train station?" Excitedly I changed into my finest threads and rushed off to meet the girl. Back at Netherhall Gardens, with a few hours to spare before Mother returned from work, I "became a man."

We performed in the front window because I knew the old people opposite, who were always peeping through their curtains, would get aggravated. But it was over very fast. Afterwards I thought: "Oh God, this is terrible. Now I've got to see Alexis out, right back to the station." It was not her fault; I had no idea what I was doing.

Soon after my liaison, I was devastated to hear that Eddie Cochran was dead. The car he had been riding in up to the airport with Gene Vincent was totalled. Gene escaped with injuries that accentuated the limp he already had. At the time I was convinced that Eddie had died for England, to light an eternal flame for rock 'n' roll in the hearts of the nation's youth.

I'd decided I was out of Wellingborough after the exams,

although John's parents had arranged for him to stay on. No manner of persuasion or pressure from Celia could persuade me to stay any longer. As a capper, the school wrote her a letter stating, "Andrew may do well ... but not here." But Wellingborough had indeed prepared me for the rest of my life.

It was good training for life, perhaps not the life I had planned for myself, but, nevertheless, it worked. School was like being in rehearsal, and leaving school was like going on stage. We rehearsed a movie called *Life*, and I owe that place the way Al Pacino says he owes Lee Strasberg. They gave me the tools. Destiny had been declared.

Cliff Richard

CHAPTER 4

my east end neighbour in north west london / frank norman - from prison stripes to chalk stripe / falling in love with the girl up the hill / the french new wave raves over london / "somebody has to let you in" - peter meaden opens the door on soho / a passion for fashion - it begins / tracing for a living / first glance at belgravia / french new wave shakes over british cinema

Rid of the country at last and back in London, I got on with my life. To pay for my fun and to avoid at all costs more hectoring from my mother, I determined to find hire worthy of the workman.

In Piccadilly, opposite the Rialto Cinema, I spotted a notice for a part-time sales assistant in the window of Adams, a small conservative men's clothes store. The old man who owned and managed the shop liked what he saw and heard from this smartly dressed, well-spoken school-leaver and appointed me on the spot. The window was drab; so was the clientèle. They didn't get the overflow from Daks or Aquascutum, just a few world-weary travelling salesmen on their way back to Leicester.

Within a few days, Harold, Adams's full-timer, knew he had a new tuner for his fiddle. Life had more hazing in store for me, it seemed. Five years older than I and East End bred, Harold threatened to beat me up if I didn't follow his orders, which were: "At closing, take a few garments into the changing room, put them on under your mufti, say 'Good night,' and wear them out." I coughed them up to Harold in the Piccadilly Circus tube station men's room, long a familiar scene for the illicit *rendezvous*. If Harold judged an item too naff to move on, he'd throw it back at me with, "'Ere. That looks good on you." Thus I was forced to steal bread off the table of my new family, which seemed a poor exchange for remaining in Harold's good graces.

Game, set, and clobber that never matched. It wouldn't have been so bad had the clothes from Adams not been so, well, as Harold would have it, naff. For the most part old Mr. Adams sold apparel I wouldn't be seen dead in. While rethinking my entrance into the working week, I decided to rest up for an early summer holiday, and spend some of that quality time with my mother - time that was rapidly becoming scarcer as my life became my own.

Juan-les-Pins, the then fashionable south of France resort, was our destination. By this time, I actually felt liberated via "Andrew may do well ... but not here." My mother's influence over me in the career department was on the wane. With a spring in my step, I would transform my dreams into reality. The film in my mind would soon leap off the screen onto the streets ...

Oh yes, I would work hard, but I had no intention of applying for the traditional school-leaver's apprenticeship: clerking at some boring, average company, where I could only expect more dress codes, more restrictions on thought, speech, and hours - more frustration - an establishment lifestyle that disincentivised discipline in order to maintain the *status quo*. I was more than willing to overcome frustration, already had a dress code, and had no doubts about my discipline and grip.

While we packed, Celia expounded upon her objections to our upstairs neighbour, Frank Norman, who rather enjoyed being the block's leading celebrity. "He comes home drunk at all hours with a different girl every night." My mother's eyes shot lasers up through the ceiling to the Norman residence. "It's not a life," she concluded, but exactly why Mr. Norman had no life remained one of Celia's secrets.

I admired Frank Norman. In his thirties, he had the sort of butch, languid features that would drive Pier Paolo Pasolini, made dangerous by the intersection of his long scar with his smile. Norman draped his tall frame in the same barrister pinstripes worn by the lot that had prosecuted him. He was an East End ex-con, who had repaid his debts to society as the guest of numerous of Her Majesty's prisons, then turned his life of crime into a well-paid afterlife in entertainment. Frank moved northwest to Hampstead to join all the other well-heeled cons on the hill. Mother was forced to share her would-be genteel neighbourhood with some of the most interesting people in London.

In fact, Frank Norman was one of the original working-class heroes of the *glitterati* (cf. the more unfortunate debacle of Jack Henry Abbott, championed by Norman Mailer *et al.*) Norman wrote *Fings Ain't Wot They Used t'Be* in the 1959, the musical comedy version of *The Last Angry Man*. With staging in 1960 by Sean Kenny, music and lyrics by Lionel Bart, and sponsorship by Joan Littlewood, the production of *Fings* kicked open the doors of the West End theatre with a disregard for conventional opinion that I could completely relate to. As could John Osborne, who by now had achieved fame and was starting to look over his shoulder in anger or fear: "Lionel Bart, booted by the genius of Joan Little-wood into soupy crash-bang wallop success with *Fings Ain't Wot They Used t'Be* ... achieved a knees-up for the nobs ..." as he wrote in his autobiography.

Upon our return from Juan-les-Pins, my final Wellingbo-rough results were waiting. I'd got one "O" level in English lit, and just in case the pen were not to prove mightier than the sword, I'd gained second-class proficiency in rifle shooting. The report hemmed and hawed about my "ability" ... and my "inability" to use it. You know the rest.

****

Sheila Klein was the beautiful, waifish, ethereal fifteen-year-old daughter of a well-respected psychoanalyst father and sculptress mother. They - Sheila, her three brothers, and parents - lived at the right end of Frognal, on the right section of Hampstead. She attended art school in Shepherd's Bush and studied sculpture part-time at St. Martin's College. She hung out with her school friend, Linda Keith, an actor's daughter who lived over in West Hampstead. It was Tanya Gordon - then coffee bar girl and fellow French art film devotee, later famous as fashion designer Tanya Sarne, O.B.E. - who introduced us.

I felt like a thoughtful French New Wave (*nouvelle vague*) movie, so I rolled the credits and appeared on location in Hamp-stead Village's thriving beatnik scene. An arty vibe pervaded the Witch's Cauldron, where the young and mainly affluent religiously posed and preened, as they drawled quasi-cultured monologues over well-nursed cappuccinos. I, of course, stood apart from this dishevelment. Their uniform of scruffy, shabby jeans worn under large and holey sweaters hid a universal preoccupation with get-ting (or not getting) laid.

I was trying to sell my imported Elvis singles. Thinking I would have a captive market back home, I had spent my allowance in France on forty copies of "It's Now or Never." It was certain to be hot, since it was as yet unavailable in England until his copyright dispute over "O Sole Mio" was resolved. I would have turned a greater profit had I invested in Juliette Greco or Jacques Brel. I didn't sell many discs in this dalliance with retail - the bohemian punters wanted the Modern Jazz Quartet, and the neighbourhood Jewish kids refused to be conned.

Gina, a pale beatnik wraith whose parents owned a Greek eatery on Heath Street south of Church Row, yanked me outta the Cauldron, away from the dregs, and up to the Hampstead Everyman Cinema on Holly Bush Vale to catch a Chabrol film kicking off the French New Wave season. She led; I followed.

Gina and I were slim and pleasing - to each other, and to those who wondered whether our bodies kept the same timing because we shared the same spring and smile in the night to our step. They didn't, but Gina and I enjoyed the game, the complement our spirits were to each other, and to those we did keep time with. Opposites don't always attract, sometimes they just look good together; her spirit was unharnessed, unbroken, a mod pop bundle of joy.

Perhaps more than her own eventual Peter Meaden, she introduced me to the space between notes that lives above gender, for that space occupies a room or two, and Peter lived out on the ledge. I remember the moment we were not above it, and we could, but would not get attached. We were on the slope that takes you away from Hampstead High Street down over Frognal and down again toward the Finchley Road where, up on the hill away from the traffic, Gina lived with her family. Gina took note of the moment too; we both laughed it off. I blushed, her eyes furnaced above the pale mask she wore. My hand wondered how pale was the rest of her as our arms clasped around each other a little tighter to preserve and bottle the moment. Laughter and love went together, we settled for harmony, we'd both just been and felt effective jazz.

We picked up our pace and strode on up the hill toward the Heath and the Everyman. I would occupy this space with several significant others in the very near future, but Gina was a first of her kind.

We walked the minute or two south toward Fitzjohn's Avenue where, snugged in the last cluster of shops, we snacked and nattered in the warmth of Gina's parents' Greek eatery. I held

the cup the way I wanted to hold her hand. I had seen some leaf-
lets on the earlier life of the Everyman and was now an expert,
holding forth to Gina about how the cinema had once been a live
theatre and had housed an earlier angry young person other than
our good selves and *le bonfroglot*.

Thirty years earlier than John Osborne, in 1924, the young
master himself as pop personified had written and starred in his
first number one and controversial smash, *The Vortex*. The young
master? Noël Coward.

Gina and I didn't care much about the matters that weighed
The Vortex: drugs, homosexuality, and mother's little penchant for
toy-boys. For me, one had been left resting on the mantelshelf at
Wellingborough, the other resided in Soho, and my mother's only
little penchant was for her toy-boy to get some decent work.

What gobsmacked us was the shock Coward caused, the
uproar amongst his peers and elders - that's what it was all about,
the cry to have the play removed from the stage of life, not dissimilar to a later hue and cry about the Stones. We didn't fall for
the cast or the hoopla, we were both too high at the pride of our
lives to be interested in the grotty malaise. We fell for the move
forward in life - the arrival, the charisma of Noël Coward making
his indelible mark ... the event.

The falling down in life to powder and flesh we knew
naught about yet. We were happy, deviant, free, New Wave divas,
and we wrapped ourselves in all things Noël, hot lemon tea, and
moussaka. We forgot about that blush of fate earlier on the hill. We
strode back out onto Hampstead High Street, bidding *adieu* to that.
School was now out, shops were now near closing, Hampstead
and its heath were alive with cars on their way home. The other
kids marching on the block were different. Somehow they knew
where they were going and didn't like it, whereas Gina and I did
like where we were going and our stride was already there.

It was the new cinema that we were on our way to see that
seduced and hooked me instantly. Springing from the political atmosphere that had inspired the New Left, it ridiculed commercial
cinema. The work demanded plots and exemplified themes relevant to the struggles of reality, stirring me to dress down and attitude up.

I happily let the wave wash over me. Claude Chabrol was

a man after Laurence Harvey's many hearts - he financed his first film, *Le beau Serge*, with an inheritance left to his first wife. It introduced Jean-Claude Brialy, whose cynical screen personality, lively temperament, and courtly manner I identified with and adopted immediately. The Chabrol style in *Le beau Serge* and *Les Cousins* via Brialy was curiously detached and I liked it. The props were a New Wave haircut, textured clothing like Shetlands, cords, and *le duffel-coat*. A return to brogues on the feet, the "moouvement" of the hands to express my heart, and I had it down. A beige wool-and-cashmere driving jacket from the Adams booty proved to be a wardrobe coup for this new movie.

When life demanded something a little more brittle, I would change reels into Jean-Luc Godard, get *Breathless* and allow for jump-cuts and unsteady hand-held moving shots. Godard reshaped film syntax while paying homage to the American gangster movie, as Jean-Paul Belmondo reinvented Jean Gabin by way of James Dean meets Humphrey Bogart. That role was a stretch for me at sixteen, so I usually calmed down into the more comfortable and laconic Jean-Claude Brialy mode.

I may have left Wellingborough but I was still at school. But don't let my French New Wave languor fool you. I was hard at work, as were many others.

This underground cinema movement was radically different, philosophically and visually, from anything we had ever experienced on screen before. The Hampstead Everyman, champion of the New Wave in London, was manna from heaven for my friends and me at the time, as we celebrated *la différence*. As the sixties gathered momentum, the French New Wave would heavily influence the British arts, initially in film and theatre, by engendering the British Free Cinema, helmed by Karel Reisz, Tony Richardson, and Lindsay Anderson. This trio of young British *auteurs* brought a new kind of internationality and sophistication to English-language films with *Saturday Night and Sunday Morning, This Sporting Life, Look Back in Anger, The Entertainer, The Loneliness of the Long Distance Runner*, and *A Taste of Honey*. Tony Richardson and John Osborne formed Woodfall Films and would later go for the whole nine yards with *Tom Jones*, winning an Oscar in the process. *La nouvelle vague*, spearheaded by Chabrol, Godard, Truffaut, Rivette, and Eric Rohmer, still makes causes and harvests effects on filmmaking to this day.

Its visual style trickled down into the fashion world via André Courrèges's bold, stark, scientifically precise, mathematical beauty. Pierre Cardin's vision was to become the most highly franchised designer name in history. Let us not forget a little schpater pop music from the Beatles and the Stones. The French films' sparse, grainy, b&w look would dominate early images by the beat boom's leading lights. The Stones input came direct from *moi* via the Everyman, plus what they brought to the table, but the Beatles got their attitude in Hamburg under the tutelage of Hamburg's Star Club and their German friends.

It was at the Everyman, too, that I met the light of Gina's life, Peter Meaden, who would provide both fuel and beam to so many lives, save his own. I came, I saw, he conquered.

Peter Meaden and I bonded on the look of American jazz style from the backs of album covers, downloading life into the simplicity of the complicity we shared, and concentrated on that. We found each other's anger and reinforced our ambitions. We honed each other's humour, band-aided each other's social sores, and fronted the lot with the totality of that. Peter had been out and about longer than I, so I happily fed off his learning.

He worked by day at an American-style ad agency at 63/69 New Oxford Street (in the same building which would later house my Immediate Records company). We began to meet regularly after work and comb the West End and Soho. We'd check out Austin's on Shaftesbury Avenue, a clothes emporium specialising in American imports, the best and latest in modern jazz style. Endorsed by the cool and knowing of the day, Austin's was a feast of reversible houndstooth and herringbone, staggered vent jackets, worn with broadcloth button-down, pin-through, and tab-collared shirts. Neither of us could afford to buy anything from this style palace, but we guzzled up the styles regardless, walked and talked a mile a minute, and were busy making plans.

"John Michael," *né* Ingram, owned two hip men's shops: Sportique on Old Compton Street and his flagship John Michael store on the King's Road. For the most part Sportique's fey clobber was ludicrous, unless you were swarthy, wealthy, and gay. John Michael, on the other hand, with its formal grey flannel suits, and striped or gingham round-collared, fly-fronted, well-tailored shirts, was another fashion plate we could ill afford, but we badly wanted. So I did starve a little for a superlative skinny wool knit tie and gingham tab-collared shirt.

At C&A's in Marble Arch, on a high-floor back-rack, Peter and I found a few lightweight, staggered-vent suits, cheap and in amazing colours. Ninety-nine percent of British men's suits were still postwar grey or black. Bottle-green mohair with a paisley lining was a visitation to be celebrated, and coupled with side-laced suede ankle boots we had heaven on earth and thrills on our feet.

Peter introduced me to a different form of nightlife, a different form of life - Soho. Our first port of call was the Scene Club, behind Piccadilly, just off Windmill Street in Ham Yard. It was run by Ronan O'Rahilly, who later started Britain's first pirate station, Radio Caroline. The Scene was a smoky, loud haven for the disenfranchised working class, where white-on-black soul was the soundtrack till dawn's harrowing light. Having grown up in the relatively rough district of Edmonton, Peter was attuned and passed for one of this crowd, whilst I stayed close to the edge watching the kids speeding on pills and good music, posing more than dancing, jaws frantically chewing the night away. Three-legged legless mod monsters, pilled to the walls of aurafide stress, bound and bonded by sound and dread of the job on Monday.

We'd move over four blocks left and right to the Flamingo on Wardour Street and a funkier, jazzier crowd. On Saturday the Flamingo was the only Soho venue serving drinks and playing music all night, giving itself up to black R&B, Atlantic, and early Stax-type fare. An exotic mélange of Soho sex and underground sorts, gangsters really, usually crashed in late after disposing of earlier engagements. Rik Gunnell and his brother John ran the late-night Flamingo, so it was very safe, which, when you think of it, is the perfect atmosphere for a club, decadence without the possibility of violence.

I followed my leader Peter and what with the leapers, our life was a party and I, too, was grinding my teeth down to the bone. Sometimes we'd head back to Hampstead for rest and more partying, and sometimes I'd go back on my own. I'd stop off and tell my mother: "I'm home."

If I was with Peter, we would bathe (he'd shave), change,

collect Gina, and we'd step out to the Hampstead raves. With Peter's motorbike and sidecar, we'd park in the hedges of well-to-do addresses and crash the parties of wealthy Jewish would-be arty girls whose parents had gone away for the weekend. Though more often than not, I'd leave Peter revving in Soho and head for Hampstead on my tod. I should think that when Peter finally did come home, Gina gave him a well-to-do settled look. Peter would have done well to have embraced and grown into what Gina was offering. But to Peter, homelife was backstage, between shows, on the nod to mod, and therefore not to be.

With all the partying, I never stopped looking around for places to present myself. The London *Evening Standard*, one of the two evening papers, had just started a weekly column on men's fashion called "Mainly For Men." It was a pioneering feature, dealing with a hitherto undiscussed-by-men subject - their clothes and their lifestyle. "Mainly For Men" was edited by Angus McGill. I bombarded him with calls, enthusing about his clothes, my clothes, any clothes, praising the column, and life in general. Mr. McGill responded with an invitation to his office.

I had exactly that, a bit of a write-up, my name and mug in the paper, the energy to turn that moment into work. Peter and I decided to form our own public relations company. I imagined I had visibility, the article had given me balls I had to live up to, so I'd front it and Peter would moonlight, supplying the stationery and printing out of his day job's back door. We called it "Image" and our slogan was "Feet's Ahead" atop a sketch of two bare feet.

Peter and I scrambled our nuts as to who we'd land as our first client; we'd sent out a hundred-odd enticers to major clothing manufacturers and stores - to no avail; we weren't in the loop. I knew that the owner of Sportique and John Michael - John Michael Ingram - lived in a cul-de-sac off the same Frognal street as Sheila. I reverted to type, knocked on his front door, hustled through it, and lucked out. The first gig we got was to design the invitations for a reception at the recently opened John Michael in Bond Street.

The invitations we designed for the fashion show were written on a shirt cuff peeking out from under a chalk stripe suit: they were a complete success. John Michael was duly impressed and asked Image to design a brochure for his upcoming Sportique boutique spring collection. Peter and I went to work tracking down and ripping off all the fashion spreads in recent issues of American *Esquire*, tracing and replacing the American gear with the Sportique gear. We came up with what we considered a genius storyboard for the brochure. Entitled *Sportique Takes a Holiday*, the visual narrative followed a film director named "Ted Wayne," travelling in a T-Bird, traced from the *Esquire* ads, to the south of France, picking up a young blond hitchhiker named Lance wearing "Sportique's new denim shorts, available in pink, grey, and blue at only 59 shillings and sixpence ..."

We delivered the finished brochure, underwritten by Peter's unsuspecting ad agency, to John Michael. He was more than a tad taken back by the overtly gay subplot of the brochure, its drawings, and text. Homosexuality was still a criminal offence, and the brochure could appear offensively mocking to John Michael's sensitive show biz clientèle. JM politely sacked us, leaving the matter of payment up in the air on Queer Street.

We may have been down but, before they could even start the count, I went chasing the King of Carnaby Street, John Stephen. He had claimed the schmater crown when he opened up in 1958. He racked up huge sales by retailing clothes so body-conscious and sexy that it was less of a problem to afford them than to fit into them. I was granted a fifteen-minute a.m. audience.

Glaswegian sped-up elf that Stephen was, he ate me for breakfast and spat me out as he raced toward lunch at a table reserved for him alone. Having single-handedly invented Carnaby Street Inc. in a blaze of youth power, he belittled Image and me for taking up even this much of his time. Luckily, the not-to-be-denied Peter couldn't make the meet - he was attending to his day job. JS was in rapid-fire braveheart flow, informing me he'd rather use a more upmarket ad agency, one already operating in the world he was going to be a part of.

In a matter of a few short years, we would both become tycoons of teen, creators of franchises the public adored. Stephen's empire would include eighteen mod clothing shops, of which six monopolised the street of dreams. Wearing John Stephen's clothes would compete with playing guitar or drums as a lad's first real commitment to banddom.

Peter Meaden had warned me to stay out of Stephen's way, but I had not heeded him, and for my trouble got a good common-sense hiding along the lines of, "Be prepared, don't insult, and don't hustle a hustler!"

We moved on to our next entrepreneurial folly. We discovered we could rent our local Hampstead Town Hall free for the evening if it we were fundraising for a non-profit entity. Accordingly, we formed "The Hampstead Literary Society" to qualify, and booked the Town Hall. Then we began advertising a "One Night Only Rhythm and Blues Extravaganza." This was not the all-knowing Soho of the West End. This was superficial, out-of-it, cappuccino land, whose gullibility I once again counted upon.

The night's entertainment was hardly R&B. The first act were "Direct from Their Successful German Tour," because the bass player had just spent his holidays in Bavaria. Next up were the then Gordon and Peter, who as Peter and Gordon later hit with Lennon and McCartney's "A World Without Love." Peter Asher survived that round to become one of the seventies' and eighties' most consistently successful managers and producers. His work with Linda Ronstadt and James Taylor was one of the era's highest earning cross-cultural transmigrations.

We managed to end the evening with no R&B at all, topping the bill with Marc Conquest (a name even Larry Parnes had passed on, but then we were "not for profit") direct from his successful engagement with Gordon and Peter earlier that same evening. The part of Marc was played by Gordon Waller. The food sold by Gina's Greek restaurateur ma and pa failed to quell the universal demands for refunds as Peter Meaden and I skipped out the back door, fifty-seven quid in hand. We moved into the Chelsea Town Hall with the same scam, but we'd forgotten the King's Road was an experienced old whore, and the scam fell flat on its face with our Hampstead profit disappearing down Chelsea's drains.

Back at 19 Netherhall Gardens, I tore open an envelope to get to the first letter addressed to Image. It was from a major American clothes designer, Emerson Mead Jr., whose first para boasted of twenty-seven retail outlets on the American East Coast. The letter explained that Mr. Mead Jr. had been on a buying trip in London and chanced upon the "great" *Sportique Takes a Holiday* brochure. Were Image interested in designing a brochure for America? Could the directors meet him in ten days time - in Liege,

Belgium - to discuss the matter?

"Let us check our schedules," we joked, "we can't over-extend." We couldn't afford to fly so we booked on the boat. Peter and I shivered in our lightweight jazz suits as the bitter cold of winter kicked in on the night ferry across to Ostend. With only enough for half a ham sandwich and half a bottle of brandy to keep us warm, we caught a train to Liege in the morning, arriving in good time for our meeting in an expensive but antiquated hotel in the city centre. Liege was decrepit, dull, and boring. It could have doubled for Newcastle-upon-Tyne. After an hour's wait, we checked with hotel registration and found out there was nobody by the name of Emerson Mead Jr. staying with them. The awful truth began to sink in: we'd been had, revenge perhaps for all the fashion and R&B scams we'd pulled back home. The original letter was a hoax.

During the cold and penniless hitch back to London, we both agreed that the prospect of continuing as partners in Image was too much. Peter needed to buckle down to work or risk losing his prestigious job at the advertising company. Though at the time we were furious, lockjawed, and into kill, we both secretly admired the scam. By the time we went our separate ways, Peter knew almost too much for his own good. He was young, but close to being jaded, and couldn't separate the dross from the gold. Reality was out of kilter with his expectations. We said goodbye, taking leave of our good selves till we met again in '64.

Peter went back for a while to New Oxford Street. After experiencing Adams, John Michael, Sportique, R&B Nights in Hampstead and Chelsea, demoralised by an expensive hoax, I was tired and needed to rest "between shows." I met up with a transplanted American teenager, Chris Harris, at a party in Hampstead, he and the attractive Susie Ornstein slumming north from their residences in Belgravia. Chris's father, Leslie Harris, had crossed the Atlantic to become manager of Incorporated Television, the company that made programmes like *Danger Man, The Baron, Ivanhoe, The Saint, Robin Hood, Four Just Men,* and ultimately, *The Prisoner.* I accepted Chris's gift of friendship and spent my time-out restoring myself in the womb of the to-the-show-biz-manor-born.

Incorporated Television Corporation was a subsidiary of Lew Grade's Associated Television. ATV, as it was better known, had since 1955 been part of Britain's only alternative television channel to the BBC. ITC provided all its episodic adventure needs. Lew was one of three Jewish brothers, who between them built Britain's most protean show business empire. Their influence and business interests stretched above and beyond, their position in entertainment was unassailable. Lew not only owned ATV and ITC, he also owned the Stoll and Moss Empire Variety Pantomime and Summer Season and a rich theatre chain comprising the Palladium, Drury Lane, and Her Majesty's, plus fifteen provincial theatres. AP Films, which made *Thunderbirds*, also belonged to Lew Grade, as did 60% of Pye Records.

Lew's brother, Leslie, chose the performers for ATV's finest hour, *Sunday Night at the London Palladium*. He co-owned London Management, London Artists, and the Harold Davison Group of agents and impresarios. The client list read like a who's who of the show biz world: Dirk Bogarde, Albert Finney, Laurence Olivier, Ralph Richardson, Julie Christie, Noël Coward, John Gielgud, *et al*. The Davison Group acted as U.K. reps for Frank Sinatra, Ella Fitzgerald, Duke Ellington, and Count Basie (and soon the Animals, Dave Clark Five, Lulu, and the Hollies). Leslie also had a 50% interest in Elstree Studios, which made, amongst many, the Cliff Richard films. The third brother, Bernard Delfont, owned more London theatres, produced shows all over Britain, virtually monopolised the pantomime and summer season industry, and had an interest in London's Talk of the Town nightclub.

I was charmed and fascinated by this Chester Square, Belgravia view of the world. I looked forward to meeting the Grade brothers' debonair Yankee import, hired to select escapist adventure fare for our clothcap-discarding lower middle classes, who agreed with their Prime Minister, the Right honourable Harold Macmillan, that Great Britain had never had it so good. Chris's father looked as if he'd stepped straight off an American movie set, tanned with immaculately styled grey hair, grey suits, and "elder statesman" striped pin-through collared shirts. Wool ties, not silk. I slipped into my eccentric cousin Jean-Claude Brialy role from *Les Cousins* quicker than you could say "left-hand drive" and relaxed with this well-heeled set.

Chris's gal-pal, fellow American Susie Ornstein, was the daughter of Bud Ornstein, who ran United Artists in the U.K. It's a small small world in which there are no accidents: Under Ornstein's helm, United Artists would get both the eventual Beatles movies, *A Hard Day's Night* ('64) and *Help!* ('65). After a first marriage to entrepreneur John Fenton, Susie settled well with Neil Aspinall, who started out as a Beatles roadie and now headed up their ongoing Apple Corps. I had a crush on Chris's black convertible T-Bird and a bigger one on Susie.

Basically I was an all-American boy. From film and TV to songwriting credits, I just wanted to know the stories and motivational factors behind these creators of three, thirty, or sixty-minute dreams. As regards the three-minute wonders, I had noticed that U.S. songwriters - Goffin/King, Leiber/Stoller, Mann/Weil, and Pomus/Shuman - had their names on the labels beneath the titles of an astonishing number of U.S. top twenty hits. I read up on the famous Brill Building, New York's 24-hour music factory where hits seemed to fly out the window. The table for this musical feast was set by hosts Don Kirschner and Al Nevins, whose Aldon Music was the first independent power in music publishing. Aldon had its ears on the street and had writers who knew where to put the bomp, young writers who had the talent and suss to take everyday facts and phrases of life and turn them into teen-dream reality, to take us up on the roof and under the boardwalk and create a body of work that exemplified the American pop art of the moment.

At home, an innovative television series featured Anthony Newley. *The World of Gurney Slade* was an off-the-wall perspective on life directed by one Ken Hughes. Mr. Hughes had made his reputation as a reliable director of British B-films in the early fifties. With a feel for American dynamics, Hughes often employed actors with faded stateside marquee value to light up a mundane genre. His Columbia Pictures Paul Douglas starrer, *Joe Macbeth* (1955), a mobster take on the bard, was way ahead of Coppola's later Corleone saga. Ken Hughes, with his ability to flit from pre-Monty Python mirth to Shakespearean mobsters, was a man I just had to meet.

He was in the phone book living in a flat on Elgin Avenue. I called and he invited me by. I tripped down to his basement pad to be greeted by a bohemian, yellow-grey-haired, mad professor Goon Show boffin who invited me in for a chat, some biscuits, and tea. It was a time when not everybody was a star, and Mr. Hughes seemed as pleased by my interest as I was with his openness and candor about the canvas of his life. As with Kenneth Hume, Harold Lang, and the others, when I recall these events I may come up short on detail but I hope I've conveyed the fondness I have for them and the time they gave me.

It was another glimpse of how those special moments conspired to happen: A man's imagination becomes a vision, he works that vision, and his vision becomes the "reality" of entertainment. I would hurry back to Frognal and Sheila, would try to describe this wonderful, magical world, and probably did.

My mother told me in so many words to shit or get off the pot. She couldn't call Chris Harris a bad influence, but she thought I was a fish out of water, gills pumping, out of my league. In my mother's book you didn't trade classes, so in a sense Mummy took the T-Bird away and Chris with it. Sheila she considered a troublesome distraction, though perhaps competition would have been a better word. It was back to, "Shape up or ship out," "Buckle down, buckle up," "It's time to get normal," "Get up, go to work, wipe the stars from your eyes and elsewhere." I told her I got the picture. I may have saluted, gifted her with lip service, but I lied. She thought I was sliding way off the rails and told me to stop spending hours with the old vagrant who'd made his abode on the wrought iron bench outside our house.

Somebody has to open the door - designer Mary Quant opened it for me.

CHAPTER 5

the king's road - how the west was won / mary quant takes over the look of young britain / a ginger zit in mary quant's court / the cool school - quant by day, ronnie scott's jazz club by night / work as art and life as hard work / having the first of my more than nineteeen nervous breakdowns

Chelsea had come on to my reality radar screen. Since I'd have to appear to be following Celia's direction, I pretended to look for a regular job, 'cause who knows, with her quirkiness I could be out of house and home if I didn't get one. I had seen my mother turn on people, and I didn't want to be one of them. But "regular" was still the last thing on my mind. It may have seemed I was busy with the want-ads and Yellow Pages, but I was really reassessing the King's Road.

At the centre of this chinless Chelsea scene (as shallow in its own way as that of Hampstead Village) was a thriving, industrious, and chinful King's Road boutique called Bazaar. Owned by Mary Quant, her husband Alexander Plunket Greene, and their partner, Archie McNair, Bazaar opened on an elegant shoestring in November 1955 and swiftly galvanised the pioneering young things that became their earliest patrons. Bazaar's fashions brought the expressive sexiness only a few daring women would as yet act out in their bedrooms into an uptight work place transformed by feminine youth. Mary Quant would give the New Workers their cockney-Chanel non-uniform uniform at a price the suddenly eager shoppers thronging the high streets couldn't resist.

The Quant Look came to be topped off by the strikingly functional and sexy statement that Vidal Sassoon brought to hair. Iconised by photographers Bailey, Donovan, and Duffy, Quant's empire was the one true manifestation of pop in the years between the archetypal rock 'n' roll of the mid-fifties and its eventual second coming with the Beatles in the mid-sixties. Quant was naturally the place I wanted to be. I learned that the Bazaar business office was at the back of Ives Street, close to Draycott Avenue. Nervously I knocked on the door; it was opened with kindness, and suddenly I was in.

When you're on, you're just blind, going through it, getting the job done, so you don't actually remember the moment, though you'd better be in it. That's why it's difficult to remember what I said when I walked in. Hopefully I listened; I doubt it. I can remember the rehearsal, and I can remember arriving. The next thing I remember is leaving Archie's office and *voila!* ... I had the job.

Well before 1963 changed the face of music as we knew it forever, Britain had already got a pop business - fashion. This new rock entrepreneur took those established freedoms and applied them within the limited safe world of the music business, where they appeared innovative. Six months after leaving school, qualified to do zip, I was suddenly out of the slum and way ahead of the pack. I'd been very lucky. That's why, for me, Quant Ltd. was such great training, because at first fashion was the fashion, then fashion became music. So I had a head start on those of my peers who remained in Soho.

I helped Mary dress the windows, which was my training for record cover design. I poured drinks for journalists, which made me realise that liquid can become print. I walked the dogs of famous models, which taught me how to handle stars - and I learned how to throw parties. It was amazing to watch. The three of them, Mary, Alexander, and Archie, were in total harmony. They didn't need words and when they used them, so very well, they could finish each other's sentences. There was love, and it was apparent. In their own fashion, the Quant trio were very disciplined, but they really improvised the whole thing. I will always thank Mary, Archie, Alexander, and Vidal Sassoon - whom I spent much time watching as he changed the shape of hair forever - for teaching me about fame, fashion, money, and how to have fun getting it done.

I got my next press following the Angus McGill piece due to this madras suit I'd had made at Burton's and copped from one of Alexander Plunket Greene's. I was chatting up Iris Ashley of the *Daily Mail* one day, complaining about how madras creased and she wondered how I could afford what to her looked like a fifty guinea suit. "Was I using the same Savile Row tailor as Alexander?" I explained about the Burton's deal, which put no proviso on style or material. We laughed about the argument I'd had in there when I requested my suit-to-fit be made out of madras. Eventually I'd even got them to make madras-covered buttons.

She sent a photographer down to Bazaar to photograph me, and the next week it was all over her fashion page in the *Daily Mail*, "The Boy Who Beat Burton's."

The Bazaar shop in Knightsbridge was run with nutty style by Susie Leggatt. She had originally managed the King's Road store and was the original Quant girl, a notorious, beautiful creature. She had a quality that drew you to her; I loved her, so did the rest of our world. Susie had a heart of gold and helped make me feel a part of the wonderful Quant family.

Five months out of school, I'd jobbed up, lucked out, and was in the middle of a movement. £7 a week and an education. My mother was pleased, and I was in heaven. I wanted the excitement of the Quant day to extend into the evening and take up my weekends, too. It was an addiction to a rarefied air. Before Sheila could say "no," I'd arranged an appointment for her to see a top model agency. Next came a cut from Vidal Sassoon and a photographic session with Crispian Woodgate.

I had begun to become more aware of my black moods, relentless unexplainable depressions that would always arrive to hack into any elation at life's good turns. I made up for it with front row seats to see the Everly Brothers backed by the impeccable Crickets on opening night at the New Victoria. I'd never heard anybody duplicate their records so smoothly on stage; they may have been singing to the audience, but for me they were singing to each other. At Bazaar the next day, Susie Leggatt and I swapped gossip about the Everly Brothers. She'd heard they were getting "speed shots" from a crazy doctor in New York. I had no idea that within half a decadentade I'd get to meet him.

Working for Mary Quant and Co. was akin to being in the right movie. They knew that they had recognised the right moment and turned a London "cult" into a worldwide success, retaining control through independent production. I was getting an education and call to arms that would cause and effect my later work with the Stones and Immediate Records. It was amazing, there was a joy to work. The morning walk from Knightsbridge tube station would oft be pleasured up as I approached Ives Street to a good morning honk 'n' wave from Alexander and Mary arriving in their brash open two-seater gold Renault. The teacups were thin, the carpets were thick, the banter productive, and life did not end up on the cutting room floor.

After a Bazaar day I'd invariably end up pacing Soho rather than heading home to Hampstead. Sheila was studying for finals and we'd catch up with each other on the weekend. I'd forego Soho for home when the tube showed *Johnny Staccato*, which starred John Cassavetes. Cassavetes would take his *Staccato* paycheck and start a virtual American New Wave of his own with his 1959 directorial debut, *Shadows*. Elmer Bernstein's cool Capitol discery single evoked a stylish jazz-gangster New York for me, where private eye Johnny Staccato solved cases from his office in a basement jazz club.

Staccato-inspired, I started to hang around Ronnie Scott's, the famous Soho jazz club at 39 Gerrard Street, taking stock of the customers and musicians passing in and out the club. The musos were all very "cool," oft dressed in clothes from Austin's, reeking of the influential *Man with the Golden Arm* and *Sweet Smell of Success*. Alternative garb was African root-suits, the very best of your heritage courtesy of Edgware Road.

I wanted in. Pete King, Ronnie Scott's partner, answered my call. I didn't bore him with the Quant details but cut to the chase, "Is there any work available?" That's how I got everything. There was no word of mouth or anything. It was like, "Where do I want to work?" Then I went and banged on the door.

Straight from work at Bazaar, I caught the 19 or 22 red double-decker bus (Upstairs plleezze!) from the King's Road to Shaftesbury Avenue. I worked at Ronnie Scott's seven to midnight throughout the week and to 1:00 a.m. on Saturdays. I checked coats on the cloakroom, showed people to their seats, and brought in food for the patrons from the Indian restaurant over the road. The music I got to hear live at Ronnie Scott's was world class - Ahmad Jamal, Les McCann, Dizzy Gillespie, Thelonious Monk - and one musician who made a lasting stylistic impression:

Harold McNair was an alto flute player in his own quintet. He was so cool, he was supercool with a smooth American edge to him. He simply beamed. In his houndstooth suit he evoked and matched Miles Davis posing in his raglan-sleeve, one-button, houndstooth jacket for a fashion layout in *Esquire*. Harold beamed; he was just there. He played so well and knew how to handle the spaces.

I can't even recall what the wages at Ronnie's were or what the tips amounted to. It didn't matter, I was having the time of my life. Every night I went to work knowing I might experience greatness, and I often did. Down the block from Ronnie Scott's, on Lower Wardour Street, Rik and John Gunnell hosted late night's at the Flamingo. I signed on for the after-midnight shift. John was on the door at the Flamingo and Rik's wife used to work with me behind the burger stand. There was no drinks license so we'd serve the scotch from there in coke bottles. A great old Soho character called Gypsy Larry warned us if the fuzz were coming in to raid, though I think the police sometimes called ahead as well.

The three jobs would eventually get to me. I didn't miss a social life, work was very social and the run proved to me that this life I had dreamed of existed. It functioned every day, it got up, it went to sleep, and it was for real. It was possible. Mary Quant was just doing what came naturally; she, Alexander, and Archie got up and worked at it, that's why they succeeded. Ronnie Scott and Pete King were devoted to their club and the music. None of the people I was working for gave me a headache. They stood up for what they were in front of. I was very lucky that all the people I worked for had that advantage in life. I never met anybody who moaned. Everybody was very happy. They were all doing what they wanted to do.

My mother resigned herself to Bazaar; after all I had gone out and got a regular job, but when I added the night gigs she exploded and accused me of treating her flat like a hotel. I rented a room at the bottom of the hill on the lower end of Frognal and moved out. John Douglas, my Wellingborough partner, came down from Northampton to try his hand at London. It was only one block from my mother's house. The flat had a gas meter and I couldn't handle that - putting money in the thing for heat. Also, I could see my mother's house from the flat. After about three months I moved back. I didn't move out of home again until I moved in with Mick and Keith.

The work schedule was getting me a little nuts, I was sleeping four or five hours and going full out the rest of the day. I wanted to be able to see Sheila on my schedule. One evening I went round to her house and was angrily informed by Dr. Klein that his daughter was not allowed out until she had finished the washing up. I got furious, pulled out a starting pistol I carried, shoved it in the good doctor's forehead and instructed him to "Analyse this!" I was losing it somewhat.

I was taken aback when, many years later, I first heard Archie's notion that I had abused my mother. I don't recall the incident he spoke of, and cannot imagine Celia would have tolerated such behaviour and allowed me to live under her roof. I have a Polaroid in my mind of the cramped first-floor bathroom of Netherhall Gardens that has one of us in the bath and me screaming. Did I strike her? I was certainly capable of speaking to her so abusively that violence was done. In that Polaroid I can recall being repulsed by her flesh. It doesn't surprise me that I would suppress the memory of this traumatic walk on the wild side. I do remember appreciating Archie's solicitude.

Six months of juggling three jobs had exhausted me, I was burnt out and getting irrational, rude as well. Del Shannon was number one with "Runaway." I guess that's what I was about. I packed a suitcase, tied a Union Jack around it, hitchhiked and boated my way out of England, heading for the south of France. I left letters of regret and departure, thanking all and promising I would return ...

London, 1956

CHAPTER 6

riding the french new wave in person / looking for bardot, belmondo, and beyond / begging for breakfast from well-to-do brits / robbing and rolling a pederast 'cause i cannes / smack in the middle with you - ray charles and the antibes jazz festival / an important lesson in manners from a yank on the lam / back to london and walkin' the dogs

Marc Guebard had sent me a postcard urging me to come to where the action was. He bragged about meeting the actress, Shirley Ann Field, and why not, so would I years later; and into this I read a life on the game, Marc's great looks giving him gigolo potential.

I'd taken the ferry to Calais and train to Paris, intending to hitch from there to the Med, but dressed in lime-green angora sweater, jodhpurs, riding boots, a Sherlock Holmes deerstalker hat, and a Union Jack flag around my suitcase, I was attracting the wrong kind of attention. Somehow I ended up in the bad part of an Arab district on the outskirts of Paris and spent a tense few hours. I was not assaulted physically, although my costume might have had it that I was asking for it, and, as eyes can suggest and undress you in a most disturbing way, I was glad to find the free-way south.

It was 5:00 a.m. and raining, there were six lanes of howling traffic, none of it stopping for me except the cops. The policeman was kind and explained that I was breaking the law, that one was not allowed to solicit rides on France's finest roads. He realised I was hungry, tired from the journey and my near-miss in the Arab section. He had a heart and drove me to his *Clockwork Orange* in-dustrial flat block. He woke up his wife, had her cook me break-fast, which I gratefully wolfed down, chased by strong black tea as the sun was coming up. The good gendarme drove me another mile to his precinct and parked me in a cell for an hour while he did the day's paperwork. Then it was back to the freeway. The cop stopped all cars going south, and to the one that was going the furthest, he said, "Please take him," and she did, not only into her Mercedes but also into her bed once in Lyon. That's how I got through France.

It was a time that allowed for kindness: that breakfast, that Mercedes, that bed. It was before drugs, terrorism, sex with children, and sex with the dead. Nowadays the cop couldn't trust me and I'd probably be stoned. Neither could the kind lady risk teaching me some *amour* for fear that one of us had another agenda. Now not much remains that pure.

I arrived in St. Tropez two days after playing Laurence Harvey to my Simone Signoret in *Room at The Top*. I found Marc Guebard living in a tent on the outskirts of town, so we rolled up the tent and headed for it. The colours, textures, people, and the very air of St. Tropez are life-giving. They make you feel very well. But as the light turned to night, our first reel of jetset life was changed to a second one much less fun. We had no villa to hide away and rest in; Marc and I found ourselves stranded on the lonely, narrow alleyways of St. Tropez. We were promptly arrested for vagrancy and spent the night locked in a fish market with a police guard, as the jail was full. The stench of fish was awful. You had to sleep in this dirty tunnel with a cop at both ends. They really were teaching you a lesson - get out of town.

The days were great. You didn't need money - you were amongst it. Enjoying the play of sun and water, 'twas almost as if some of it rubbed off. Anyway a hunk of bread and cheese was all you'd need in St. Tropez till the night. The second time we got locked up in the fish market, I persuaded Marc it was time to move on. I was sure we could hustle the streets somewhere else for a loaf of bread without this nightly cattle-call for the hotel-less.

In Cannes there were more Brits and we didn't stick out. Begging was part of the action; most of them drew their Picassos on the pavement for their daily bread. My art was the gift of gab so I rehearsed a good story, then started to beg.

In my best public school accent - even my mother would have been proud - I vultured the Promenade de la Croisette's circumcised and wealthy. Marc, who just couldn't allow his handsome face to look hungry, stood off to one side. "Excuse me but my allowance hasn't arrived yet from my mother and I haven't eaten, if you could lend me ten francs and tell me what hotel you're staying at, I'll get it straight back to you."

Enough people believed me for us to get by; and why not? It was true. I met an interesting bunch of characters while out on my daily schmooze: the TV-directing Adonis, Mike Mansfield; our own diminutive King of Mirth, Arthur Askey; Alex Strickland, the record store owner who gave me good and kindly counsel about my future in his biz. All gave me a look that said, "You should know better," but they still gave up the price of a meal and a grin. And they all remembered me in later years when our paths happened to cross. I'd also often cop Larry Parnes and Lionel Bart cruising the Croisette, enjoying their limelight, starring, and strolling successfully between lunch and tea.

You can only hustle the same corner for so long. Tucked behind the main drag was Jimmy's, a bar that was wall-to-wall photos of Alain Delon, Jean Gabin, Edith Piaf, Yves Montand, and La Bardot. I strolled over to Jimmy's, trolled in, ordered a soda, and came on coy, carefree, and gay. Within thirty minutes, I got picked up. Once inside the guy's apartment, he served me a drink and made his move.

He attempted to kiss me, and I smelled his repugnant, garlic-infested breath. I didn't mind eating garlic, but I drew the line at being kissed by it. I pulled away and the French guy knew something was wrong. Then I made my move. I worked the young innocent boy in an old poof's apartment: Pay up or I'll call the law. He didn't have much in readies and his clothes were awful and wouldn't have fit. The guy was cowering on the floor, squealing, "Take what you like but don't hurt me." I kicked the old poof in the stomach, left with 120 francs in hand, a bad taste in my mouth, and a cruel and criminal act on my conscience.

So many of England's finest had invited me into their homes, entertained, educated, and improved me without so much as putting a pinkie finger on my knee, and I repaid my debt of gratitude to this way of life with thuggery and violence. Once was one time too many.

Marc moved back to happier stomping grounds in St. Tropez. I decided to stay in Cannes and rented a room, continuing to hustle the Croisette three or four times a week, which prevented overkill, allowed me to rotate into a fresh batch of tourists, eat, and pay the rent. My new pal and roommate was an ex-American soldier, Pete Fanning, who'd fought in Korea, and was now drifting around the world. He showed me a suitcase full of marijuana, which he'd bought in Morocco. I'd seen people under the influence but I'd never seen the farm. Pete wouldn't actually let me smoke anything, but I couldn't help but get high with the help of my friend as he sucked on his spliffs and grinned. Pete would spliff, grin, and get horny, pull or pay girls back to the room, and I would be given marching orders to head for the Croisette.

On one such evening stroll, I sniffed the pungent herb that perfumed our little room. I followed the aroma around the corner, and there stood the man, Pablo Picasso, casually pulling on a spliff whilst checking out his own work enshrined in an art gallery window. The artist looked totally contented with his lot and at one with his Cubist glass-arts. He cut an impressive figure, minotaurial in his tight French striped T-shirt, his espadrilles hugging the curb. It was a power moment for *moi*, and I guess if I had thus far ignored ganga due to my jazz experience, from this Picasso moment, I embraced the idea of marijuana as another staple tool of creativity. I decided that if marijuana hadn't shut down Picasso, then, when opportunity reared its bud, I'd let it into my life.

I hadn't been doing too well on the Croisette of late so I packed my bag, ran out on the rent and Pete Fanning, relocating in the next paradise of opportunity down the coast, Juan-les-Pins. Within two days of arriving I'd landed two jobs. The first was in a staid men's clothes shop, where I charmed the owner into having his shop's windows dressed twice a week. Gig number two was majordomo at an English tearoom called Butler's, situated at the tip of a peninsula of buildings overlooking the lapping blue Mediterranean. I had been there before in another season with my mom for tea and scones. The Brit owner's French wife, Madame Butler, remembered Andy well, as I did her, so I set about waiting on tables and serving Brits. Here I met Jeremy Paul Solomons.

Juan was a massive film set. The lighting was incredible. They had a form of light that England didn't even know about yet. The rock 'n' roll clubs were amazing. They were all open-air, hidden behind a row of hedges. You could hear the music from the street. Juan-les-Pins was where the French rock 'n' roll stars went for the summer, because it had a younger crowd. The French rock 'n' roll stars were great. In the winter they would go shopping in America and claim they were on tour there.

I knew my French rock 'n' roll from ay to zee via *Salut les copains*, the glossy colour music mag that took its pop as seriously as *Cahiers du cinema* did film. Another plus of French pop was they didn't truck in singles; for the most part, it was E.P.s, four sides at

45 rpm, packed in a glossy picture sleeve. Eddy Mitchell was the Belmondo-meets-Eddie-Cochran-of-Frogpop. Dick Rivers, with his Chaussettes Noirs, did a young pre-crippled Gene Vincent. In France, original pop meant, "Who do I cop?" The legendary Johnny Hallyday, the everyman of France, had it down to an effortless knack: Each year he'd clone last year's American flavour, and Hallyday it up into art. His enterprise was a family biz, with his brother and manager an actual part of Johnny's act - "Laydeees an' Geentleman, my manager, Lee Hallyday!" Johnny was on top, ahead of the pack. He played the Juan-les-Pins casino. I couldn't afford the price of admission nor did I have the white smoking duds required.

The raucous rock 'n' roll legend in his own mind, Vince Taylor, with his Playboys, was now a legitimate star in France. He had said, "Fuck it, if Elvis can't make Europe, then let me be first in the land of second best." Vince moved with rockin' aplomb from the 2 I's basement in Soho to greatness in the land of de Gaulle. David Bowie must have caught this incredible performance, for later he named Taylor as an inspiration for his Ziggy Stardust. The refreshing thing about rockin' on the Côte d'Azur was that in France, rock and pop were celebrated, whereas in England they were merely tolerated. In England the warnings were muted but persistent: Do not get above your station. In France an entertainer's success was welcomed and applauded, not scorned. France had a completely different notion of class society from England.

The Antibes Jazz Festival was the highlight of the Juan summer season. In the pebbled park at the back of the casino under the shadow of Hôtel Cap d'Antibes, a giant wondrous shell was erected out into the water. For a week a few thousand people were lucky enough to be able to enjoy cool music in this cool Juan locale. I got a gig at the festival gofering for pianist Les McCann, who named me "Sea Breeze," as I was so fast and light on my feet going about my duties.

I got to enjoy the Les McCann Trio; Count Basie and his Orchestra; Lambert, Hendricks, and Ross; and the absolute master, Ray Charles. I felt that if God made the world in seven days, he had then decided on an encore and created the Antibes Jazz Festival. I never witnessed such a stellar music-and-people event till Monterey Pop in 1967.

One disconcerting moment in the midst of all this sheer joy
was the sight of Ray Charles shivering in junkie time on a rock
looking out on the Antibes blue, clutching his overcoat around
him to ward off his withdrawal shivers in the noonday sun. He
appeared very lost at that moment.

I had learned at Ronnie Scott's that there were two kinds of
jazz musicians: those who did and those who did not. I had to be
at the festival in the morning to help set up the stage, which is when
I saw him. It's very clear in my mind. It was scary. I think he only
had the problem for another couple of years. He was OK when he
was onstage but his offstage life appeared to be in disarray. It was
a very heady image. I would later use heroin; it was sheer pain, not
pleasure, that took me there, but seeing how Ray Charles behaved
in France helped to squelch any regularity with which I would take
up the drug. If I was totally opposed to my mother, my masters at
school, or my employer controlling me, I was certainly not about to
give up my freedom at that time to a drug. I could see clearly that
Charles was not in control of his own life. When life was as beautiful
as it was around you, it seemed a silly thing to be shivering in the
sun. It was an image of somebody who was not really up for anything. The smack was in control - which seemed a waste of a life.

I did well between window dressing, Butler's Tearoom,
and the jazz festival gig. I'd stopped sleeping out and got myself
a garret on the road to Antibes, and still had enough for water
skiing lessons at the Cap. My landlady warned me not to go farther, meaning be careful if I went out at night to the Cap. "The English pederast ..." she said - meaning the writer Somerset Maugham
- was living out his days on the Cap amidst whisperings that young
men went out there in the night never to be seen again. Maugham,
who was about eighty, was rumoured to be taking life-prolonging
injections made from the cells of the disappearing young men. In
fact the doyen author would blanket his knees for the drive to
Vevey on Lake Geneva. There he dared hope that the cells of un-
born lamb which he welcomed into his aged corpus via a needle
would extend and rejuvenate his life. I would do the same myself
some twenty-five years later.

One afternoon as I was window dressing in the glare of a
harsh afternoon sun, the six-foot-four, good-bad-but-now-ugly
Pete Fanning caught up with me for skipping town on him and

the rent. He threw me up against the wall, and the summer tan drained out of my face, as the bells of Wellingborough rang in my frightened head once more. I was sure I was about to get levelled when Pete seemed to change his mind and dropped me. He told me he figured I'd got the lesson. I had. I didn't run out on the rent again. It was already September and it was time for the type of Brits who haunted Juan to be back at work. Butler's would soon let me go, the town would wind down, and by the end of the month it would be dead, so I decided to come up with a fresh start and check out Monte Carlo.

I may have got fifty or so quid, and I closed up the garret in Antibes for one last move-on. I was trying to stay ahead of the end of the season, so I got down to Nice. With my passable French, I worked the door at a striptease club to get as many American sailors as I could to come in. It was a very tame strip club. There wasn't anything particular seedy about it. I saw a few of the shows but they weren't really that interesting. The girls didn't really strip, though I had promised the American sailors a lot more. A magician who used to perform between the girls had these three amazing leopard-skin drape jackets, tinted blue, silver, and red. I really wanted one. They were the ultimate rock 'n' roll jackets. He had them specially made; you couldn't buy them in the shops.

So I stole one. It was a thoughtless and criminal move. The writing was on my wall; it was the end of the summer. I was starting to make mistakes and the backstreets of Nice were no place to be foolish. I headed for the front and the English church where I knew the vicar was a friend of Wellingborough's Reverend Pitt. I explained my circumstances in a roundabout way and walked out of there with a God-given £50. I thanked the Rev. and stepped over to the British consulate where I knew you could surrender your passport and be repatriated, with the consulate paying for your train ticket home. I was too tired to hitch, life was suddenly a bitch, and in thirty-six hours I was home.

****

I bathed in the warm welcomes I got from Celia, Alec, and Sheila and pondered what I would do next. I knew I'd better make my own plans before my mother started setting up some rigid rules.

I put my hand on my heart and called Mary Quant and she was good enough to see me. She could not take me back, natch, but she could ring up a Peter Hope Lumley, who, from Knightsbridge overlooking Beauchamp Place, ran a thriving PR company and model agency, to see if there was something I could do over there.

James Dean said, "The stage is like a religion, you dedicate yourself to it and suddenly you find that you don't have time to see your friends, and it's hard for them to understand. You don't see anybody. You're all alone with your concentration and your imagination and that's all you have. You're an actor." I understood that, later re-reading it in the preface of Terence Stamp's autobiography, *Coming Attractions*. Thanks, Tel ... I have only had the pleasure of knowing the other brother Stamp, Christopher, on a first-game basis, but I have always had time for the example and aura that T. Stamp has given us on both the screen and the page and in their parallel explanatory duties. This other half of the Stamp collection, from the early *Billy Budd* and *The Collector* through *Superman*, *Wall Street*, and the priceless *Adventures of Priscilla, Queen of the Desert* has handled his lot with Zen aplomb. It's a rare man who has grasped the meaning of being one; which is a fabric and station of life that Mr. Stamp wears and tells well.

In 1961, public relations, like the advertising business, was considered slightly "wide boy" and not quite a career, an attraction in and of itself to me. But from his plush first-floor offices on 54 Brompton Road, Knightsbridge, Peter Hope Lumley had brought some solid substance to PR. He added the comfort of "yesterday" to the selling of "tomorrow," with a conviction that tomorrow could be now. His office suited him: oak-desked, deeply cushioned and carpeted, perhaps frayed, but nonetheless providing a fitting backdrop to a man of no nonsense, cardigan'd, striped-shirted, and well-brogued as he was. The pace of life and texture of personality were not as fast and gleaming as they had been at Quant's but the firm was solid quality and became home. I was welcomed very warmly and the stars gave me another good chance.

My Quant pal Susie Leggatt had come from Bazaar to head up Hope Lumley's model agency, simply called Model Agency. I did all sorts of odd jobs for Peter and the Model Agency. I walked their dogs, for one. Walking the models' dogs, I would attract wolf whistles from workers on building sites as I cruised past with a

couple of terriers and maybe a pekingese or two. I used to encourage, but never acknowledge, this by wearing a very stylish
gold overcoat, a gift from Alec that I'd camped up by adding a
huge spy's fur collar.

Thus far the only good who died young had been my idols
on the screen and stage, but now it was beginning to be those who
had been good to me in real life. I remember Susie well.

I made deliveries back and forth to the Hardy Amies house
on Savile Row. Every visit I ran into the incredible looking Amies
director, Bunny Roger. If I thought I had nerve, this apparition
made mockery of the mere thought.

His idol was the author and cartoonist, Max Beerbohm.
Bunny was unapproachably aloof but I learnt enough from him by
just looking. He paid meticulous attention to every detail of his
appearance. Everything he did was a piss-take and a celebration.
He looked almost sixty but he used to prance about in the most
amazing three-piece chalk-striped suits. His jackets were so tight-
waisted that they flared out like a skirt. The trousers were tighter
than drainpipes and his shirts had high, rounded, stiff-starched
collars. His lips were permanently pursed, and he always wore a
grey bowler hat, pearl tie-pin, make-up, eyeliner, and a carnation.

Hope Lumley heard stories, perhaps from Celia herself,
that I was beating her up. Again, I do not recall knocking my
mother about in any way, shape, or form. It was not part of my
lifestyle. She would have never spoken to me again had I behaved
in such a way. But I can imagine his using a story as dramatic as
that to offset my being late for work. It would take an excuse that
dramatic to cover for what I agreed was as heinous a breach of my
own work ethic as of Lumley's. I would also not have put it past
myself to persuade my good pre-Sheila friend Diana to make calls
claiming to be my mother. She was a good sport and would have
been up for it. If you're going to be late, make it into an event.

That my colleagues at both the Quant and Lumley shops
remember me as abusive of Celia suggests that there were indeed
strong psychological and physical undercurrents at work between
us. Certainly my position as a messenger boy in the fashion business was not her idea of job security, but I was satisfied that I had
conformed more or less to her wishes as well as my own ambitions.
Her continued criticism was therefore irksome and, I felt, unfair,

yet now I see that her mistrust of my new friends and employers was a reflection of her own feelings of rejection from fashionable society, which she was sure would be visited on her offspring. Perhaps, in her own way, she was trying to spare me the heartache of "illegitimacy" and class insecurity with which she tortured herself.

In hindsight, Celia, like most of her generation, was completely unprepared for the advent of the meritocracy so applauded by Vidal Sassoon. She didn't realise that in the world in which I now had a toehold, a hyphenated name got you no further than the switchboard if you didn't have "it." I would not necessarily recommend that Aquarians live together, as my mother and I were forced to do: We bury our agendas deep and our frustrations simmer coldly. If my mother had changed reels on me without my permission, I may well have whacked her, *Psycho*-style, in the bath and blanked the act out. That cause may or not have been made, yet regardless, the effect was simultaneous and a good deal of my time these days is spent studying, taking responsibility for, and handling my less enlightened actions.

Peter had warned me he couldn't afford to keep me on and I dutifully told my mother. She took it as an opportunity to pressure me to secure a "proper job with a stable future." Oh My God!

Years after the Stones and Immediate Records, I was talking with my mother about life. She remained unimpressed by my fame and success, very unimpressed as a matter of fact. She just said, "Yes Andrew, that's all well and good but when are you going to get a proper job?" Well, mother, so far, so good ...

Pablo Picasso

*Kent Walton: actor, wrestling commentator,
and host of ITV's "Cool for Cats"*

CHAPTER 7

*an appreciation for park lane and the older successful single woman /
first brush with the british vinyl barons / one last shot at a regular
job / one week with the terrifying joe meek / dusty springfield's
brother and a lover of dancing glide me one step nearer the flame
of pop / the flame begins - into pop school with manager ray
mackender and his venus in bleu jeans*

> "Keep away from people who try to belittle your ambitions.
> Small people always do that, but the really great make you
> feel that you, too, can somehow become great."
>
> - Mark Twain.

I scoured *The Stage* magazine for anything but a proper job. This
weekly trade rag customarily listed the managers and agents of
those few acts lucky enough to be working. An ad for actor Jess
Conrad caught my attention. Jess was a singer signed to Decca
and had hit number eighteen on the charts with "Mystery Girl"
in 1961. He was a protégé of Jack Good and had appeared often
on ITV's replacement for Good's *Oh Boy!*, *Boy Meets Girls*. Since
then, Conrad's recording career had languished, and he was
hoping to pick up the pace with his latest single, "Pretty Jenny."

Monte Mackay managed Jess from a theatrical agency
owned by American film producer/agent Al Parker. When I met
her in their offices just off Park Lane, she reminded me of the sophisticated and sexy Lauren Bacall as the literary agent to James
Caan in *Misery*. Miss Mackay was sufficiently impressed with
my cheek to invite me to her home for a follow-up. Monte lived
in Grosvenor House - hallowed ground for me, as it also housed
Laurence Harvey and Jimmy Woolf.

Room service delivered tea and biscuits, and I presented
myself as the press-cutting saviour of Jess Conrad's recording
career, albeit I had no business card or private phone number.
Monte Mackay was interested in the good-looking Conrad as an
actor and was indifferent to the world of pop music, but she gave
me a month to work my magic.

Tubing down from Hampstead to all points of the West

End, I got no joy and even less print for the "Pretty Jenny" single. I made one visit to Conrad's record label, Decca, and found that *Expresso Bongo* was not fiction: Wolf Mankowitz must have done his homework in the same tired lino'd offices. The music industry had none of the creative spark and optimism of the fashion industry I had recently left, nor did its denizens dwell in the house of good manners.

Taciturn businessmen controlled Decca with an apparent aversion to style, reflected in the ruthlessly staid Decca offices. They did not even appear to like or listen to pop music - they could have been selling baked beans for all they cared. Their interest was the tins. Dismayed by their apathy and appalled at their poor taste in clothes, I was repelled back onto the Albert Embankment from whence I came. Decca had its own press department, thank you, and was ready and able to service the every requirement of its *artistes* - no need for the likes of me in this scheme. Isn't this where I came in?

Powerful agents and managers still regarded record companies as the valet parking of stardom: spaces for their cars, the stars, that might get spattered with bird droppings or come back immaculate. In those days, your client warbling on the airwaves meant more money for the panto or summer season. The singer/ manager combo's relationship with the A&R manager, who found the songs and matched them with the acts of his choosing, was crucial. The A&R fella - A as in Artist, R as in Repertoire - would select the material and give it to the artist - *in that order* - unless the artist had already scored a hit or two. The U.K. business turned a blind eye to the reality of America. The British recording establishment wishfully hoped the Furys and Wildes would all disappear and we'd return to the pre-hula hoop safety of lush Mantovani. We were a long way from self-contained artists who would march over the "extended play" (EP) and demand the "long player" (LP) to cover the things they had to say. For the progress we'd made, we could thank Cliff, the Shadows *né* Drifters, and scribe Ian "Sammy" Samwell, for "Move It!" as well as Norrie Paramor, their A&R man, who allowed their will to be done. Let us appreciate Jack Good and Rita Gillespie as pioneers of multimedia with the always threatening, persuasively hopeful *Oh Boy!* And let us remember that Eddie Cochran died for rock 'n' roll on the playing fields of England. This would have to do for the mo; the Beatles were still polishing their chops in Hamburg.

I found myself up against a brick wall: I couldn't do anything for Jess Conrad except smile a "game's up, own up." We met in Mackay's hotel suite, and I was mightily impressed by the all-knowingness between the singing actor and his agent/manager. I wanted more. I liked Monte Mackay. She didn't feel threatened by a kid trying to stir things up in her shop. Rather, she seemed a guiding light - a professional beauty, who loved her work and brightened her world. Her example of decorum and vitality made her world the one I wanted for myself.

My month was up - I hadn't landed on my feet, and Jess hadn't landed in the charts, so with a bow and wave, it was back to Hampstead and Celia's agenda. I might talk to the tramps but I was not about to join them. My first attempt to adhere to her agenda had me bounding down to Mayfair and the 15 Hays Mews address of an old school PR firm, the Leslie Frewin Organisation. I managed to get in and pass an audition, and was happy to return to Hampstead to report to my mother that as of the following Monday I would be assistant to the assistant of account executive Stuart Valdor.

From day one I realised I was not going to enjoy working at the Leslie Frewin Organisation; it was Wellingborough in a Mews setting. I was quickly reprimanded over my suit - "too flash," and my attitude - "too casual." Stuart Valdor meant well and attempted to take me under his wing, but, Valdor aside, they were all used-car salesmen putting on Heseltine airs, as interesting as the label copy on the back of a packet of fags. On the spiv food chain, public relations was the new upmarket goldmine. To put a finer point on it, at the time, I regarded the press agent's lot as an honest one: You did your pitch, and you and your client were hopefully rewarded in ink. "PR" as practised by Leslie Frewin and associates spent more time assuring and shaping the client, it seemed to me, than going for the ink. PR appealed to the way an artist felt about himself inwardly, rather than the way the paying public felt about him outwardly. It was all fake and sleight of hand at the LFO. Their most exciting client was the British Menswear Guild, a consortium of staid U.K. clothes stores and manufacturers, like Aquascutum, guilded together in a boring, panicked, monolithic, monopoly of self-preservation.

I found more to interest me in the company founder, Leslie
Frewin, than in our customers. Author of several self-published
spy novels, Frewin had set up a self-contained independent production system long before "vertical integration" was a buzzword.
Unfortunately Frewin's top-floor office was considered almost
sacrosanct by his staff, and certainly out of bounds to inquisitive
assistant juniors such as I.

Between the rules and the catty competition, this job more
than any other I'd taken was like being back at school. To progress
up the ranks, I would have to cultivate a patience I neither had nor
wanted. My very being was anathema to all and not encouraged
nor invited in, but I had given my word to my mother and was
doing my best to keep it. Yet the mutual disdain with which my
co-workers and I regarded each other certainly meant my days
were numbered.

Due to the influence of rebels like Tony Meehan, independence was becoming my mantra. Leslie Frewin didn't figure into
my vision. I was moonlighting before too long - it had to be. *Cool
for Cats* was ITV's midweek pop music showcase and the programme's presenter, Kent Walton, was a minor celebrity. I was
more interested in the lead dancer in residence: Peppi brought
the show to an end each week, gyrating to the play-out record.

Despite Peppi's visibility, he hadn't had any press, so I figured with beginner's luck I'd be able to get him something. I had
to ... the guy was on a television show every week and a Yank to
boot. Just by the law of averages, I had to be able to get him five
or six press cuttings from somewhere. All I had to do was get in.

The company who made *Cool for Cats*, Rediffusion, had their
offices in Holborn. I stood waiting outside, amongst a small crowd
of kids looking to see Kent Walton or anybody. My screaming
days were over; it was time to get a move on. When Kent finally
appeared, I employed myself in officiously shooing back the kids,
and led Walton to his parked Mercedes. In that teaked beige mas-
tercar, Mr. Walton moved from minor to major key before he could
ignition-up as I leapt in the back seat behind him. Before Walton
had a chance to protest, the surrounding fans forced him to put
his car into motion.

Long before a quietly raging Robert De Niro pulled the

same trick to get himself close to Jerry Lewis in Martin Scorsese's *The King of Comedy* (1982), I knew the grift well. By then I was living in Manhattan, officed "*chez* Freddy Bienstock" at the hallowed Brill Building. During the filming - proving that the apple falls not far from the tree - I ligged my way into a small walk-on part in the film.

To me, Mr. Walton was a B-player, so I figured I could easily force my way into his affections. I was optimistic. Unlike some of the other people I pushed myself upon, I must have been a real nuisance to him. Like everybody else, I wanted something: two audience tickets to the next *Cool for Cats* and I got them.

I took Sheila to the show and afterwards we hunted Peppi down. A nice guy, he got hooked on my attention and enthusiasm, but said he'd have to check with his manager, Tom Springfield, about taking me on as his press agent. Tom was naturally a little pissed off that I'd got to his act backstage. No newcomer to show biz was Tom, a founding member of sister Dusty's Springfields. Before "You Don't Have to Say You Love Me," Dusty and brother Tom were Britain's answer to hootenanny and the Springfields had a deal of their own on Philips.

To prove that no good deed goes unpunished, Tom would later manage the *Georgy Girl* Seekers. Dusty, of course, went solo as she should, while late Springfielder Mike Hurst went behind the lights to discover Cat Stevens. Hurst cut both Cat and my own First Lady of Immediate, P.P. Arnold, on "First Cut is the Deepest."

Peppi brought me back to Tom's office for another audition. Tom saw straight through my act, smiled a knowing smile at my hoisting his client aloft into dreamland, and took me on board for a month at a fiver per week. The arrangement was too loose to give up the Leslie Frewin day job, but I took great pleasure in making Mr. Frewin's org work for my newest client. At closing time, I'd find an empty cupboard and hide away in it until the rest of the staff had left the office. Then I'd chop-chop to the company telephones and hustle Peppi till Fleet Street headed for home or local. I kept one ground-floor window open, "my front door," through which I could receive my client Peppi and leave each night.

The Peppi I longed to introduce to a mass public was at best vaporware, and his lack of tangibility combined with a modicum of notoriety yielded a scant few inches of print, just before the end of my thirty-day trial. Once again it seemed I'd been cause out of faith in effects: Tom and Peppi, once skeptical, were generous in their praise but couldn't afford to waste any more money on PR. The reality was, there was to be no new season of *Cool for Cats*. The show faded from the screen and, with it, Peppi's U.K. TV career.

I was pleasantly surprised at what I had achieved for Peppi. The small success I'd had and the contacts I'd made raised the ante that the Leslie Frewin office was unwilling to put up: clients of my own. Later, when I had the means, I attempted a gesture of thanks, producing a single released on Decca in 1964, an enthusiastic reworking of Gene Vincent's "Pistol Packin' Mama."

H&R - homework and research - was my passion. British rock 'n' roll had once again reached an all-time low; performers who'd had magic moments had become tame and lame, knocking out slushy ballads, from sex 'n' shake to slop 'n' rot, *en route* to becoming "all-round entertainers." In England there was going to be no new Cliff Richard. It was all quiet on the sexual front. The future offered by Harold Macmillan and Leslie Frewin was reflected in the music they all hoped I'd listen to. Yet I was beginning to meet people who wanted to make a different kind of music, with their own hands, so to speak.

Shel Talmy wasn't the only newly-hatched independent producer trying to shake England out of its doldrums. There was also the truly unique Joe Meek. I went up to his studio on Holloway Road. He was recording a vocal version of "Telstar" with this fifteen-year-old kid, Kenny Hollywood, and I was hired to work it. Joe Meek really scared me. He was immaculate but seedy. He had a suit and tie on and more grease in his hair than you could imagine. He looked like a real mean-queen teddy boy and his eyes were riveting. There were shotguns in his studio, shotguns in his head, even then. The Kenny Hollywood single, "Magic Star," sank without trace and the only cuttings I could get on young Mr. Hollywood confirmed that he wanted to go there. Later, Joe said, "Andrew Oldham had a couple of months with RGM Sound as a public relations officer but got bitten by the recording bug and buzzed off."

In 1967, aged thirty-seven, on the eighth anniversary of Buddy Holly's death, Joe was awaiting trial for soliciting/cottaging in a Holloway toilet. His landlady went upstairs to confront him about making moves on her grandson. He blew her head off with a shotgun and then did the same to himself.

I started looking for another star to swing on: In the latest issue of *Melody Maker* I paused at an old photograph that had been used to launch teenage singer Mark Wynter when he was on Decca. His new label, Pye, had recycled the Lionel Bart-staged glossy to announce his signing. Mark's mentor, Ray Mackender, would become one of the first men in the pop field whom I respected enough to work for rather than imitate. A large and imposing man's man, Ray's lifestyle put him at odds with the time: He was born either too late or too early to be able to be himself. His love of show business was an inspiration and education to me.

Ray Mackender was as unlike a manager of the day as it was possible to be. For a start, he only handled one act. He also kept up a day job in the City, as an insurance broker at a subsidiary of Lloyd's called Bland Welch and Co., Ltd. Ray's double life was also marked by his desire to be surrounded by youth.

More than anything, Ray was a Cliff Richard fan. After meeting his idol during a taping of *Oh Boy!* at Hackney Empire, he'd started deejaying. Soon Ray was ghostwriting articles on behalf of Cliff for *NME*, coming up with crazy stories like Cliff thought Father Christmas came on a white elephant. While deejaying, Mackender came across Terry Lewis, a seventeen-year-old supermarket worker who did a bit of singing. Terry Lewis transformed into Mark Wynter.

Ray took too much vicarious pleasure in his youthful friends to pay mind to the taboos of the day. I realise this now in retrospect; my own upbringing had been too sheltered for me to understand what Ray was really about. He was a great boss and encouraged me to break away from establishment flackery, and to nourish the one I was with - myself.

The Aquarian magic among Ray, Mark, and me worked threefold. The Tony Hatch-produced "Venus in Blue Jeans" would soar into the charts, eventually rising to number four (October '62) and staying in the charts for fifteen weeks. I quickly resigned from the Leslie Frewin Organisation, worked for Ray and Mark full-time now, and did this despite mother's complaints that I was throwing away my future.

Ray Mackender was a total league of gentlemen. He let me

into his life and taught me how to work. He gave me his press
lists and contacts, his fire, his agenda. Ray's incredible respect for
show business influenced me greatly. His discipline complemented
my ambition. I enjoyed him setting me tasks and then delivering
on them. Alas, Ray was a tad too early. If he'd had the muscle of
the Moptops, like Brian Epstein, he would have had his day. But
Ray was too educated, too early, and cared too much.

Ray gave me the names and numbers for a crew of show
business journalists that covered the length and breadth of the
Isles. Between them, they appeared in almost every local newspaper from London to the middle of nowhere. I worked the
angle of volume diligently and had earned a list of contacts for
present and future use, a kind of legacy from Ray to me.

I was so close to Ray and Mark that for the first time I understood how the business enjoyed caressing success into being
by belief, leavened by good manners. I would briefly debate in my
mind the extent to which Ray and I manipulated Mark, but that
turned out to be a red herring. Our enthusiasm was undeniable.
I didn't have to tell Ray and Mark what I wanted to do: I was doing it. I could speak about what I was doing and feel confident it
would be received in the spirit in which I intended it. Hindsight
being what it is, this was the beginning of the happiest time in my
life. I was in a unique position, a publicist in the world of pop 'n'
rock. At only seventeen, I joined Les Perrin and a handful of others
as a pioneer.

Within a year my own list of clients would be impressive:
Mark Wynter, Kenny Lynch, Chris Montez, Johnny Tillotson,
Brian Hyland, Phil Spector, Bob Dylan, the Beatles, Jet Harris,
and Tony Meehan, the Little Richard/Sam Cooke tour. Save Mr.
Dylan, they'd all had hits, and hits made my world go round.

The other indie press agents were all boring; worse yet, they
were mostly former journalists, elbows and minds rubbed raw by
booze. I was the new cock of the walk, the new game in town. I came
from a different world: Mary Quant, Alexander Plunket Greene,
Vidal Sassoon, Hardy Amies. I reeked of *Vogue*, not *Melody Maker*.
The world of David Bailey, Terence Donovan, Brian Duffy, photographers whose work for the new world designers, crimpers, and
fashion mags had already, beats and shutters ahead of rock 'n' roll,
U.K. style, sent a message to the world that the British were coming.

Just as Elvis begot Pat Boone, Cliff begot Fury, Doris Day ended, and Monroe took the night. As later the Beatles allowed for the opposite Stones, so the dark side of entertainment in movies and theatre of the late fifties and early sixties had reached out and hit Broadway and the art cinemas of New York City. Osborne's *Look Back in Anger*; the works of Behan, Wesker, Pinter, Norman and Bart; *Saturday Night and Sunday Morning*; *The Loneliness of the Long Distance Runner*; Bryan Forbes and Richard Attenborough's *The Angry Silence* and *The L-Shaped Room* all took their cue from the French New Wave and New Brit Theatre, scoring as art hits in the U.S. Then came the lighter side of the British coin, the flash of fashion, and for a flash I had been there and took that moment to where I moved on.

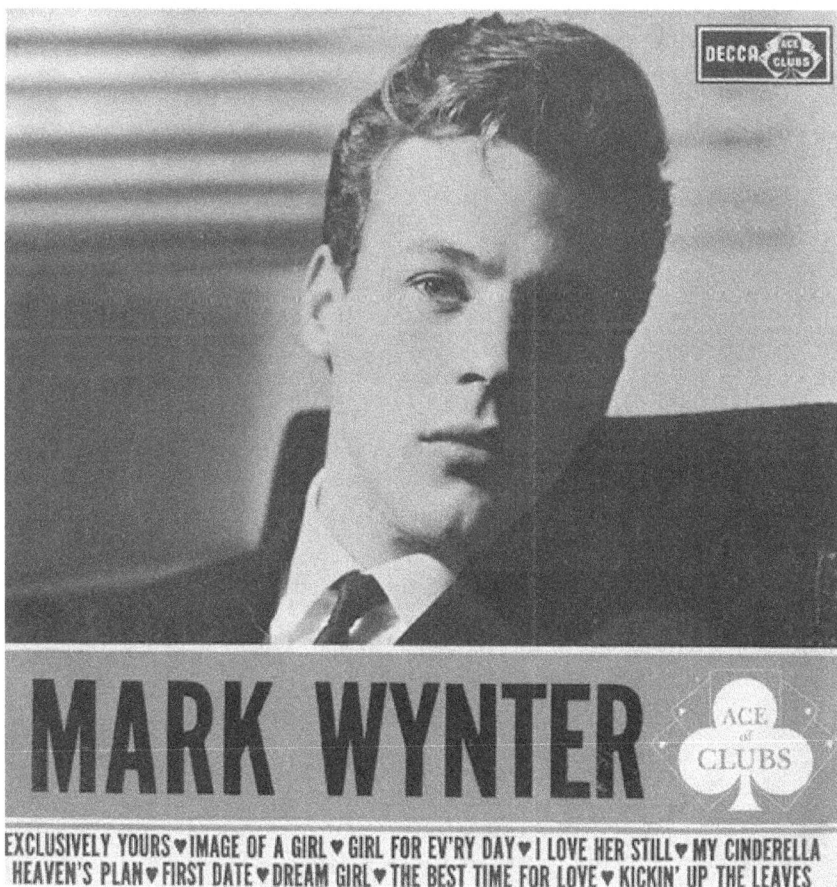

Everyone loved Princess Margaret.

CHAPTER 8

*my first american pr clients and the enlightening tony hall / an
audience with god, his client christ, and a ten day gig here on earth
- albert grossman and bob dylan / a spark of life: mr. tony king /
movie moments - before the beatles with director richard lester / a
schoolboy crush - miss jean lincoln / i get better lighting and i meet
don arden / a christmas gift for me - phil spector*

I didn't see Ray Mackender from 1965 until the year he passed on
in Toronto in the early nineties. Ray, after Mark Wynter, moved
out into the world and became his own act. He stopped pretending,
both by day and by night, and gave up both his jobs to travel the
world. He worked in Australia and Tahiti as a short order cook,
as a tour guide in the mountains of New Zealand, and as a cruise
line social director, visiting ports of call all over the world. Ray
gave up on London and when rock dropped the pop and tough
nuts took over the town, Ray moved on to another berth. When I
saw him that last year before he died, he still had that shine that
drew me to him, that light for those with the wherewithal and
the discipline to hone their talent into manna from the stalls to
the upper circle.

   If my recollections of the business in the early sixties make
the artist appear to be a necessary evil, I'm not exaggerating. One
young record industry promotion man decided to swim against
the scumline. The Decca office that Tony Hall set up in Great Marlborough Street became the place to go. Hall took over the third
floor, had his wife Mafalda decorate the offices, and left the main
area to be used for receptions to welcome American *artistes*. The
atmosphere of the offices reflected Tony's personality: loose and
cool, totally different from Decca's Albert Embankment H.Q.

   The visiting American stars and their managers used to stay
at the Stratford Palace Court Hotel on Oxford Street. I stopped in
regularly to hustle whomever I could buttonhole. As most of the
managers I spoke to were hustlers themselves, they appreciated
my candor. It made sense to hire someone who would be solely
devoted to their act, with them all the way for the week or so they
were in town.

   I managed to feather my nest with short-term assignments

from Brian Hyland ("Sealed With a Kiss"), Johnny Tillotson ("Send Me the Pillow That You Dream On") and Little Eva, who went from babysitting for Carole King and Gerry Goffin to brief stardom with the "Loco-Motion." The U.S. acts were very nice, thank you: quiffed, coy, and in the top twenty. I loved the way they enjoyed their fifteen minutes over three, but it was their Yank managers that made a deep-screen impression; there was nobody like them working the music side of the street in England. These guys oozed and pored the sweet smell of success - Las Vegas and Broadway version.

Johnny Tillotson's bloodhound, the affable Mel Shayne, was as Las Vegas as the neon sign over the Sands Hotel. On looks alone, Martin Scorsese would have hired him as a technical advisor on *Casino*. Brian Hyland's minder was Sidney Falco grown up: Sam Goldstein, renamed Gordon, as in quiet and Flash, was an inventive, wiry show-me-the-money Jerry McGuire via Damon Runyon. English managers, however competent and loathing they may have been, still felt they had to make excuses and curtsies for their lot as pimps. Americans came without shame and I loved them for it.

At the Cumberland Hotel, Marble Arch, I bumped into another American manager, Albert Grossman, a one-off among the wanna-beez, the calm above the norm. His young charge, Bob Dylan, was in London to play a minor role as a hobo in a BBC American-beatnik-style television drama written by Evan Jones, *The Madhouse on Castle Street*, whose only known copy was erased by the Beeb in 1968. Dylan got to perform four songs: "Blowin' in the Wind," "The Ballad of the Gliding Swan," "Hang Me, Oh, Hang Me," and "The Cuckoo." I got a fiver to handle him for the week in December 1962.

At the time, Grossman was a very casually dressed, neat, grey-haired guy, nothing like the ponytailed wildman of Woodstock whom he would later become. He looked like a well-to-do lawyer in his weekend clothes. His devotion to Dylan, even then, was apparent. In a world of agents it was refreshing to meet someone like that. As for Dylan, he was "Bob Dylan" already, as he's Bob Dylan now. It wasn't an act, even if it was. He had the magic and the words of life already. But it was Grossman's singular devotion that impressed me. To be sitting in a small hotel room, giving all his time to just one artist. They were both very happy together. They acted like they knew something we didn't know yet.

Grossman was still only in his thirties, though prematurely grey. A Jewish hustler from Chicago, he was on his way to becoming the most influential American management figure of the sixties. Intuitive and gutsy, he already had a firm grip on the street-level New York Greenwich Village folk scene. Along with Dylan he managed Odetta and Peter, Paul, and Mary - who in a few months would be the first of his acts to break big with a cover of Dylan's "Blowin' in the Wind." It was written that Grossman broke two acts at the same time: PPM and Dylan. But it would be 1965 before Dylan's own platters broke through as national pop anthems with "Like a Rolling Stone." While I managed to secure some press for the unknown-in-Britain folk zinger, Albert Grossman was reinventing and ahead of the game, turning the quick buck into the long buck.

Soon all my English pop acts were top acts, and Ray Mackender's education in show biz tradition was fortified by the street smarts I picked up from the Yank travelling salesmen. Their attitude toward me, was not "What Do You Want?" but "What Can I Tell Ya?" The days were happily B.R.P. - Before Rampant Paranoia. Everybody shared and the shills were alive with the sound of music.

Tony King had the spark of life, still does. There was a great energy being given off at that moment; we knew we were somewhere, even if we didn't quite know where. Work was given an extra kick by the two Tonys, Hall and King, not being housed in Decca's main funeral home, 9 Albert Embankment, that held Sir Edward, Bill Townsley, Dick Rowe, a host of civil servants, plus old soldiers and pensioners from World War I manning the doors.

When I offed the elevator and entered the two Tonys' suite, I felt love and felt at home, whether I dropped in at tea-time, for a natter or a shop, or arrived six-thirtyish to a smoke-filled reception: The smoke cleared whenever I caught the gleam in either of the Tonys' eyes. There were a lot of great receptions that I and Keith Richards and others would sometimes be invited to, and sometimes crash, and on occasion it was not as amusing for Tony King as it was for us. We were the mad hatters, functioning in a world that the Albert Embankment nutters still thought quite mad and silly, but knew now was definitely not going away. I've said that the publicity agent period, as mad as it was, was also the calmest, happiest time of my life. Then came the Stones. Then came the real work and real madness.

I didn't see Tony King for a while. He'd started in the Decca promo department, then joined me at Ivor Court to launch Immediate Records and promote the Stones before moving on in 1966, to work first for George Martin and his AIR production house; then in the seventies for John Lennon, Elton John, and the RCA disco department (bet that was fun); and by the mid-eighties, finally full circle, P.A.-ing for Mick and the Stones, surviving many years of Mick, then moving back to our pal Elton. Tony remains a very thoughtful being, whom I love, who speaks well of and to, dresses well, shops well, keeps well, and laughs well. One of his gifts, whether with me, Mick, Reg, or Lennon, is that Tony would only put up with the very best of you, and had the ability to help you find it.

I was now spending my time between shepherding American one-weekers-in-London and looking after Mark Wynter on the Larry Parnes-produced package tour of the U.K. starring Billy Fury. At the Britannia Pier, Great Yarmouth, I finally got to meet Fury and, more significantly, Parnes.

Fury was not up to the fantasy; he was not only stoned, he was bored. As David Bowie said later, sometimes it's better not to meet your idols, that way they stay intact. Billy was not intact. Parnes, on the other hand, lived up to my true pop Diaghilev image of him, a rare blend of art, money, and sparkle on the job. Mr. Parnes was a captain alert whilst his *artiste* seemed to be floundering, without structure, a Nijinsky to the maestro. I do not recommend piers in Great Yarmouth as the place to meet those who've shaped your life thus far.

Straight off the "Rock and Trad" tour, Mark and I headed for Twickenham Film Studios. Mark, as part of the transformation to all-round entertainer, was to star in the Milton Subotsky-produced *Just for Fun* (directed by Gordon Flemyng) and I was along to make sure everything went smoothly.

At Twickenham another film was also being shot, *It's Trad, Dad!* (a.k.a. *Ring-a-Ding Rhythm!* directed by Richard Lester, later to direct the Beatles on film) and to keep costs down many of the cast featured in both movies. Both films were poor imitations of the American rock 'n' roll B-movies, with little plot but packed with plenty of current pop acts. Amongst the likes of Helen Shapiro, Bobby Vee, Dusty Springfield, the Crickets, Joe Brown, the Tornados, Jet Harris, Tony Meehan, *et al.*, Mark was treated like a true star as he was acting with an "A," as opposed to miming his perhaps next hit single like his fellow cast members.

We shared the same room in a bed-and-breakfast near the studio. We had to be on the set at 6:00 a.m. Every morning Mark would go through this marvelous little routine: get up, creep off to the bathroom to wash, shave, put on a little make-up, and fix his hair, then get back into bed, and pretend to wake up again, yawning and stretching. Eventually he'd sit up and say, "Well, Andrew, time to set off for the studios." He was convinced I thought he always woke up looking like that. I just thought it was great; he really was looking after his image! I loved it. If I don't think you're a star, I have a hard job selling you. I liked the fact that Mark was on for me.

In my role as deputy manager, I soaked up the glamorous atmosphere. Although press people visited the film set, I had enough spare time to be happily engrossed in the filming process, chatting with producers, directors, and cameramen, and watching them on the job.

My name was getting out there; it was a wonderful time of simply being and doing, when I had no concern about what others thought of me or my progress. Jean Lincoln was another doer working for the Bernard Delfont Agency, which operated out of a second-floor spread on the wrong end of Jermyn Street, above the back entrance to the Piccadilly tube. Notoriously lethal agents and managers, amongst them Billy Marsh, Keith Devon and Mike Sullivan, manned the agency.

Jean worked closely with Mike Sullivan, helping him book Shirley Bassey, Ron Moody, and Shani Wallis. She also exclusively managed Kenny Lynch, so we met and talked about me handling Kenny's press. When I try to recall the actual meeting, all I get is lights and action - her eyes, beauty, and spirit signifying that I'd met one of the big teachers and best friends of my life, whom I immediately felt I'd known in another.

Jean had met Kenny in 1960 at one of his regular club bookings, Romano's, run by Mervyn Conn on Soho's Gerrard Street. Two weeks later she'd arranged an audition for Lynch with Wally Ridley, A&R at EMI, who signed him to an EMI subsidiary, HMV

POP. His first few singles all stalled at the lower end of the charts, but Lincoln was sure lightning would strike twice with Kenny's cover of Goffin/King's "Up on the Roof," a proven smash for the Leiber/Stoller Drifters in the U.S. In 1961 the Drifters had scored so big with the classic "Save the Last Dance for Me" that Cliff's own Drifters were forced to re-badge themselves as the Shadows.

Kenny Lynch is a sophisticated braveheart with a great many textures. His talent, sense of humour, Shetland skin, and big heart. He just fits together and lives in the comfort zone.

Jean introduced me to Roy Moseley, who handled Jet Harris. When Jet left the Shadows to go solo, he had a hit with "The Man with the Golden Arm," a Jet-come-lately cover of the title theme of the 1955 film produced by and starring Frank Sinatra.

Jet had recently formed an instrumental duo with the other ex-Shadow, my neighbourhood finishing school master, Tony Meehan. They had "Diamonds" coming out, and I got to rep Jet on the Little Richard/Sam Cooke tour for ten minutes. Two years earlier I'd been sneaking away from Wellingborough to see the Shadows and Emile Ford at the Granada Kettering, putting Vim in my hair to have the kind of blond fun I imagined Jet was having. Jet was James Dean on bass, the man who took the bass electric and made it a star.

Jean was my mother, my father, my very best friend. There was nothing we didn't share as we played the game of life. She showed me show biz - the whole block, how her world worked. She showed me where to play and where not to. She was my guide, my muse, my angel. She left for America some years later. We would end up living in the same block on Central Park West in New York, and there she died. She remains one of the faces always smiling over me.

The Delfont Agency didn't give a damn about the act unless they were over fifty or behaved like it. This was no happy show business vibe . This was a very austere monopoly, there was nothing glamorous about it. But in the middle of this, at two formica tables, were Jean Lincoln and Roy Moseley, who both had the smile and made it worthwhile.

I'd got the Little Richard tour through getting up the front to tackle Don Arden. Born Harry Levy, Don Arden was once the most famous Hebrew folk singer in Europe. He'd also worked as a comic and MC repped by impresario Harold Davison, who'd brought to the U.K. Count Basie, Duke Ellington, and Frank Sinatra. By the late fifties Arden had retired from the stage and gone into business as a promoter of rock 'n' roll.

He'd quickly established himself as the most talked about rock 'n' roll concert promoter of the day, the principal European agent for the whole rock 'n' roll pantheon: Gene Vincent, Sam Cooke, Jerry Lee Lewis, Little Richard, Brenda Lee, the Shirelles, Bo Diddley, Johnny Preston, Duane Eddy, Chuck Berry, Ray Charles, Fats Domino, Bill Haley, the Everly Brothers, and many more, even Jayne Mansfield. Teddy boys elevated Don to cult status and the punters made him rich. Counting stubs on the many hundreds of thousands of tickets he sold, Arden had grown wildly resplendent.

So I was off the tour, but in Don Arden, I'd made a friend for life. If you wanted to be in show business you just stood next to Don. I'd had the time of my life, I'd witnessed two greats, a nightly triathlon of rock, pop 'n' stomp, fought out between the oh-so-wild Little Richard and oh-so-smooth Mr. Cooke.

My dance card of life was getting fatter, richer, and info'd up; people were very giving. They were competitive, but the competition was not driven by fear. That's one of the courses drugs would bring to the menu, seasoned by success, a heavy toxin for most, digestible by only a few. Meanwhile "the greatest records ever made" were being made and made again. The Four Seasons' "Big Girls Don't Cry," produced by Bob Crewe, was at number three in the States and Phil Spector's "He's a Rebel" by the Crystals was number two. In England, Rolf Harris and Frank Ifield held those spots.

I found out the number of Mother Bertha Music, Phil's publishing company in New York, and got hold of Danny Davis, who ran it. I told him I could get Phil in the British equivalent of the *New York Times*. Two days later he sent me a telegram saying "Do it." It was a breeze, because I already knew that Maureen Cleave was going to write about the man. All I had to do was get to the airport with Maureen and act as if I had arranged it all. This I managed to do. After Maureen's feature in the *Evening Standard*, the music press was easy.

In his bright red corduroy jacket with black suede patches on the sleeves, Phil looked more like an act than most acts, and behaved like one too, upsetting the staff at the Mirabelle. His appearance and attitude would just upset people. Little men in red corduroy jackets and shades simply did not alight from large Rolls-Royces in Mayfair. Phil set the example. I was infatuated with him. I'd spent my time till now being polite, but now I had the opportunity to model myself after a perfect little hooligan. I picked up image and energy from Spector, and used all of what I thought were his principles when I produced the Rolling Stones' records. I had no idea of how he actually worked in the studio. I was very proud when Bill Wyman later said, "Phil Spector had the 'Wall of Sound', we had the 'Wall of Noise'." Even though it wasn't said as a compliment, it was.

Spector didn't just change my point of view, he helped me change my life, and some would have it not for the better. But he did change the way records could and would be made and elevated record production to commercial art. He moved the meaning and status of record production out of the backroom, on to the main lot. In scale and presence he was to the record biz what Orson Welles was to Hollywood. "You've Lost That Lovin' Feeling" and "River Deep - Mountain High," like *Citizen Kane* and *Touch of Evil*, could not be created merely by recreating what had been successful in the past. The pressure to repeat that one puts on oneself is almost unbearable. Phil stood and delivered for John Lennon but that was his last call. I don't see much difference between Welles at Ma Maison and Spector at the Rock and Roll Hall of Fame. For me it's either work or stay home, and three cheers for Steven Spielberg. Spector got recognition for his craft and, one way or another, he picked up the tab.

That Christmas came as an unwelcome interruption. I did my best to enjoy a quiet break in Hampstead, dividing my time between Celia and Sheila. Celia made a fantastic Christmas cake - heavy with liqueur to ward off the bitter cold, and somewhat under the influence, I took Sheila out in the snow on Hampstead Heath.

CHAPTER 9

who are those magical scruffs in the corner? meeting the beatles /
long distance phone calls are expensive - brian epstein gives me a
job / a few words from johnny jackson / doing pr for the beatles,
watching them do pr for themselves - their second greatest gift:
selling themselves / already time to pick a favourite beatle / on
the road with the fabs - the roar of the whole world in one small
midlands town, and the smell of tomorrow / somebody up there
likes me - and tells me about the rollin' stones

1963, and the sixties as we knew them began. Jet Harris and Tony
Meehan entered the *NME* charts at number ten with "Diamonds,"
Mark Wynter sat at number eleven and Kenny Lynch at number
twelve. The Shadows, Elvis, and Cliff held the top three *NME* spots.
America was "enjoying" a respite from real rock with Steve Lawrence at number one warbling "Go Away Little Girl," the number
two and three spots taken by the U.K.'s own Tornados with "Telstar"
and Chubby Checker with "Limbo Rock." Rock was indeed in limbo,
so auld lang syne, say goodbye to the old and bring on the new.

On January 13, two weeks before my nineteenth birthday,
I was with Mark Wynter in Birmingham for his appearance on the
top pop programme of the day, ABC TV's *Thank Your Lucky Slurs*.
Filmed live on Sundays, the show aired the following Saturday
early evening. Watching in the wings, I was spellbound by a new
British group making their first appearance on national television.
The Beatles had landed with their second release on Parlophone,
"Please, Please Me," and I wanted to know who was driving their
plane. I can clearly recall the buzz of watching them rehearse.
They weren't that different in appearance from the other acts -
they were all wearing suits and ties. What was unusual was their
attitude; they exuded a "fuck you, we're good and we know it"
attitude. You normally didn't see that in an act making its first TV
appearance. Of course that attitude was compromised as soon as
they became the famous Moptops, when it didn't really matter
who they were but who people thought they were. Soon enough,
the boys would vacillate between being obnoxiously themselves
and hiding any semblance of their true personalities to avoid the
hassles that followed them everywhere, no matter what they did.

I asked John Lennon who their manager was. He stuck his thumb in the direction of an elegant looking man standing in the hall. Brian Epstein radiated success in his expensive overcoat and paisley scarf. I studied this unpop-looking hotshot for a mo and quickly decided he was well worth a shot. He was obsessed and I wanted in. When I sized up the Beatles and Brian, I realised that these sixties were not only happening to me. I'd picked up on it just months earlier from Grossman and Dylan - it was hypnotic and life giving. There was nothing calculated about artists like Dylan and the Beatles; they were simultaneously omniscient and naïve.

We took each other's measure and passed the tests. Epstein complained that Parlophone were not really helping him to promote the group and perhaps, yes, I could do something for them. Maybe they did need somebody pounding the pavements for them in ... London, which he pronounced like a man getting rid of phlegm in his throat or a stone from his shoe. Brian already had the only guy he'd impressed at Decca, Tony Barrow, industriously moonlighting PR on his behalf, but he needed someone he could call his own, and I was it. The record was great and so was everybody.

When you sat down with Brian you knew you were dealing with a man who had a vision for the Beatles and nobody was going to get in the way of that vision. He was convinced that eventually everybody was going to agree with him. That gave him the power to make people listen. He'd say, "I believe this," and you'd believe him, so when he said, "I want this done," it was do-able. That Brian was somewhat to-the-manor-born gave him both a self-assurance and an entrée with the stubbornly middle-class label managers he had to deal with. At *Thank Your Lucky Stars* Brian merely stood watching his boys, yet his belief and their talent permeated the room, and would soon, thanks to TV, permeate the Isles, north to south. In those early days, Brian's presence, the Beatles irreverence, and their mutual pleasure were all conveniently merged.

So I moved on. Ray wanted me to work the last days of "Go Away Little Girl," but it was time to leave Great Cumberland Place and find my own office. Walking through Covent Garden after a lunchtime pub 'n' hustle I told *Melody Maker* scribe Don George of my need, and he recommended I call on Eric Easton, who had a small backroom up for rent at his Regent Street office. Eric Easton ran a little booking agency representing Julie Grant and guitarist Bert Weedon. He also managed *Thank Your Lucky Stars* host deejay Brian Matthew and the absurd, pianistic Mrs. Mills.

Eric was grey-haired, grey-suited, and in his mid-thirties - to someone my age that put him over the hill, but for work space at only £4 a week I decided to like him and his fifth-floor Regent Street office, which looked out over the back of Piccadilly.

I'd read somewhere that Aristotle Onassis had a recipe for success from his early days. It consisted of having a good address, be it a basement or an attic, a good suit, and a suntan. I now had a good address, had had a good suit for a while, and the suntan came courtesy of some make-up.

I settled into Eric's office fast, promoting every media contact I had, which now covered a wide range of publications: *femme* teen rags, "serious" music weeklies, lightweight pop periodicals, national and provincial newspapers, and upper and lower fashion magazines. The Beatles and Epstein came down to London once every two or three weeks, staying for two days in a hotel on Sloane Square adjacent to the Royal Court. I got them lots of ink, which wasn't too difficult. By summer Epstein's obsession would go national and the more tuned-in amongst the press could already smell pop blueblood.

I scored a coup when I got them into *Vogue*, although Adam Faith had come out as a pop debutante in *Queen* magazine a year earlier. Norman Parkinson photographed Faith in a white suit, white Anello and Davide boots, and black button-down shirt surrounded by dancing mod babes of the deb class. Parkinson's black-and-whiter was a precursor to later *Vogue* face-of-the moment spreads, featuring Stones and Beatles draped by this year's girls. Nothing is original; it might seem to be, though, depending on your timing ...

Johnny Jackson:

People who don't know see a lot of pictures, headlines, blurbs, and puffs, they hear a name being talked around and straightaway they start counting how much money it means in the bank account of the overpublicised one. But if publicity was dough, every little starlet in town wouldn't be plotting how to marry a millionaire - she would be one. Similarly with me and Bongo. We were making a big impact but there was still a lot of merchandising to be done before you could say that my property was a solid investment. Certainly *Expresso Bongo* was running away but, if you remember I had sold Garrick Records the whole show outright for £50. Stupid of me - but poverty and Mr. Mayer had taken advantage of both my good nature and judgment. All the good that particular bestseller was doing us was in newspaper clippings.

Of course, Bongo was picking up television fees here and there, but booking agents just laughed and laughed when I asked them for a hundred a week for him on tour. According to them, in the provinces the public didn't watch television or read the newspapers. The reputations were made here, in London, the Smoke.

Just as one can buy a ready-made or bespoke suit, rock 'n' roll offers two kinds of stardom: cheap, off the rack, and disposable, or costly, custom-made, real, and durable. Only those gifted with the gab of song, or manna from God's own publishing wing like Cliff, get an opportunity to tailor a career for the ages. Ignoring all the beware signs, our greatest street scribes run the red lights meant to keep pop at the top. If you're not sure about who rock 'n' roll belongs to, it surely isn't yours. Rules are there to be tested and broken, as is your mind, body, and spirit. History only serves the revisionists as they realign the rules of conduct for your next fucking. The only lessons that survive are clear instructions on such matters as to how to clean your bottom. The Beatles recreated the rules of survival, destruction, and rebirth. On each generation their impact was total. Their cause and effect was seen and heard on every avenue of the bop and pop boulevard; their songs were, are, and will always be hits.

Down in the Smoke, Brian Epstein was rather snotty about the press so I got to be "manager for a day" when the attractively scattered Moptops came to London to squeeze in some radio shows and press interviews. The 31 bus provided a leisurely, pleasant and dream-filled excursion, always a good ticket to ride over its unusual route from Hampstead to the back end of the Kings Road. A hop, skip, jump, and nod past Bazaar and John Michael, and I'd be in that solid Sloane Square, Royal Court'd and W.H. Smith'd.

The Beatles greeted me in the lobby of a small hotel facing

Smith's with the wonderful fact of that time - they were *The Beatles*. John Lennon was Everyman: I'd love to have been in Stu Sutcliffe's place for a while back then and had a mind-polish from John. As it was, I took what I could get. He was loud, rude, and a lout, but we would line up on the same side of the street and shout about life to others. I never knew John Lennon very well, but the times I spent with him were perhaps a mindmapping experience for us both. He looked, I floated; I looked, he floated. I could sit next to him in a cab or a club, and regardless of whatever war we were both fighting at the time, I found peace around him, and I think it was mutual. Oh, I had laughs with him, but in his physical presence I breathed a sigh of relief - around John life was always easy.

Paul has always been another chapter, his curiosity was honed and skilled. He didn't, like Lennon or me, crash his way through life's high street. John and I scattered broken dreams in our wake in order to preserve our own reality. At once innocent and crafty, Paul never seemed to realise he was centre-stage, which he always was, and perhaps that was a saving grace for his sanity as the world smothered the Beatles with its approval. George was already on his journey, and Ringo was clear from the off.

We'd cab around London to visit such musical scribes as Penny Valentine and Keith Altham, or to thank Chris Hutchins for his coverage of the news today. Paul would look at me and wonder where we were going, and John would know we'd already been there.

In Los Angeles in early March 1974, John Lennon, Tony King, and I found ourselves together at Lou Adler's Rainbow Club. With Lou Adler, I was with another of life's good twins. Lennon had impulsively jetted west on what would be the start of his notorious lost weekend with Harry Nilsson. It would be the last time I saw John in physical form, and the descent into Hollywood hell had not yet begun for him. He had left New York so suddenly he hadn't organised a place to crash. As I was moving out of Lou's Bel Air guest house and returning to New York, after a nod from my host I handed John the keys to the Stone Canyon abode. I was sober that year of mind games and reasonably clear apart from my service in the marching powder and pill brigade, my flair for biochemistry maintaining a reasonably psychotic, Ritalinish even keel. John and I wished each other the very best of love and life as we toasted with cups of coffee, enjoying the pleasant irony that neither of us was pissed at midnight on the Sunset Strip.

At my behest, *NME* announced that the Beatles had joined Helen Shapiro, Tommy Roe, Chris Montez, and Kenny Lynch for a month long U.K. Arthur Howes-promoted package tour kicking off in mid-February. Unbeknownst to me, I would get to tour the U.K. and see the world.

After an early show in Birmingham I was woken at home by a telephone call from Jean. The tour had moved on and left Kenny's luggage in Birmingham. She was driving up there to collect it and wanted me to keep her company. I agreed on one condition - she let me drive. I needed the practice. We got stopped by the police on the M1; I didn't have a license; the Mini had tinted windows; it was all suss. Somehow Jean managed to bluff the cops with some show biz talk and we were waved on, but I was in such a blind panic that I couldn't hit the right pedal. "Put your foot on the left," whispered Jean, but this just confused me even more. Now the cops were walking back toward the car to see what was wrong. I had to fake a cramp in my foot and ask the policeman to put my foot on the right pedal ...

Chris Montez was very shy and untravelled. I didn't grasp that perhaps the nineteen-year-old Chicano "Let's Dance" star might not speak much English. He was a very nice guy, gamely struggling on stage to get through a "full" set. Like most American acts reared on the Dick Clark "Caravan of Stars" tours, he was used to doing two numbers at most. In Britain he was asked to play a six-song, twenty-minute set.

Chris's enigmatic manager, Jim Lee, had hired me to publicise his boy for the duration of the tour, and I was now representing three major acts on the bill. Lee gave me some vital tips on the music business that would deeply influence how I would hone my potential. He sat me down one night after the show, and explained that he wasn't just Montez's manager but he'd written, produced, and published "Let's Dance." In America, Jim Lee was also the "independent" record company, and worldwide at the end of the day, he reckoned to make about $1,000,000 from the single.

Lee had a realistic sense of life and humour, knew he'd been lucky, and didn't intend to try to repeat his success. He had no desire to stay in the music business. He wanted to get out before he got sucked into believing that he could turn loaves and oafs into stars. He was looking forward to getting out, investing his million-dollar profit, and living happily ever after. I never heard of him in the music biz again and hope he got his wish.

The Beatles were fast becoming a national treasure, each new single replacing the previous one as the national anthem. Chris Montez, who had been the original headline act, was no doubt relieved when told by the tour's promoter that the Beatles were now going to top the bill. At the Granada Theatre in Bedford, I stood at the back of the stalls beside Brian Epstein, who'd been slightly apprehensive about the lukewarm reactions his boys had been getting "down south." This night, though, there was a tangible sense of mad hysteria rising all over the theatre, and with the arrival of the Beatles on stage it rose to a frenzy and took on a life of its own.

The kids broke all the backstage windows. It was pandemonium. On stage, you could not hear the Beatles for the roar of the crowd, and the roar I heard was the roar of the whole world. You can hear something without seeing it, in the same way as you can have an experience that is beyond anything you've had before. You don't have to be clever, you only have to be a member of the public. The noise that night hit me emotionally, like a blow to the chest. The audience that evening expressed something beyond repressed adolescent sexuality. The noise they made was the sound of the future. Even though I hadn't seen the world, I heard the whole world screaming. The power of the Beatles touched and changed minds and bodies all over the world. I didn't see it - I heard and felt it. When I looked at Brian, he had the same lump in his throat and tear in his eye as I.

Before he returned to California, my new best friend Phil Spector had left behind some pearls of wisdom, which at the time did not seem relevant to my PR-driven lifestyle. But within a few rollin' months his cautions would prove to be invaluable. Phil had been impressed with all he'd seen in the U.K. and was looking further ahead for me than I was looking for myself. He told me that if I ever found a group to record, I should on no account let them use the record company's studio, or sign the act directly to the recording company, but instead should pay for an independent studio session myself and afterwards sell or lease back the tapes to the record company. That way, Spector explained, you keep control and you earn much more money. Now, in my present cuffed-hand-to-big-mouth existence, I had no thought for "real" money, but control I thought I understood. And I loved the idea. What Phil didn't mention then - perhaps he didn't know it himself - is that having this much control can alienate one from what one loves best and can lead to a personal life out of control.

My lunchtime port of call was the De Hems pub, just off Shaftesbury Avenue in Soho. It had been a gangster hangout in the twenties, but was now the acknowledged watering hole of the British music business. Journalists, managers, agents, and promoters would meet there to seal deals or swap gossip. For me it was the perfect place to hustle for clients over an orange juice. My main De Hems hustle was *Record Mirror* editor, Peter Jones. The burly, big hearted journo made up in *Record Mirror* space any *NME* deficiency I might suffer. With only two thirds of *NME*'s circulation but twice the space at times allotted to my clients, Peter's *Mirror* often saved my week in clippings. I would head for De Hems with a list of five acts and settle for getting three out of five into print.

This day, Jones had had enough already. "Oh, Andrew, we did him last week, we can't give you any space." He was telling me to shut up, drink up, and count my blessings. Then, "Listen to me for a change." That allowed and given, he went on to explain that a colleague, Norman Jopling, had just written an article about a fledgling R&B band called the Rollin' Stones. It would be appearing in the following week's issue of *Record Mirror*, under the headline "Genuine R 'n' B." Jones had not seen the band but Norman Jopling's enthusiastic write-up made the Rollin' Stones sound really wild. It was unheard of for *Record Mirror*, or any music weekly, to write about a band before they had single hovering on the lower rungs of the charts. The Rollin' Stones didn't even have a record out. Jopling's going to bat for these newcomers intrigued Jones, and Jones attempted to intrigue me.

Truth be known, I didn't give a shit. I was still smarting over the two clients whom Peter Jones had refused to touch and hoped that by listening I would be allowed to hustle them back into his good graces. So I listened to Jones's story of a musical evolution I had yet to give two farthings about. "As the trad scene gradually subsides, promoters of all kinds of teen-beat entertainment heave a long sigh of relief that they have found something to take its place. It's Rhythm 'n' Blues, of course. The number of R&B clubs that has sprung up is nothing short of fantastic," Jopling was to write in the May 11, 1963 *Record Mirror*. I think it was all of three, but journalists are entitled to their own hypes. "The hip kids throw themselves about to this new 'jungle music' like they never did in the more restrained days of trad."

The Rollin' [sic] Stones where I met them, at the Crawdaddy Club in the Station Hotel, Richmond.

CHAPTER 10

*: i say hallo to the rest of my life - ladies and gentlemen, the rollin'
stones / the system and how it was and forever shall be against
you / i help brian epstein say no to the stones and get a yes without
sympathy from a devil / sorting the stones out and removing one
from my shoe / first recording sessions - a pool with or without
water? let's not even ask if we can swim / decca records sign the
stones then try to fuck me for them - an industry standard / last
stroll through soho as a virgin - work as a hooker begins*

There are no accidents and Peter Jones was the conduit to my
destiny. I was probably forty-eight hours ahead of the rest of the
business in getting there, but that's the way God planned it. I met
the Rollin' Stones and said "hallo" to the rest of my life.

1963 was a very good year, and a very fast one. Late '62
through April '63 had me busy, secure, and content with my lot.
I hoped my mother had noticed, and had told Alec as much.
Alec's approval was just as important to me, since if he thought I
was doing OK, my mother would go along with him.

I wasn't just dreaming - I was doing. When asked, I didn't
have to conjure up what I wanted to do (just as well, as I still had
no idea): I could spout about what I was doing. I was a publicist
or press agent in the world of pop music and rock 'n' roll, and I
was in a unique position. It was a new field, that of an independent, self-employed publicist; there were only a few of us. The
mainstays were all employed directly by EMI and Decca (major)
or Philips and Pye (minor). The tedium of supporting a crumbling
system prevented them from enjoying the incessant beat of revolution booming out of Liverpool. Best case? Guitars would disappear as fast as hula hoops and Davy Crockett hats. They could
go back to sleep over their pints after that.

Now, all my money, save what I gave to mother out of respect, was going on music and clothes. Each day I would spring
forth new, soundtrack intact, wardrobe mistress to my own ethical
grooming, with God handling my lighting, backed up by schlap.
Broadcloth blue, tab-collared shirt, jet black wool tie, three-piece
suit complete with cuffs on jacket and trousers, flair-waisted jacket *á la* Bunny Roger with inverted vent, spit-and-polished side-

laced black booties: a smorgasbord of crossed cultures to fit the
mood the day required. One enjoyed both the charm of Harvey's
Johnny Jackson and good spark of Tony Curtis's Sydney Falco in
Sweet Smell of Success. Better yet, I was free as a bird with no J.J.
Hunsecker (Burt Lancaster) to be kowtowed to. I had both the
sense and the good taste to avoid Mr. Harvey's hand-rolled wing
collars, ordered from a Jermyn Street establishment I could not
patronise; I lived on the via of broadcloth tabs.

So it was with fitting in and standing out that I pondered
on when it came time to pick my clothes for the trip to Richmond.
When would the dismal anti-fashion of the Witch's Cauldron be
behind me? I wondered. I anticipated a very beat outing, slumming
in the south of town. Jumper, slacks, hush puppies, I thought did
rather a good job of muting my ambition without undoing my
grooming. I said "goodbye" to my mother that late Sunday afternoon the 21st and strolled from our flat down Frognal to the Finchley
Road British Rail line, which fortunately ran every forty minutes
ten stops from Northwest Hampstead to Southwest Richmond's
hilly streets. It had been a beautiful day for April, and as I alighted
from the train at Richmond the sun was lingering, loath to leave
day for night.

Opposite the train station was, naturally enough, the Station Hotel. The Rollin' Stones, I'd been told, would be playing in
a room that had an entrance at the back of the hotel. I crossed the
zebra and headed down a long alley. On my right was the Station
Hotel building, and to my left, the British Rail lines running farther southwest and back north again.

For the first few strides I was alone in the alley with the
sound of my mind and my footsteps. Halfway down the path I
saw that I was not alone - there were two figures ahead of me, one
with its back to the wall, the other facing the other, arms against
the wall. I got closer; they weren't discussing, they were arguing.
A girl was against the wall and a boy was pressing his point.

As I passed them I tried to be invisible, looking away from
them, but not quite. The three of us acknowledged each other, I by
picking up my pace as I passed by, they by pausing. He gave me
a look that asked me everything about myself in one moment - as
in: "What are you doing with the rest of my life?" His lips looked at
you, seconding that first emotion. He was thin, waistless, giving

him the human form of a puma with a gender of its own. The girl was a bridge to reality. They were both very earnest, hurt, and similar: pale skins, brown hair, and flashing eyes -and both, very attractive in their similarity, in heat; in the shadows of the pathway, I wasn't sure who was mommy and who was daddy.

I edited all such thoughts out of my mental movie and quickly put a coin in my juke box and walked on by. Later I found out that the Romeo and Juliet in my path had been Michael Philip Jagger and Chrissie Shrimpton on their first date, first fight. I turned right to the back entrance of the hotel, and bumped into a big enough queue to make the night promising. The next half-hour went by in a moment. I do that in queues or whilst waiting; I change time. It was time for the cutting room floor anyway.

Finally, in the dark and sweaty room, the Rollin' Stones, all six of them, took to the stage while the nattering, half-pint-sodden, hundred-odd couples seemed ready for what they were about to receive, and went apeshit. So did the group - they didn't seem to start so much as carry on from a previous journey. I was already standing up but what I saw, heard, and felt stood me up again, as the remaining air left the room from the whoosh of hundreds of waving hands, dancing feet, and heaving bodies, having sheer, sheer pleasure.

I wasn't familiar with the songs or the sound. R&B to me had been Elvis's "A Mess of Blues" and a bunch of "interesting" Chess 45s released on Pye in the U.K. that bubbled just inside the top fifty for a paltry week, and so of no interest to me. They were of much more consequence to this Michael Philip Jagger, who regularly petitioned Pye to release more Bo Diddley records. The stuttering beat spoke of sex the instant it started its little dance in my heart.

Thinking was suddenly not required - redundant. The room was as one, the music and audience had one particular place to go, a place I'd never been to but was happily being drawn to. The Rollin' Stones were six who became one. Three were backed against the wall: on the left, one Bill Wyman, on bass, to his right a large amp I'd only seen in ads and Charing Cross Road store windows. He stood like the statue who became a celebrity, concentrated, nonchalant, picking his instrument in an upright "shhhoulder-arrrms" army drill position, perhaps as a result of having seen service as Bill Perks for Queen and country. He was gaunt, pale, almost mediaeval in a way.

The drummer appeared to have been beamed in, and it seemed you didn't as much hear him as feel him. I enjoyed the presence he brought to the group as well as his playing. Unlike the jacketless other five, he had the two top buttons of his jacket done up meticulously over a just-as-neat buttoned-down shirt and tie, unaffected by the weather in the room. Body behind kit, head turned right in a distant, mannered disdain for the showing of hands waving at 78 rpm in front of him. He was with the Stones but not of them, kinda blue, like he'd been transported for the evening from Ronnie Scott's or Birdland where he'd been driving in another Julian "Cannonball" Adderley time and space.

He was the one and only, all-time man of his world, gentleman of time, space, and the heart. His rare musical talent is an expression of his bigger talent for life: I'd just met Charlie Watts.

Back stage right was an odd man out. Sometimes on piano, sometimes maracas, he had a Popeye torso, a William Bendix jawline, and a bad Ray Danton haircut. He cared for his "little three-chord wonders" till the day he died. As time went by he would pay me this compliment: "Andrew Oldham? I wouldn't piss on him if he was on fire." Yes, the real deal, sixth Stone, Ian Stewart.

The front stage three took in and gave out from stools, nicely opposite their striving audience. From stage left: black as night, hacked hair, maybe baby-hacked face atop a war-rationed baby-body channelled into his guitar. This hollow-cheeked one effected an alchemic exchange in cool-hand heat with himself, and turned on a dime with alacrity.

I wasn't sure tho', which was which and who played what. Such were the six-stringed exchanges between Keith Richards and the incredible blond hulking hunk stage right. Brian Jones's ugly pretty, shining blond Barnet was belied by a face that already looked as though it had a few unpaid bills with life. His head, having forgone a neck, slipped straight into a subliminally deformed *Greystoke* body. Undeniably, one half of two with one great guitar sound. Yet, of all the six, Brian was the one whose eyes darted around the room (save Perks on the perennial pull), wanting to suss the reaction right now and not able to wait for the acclaim or applause between songs. Although he bathed in that too, like somebody having sex, rolling over, smiling, and saying, "Next time, its your turn ..." Our own Diana Barrymore.

Finally, centre-stage front, was the boy from the railway towpath: the *hors d'oeuvres*, the dessert, and meal in between. On that tiny stage, when I took in the Stones' front line, I saw rock 'n' roll in 3-D and Cinerama for the first time. There had always been a succession of Ones: Elvis, Johnnie Ray, Eddie Cochran, and more. Then at the New Victoria Cinema I finally saw an act on stage that didn't cheat. The Everly Brothers sounded like their records, the Crickets backing them superbly. In particular Jerry Allison "be-bom-de-boomt"-ing" his way through "Till I Kissed You" and "Cathy's Clown." I saw double, not for the last time: Don and Phil Everly enjoyed their forever moment of music, and oh, what a feeling, as one voice lay on top of the other, reversed, lay together, sideways - always sounding as if the girls they sang about were a front for this Lord-approved and given musical incest.

Yeah, I know. It's also called purity.

Mick's voice was the first of many things that struck me as I watched Brian, Mick, and Keith work with, and in spite of, us and each other. It wasn't just a voice, and it was much, much more than a rendition, a mere lead vocal. It was an instrument, a declaration, not backed by a band, but a part of the band, their decree. Mick moved like an adolescent Tarzan, plucked from the jungle, not comfortable in his clothes. Probably that night, a drip-dry "Tern" white shirt and loose black string tie, Take Six midweight trews around a body that was still deciding what it was and what it wanted. A positive question of opposites.

Sorry folks, it's eyes down for a full house; you've paid your money, just turn the page. I can't be clever and experienced, subtle, or oblique about this. We are talking about one of the three most proficient entertainers of the twentieth century and the group that defied time, all bets, and most drugs to close out the century as the world's greatest rock 'n' roll band. I can only embarrass you, not me, and have you chuckin' up, were I to put in here an "Oh God, how embarrassing!" from Mick's childbearing lips, or even an "I saw how you felt, 'twas true" from Charlie. A nod from Keith would certainly be fitting, and from wherever he may be, Brian would suggest, "Enough about me, what do you think about me?" I can only tell you what I felt and attempt to take you there.

I'd never seen anything like it. They came on to me. All my preparations, ambitions, and desires had just met their purpose. It was a feeling of all the elements falling into the right place and time, catching all the dualities. The music was authentic and sexually driven by the three on stools and the bottom end behind them. It reached out and went inside me - totally. It satisfied me. I was in love. I heard the anthem of a national sound, I heard the sound of a national anthem. I heard what I always wanted to hear. I wanted it; it already belonged to me. Everything I'd done up until now was preparation for this moment. I saw and heard what my life, thus far, had been for.

The look the puma had given me in the alley kicked its heels into my life and made sense. I stopped thinking; I had no programme, no thoughts on what suddenly felt like the norm. Life was not second-hand in this moment. Yes, at the Granada Bedford I had stood with Brian Epstein watching the Beatles and feeling the world. But it was third hand, not mine. Yes, I was there, but had no real cause nor effect in their lives; I wasn't that to them, and I was never meant to be. I saw you standing there and thanks for the memory. But here I was in the eye of the storm; I had stopped thinking, or more accurately, scheming, and I was feeling ... great.

Before the pill, when sex was still a delicacy, teenagers had it artificially inseminated through vinyl and live gigs. The audience at the Station Hotel Crawdaddy Club, getting off on the Stones, were as flushed and happy as if they'd had the real thing. As for your actual R&B, it didn't mean dick to me. I have always maintained that if it had, I might have had an opinion about it and missed the totality of what hit me - I was just bowled over by that totality. Ignorance was bliss.

The set over, I didn't have the bottle to approach the act on the spot. What I'd seen was amazing and somehow I felt lacking, unprepared. I needed time to get my act together and consider my move on the band. On the oh-so-slow train back to Frognal I was dizzy from the experience, a comeuppance considering my low expectations for the evening. I mentally bounced all over the train. I'd never had career conversations with myself thus far - I just got on with life, happy in the action of the moment it had bought me or I had grabbed. Wants and needs in order, lucky in love and at one with my life. That Sunday changed all that: I felt their force and I wanted in, I felt a God-given invitation to Jagger, I'd let the band wave over me, and got the reason for all my experience and gains, this was no third-hand, once removed feeling: I was feeling something I belonged to. I was already theirs, and theirs was the world ...

Now, to get acts work you had to be an agent, you had to have a license to be one, an agent's license was issued by the London County Council, you had to be over twenty-one to get this license, and you had to have your own registered offices. I was not in that business. I couldn't see siphoning my enthusiasm down to a Delfont: "Well, the boys are free the third week of April." Climbing down from the sky, I started to mark out my next set. I knew what I could provide the Stones, but that would not be enough. The band's daily bread was live work, and I didn't arrange that kind of thing, agents did.

I phoned Brian Epstein at his home on Monday. The Beatles' manager might not have wanted to hear that his London press agent had seen God in the Rollin' Stones (having already discovered over a year before that God was the Beatles). If Epstein got involved in the deal, I would have to play second fiddle. I really didn't want to do that, but I decided to go for polite, falling back on the manners I'd been raised to have, and a sense of social etiquette I was coming to have.

Brian was in, and out, an increasing occurrence I could not fathom nor dwell on. I informed him that I was resigning from his NEMS Enterprises Ltd., that I'd seen this group called the Rollin' Stones, and wanted to devote myself to them, try to become their manager. "I really think they're great," I told Epstein, "and when I see the Stones again, if we can agree on a deal, there are so many things I can't handle on the organisational side, like getting them work - would you be interested in coming in with me on it?"

Perhaps because Brian Epstein was already frantic from working the Beatles, Gerry and the Pacemakers, Billy J. Kramer, and Cilla Black, he didn't really hear me, perhaps I wasn't that loud. Whatever - Epstein chose to pass on the offer. He thanked me for letting him know so politely about my resignation.

The good news was that I would not be leaving Epstein without a London pavement pounder. Brian had managed to per-suade Tony Barrow to leave Decca and work full-time at Eppy's newly opened London office in Argyll Street. I was relieved. By instinct I knew if the Stones joined NEMS then they would be following a trend, not setting one. I was pleased that Epstein had turned down my offer over this band I didn't yet represent, and I was happy to have ended my working relationship with Epstein on good terms as he wished me goodnight and the best of luck.

By Wednesday, I was back down at De Hems. Perhaps my desire to become the Rollin' Stones manager was unrealizable? I practised on Peter Jones, to see how convincing and real I could make it sound, running all the angles past the *Record Mirror* editor. I double-checked with Jones about Giorgio Gomelsky, asking him, "Are you sure they're not signed?" Gomelsky was the promoter of the Station Hotel gig and there was an understanding between him and the band about management, but Peter Jones thought there was nothing official or signed.

Back at the back of Eric Easton's office I was agitated as I considered what I knew was the inevitable move, the man sitting next door. Putting it off, I stared out of the office window, immune to secretary Janice's well-meaning effort to lift my obvious gloom, meditating on the high-class hookers entering and exiting a club at the top of Lower Sackville Street. I mused that Eric had treated me benignly. "That Andy," he'd told Janice, "What a case he is, but a nice lad. He's trying it on today, he told me the Everly Brothers were all about incest."

Eric Easton was an agent, could get the band work, and could finance the recording operation I had in mind as a must. From the Stones' point of view, Easton would seem a solid partner - together we'd look like some Machiavellian show biz partnership. "Yeah, it would work." I laughed my best Johnny Jackson laugh, stopped checking out the working girls, and got ready to pimp. Janice heard the laugh and flashed me a smile of relief.

"Hey, Eric, Got a mo?" He did. I sat down opposite him and offered him "the chance of a lifetime," three cheers for me. I enthused about the potential of the Rollin' Stones: cash, cash, cash. Did Easton fancy being partners with me in a proposed management deal with the band: money, money, money? Did he see how well the Beatles were doing: blah, blah, blah? These Rollin' Stones could really make it: big, big, big. George Harrison of the Beatles digs them, he's been down and seen them: knock, knock, knock. They stand a big chance of becoming a big hit outfit: get it, get it, get it. Peter Jones recommended the boys without reservation: got it, got it, got it.

"You know I don't really like this new pop music, Andy," he said. Easton was happily married with two children and lived in a terrace house in Ealing. His one luxury was a caravan on the South Coast. I knew it would be difficult to get him to leave his house on a Sunday evening to check out the Stones at the Crawdaddy. Watching *Sunday Night at the London Palladium* live on TV was for him like going to mass. Easton finally agreed: "I'm making a huge sacrifice, Andy, to be missing my Palladium show, so they better be good, that's all I can say."

The next Sunday I stood outside the Richmond train station waiting for Eric Easton, worried he'd become fascinated with another old-timer on the box and not show up at all. When he did I breathed a mighty sigh of relief and steered him toward the Crawdaddy. Inside I watched Eric watch the band. Eric Easton accepted all, smiled and said, "Alright ..."

I went up to the bandstand after the show and asked Charlie Watts for the leader of the Rollin' Stones; he pointed me toward Brian Jones. I approached Jones and told him how great he was, and that me and this agent Eric Easton were in partnership and "would really like to do something with you." Then I pushed Eric forward to fill in the holes.

Easton reiterated to Jones that he was an agent, that I worked in publicity with the Beatles and that we'd both been very impressed with what we'd seen, and would Jones like to have a meeting to discuss the possibility of working together? Brian seemed keen and telephone numbers were exchanged, Brian promising to call Easton's office on Monday or Tuesday morning. I breathed a sigh of relief and left the Crawdaddy Club in raptures, convinced that Eric and I had done enough to secure the band's signature and my future.

Brian Jones, accompanied by Mick Jagger, came up to Eric's office as arranged at two o'clock the next Tuesday. We sat down and played mixed doubles. Eric Easton, former pier organist from up North, now a nigh-on fortyish, unassuming slightly greying, bespectacled open-faced man, sat behind his desk with a twinkle in his eye. Eric had that twinkle from the time I met him, on most occasions, till sometime in '65. He got the money, I hope he got a life and got the twinkle back.

When Sean O'Mahony called me in the early nineties and informed me that Eric would soon be leaving his body I placed a call to Eric in Florida to attempt a closure to all our acts on this earth. Eric came to the phone, but didn't really want to speak with me - his call. But that '63 day he was all mouth and good with it.

To me, anybody over twenty-five or twenty-six was forty-ish, including Bill Wyman. On the other side of the desk from Eric sat a furtive Brian Jones, all sham, shampooed, and spotless, ready to act as spokesman for his group. Mick and I sat in neutral corners waiting for the first round of this two o'clock bout to begin. Two o'clock was a very reasonable rock 'n' roll hour, years later ten o'clock meetings would be set by the men with the money to see if one could get up and not fall over. When we'd small-talked enough, Eric cut to the chase and restated our interest in the Rollin' Stones. "We're not promising we can do anything for you, we'd just like to try," he told Brian.

Eric asked if there was anything contractually stopping the band from signing. Brian said that Giorgio Gomelsky had wanted to become their manager, but nothing had been signed. Gomelsky wasn't in London to defend his corner, but in Switzerland, making funeral arrangements for his recently deceased father. "Gomelsky will be making funeral arrangements for his Rollin' Stones impresarial career," pimpresario Sydney Falco whispered in my ear, as Brian let us know that the band were fair game.

I was fascinated by Brian's position as group spokesman and leader. A short year later, when my knowledge of the structure of groups had increased, i.e., I was an expert, I realised that almost every group had a manager until they had one. Meaning that until a group had decided on management or management had decided on them, and the real deal was in to help one and all up the ladder to money, fame, and fuck everything in sight that moves (a.k.a. sex, drugs, and rock 'n' roll), a member of the group either found or elected himself to the position of frontman, sounding board, keeper of the cash, and Checkpoint Charlie into whatever world in which the group lived.

Then two things usually happened: The said "temp" manager got no joy from phoning dozy drummer Dave five times to make sure he got to the gig or rehearsal on time, or got no spurt of power from holding a few quid for a few hours, and so welcomed getting back to just the band and the music. For the other cast of managers-in-waiting, things weren't quite so simple and they started to get a little fucked up.

They'd enjoyed holding all the cards, even for a few minutes, from the rest of the group. They'd relished the importance of telling the other anxious band members what had transpired during the day and what might happen the next week. They were the first to hear good news, and they were bearers of needed data, heeded by default. The rest of the band gave full attention to the spokesman. Though, if he thought about it, he knew that actual management was needed for the dreams and reality at hand, he would never get over the loss of power, that moment of secure importance. For some, it dimmed the pleasure of all the good things to come. So Brian sat across from Eric Easton and began the long goodbye.

"Please tell us what it is you think you could do for us, Mr. Easton," Brian said, allowing a nod in Mick's direction.

"Look, lads," Eric began, the northern lilt in his voice seeking to convince. "We really liked you, and both Andy and I would like to manage your careers, we'd do the very best we can for you. But I have to make it clear, we'll make a real go of it, but we're not making any promises about anything to you."

"What does that mean?" entered Jagger.

"Good one," I thought, "I like this Jagger." Four words to the point and not cock of the run like Jones's "What do you think you could do for us?" routine.

"What's that mean?" said Eric, lilt travelling further North, turning toward Mick, slight pause. "Mick, it's that neither Andrew nor I are in the business of making promises to you in order to get you to sign with us. I'm not going to tell you you'll have a hit record, or even a record. It doesn't work like that and I'd have to be mad to tell you any different."

"Get mad, Eric," I thought, "get mad." The man continued, "I have no idea what might happen to you ... or whether others will agree on your potential. But we'd like to make a go of it, we think you've got the potential. We think you're really good."

Brian was back in the game with "Eric, what is it about us that you think is good, what about us did you like, is what I'm saying?" Oh, cry me a river! Even Mick squirmed. Then it was my turn.

"What we like is that you've got it - I don't know what that is but, whatever it is, you've got it. It's like with the Beatles, I remember the night in Bedford they took over. Two weeks into the tour and they'd taken over. I stood at the back with a lump in my throat, you felt what was coming, the crowd roared and you felt the world, the hairs on my hand stood up, the lump ... it's instinctive, natural, and I know that the public will demand an opposite, for every kid who wants to take his Beatles home there's another who doesn't want to share, and it'll be you that he won't want to share. And when I first saw you, when Eric and I saw you, we knew it was you. I know you've got it, and I want to do what I can to help you get it."

I don't remember the rest of that meeting. I was too busy recovering from my own applause.

Stars must be killers, always striking first and last. They have to be so totally obsessed and paranoid about this year's vision of themselves, that it's beyond obsession - it's reality - logical and natural. There's no remorse when they kill, no regrets when they pimp, and no shame when they whore. And it's really a fair exchange: The world needs them and they need the world. A star is a star is a star, and a fixed race would be nice if you could arrange it ...

The Stones all agreed to look at an agreement that Eric would prepare, Brian calling back and telling Easton to start drawing up the contract. I'd told Eric that the contract must be for a management and a recording deal; as managers it would be in our best interest to create a company to supervise the band's recording sessions and then lease the finished tapes to which-ever record company to manufacture and distribute.

I had a lot of reasons for this, the first being control. From catching a few minutes of a few sessions, I knew what major record company staff producers looked like, glorified civil servants *avec* pipe. I had no truck with the swimming pool atmosphere of "OK boys, you can hear a playback, it's great ..." A Romans-and-Christians pecking order obtained and, as such, an act with an opinion as to what it was about would be thrown to the lions.

This was not a conducive setup for Stones recordings, what-ever that meant. I was sure, however, that what I'd witnessed in Richmond could not possibly translate to that meat-market environ-ment. As comfortable as the Beatles had seemed in the few minutes I'd caught of them at Abbey Road, I didn't see it working for the Stones ... or me. I also firmly believed that stars should be stars to everybody. I wanted the record company to sell the band as stars, not as mere mortals whom they'd seen sweating in the studio for the man.

Pragmatic Eric, however, was not into my utopian autarchic agenda and was concerned by one small detail, "Yes Andy, but who's gonna make the records?" I told him, "We will, Eric, we will."

I suggested that we call our independent recording company "Impact Sound" and Easton registered it. Later, I learned that "our" company was registered solely in the name of Eric Easton Ltd., cutting me out. Thus Eric slid into the driver's seat, little Andy being an excited and trusting minor jumping up and down in the back seat. The northern slag next set about drafting the contracts whereby as managers we would take 25% off the top of everything, Impact Sound paying for the sessions, taking the larger percentage for time, trouble, and "investment," giving the remainder of the receivables to the group, which would still amount to a good three times as much as an average recording company artist's royalty. It was not the time to debate the exact fairness of that arrangement with Eric; he'd translated my art into commerce as I'd asked him to, and we needed to maintain a united front to the unsigned group.

The band accepted me because we had the same interest. They'd listened to me because we could identify with each other. Mick and Keith, especially, could be art-yobbo layabouts in search of a good time rather than a regular job. But at the same time, they were as ambitious and proud as panthers, and prepared to work at it, knowing I'd pound their beat for them. The security for the band was Eric Easton. They'd at least have work, worst scenario, whichever way the records and the fifteen minutes went.

The group approved and Lewis Brian Jones signed the management contract, which was to run for three years. He then had to admit that he could not sign the recording document as the band already had a recording agreement with IBC Studios. Hitherto Jones had maintained the Stones had nothing concrete, signed or otherwise, with Gomelsky or any other party. I was totally shocked, Eric less so, by little LBJ's revelation - this could shut down my whole movie. I wanted to throw the runt to the whores.

Brian had entered into a deal with IBC studios in January 1963. IBC provided the band with free time and their house engineer, Glyn Johns, and in return IBC had a six-month option on the Stones tapes. IBC had unsuccessfully tried to sell the five-track demo to every label in town, and had more or less given up on the group, but a contract was a contract. The IBC deal ran on until July, and that seemed like waiting for the millennium. Even Norman Jopling's article could be turned against us if some record company woke up and went for the band.

IBC Studios was owned by George Clouston and Eric Robinson, both straight and successfully out of the big band era and not clued up or into pop. Glyn Johns had an agreement with them that he could bring in any act he liked to demo, the tapes remaining the property of IBC.

We told Brian to ring up IBC and tell them things were not going well and that he had got an offer to join another group, which involved a recording contract and a potentially bigger future than he might have with the Stones. As Brian Jones's was the only signature on the contract, this would mean that if IBC agreed "not to stand in the way of his new future" and let him out of the contract, they'd be letting the whole group out.

A well-rehearsed Jones went to the IBC Studios at Portland Place and explained to the studio brass, "Look, my parents have agreed to put up £90, for the cost of the sessions, and will pay it to you if you let me out of contract." Clouston, with the best intentions, comforted by the promise of £90, and faced with a belligerent Brian going, "Me, Me, Me," agreed to let Brian (and so the Stones) out of the contract.

When Glyn Johns found out, he felt he'd been run over. Brian or the group told him they were going to be recording for Impact Sound and he opined that Andrew Oldham couldn't produce juice from an orange. He refused point blank to engineer any further sessions for them. Eventually, reality and talent would prevail and happily Glyn got over it to engineer my later Small Faces hits and other Immediate acts, become an Immediate act himself for a short while, and record the Stones again when we returned to recording in England in late '66. Glyn enjoyed a good relationship for a while with the group after they and I went our separate ways, but that's a lot of orange juice under the bridge of hits.

The IBC deal was done, they signed with "us," and it was time to go to work on getting recorded and released. Their job was to pick the five songs out of their entire repertoire that were the most commercial. I left them to it. They were supposed to know their part. That Thursday afternoon at a Wetherby Arms rehearsal, I was happy to inform the Stones that we'd booked time at Olympic Studios for Friday, May 10. Nobody discussed how the sessions were actually going to be produced; we just sort of mumbled our way through that one, the less said the better till D-Day. We eventually chose three songs to record, one being an obscure Chuck Berry number, "Come On," which had never been out in the U.K.

I picked Olympic, got Eric to book it, he telling me how little money we had. Keith Grant, the studio head at Olympic, recommending "young" Roger Savage as being suitable for the Stones and us, trying to get as much as we could done in three hours on forty quid. I hadn't checked out the place. The control room was upstairs, and I didn't like that because it was like a machine gun turret - one is literally talking down at the act. The session was cold.

It was, "Time's up," five minutes to six. I thought we were done and Roger Savage asked me, "What about mixing it?"

I said "What's that?"

He explained that the basic recording had been made on four channels and we now had to reduce them to stereo and mono for public consumption. I said, "Oh, you do that. I'll come back in the morning for it." Because, I figured, if I wasn't there I wouldn't have to pay for it. I also floated the idea that I thought the electric guitars would be plugged straight into the studio walls so that nobody would ask me to pay for an amp. A year later I was an expert and nobody was going to stop me from divining exactly how four channels would be pared down for public consumption.

At that time none of us knew a thing about recording. The entire process was a new mysterious experience for everyone. The recorded results fell somewhere in that flawed middle ground between what the Stones wanted and what I wanted. Quite simply, it would do. It wasn't Willie Dixon and it wasn't the Ronettes. Now we had to get the product out, get a record company. The most logical place was Decca: After all, they'd turned the Beatles down, maybe they'd panic and sign us. I didn't believe in knocking on ten doors, I believed in picking one and kicking it down - Decca was it. The Rollin' Stones didn't have to perform to get a record contract; Eric and I did.

In the eighties I met Dick Rowe's son, a lawyer at Sony. I asked him how his father was, and he said, "Dead." And that seemed to be that, no great loss, or perhaps he just felt it was none of my business. I asked him why he'd become a lawyer and he replied, "Look at my father ... that's why." I felt I had to remind him that, in my life, Dick Rowe was not the man who turned down the Beatles but the man who helped me to my great break, the man who signed the Stones. Don't let the pipe or the self-depreciating remarks fool you, Dick Rowe was good at his job for a very long time; anybody can have a hit, but can they have another, and another? I've never seen George Martin work, but, like you, I've heard it. With his other acts - Cilla Black, Billy J. Kramer, and the like - he was your competent producer. With the Beatles he was obviously so much more: the glue, the guidebook, the translator, the subtitles to brilliant foreign ideas. The only time the Beatles ever contradicted what they were all about was when they wrote "You Can't Do That."

Dick Rowe enjoyed a remarkable run and held an exemplary track record starting in the early fifties with David Whitfield, the Beverley Sisters, Winifred Atwell, Jimmy Young, and Dickie Valentine, all huge long-term sellers. When rock 'n' pop showed up, he still came to the table, signing Tommy Steele and Billy Fury. Rowe did two of the first tape-lease deals in England, for Eden Kane and Joe Meek products, including the Tornados and "Telstar." He also signed Tom Jones, Engelbert Humperdinck, Jet Harris and Tony Meehan, Them, the Moody Blues, John Mayall, and many more in addition to, of course, the Stones. That is some track record, plus he was a good guy who didn't attitude me, happy with who he was, thus having no need to rain on this upstart's parade.

Eric was already dialoguing with Dick Rowe, who'd recently had his ear bent about the Stones by George Harrison when they were both on some talent panel at the Philharmonic Hall in Liverpool. The die was cast. I cemented it by phoning Maurice Clark, who ran Jewel Music out of Chappell's and had the Chess Records publishing catalogue. I told Maurice that his catalogue was the meat and potatoes of the Stones act, which it was. Why didn't he be a sweetheart and call Dick Rowe, tell him he's seen the group, they're the best thing since sliced bread, and Dick had better move fast as EMI was hot for them?

Dick Rowe moved, the tape-lease deal was, in principle, agreed upon, then came the bombshell: Decca had a weekly product meeting and it had been decided that "Come On" could be recorded better. Dick Rowe suggested to Eric that the Stones go back into

the studio with a "perhaps more qualified producer," Michael Bar-
clay, whose Eden Kane empire had started to dissolve into a one-
trick pony and was now being gold-watched by Dick Rowe.

The following Saturday, the Stones went to record at Decca's West Hampstead studios, a little pissed off at having to record
the song again. I didn't attend, but stayed home biting my nails.
On the left hand, I wanted the best for the band, and on the other,
and I'm right handed, I wanted the best for myself. After the session, Mick called me at home and reported, "It didn't go well, in
fact it's worse than the Olympic session." Phweww ...

Dick Rowe took both versions of "Come On" into the Tuesday product meeting at Decca. In the afternoon, he called Eric to tell
him that Decca preferred the Impact Sound version. "Come in and
we'll sign the deal," Dick said. It was a huge relief to have everything
back on again, the Stones were now on Decca via Impact Sound
and "Come On" was scheduled for release on Friday, June 7, 1963.

I've always had my doubts about the whole re-record soap
opera and feel that Dick Rowe was doing his best as a company
man to get the group signed directly to Decca. With Impact Sound
out, Decca would have paid a much smaller artist's royalty to the
Stones. I just cannot see these suits sitting around their old oak
table at their product meeting deciding that "Come On" could be
recorded better - top weight, they'd be wondering why it had been
recorded at all. Meanwhile Easton set about trying to book gigs for
the band and to arrange radio exposure around our release date:
"I've got these lads, and Andy seems to think they've got a future."

Late in the day, after a liquid lunch with Peter Jones at De
Hems, we took our last orders - marching orders - and I headed
north for Old Compton Street in the afternoon sun on my route back
to 93/97 Regent Street. It was still a different Soho in the early sixties:
The hookers kept their shrines on the second floor, not on the pavement and in your face; the streets were reserved for characters, cappuccino action, nerve, real verve and chat, most of it about music.
The streets reeked of chutzpah; skiffle was dead, long live pop. Alex
Strickland's Soho Record Centre on the corner of Dean and Compton
blared the future, now it just blares upfront sex and "marital aids."
Oh, there was Johnny Danger on the third floor holding life's markers;
evil indeed lurked behind the façade, but what a façade; when they
filmed *Absolute Beginners* in 1986 they forgot the rum in the punch

and alas, it was all façade. I passed the 2 I's on my left, still squeezed between a deli and Heaven and Hell. I even managed a fond nod in the direction of Sportique. Walking the streets of *Expresso Bongo*, my heart went boom as I crossed that room, ghost riders in the sky. I blinked to keep my eyes dry, sussed I'd taken the long route in order to wave goodbye. I was on a final lap of honour, it was time to get on with it, and as I crossed over Wardour Street, I said good-bye, thank you baby, and amen.

The other side of Regent Street, five quiet floors up, Eric called me into his office. No offer of tea, just a sigh, as he told me he'd learned that our lads had failed their BBC radio audition. Mick Jagger's singing voice had been deemed either "too black" or "just not good enough," take your pick. To Eric, this was a death knell to our progress - to line up live work he absolutely needed the tag line, "They're on the radio in three weeks."

Due to union rules, for the BBC to consider spinning a new homegrown platter, the act had to be worthy of playing live on the radio, hence the audition. Easton, perennial cigarette in gob and a suit that matched the colour of the ash, was anxious the Rollin' Stones should pass BBC muster. I ashened in demeanor when Eric suggested we might have to sack Mick Jagger.

If they did not appear on nationally popular BBC radio shows like *Saturday Club*, the Stones single was certain to be rejected as well. Eventually, the BBC had to have them: The press I was getting for the group, the buzz, fuss, and belief building around the scruffiest band in the land, along with an orchestrated barrage of letters from disgruntled fans forced them to schedule a token second audition. Was this the birth of hype or a miscarriage? I'll live with it.

On the subject of Mick's adequacy as a vocalist, Brian and Eric had already had a summit powwow - Oh God, how fast we all become experts! - and decided that nothing should be allowed to get in the way of this "great opportunity," including Mick. Ian Stewart, who overheard the conversation, told us that Brian agreed with Easton, noting that Jagger had always had a weak voice and "has to be careful if he wants to sing night after night, we'll just have to get rid of him if necessary."

Radio was that important, your fella, your never-let-you-down date. For me as a manager wanna-be producer, live radio was a grating necessity, a ludicrous opportunity to prove that your records were manufactured and not real. I realise that my opinion was singular, in a definite minority. Fandom loved to hear its fave in all shapes, sounds, and less-than-perfect condition; for me it was akin to putting laddered nylons on the runway. A few recordings made in Radiolandia remain tip-top and magical, but the odds at the time of pulling that off were stacked against you. You entered a drip-dry world of wool ties, cloth ears, and malicious civil service disdain. Oh, there was an occasional producer with a glint in his eye for the music as well as the hopefully gay young thing that emoted it. One met an occasional open-minded engineer, facility intact, of good heart and open ears. Given that rare combo, some gems managed to get onto tape.

Many of the BBC studios were no better than the servants who toiled in them, but a few of the broadcast sites were gold, structured to capture resonance and kiss the sound of music straight to the stalls of your heart, then, piped by pure tubular technology, to your hearth and home. Old concert halls that had been Henry Hall'd, Vera Lynn'd, Ted Heath'd, and Bert Ambrose'd; Camden Town vaudeville halls that had sheltered war torn Londoners and offered them good, blue, belly laughs; theatres that once had amplified his master's voice, when Noël Coward polished up the worker's brain, rinsed it with wit, camaraderie, verve, nuance, and aplomb. Mr. Coward had addressed the chore of war over the sound of sirens, rationing, and being poor, crafting for everyman an edutainment as he did his best to put food and warmth on the table of thought.

Most of these wonderfully sound acoustic centres were by the late fifties electronically bankrupted by the advent of nickelodeon sight and sound and some had been taken over by the BBC motley crew. It was on those ne'er visible boards that the Stones stood, while beatdom hovered between doubt and fame and, against the staffed odds, a lot of good shit did shine through.

Back at the offices of Impact Sound, the Cinemascope was on the wall of battles to come, but this time Eric had not thought it through and backed off when I snarled, "So Brian sings?" I'd already heard Jones's backing vocal attempts and the Big Bopper could rest in peace. Easton, in what would become his familiar line of attack, accused me of "caring too much," suggesting that I was too influenced by one of the guitars and the vocal refrain. When you are at a certain age you see everyone who is above that age as old. To me, Eric Easton was old; he seemed set in his way and eager to be a successful part of the establishment and in his world; you didn't go out with the act, you told jokes about them.

Sean O'Mahony, using the *nom de guerre* "Johnny Dean," launched *Beat Monthly* in March 1963. Sean was an old PR contact of mine. I liked the man. He had a wry, composed mind and was not put out by the new beat in town; in fact he welcomed it. I introduced Sean to Eric Easton and the two contemporaries became close friends as they conveniently lived a mere half-mile apart from one another in Ealing. I thought Sean would be good for Eric, and a good sounding board for my relationship with him.

It soon became apparent that Decca was going to do very little to help me promote the single. They took out one advert for "Come On," a quarter-page strip in *NME* devoted to four groups. "One week and you're on your own, my son," was the Albert Embankment motto. The fact that I had not delivered a national anthem was neither here nor there in my book - belief was the thing: Here's my kill factor, now show me yours.

Decca's basic attitude was, "Well, we've got them, no one else can have them." Records or acts didn't get launched, they just got thrown against the wall. There were no adverts proclaiming how great the first Rollin' Stones record was. There was no build up by the record company. There was no support from Decca. It was just another group. You didn't even get three weeks devotion. With a single you got a week, and the next week they had another batch of singles to bash against the wall. As Tony Hall had it, if you had the magic, you got the airplay. We had the magic, but we hadn't got it on vinyl yet. All of these hard facts helped the Stones to become what they were and are.

Now I needed to feel good and have the band feel good, so I got the Stones ready for photos by doing what I did best: I took them shopping for free gear.

I made my first visit to the infamously rank and scummy 102 Edith Grove flat to prepare the band for the Embankment snaps. The worn dirty lino in the kitchen and the gas meter in the hall appalled me. There was no telephone and the place smelt like a never-ending fry-up.

I had met photographer Crispian Woodgate on an earlier PR episode. In 1963, it was traditional for pop groups to pose for publicity photographs frozen, bland, and blank, all uniform, rigidly smiling in a softporn lit studio. Down at the Embankment, I put the Stones, minus Ian Stewart, up against a grim looking wall near the river. The group were "sorry" to have "forgotten" their recently acquired apparel and wore their own clothes.

That look, that "just-out-of-bed-and-fuck-you" look - the river, the bricks, the industrial location - was the beginning of the image that would define and divine them. Word got out that the results of the Embankment photo session were "disgusting." The Stones were unkempt, dirty, and rude. I loved the photos, got the picture, the penny dropped. I thought we were all in the same biz, that the press and photogs had seen it all before. I was wrong. They hadn't seen anything yet. I went home, put the kettle on, drew a bath, and soaked in the reaction.

Mick Jagger asked me to define this "fame" I kept talking about. I was taken aback. Specific objective questions will do that, and out of respect require succinct actual answers, from the heart as opposed to random bullshit. "Fame," the gift that God gave to a few until the sixties, but by the seventies had appropriated to all. I breathed deeply and said, "This is how I see fame. Every time you go through an airport you will get your picture taken and in the newspapers. That is fame and you will be that famous." I silently thanked Laurence Harvey for the line, Liberace, Lana Turner, and the late Johnny Stompanato for the proof, and moved on.

I had two more tasks on my agenda, so I met with Mick and Brian and told them that from now on, they were "The Rolling Stones." I'd informed Decca that "Rollin'" was gone, they were not an abbreviation, they were not slang. I said, "How can you expect people to take you seriously when you can't even be bothered to spell your name properly? You've taken away the authority of the group."

Then I went for the home run: "Look, from the first time I saw you, I've felt ... I can only see ... five Rolling Stones." I told Brian and Mick that it was OK for Ian Stewart to appear on records and do live radio, but their ivory thumper could not be seen in photos or on TV. I compounded the cruelty, adding that he was ugly and spoiled the "look" of the group. Plus, I was convinced that six members in a group was at least one too many. The public would not be able to remember, much less care, who the individual members of a six-piece band were. For me, six was not synonymous with success or stardom. Five was pushing it, six was impossible. People worked nine-to-five; they couldn't be expected to remember more than four faces. "This is entertainment, not a memory test," I concluded.

Hurt was not in my vocabulary, perhaps it should have been. In the spirit of the day, everyone was superficially too busy and too young for slop. That was a luxury for our elders; I had a job to do. That meant including Stu, not excluding him altogether. Far from it: Stu had the van and he played great. I took him out of the picture, I didn't take him out of their hearts, that move would have had to have been the group's ...

Suddenly I didn't have time to listen to records, I was selling them. Cliff Richard was enjoying his first prolonged spate of ballads, the worst of Buddy Holly was being re-issued, and Del Shannon was failing to follow up "Runaway." Only Roy Orbison and the Crystals gave me the spark. I didn't have time to go to the movies, I was in one. And the first reel was going slow. For the next month, Eric and I fought tooth and nail to increase the group's profile, get the band gigs, and push the record up the charts, thwarting the skeptics who predicted the Stones' early demise.

"Come On" was released on Friday, June 7. Back at the office on Monday morning, I was racing. The 45 rpm had had its first small flutter of mostly naff reviews. We needed the endorsement of a national newspaper.

The *Daily Mirror* was the biggest newspaper in our western world with a five million circulation. Patrick Doncaster's Thursday pop column was the most read musical page in the country. On my own I could probably get a sorry paragraph hidden between the pop star summer season news and the Beatles. I wanted more, so I telephoned Leslie Perrin, the patron saint of pop PR, and honestly explained my predicament. Experience teaches that it is often more productive to channel our neuroses than attempt to eliminate them: My obsessive-compulsive tendencies worked well for the Stones in those early days. My manoeuvres allowed the boys an unprecedented measure of spontaneity while ensuring that their press was anything but random. Doncaster was beyond my reach, however, and my respect for some forms of show biz tradition served us well when I approached Mr. Perrin cap in hand.

As much as I needed Leslie's good will at the very beginning, his stature and poise would become far more essential to preserving our gains a lifetime later in 1966. By then the gig was to keep the Stones out of the papers, a challenge that Leslie had met for the likes of Frank Sinatra, my intuition telling me that our publicity had become rather too much of a good thing. Leslie's loyalty to his clients far transcended the income he derived from them, and when the establishment decided they'd had quite enough of the Rolling Stones and sought to imprison them, it was Perrin who literally held Mick's and Keith's hands as they ran the gauntlet that left me too terrified to act effectively.

In those far more innocent days of 1963, an overcast Tuesday morning got brighter when Leslie arranged a lunchtime meet at Doncaster's regular pub off Fleet Street. I'd never met your man Perrin, but he'd heard of me and invited me down with an open heart to raise elbows and play with the big boys. I skidded off the No. 19 bus in Holborn and happily hopped my way to the meeting. Leslie, enjoying the hustle, smilingly introduced me to Patrick Doncaster, laughed, and departed, saying, "You're on your own now."

Fortunately for me, Pat was as much a gentleman as Leslie, and was equally amused by my forwardness. Although good form dictated my leaving Mr. Doncaster to nurse his half pint once I'd made my pitch, I was feeling Sonny Bono's songscribed needles and pins in anticipation of whether or not I'd succeeded in piquing his interest. Once again, I got a life lesson in the art of relationships.

"I've really enjoyed meeting you, Andrew," he allowed graciously. "I've heard a lot about you, about how young and persistent you are. I know that you called Leslie to find out the best way to handle me." He gave me a steady look as he let that one drop. I might be getting what I wanted, but I wasn't controlling the situation.

"Usually I don't decide till the deadline what goes into the Thursday column. But I'm going to make an exception for you, Andrew. When Leslie called me about you, we both laughed and said you should be able to get into the column on cheek alone, so ..." he said, putting his hand on my arm and slowing me down. "... you can relax, I think you'll be very pleased with next Thursday's *Mirror*."

When the column came out on June 13, I had to admit I couldn't have written it better myself. We had the headline to ourselves! It read, "Bad News is Good News for the Stones." The better part of an entire page was devoted to singing our praises, and my sigh of relief could be heard in rock 'n' roll heaven.

That Thursday, when the Rolling Stones rolled over England's breakfast tables and bus queues with Doncaster's stamp of approval, the nation, had it been listening closely, would have heard the sound of distant thunder. The Rolling Stones had sort of arrived ...

I finally had to buy "Come On" into the charts. What you had to do was convince the record company it was doing business, because the record company falls in love with you twice. Once when they sign you, and the second time when you sell. So I bought the records myself. This was before and above corruption, so no one was checking up on you. If there were 5000 retailers, all we had to know was which 450 were being reported to the charts. The trick was to send the fan club girls in to buy all the records on Thursday or Friday. Then you send the girls back in on Saturday, but the shops have no stock left, so on Monday morning the retailer calls Decca and he orders five more Stones records. Suddenly the record company believes in you, and the record is in the charts. That's how it worked.

Thanks to Eric, a *Thank Your Lucky Stars* date was firm - we needed it. He had bent the arm of his client, *Thank Your Lucky Stars* host Brian Matthew, and director Philip Jones, and pulled it off. We promised they'd be dressed like "a proper group" ...

The Stones had their first, and possibly last, national television appearance recorded, ready for transmission the following Saturday, July 13. We had a national television show! But it was a long time after the release date. Normally you'd be on *Thank Your Lucky Stars* the weekend of or after the 45 rpm release. In the life of a 45 rpm this *Thank Your Lucky Stars* appearance was rather late, almost a reprieve.

In my mind the record would then look bigger than it was to Decca. But more importantly, the word of mouth that I had carefully fomented would be made flesh by the five Rolling Stones, a feeling in search of a product. The single had reached number thirty-eight in some charts and, "fan support" or not, was not going higher. Neither was I. I was tired, a recurring black mood was giving me its warning knock, and I didn't know how to rise above it. I needed time to regroup in my own mind. The last thing I wanted was for anything to be boring. I decided to call "time out" and head back to the south of France, to Juan-les-Pins, where the stars always came out at night.

CHAPTER 11

meeting the beatles again / john, paul, and brian jones put us into the top ten / here comes my second nervous breakdown / overwhelmed and unbelievable - room at the top with fame as a severe and secure mistress / the dark damsel of depression, or being a stupid cunt / if you cannot handle being screwed - find another yard to play in / the rolling stones go to the university of the road - touring with the everly brothers / a time to move out on mum and in with the dimmer twins / goodbye jfk, and to so much more - and hallo to mick and keith as writers

Eric managed to book a hardworking ballroom tour that turned out to be a factfinding mission. I didn't venture out to a lot of these gigs, I had a lot to do plus most places north of Luton were Beatles territory so I just left it to the band to try and clobber the aliens any way they could. Anyway I'd been to the ballroom tour opener in Wisbech, and somewhere between the agony of riding in the back of Stu's van and what passed for toast the next morning in the B&B, the band applauded my effort and support and happily waved me back to hustle in the Smoke.

If this was the future as seen through a rear view mirror by the keen Nik Cohn, then I needed a detour. I don't knock the copypop movement but we needed to rise above it, and fast, or sink with it. I had a band without songs: We were akin to an aeroplane without parachutes.

At the Stones' first photo opportunity a half-dozen pop picture takers shared generously their mutual disgust at their subjects. The lens lizards whispered in my ear, "Are they really that dirty?" I quietly let on they were. I now endorsed the anti-image, so that the Stones could copyright a come-as-we-are appearance that proclaimed they were already their own men.

That day I bid farewell to that revolting, fried-up, lino piss-hole, 102 Edith Grove. On my few "rise and shine" missions to the lair I don't recall Brian Jones ever being at home. I later found out he was busy procreating in the suburbs. But I do remember Charlie Watts and Shirley Ann Shepherd-soon-to-be-Watts sharing each other in a single bed; thankfully some things remain the same. Charlie and Shirley Watts still share the same bed. One of life's achievements.

The first single arrived through a combination of wishful thinking and ignorance. I was unjustifiably optimistic about the group's ability to marshal its own career musically. "Play me the five songs you think are your most commercial" was the only command I'd issued to produce "Come On." Fortunately, I was saved the masochism of delving into the Stones' idea of their next fave five. The God that looks after Soho and its children deemed that the Rolling Stones' second single would be scribed by John and Paul: "I Wanna Be Your Man."

The Stones were rehearsing in Ken Colyer's Studio 51 jazz club in Great Newport Street off Charing Cross Road. There we had been introduced to that reality named frustration. Cover records of Leiber and Stoller's pussy-driven blackface vignettes would neither do their black masters justice nor ally me with a star of the magnitude I wanted. It was about two-thirty on a dark London afternoon, dark more so for me as we plowed the fields and scattered the Stones repertoire right and left for that hit.

Then two good seeds lent a hand. When in doubt, leave the room and take your gloom away from those who have their own row to hoe. I hopped out of the basement, flicked right on the street, and headed toward Charing Cross Road. I started to walk between and against the traffic, daring the cars to hit, run, or pause; it was all the same to me.

Then two beams of light and ale emerged from a taxi in front of Leicester Square tube station. They were a slightly wobbly John Lennon and possibly slightly tipsy Paul McCartney; at least, John was swaying visibly as he counted out shillings for the cab driver. His eyes met mine as the driver "thank you guv"d him, and they waved me over. I hurried in their direction, little thinking that this chance meeting would be yet another signpost to the top of the pops. This was the first time I'd seen them since I'd left their employ.

I didn't think they knew me well, but they did. I'd also forgotten what perceptive buggers they were. They came straight to the point and asked me what was wrong. They'd just left a Variety Club luncheon at the Savoy at which they'd been honoured and wished well, and they wished me well enough to stop me drowning in my dark afternoon: "C'mon, Andrew, what's up?"

They were in their sartorial Sunday pop best, but, freed from the pressure of the press, John had already loosened his tie.

Though they looked like they'd just stepped off the stage of the London Palladium, their casual charisma was very much in evidence, and they seemed slightly embarrassed to be caught wearing such finery in broad daylight. A liquid lunch helped to make the event go down easier - the first stop on the honour chain that would come their way for contributions to Queen, Country, and Apple Corps.

I explained that I had nothing to record for the Stones' next single. They smiled at me and each other, told me not to worry, and our three pairs of Cuban heels turned smartly back toward the basement rehearsal. Beginning with our Anello and Davide Beatle boots, we were the epitome of upwardly mobile youth style: I was wearing my customary John Stephen blazer over a gingham shirt and grey flannel trousers, while John and Paul were fabulous in their three-piece, four-button, bespoke Dougie Millings suits. With Paul in lighter and John in darker shades of grey, their gear was a mod variation of the classic Ted drape jacket, set off by black velvet collars, slash pockets, and narrow plain-front trousers.

Once downstairs the boys quickly got to work teaching the Stones "I Wanna Be Your Man." Yeah, they gave us a hit, which was certainly my oxygen, but more than that, they gave us a real tutorial in the reality they were forging for themselves: lesson of the day from John and Paul. I went from downed to reprieved to exalted as the two Beatles ran through their gift for the open-mouthed Stones.

It was a match made in heaven - the north and south of musical life, rampant youth colliding, and I knew I'd hear the country cheering. It was scary; this was the beginning of home. At that rehearsal, an inspired Brian Jones added the roar of his slide guitar, John and Paul enjoying as much as the Stones and I the spontaneity of the moment. The unfinished bridge was finished there and then in front of everybody, pro scribing in your face. "I Wanna Be Your Man" would make "Come On" sound limp by comparison. The force of the title and writers would demand attention, and the power of the collaboration and execution of same would guarantee the hit.

I let the oncoming black mood I'd tried to ward off take over and flew to Paris that eve, leaving the recording to the Stones and Eric Easton. I'd already heard it in my head and that was reality, and when I returned from Paris, it was done. I was experiencing one of my first claustrophobically painful periods of depression. I didn't understand this mental takeover. My only cure was to get out of town, to be alone with this madness, to try and calm it down, make it a friend. I couldn't get over the fateful fact that, had I gone for a walk five minutes earlier or later, I wouldn't have run into Lennon and McCartney, and the Stones wouldn't have got "I Wanna Be Your Man."

This time the let down was overwhelming. I could not afford to be seen. I just had to go. It was so very hard for me to understand why such a happy "up" career-propelling event would leave me so down. These were the first recognizable symptoms of severe manic depression - which I would suffer from and deal with unsuccessfully for the next thirty years. It was so confusing and scary, yet I knew I wouldn't scream for help.

Something in your brain is broken, your clock's overwound. Depression is a sly mistress, she offers numbness in exchange for feeling, and scolds you for staying away so long. Years before success drove me mad, I'd look at my mother, and know she knew, but my mother was too busy keeping her own hounds at bay to throw mine a bone of comfort. But she saw it and recognised it. Perhaps that's what she felt sorry about - the passing on of this flat and unprofitable inheritance; perhaps it was not about my wasting my time. Sheila I couldn't talk to - my call - my bottle was on empty and I may have killed her had she known and let me know at the wrong moment. I may well have on a later date when she dared to care, or scorn, and pull rank on this almighty and was rewarded by being thrown from a moving car. There may well have been two of her at the time, she could have been pregnant. The scream inside me could drown the sound of the underground, and the platform would scare you because you can only associate it with an invitation to jump.

Thus, I became a self-educated psychiatric pharmacologist in my driven efforts to put the pain down. When I exhausted the biochemical overdraft of self-medication, I allowed myself to believe that other "caregivers" knew me better than I knew myself, and thus endured shock treatments that resembled those of *A Clockwork Orange*, without the distinct advantage of being able to dog-ear the page and close the book. I will never enjoy the pain that is my legacy but I now realise that it doesn't have to define my mission.

Eventually, I returned to form, all positive, all "up" and all front. But this lack of control over fate and my moods alarmed me, and this first in a series of career highs, followed by uninvited and unexplainable lows, left me unnerved and dumbfounded.

My head was clear when I returned from Paris a few days later. I was back to my old self. My abrupt mood swing may have mystified the Stones, but I offered no explanation for my absence. All I wanted to do was hear the result of the recording session. It sounded great. For the B-side the group made their first stab at constructive plagiarism with a bluesy instrumental called "Stoned."

Whilst I had been away, Eric Easton had done more than handle the recording session. My co-manager and partner had made a move on his own to handle the disposition of the B-side composition. Eric had explained to the band the obvious fact that "Stoned," as an original song, needed a publisher to collect royalties due it, and recommended the band publish the song with "some good publishers" he knew over on Denmark Street, Southern Music.

Eric Easton was in fact acting duplicitously and had forgotten to mention to me or the Stones that he already had a joint publishing company with Southern, called South-Eastern Music (which would co-publish "Stoned"). Easton would have Mick and Keith assign a few more songs into this arrangement before the three of us put a stop to it early in 1964. The actual details of the intercompany arrangement between Southern and Easton emerged years later when the other shoe dropped. Despite his seeming so straight, Eric was just plain criminal at times, representing that "Southern are a good outfit, lads; they'll make sure you get paid properly ..."

The publishing scam nailed the coffin of my relationship with Eric Easton shut. No doubt to distract me from his own bad faith efforts, Eric constantly needled me about my personal relationship with the band. He felt I could not be objective about their career as long as I was under their influence as friends. He was asking me to make a crucial choice between him and the band, as if a long-term partnership with Easton could fulfil my lifelong aspirations. All I had to do was dream, and Eric would worry what scheme I was up to. There was never any real trust between Eric and me, and those days in which I was winning the trust of the group were indeed perilous.

Still, for the moment, Eric and I presented a united front to convince the media and teenagers of the British Isles that they needed the Rolling Stones in their lives. It was not time to fight openly with Eric, and remember, at the time I had no real evidence of wrongdoing, only the prejudice I had against who he was and what he did, and a suspicion that my commitment to the Stones was not taken altogether seriously.

Meanwhile the Rolling Stones themselves were struggling with the physical and emotional demands of their first tours. If the Stones thought the ballroom trek with its alien and indifferent audiences was an ordeal, they were about to find out the real meaning of hard work. On September 29 they embarked on the Everly Brothers theatre tour. The schedule was exhausting, with two shows a night, and only three travel days off in a relentless thirty-two-day schedule. The tour with Don and Phil was to the young Stones what Hamburg had been for the even younger Beatles, and it is hard to see how they could have become the most durable touring band of all time if they had not suffered this thankless first rung. Night after night they fought to win over audiences that at best found them a poor substitute for the Beatles. I may have emphasised the Stones' roughness, but it was the road that brought out and hardened their toughness.

The Stones rose to the occasion and started to shine the metal that has been the underlying strength of their career. Every night the band learned new tricks from the more accomplished performers they played alongside. They were determined and dedicated, and they never let us down. Winning the audience over was their mission, and they took the stage unintimidated by the stars who followed.

I was far from getting the press reaction that I wanted for "I Wanna Be Your Man." NME dispatched the single with one line: "... the latest group to try their chart luck with a Lennon and McCartney song." Though nobody agreed with me on the eventfulness of the Rolling Stones' second record, I did manage to convince several magazine editors to feature the band.

While the Stones were on the road learning their craft, I took steps to learn mine. I formed a new "postage stamp" company named Andes Sound. I needed recording experience if I was going to become indispensable. Decca wouldn't give me the free studio time I asked for, so I scraped together a few pounds and found an artist to experiment with in the studio.

George Bean was a friend of Chrissie Shrimpton, and with all due respect to the late Mr. Bean, I would have recorded just about anything. But George was one of the good guys and game. Mr. Bean, mark one, had his own group, the Runners, but I wanted to experiment in the studio with musicians, arrangers, and arrangements, and George signed with Andes Sound as a solo artist. I booked Olympic Studios and hired engineer Roger Savage and arranger Charles Blackwell for the session. We happily recorded a slightly R&B-flavoured version of the old Doris Day standard, "Secret Love." The song sounded terrible. I had no idea how to pick the right key for the singer and no idea whether the song was even in George Bean's range, for that matter. Too late, I found it wasn't.

I presented the disc to Dick Rowe at Decca, who took it into the Tuesday product meeting. He called back and informed me that although Decca was prepared to release the record, perhaps I should reconsider having my version exposed because Decca had just recorded Kathy Kirby singing the same song. Kirby, managed by bandleader Bert Ambrose, had just had a minor top twenty success with "Dance On" and was about to get the big push from Decca. Even after Dick had kindly played me the Kirby version (which had smash written into every groove), I foolishly demanded my day at the races. There was no contest: Kathy got into the top three, and I did not. Mr. Bean and the Runners went on to be featured in the 1967 Paul Jones-Jean Shrimpton beware-of-pop flick, *Privilege*.

I determined that it was just a matter of time till I got it right, and turned my attention back to the Stones. With the release of "I Wanna Be Your Man" less than a week away, I looked forward to the final dates of the Everly Brothers tour in the London area. The record reviewers destroyed us: *Melody Maker* wrote that Jagger's vocals were "lost," "which may have been the intention but not a good one." *Disc* claimed the recording was "fuzzy and undisciplined, complete chaos." In *Beat Monthly*, Johnny Dean wrote that the single would be "a top ten chart entry - all in all a great double side, well produced by Eric Easton. The Stones are rolling again."

This last review, however, did not mean much to me even though I agreed with it, Johnny Dean being Sean O'Mahony, Eric Easton's new best friend.

Despite the poor reviews, we were in high spirits at the Odeon Hammersmith when, on the last night, the Stones received their best reception of the entire tour. Though the Stones still played in their usual early slot, something was in the air, the month-long graft on the road paid off, and for the Stones it was almost a "Welcome home!" as they bathed in a reaction usually reserved for the headline act. A turning point had been reached: The compere, Bob Bain, had to stop the Everlys' performance to plead with the audience to stop shouting for the Stones.

The tour had knocked the group into shape and given them focus. They were now the hottest band south of Liverpool. With the timely help of our teeny bopper shoppers, "I Wanna Be Your Man," which had gotten good reaction in the show, was propelled into the top thirty the week of its release. The single was given real legs as the group set off on a continual run of ballroom one-nighters, which would see them flogging "I Wanna Be Your Man" through the new year with only five nights off. Putting further distance between "group leader" Jones and his merry men was Easton's foolish decision to cave in to Brian's unjustifiable demand for an extra fiver a week as payment for his now imagined management liaison duties. He would also distinguish himself as a team player by staying alone in hotels somewhat nicer than the dumps the other Stones were booked into, and by arranging his own transportation to avoid Stu's overcrowded VW bus.

But most of the news was good, for a change. Television was falling into line; it was certainly a better medium for what the Stones had to offer than radio, at least for the moment. The single's chart activity earned a second turn on *Thank Your Lucky Stars* and a first on the new pop programme, *Ready, Steady, Go!* We met Gene Pitney, who was promoting "Twenty-Four Hours from Tulsa" on some of the same shows. I'd admired Gene's musical taste and ability since his Phil Spector-produced "Every Breath I Take" and the Dimitri Tiomkin movie theme, "Town Without Pity" - defining moments in suburban street symphonies.

****

The long, unorthodox hours I was working left my mother feeling I'd been treating her home like a hotel. I was away for days at a time, only coming home to change clothes, and then heading straight back out to the job, or lack of it, as she saw it. Celia was very proud and we were hardly speaking. In Stu's van, on the way back from Birmingham, following the Sunday taping of *Thank Your Lucky Stars*, I asked Mick and Keith if I could move in with them. They said, "Yeah," and I moved in lock, stock, and wardrobe. Brian Jones had gone to live at his girlfriend's house, which he'd persuaded them to rename "Rolling Stone." Charlie Watts was in Wembley and Bill Wyman at home (in what I snobbishly dubbed Formica Avenue) with his first wife, Diane, in Penge, Kent.

33 Mapesbury Road gave birth to the Rolling Stones as you know them now, then a little dimmer but always with a glimmer, as I forced them to write songs. 33 was a circa-thirties house on a peninsula corner that had become part of bedsitter land. The terrible three - Mick, Keith, and yours truly - now had rooms in the left-hand corner of the second floor. The living and sleeping arrangements were frugal, practical, and cramped enough to require a civility between us that might have seemed out of character with the image. In the morning, I would leave Mick and Keith sleeping off the previous night's gig, and in my best and only £7 John Stephens blazer (bone buttoned by my own tailor), over the fly fronted John Michael four-guinea gingham checked shirt from my Peter Hope Lumley days, I would head to the Willesden Tube Station for Piccadilly and my £4 a week office, courtesy of Eric Easton.

Now, there was no distance to complain of, and three of the Rolling Stones' leading lights beamed as one. I talked to Mick, and Keith listened, though on occasion Mick had begun to confide in me in a manner that would have given Keith only amusement. Mick and I were as close for a while as two young men could probably become. These days I enjoy the same with my dog. I love my dog, we have the same goal in mind - her food and love. Substitute what it was that Mick was looking for and you'll find between us as fair an exchange. I gave him what he wanted and got what I'd decided I needed.

From the safety of the suburban R&B circuit to the trial-by-fire early ballroom and cinema tours, I watched Mick find out. He would put out his hand in a gesture to the audience and watch it come back empty. He would rue it, get over it, and work at it. Then he'd go out there again, put his hand out again, and it would come back full.

On the home front, this growing charisma of Mick's, and his obvious enjoyment of it, was giving Chrissie fits, which she vented in outbursts that were both verbal and physical. When she slammed the door on him, Mick would ring me at my mother's. He'd walk from 102 Edith Grove, we'd meet at a bench on the Embankment, and he'd shout and wail at the Thames and me about the confusion of being in love with oneself, one's girl, and one's life. All I could be was a good listener and manager; I was not well versed enough in the avenue of the heart to tell him how to sing that song. I was working out for myself how to commit to Sheila without feeling overwhelmed or obligated. I had my own scarcely acknowledged fears that she might throw me over.

"She shouts at me all the time, Andrew," Mick complained.

"They all do," I replied.

"But she hits me," he rejoined.

I had no answer for that one, though it occurred to me that there was only a small difference in our teenage angst between a hit and a kiss.

By six in the morning London was moving again and Mick had tired himself out. Since I was the sounding board for his anguish, we were both very tired. We'd walk off the Embankment, he'd stop being a victim, and I'd manage us into a fresh day. We walked north with a rude nod to Number 10, a smile at the statues as we picked up the pace, got some rhythm of life and strode onto Trafalgar Square. South of Shaftesbury Avenue, east of Cambridge Circus, an all-night taxi-stand cafe served us tea and a fried egg and bacon white-breaded saviour and we'd walk three more blocks to Jean Lincoln's edge-of-Soho flat. She'd awaken with a smile, put Mick to kip on the couch with a hug and a kiss, with a cuppa for me. Jean and I would sit in the kitchen over more tea and smile at what life had given us, especially each other, and laugh about what it would give us next. She'd get dressed and made up; I'd coldwash my boatrace and iron my shirt fit for the day. We'd leave Mick to sleep off his night's young agony, to kiss and make up with his gal before we'd finished our day's work and he began his. And with that, Jean and I would bound down the stairs; she'd turn left to Piccadilly and Delfont's and I'd move on to Eric and Radnor House.

When it was my turn to wonder, I'd complain to Mick about how Sheila didn't understand my commitment to work and the Stones and resented how little she now saw of me. Knowing me was becoming much harder, and I wasn't giving her the chance to catch up. Life became insular and single-minded: If you weren't prepared to contribute to the subject at hand - us - then be prepared to be left out of our lives. In a superficial way, the early dramas would flatten out for a while during this halcyon period: We would attain an easy rhythm as casual domesticity and dating went hand-in-hand with our careers for a short while. Later, after we'd toured America, we all jumped gradients too fast and a certain madness would set in.

But during our London-based run up to world domination, Mick, Keith, and I all committed to the adventure, as Keith readily took up the life he still pretty much leads years on: basically, "Let me know when I have to play, and in the meantime I'll work on this writing thing." I don't know if Michael Philip had made his deal with fame as yet; I don't think he did until we hit a few strides in America and the economics made sense to the boy's mind and training. He did math and I did airports.

So, in the Mapesbury days, a dream-come-true was our reality and for the "unholy trinity" it was fun getting it done.

I had this thing that whatever I decided people could be, they became. I got nothing but moans and groans from Mick and Keith. They were too tired from the gigs to write songs, and at the end of a few weeks, nothing had been written. One evening I told Mick and Keith I was going to mother's to eat - I was locking them in the flat and when I came back I expected a song, and they better have one if they expected me to bring them any food. It was not a real threat, it was the kind of threat you can voice to those for whom you have a great deal of affection, to let them know how deadly serious I was about the need for songs and my belief in their ability to write them.

I got back from my mother's, quietly let myself in the downstairs front door, tiptoed upstairs, and listened outside the flat door. I was happy to hear that Mick and Keith were inside working. I could hear a guitar, a voice, and a conversation. To me that meant a song.

I went downstairs again, slammed the front door noisily, went upstairs, and unlocked the flat door, smiled at Mick and Keith and said, "What have you got?" Mick, who was pissed off and hungry, told me they'd "written this fucking song and you'd better fucking like it."

Music publishing had come into its own with the advent of the piano as a piece of furniture and became an even more lucrative business when the audiences leaving vaudeville venues like the Metropolitan in the Edgware Road were able to take home sheet music of the songs they'd heard inside. Publishing evolved to promoting live radio performances; the sheet music was sold to all the local bands and to well-to-do homes with pianos in the sitting room. By 1964 you could make a mint selling sheet music of hits like "Please Please Me" to ballroom band leaders all over the U.K. The Beatles, with their growing catalogue of original songs, helped to create an important new revenue stream that became a rushing river of income, as each spin on the BBC, live or disc, earned the songwriter a fee. Publishers collected and distributed the royalties and kept half for their trouble.

I'd discovered a cheap recording studio, mostly used to voice-over jingles, that the Stones and I both liked and felt comfortable in: Regent Sound on Denmark Street. It was a mono studio and, after our haphazard unnerving experience in a four track studio, everyone agreed that recording in mono would be better. Mono had the element we needed: What you hear is what you get.

Regent Sound was magnificent. You'd pass a small reception and be straight into the studio, which was no larger than an average good-sized hotel room. The control room was the size of a hotel bathroom, but for us it was magic. The sound leaked, instrument to instrument, the right way. You'd hear the bottom end of Charlie's drums bleeding though Keith's acoustic, and vice versa, Keith's guitar delay bleeding through the drum track. Put them both together and you had our wall of noise. It was our version of direct-to-disc recording, where the placement of the instrument defined the sound that you got. We would record all of the first Rolling Stones album there.

When I'd decided I wanted to record properly there, the house engineer, Bill Farley, gave a little more, because for the first time he was making master recordings. Farley was bemused at the

Rolling Stones' ambition. An East Ender in his late twenties, Farley did everything he could to get the right sound, and put up with my style of direction, which required an engineer be more familiar with proven hits that with notes and knobs. With my "I want it to sound like ..." approach, Regent Sound entered the major leagues.

This was another indirect benefit of the production company/leased tape approach that we were pioneering. If you went into Decca studios, by contrast, you were given a very strict, usually short, amount of time to do just the songs that A&R had agreed to. You had to leave on time, because other artists were doubtlessly waiting in the wings for their turn in this expensive-to-run facility.

At Regent, on the other hand, because it was relatively cheap and they were glad to have us, we could stretch out a bit, experiment, and learn from our mistakes. I have no doubt that the feel of those early Stones records was due in no small part to avoiding the major studios, and the lessons we learned would be unconsciously applied over and over by anyone trying to build a recording track record from the ground up.

Before setting off for that night's ballroom gig, we demo'd Mick's and Keith's first batch of songs at Regent Sound, including "Shang a Doo Lang," "My Only Girl," "Will You Be My Lover Tonight?" and "It Should Be You." Not "The Last Time," certainly, but a start in the right direction.

America mourned the assassination of President John Kennedy in Dallas. In England the spirit of Christmas raved nonstop right on through to the early months of the new year; this was the beginning of the good times. An Aston Martin DB4 Vantage would provide you with advantages indeed for £3746, and suddenly the purchase was not out of the question. With all the hard work, politicking, and close calls, we still had time to enjoy our new status as pop stars.

Brian Epstein

CHAPTER 12

*mick, keith, and i are screwed by the last of the manicured jew
brigade / a little bit of england / tales of moishe levy - the math
according to roulette records / dreams are coming true faster
than i can fly / meeting tony calder and steve marriott - outside
a magistrates' court, of course / saying goodbye to saying hallo
to sheila*

People say I made the Stones. I didn't. They were there already.
They only wanted exploiting. They were all bad boys when I
found them. I just brought out the worst in them.

I had to find a home for the songs that Mick and Keith
were writing. So what if they were soppy and imitative to begin
with - they had to come to the process of songwriting through
trial and error. That takes a lot of balls and front, as you find out
what it is you really want to say and develop the confidence to
believe that others will want to hear it.

The novelty of their first loves - Chuck Berry, Bo Diddley,
Muddy Waters - had provided an edge early on, which, now that
they were recording *artistes*, could hold them back. The entire
teenage population of the British Isles could not be expected to
relate to the needs and wants of middle-aged American blacks.

They had already learned the language of R&B and now
they had to create a language of their own to speak to the masses.
"There is a rose in Spanish Harlem" is a wonderful and total concept. "You can turn off and on more times than a flashing neon
sign ..." is an example of Mick and Keith beginning to get it right
in their own idiom.

The two outstandingly successful publishers of the day
were Freddy Bienstock and David Platz. I feared Freddy's sophistication and worldliness and assumed he would eat me for dinner. I don't know why, I had no experience on which to base this
reservation. So I picked the quiet, seemingly unassuming, all business, not enamoured with the show of the biz, Platz.

The Stones and I formed two publishing entities, Mirage
Music Ltd. and Nanker Phelge Music Ltd., and assigned the administration rights to Essex Music. David was born in the wrong
place at the wrong time - Germany in the thirties - and the result-
ing murder of his family, which David so narrowly escaped, left

him deeply troubled and permanently out on ethics. He would come to feel that I did not deserve my good fortune, as if it was any of his business, and he took and allowed things to be taken from me.

A song has many potential sources of income: sheet music, the pennies paid every time you hear a song on the radio, the "mechanical" royalties paid to the writer and publisher for the use of the song each time a recording of it is sold. It all adds up, and if you have a national anthem, you are talking a lot of money. Even a minor hit is going to put food on your table. In the old world a pound would come in, the publisher would take 10 or 15% off the top for collecting the money, an "administrative charge." The remaining 85 or 90% would be divided up 50/50 between the writers and publisher. So the publisher's total take would come to 55-57.5% of the income.

In a system in which writers and singers needed the A&R man to marry them, the publisher earned his keep by being a matchmaker. The publisher was indeed doing the writer a favour by agreeing to publish and represent his work; the publisher had all the contacts and all the data on which A&R man was looking for what kind of song for which act. Without a publisher and his connections, no song, no matter how commercial, would ever get recorded.

The 1958-63 run of rock 'n' pop in the U.K. did not do much to change the business of songwriting and music publishing: Those few *artistes* that did write their own material did not do so with enough consistency or proficiency to empower them against the publisher-label establishment. Nor were most pop careers at that time hurt by the *artistes'* inability to find their own voices. The greatest of them all, Cliff Richard, did not write. His performances transcended his often hand-me-down material, with a few exceptions like the Anglo-urbanese masterpiece, "Living Doll," by the ever hit-bound Lionel Bart.

The beauty with a brain, Adam Faith, sulked to a pithy background of pizzicato strings that frequently obscured an *artiste's* originality with musical clichés. Billy Fury, when he wasn't birdwatching, occasionally put pen to paper for the odd flash of smoked realism, but we know that consistency wasn't Billy's strong suit. To move his career along, he depended on

Goffin/King covers and adequate local product. Marty Wilde did have the gift and mastered the art of song, as shown by such structurally savvy ditties as his 1960 smash "Bad Boy." Unfortunately for Marty, by the time he had it down, he'd gotten married. As a groom, Marty no longer had anything to say that a fickle, blemished, serial fan wanted to hear. He bounced out of the top ten with his final hit, "Rubber Ball," showing poorly against the Bobby Vee import, itself not the finest hour of Gerry Goffin and Carole King.

Then the Beatles changed the rules - not the rules of engagement and payment, but the total package that they delivered of songs, sound, ideas, and attitude made them as self-reliant as recording artists as they were on stage. George Martin was able to discover new pop depths within his own considerably broad musical range, although doubtless his experience with Peter Sellers and the Goons helped him to get the most out of John's and Ringo's looning. The overflow from their Jacuzzi of bubbling writing output helped Brian Epstein to become more than king of pop managers. With his stable generously supplied with Lennon/McCartney tunes, he became the emperor! I would be more than happy if Mick and Keith could just provide unto the Stones.

We were past the stage where we needed a publisher to get us recordings; I just needed one to collect. Many publishers were loath to say goodbye to the good old days and the lion's share of the money. Platz seemed forward-thinking and ready to play it my way. He and Essex Music would get 15% off the top for collecting, the rest divided between Mick and Keith or the group as writers and the two publishing companies that we had formed to cover both events.

We allowed Essex 50% on foreign cover versions, meaning that if they got Johnny Hallyday in France or Enni Boddi in Italy to cover a Stones tune, they got a larger slice for racking up extra income for us in that territory. Alas, I was not well-versed in the local foreign laws that entitled you to get 50% on the lot, Rolling Stones version as well, if you got a local cover version. Essex had a little demo studio and whacked off cover versions of everybody, but especially those songs they published, and thus they had legal right to 50% of everything ... and I mean everything. A franc would come in to the French kitty, half would stay there and half a franc would cross the English channel to be divvied up yet again. Nice work if fucking is your way of life.

I hope I've made this trail of deception clearer to you than it was to me when it first raised its hooked and ugly head. It took me a long time to digest and learn to live with the impious suppression of talent and youth that the publishing business believes is its rightful occupation. I'm still working on it.

Years later, I was told the story of two record companies bidding for a new contract with an artist of some recent success; either Bobby Darin or Tommy James and the Shondells, it may have been. One company was corporate with audited restraints on what they could pay out in royalties. The other company, which was rumoured to be Mafia-financed and run, offered eight percentage points more than their rival, and the act signed with them. At an industry conference some months later the legit record man ran into the connected one and asked, "How can you pay that much for an act? You can't be making anything on them after you pay them." The connected one smiled and replied, "Just because I promised him eighteen points doesn't mean he's going to get paid it."

Now that I was a full-fledged manager, I was taken by the idea of becoming a record producer. I understood this new role to be both a want and a need: I wanted my own version of the celebrity and madness that I had glimpsed through Phil Spector; I needed the Stones' musical destiny to become as self-determined as possible. The God that looks over Soho would probably not be providing any more Beatle-arranged-and-tailored smashes. Mick's and Keith's hits would have to be recorded by someone, and I was sure I wanted to become Phil Spector and not Eric Easton.

I have often been accused of being a hustler, a bullshit artist, etc., because many of my most ambitious projects have appeared to vanish before the ink was dry on the press release. However, to my mind, a prophecy of success is always the first step in making it reality, and as I am essentially honest and sincere about my work, predicting an outrageous outcome is the surest way I know to commit myself to delivering it. So it was that I acknowledged my agenda for 1964 to the *Record Mirror*: "Andrew Loog Oldham predicts he will be the most successful independent record producer in the country by autumn." Now I had a deadline, driven by the hard reality that any fool can have a hit, but could he have another, and another, and another, ... ?

I summoned the Stones to Regent Sound within the first few days of January and set about fulfilling this prophecy. The band grumbled about recording the day after performing "I Wanna Be Your Man" on the premiere of the BBC's new pop programme, *Top of the Pops*. The Stones had another ballroom date that evening and wanted an afternoon off.

But my own timetable was bringing out the manager in me: I planned to use the Stones as session musicians for a single I was producing with Cleo Sylvestre. The eighteen-year-old black beauty from London had once auditioned to become a backing vocalist for the Stones (in one of their previous incarnations before meeting me). Although the group quickly abandoned the idea, Mick Jagger had stayed in touch with her, and it was Mick who suggested I record her.

On the promise of a couple of quid each, the rest of the Stones agreed to play on the single. I was now doubly grateful, as I couldn't afford to pay the £7 fee that real session musicians commanded, on top of the studio time that I couldn't avoid paying. "Put it down to experience, we could all use it," I told them.

I decided to record Cleo singing a version of the Teddy Bears' 1958 classic "To Know Him is to Love Him." I remember thinking literally that if "To Know Him is to Love Him" had kicked off Phil Spector's career, it was good enough to kick off my commitment to 1964. I teamed up with musical arranger Mike Leander to stack the deck and eliminate any possibility that Decca could refuse the record. Leander, although only twenty-three, had studied orchestration and conducting at Trinity College of Music. He was on the staff at Decca and admired by Dick Rowe. He had also apprenticed with American songwriter/producer Bert Berns, who seemed to make all the Atlantic hits not recorded by Leiber and Stoller. The results of the Sylvestre session were good enough, thanks to Mike Leander's contribution, to convince Decca that "To Know Him is to Love Him" should be rush-released. This tribute to my master's voice became my first solo independent production. We got into the chart at number forty-eight, and a week later I was ready to try again.

The B-side of the Sylvestre single was a weird instrumental called "There are but Five Rolling Stones." The "Andrew Loog Old-ham Orchestra" performed the song - in actuality the Stones - with writing credits attributed to Leander and myself. I was copying Spector's infamous B-side *modus operandi* for good luck: Apart from not sharing the B-side revenues with the artist, I was shame-lessly using the situation to promote the name of the group and my own.

Meanwhile, we all needed to earn our keep by staying busy on the road. The Stones were booked on their second U.K. package tour as co-headliners with Phil Spector's latest bestselling bad girls, the Ronettes. Promoted by wanna-be Robert Stigwood and billed as "The Group Scene 1964," the tour kicked off on January 6.

The success of "I Wanna Be Your Man" spread the Rolling Stones' name throughout Britain, and on the "Group Scene" tour they were treated to their first real dose of girl-adulation. The audiences on their first package tour had largely been made up of Little Richard-loving teds and staid Everly couplets. On the '64 tour the crowds were out of their heads, thousands of teenage girls going ballistic. The group travelled back to London each night after the first few dates with the Ronettes, so that during the day I could record them in Regent Sound, before they set off for another frantic gig in the evening. Despite what I may have wanted the press and the older generation to think of us, our work ethic was never in question.

These were highly charged, innovative sessions, and I was adamant that they should include as many commercial pop songs for the looming first album as possible. Toward this end, I suggested Marvin Gaye's "Can I Get a Witness?" When it became apparent that Mick didn't know all the words, I called Freddy Bienstock, who had published the song, and Mick ran from Regent Sound to pick up the sheet music left in reception at Freddy's Savile Row office. Everyone else had a leisurely cup of tea and caught up on gossip. When Mick returned we recorded his vocal and the guitar overdubs. And that's the reason the vocal on our "Can I Get a Witness?" sounds so breathless.

The Ronettes' dates continued apace. It was a good thing our dreams were now our daily reality, because, between the tour and the recording, we were on the job twenty-four hours a day and literally had no time to dream up new ones. It was obvious from the reaction the Stones were getting that "I Wanna Be Your Man" had cracked open a whole new market for them. To capitalise on this, and knowing the band didn't have another single ready for release yet, Eric and I persuaded Decca to rush-release an EP. Made up of four as yet unreleased tracks, the eponymous "Rolling Stones" EP proved to be a masterstroke. The record stayed in the EP charts for the rest of the year! It also crashed the singles' chart, rising to number eleven.

This was truly amazing. EPs cost twice as much as singles, and for that reason were expected to sell less. The Stones' EP would outsell both their previous two singles! The most celebrated track on the EP was their version of Arthur Alexander's "You Better Move On." While R&B was still a cult, the BBC got behind the Stones' "You Better Move On" because it was a ballad. The song enjoyed the same heavy radio exposure as Dusty Springfield's "I Only Wanna Be with You" and Gene Pitney's "Twenty-Four Hours from Tulsa." For a second time, the collision between my pop opportunism and the Stones' R&B purity had ended amicably in a hit.

The angry breach that was building between Eric and me came to a head while the Stones were away on tour. Easton told me that the Regent Street office was now so busy with the Stones' business that my space would be needed and I would have to find a new office. Sure ... in fact Eric was just totally pissed off. He'd had it with me, my style of personal management, and the publishing arrangements I'd made, not behind his back, but in his face. He thought, regardless of any apparent results, that I was spending too much time with Mick and Keith, and not acting as a manager should. He just did not get that this was not a job ... it was a way of life. He was saying to any ear he could get that I was having a bad effect on the rest of the group. But to me, the only ones having a bad reaction were Eric Easton and Brian Jones. So Eric demanded that I move out of his office, and thus began the real beginning of the end of us.

I was not entirely alone in the ranks of precocious young upstarts: On a bright and brisk early spring afternoon in 1963 I had waltzed out of the Decca promotions offices with not a care in the world but caring for everything in the world. As I marched past the Great Marlborough Street Magistrates' Court, I thought I saw somebody I recognised. It was Tony Calder, whom I'd met on the Twickenham film set with Mark Wynter. Calder had under his wings a young London artist, Steve Marriott, whom he'd just accompanied whilst the cockney tyke pleaded "fair cop" to a petty offence. It was a serendipitous meeting - both Steve and Tony would become a large part of my future.

Tony and I are indeed a strange lot, enjoying our share of mutual good fortune while carrying each other's luggage for much of a lifetime. Tony is an engaged, passionate, and handsome man, qualities that would catch Sheila's attention for a while in the seventies after she and I separated. In the long haul I cannot hold Sheila against him; he didn't take anything that was not offered.

The nature of the game is that there are many who have spoken ill of and ridiculed Tony who genuinely thought they were doing me a good turn, and there are others who did not want me to have the benefit of him. I gave him the best and worst years of my life, and the best and worst of all was our Immediate Records, whose story can be told later. Although Tony might claim, "It was only business," the depths to which I would sink over the long while would have pained him; the waste of opportunity and talent would surely have put him out. We dived into the fray with enthusiasm, and we definitely changed some of the rules of engagement. Had I assimilated some of his passionate pragmatism for the game and the players, I might have saved myself some bruising.

I was scared of Sheila so, I suppose, I gradually started pulling away. I had not grown up in an environment where relationships were a given; intimacy was not the daily bread and happenstance that life revolved around. Regardless of how much love and deep affection there might have been between my mother and Alec, it was still love on the side. I was very shy and only confronted people when in character, so I was a very busy actor. Sheila offered a wonderful opportunity, to which I was slowly saying "No."

I still recall the first time Sheila invited me to make love: both the totality and the details of her comfortable first-floor bedroom at Frognal. Her bed offered the world, and I sank into it in slow, treasured motion. I can relive that freefall, isolate her body and its possibilities, the gentle dew on the window panes, the smell and texture of the fresh sheets and our new skins that kept the world out and allowed us to concentrate on this, for me, new journey.

Bodies till then I had groped with on life's dare, as door-knobs to be turned, some dicks not yet hung to be pulled on boys who knew better, and entry attempts made on young girls who didn't. A first failed stab at immortality with Alexis, the dance instructor's daughter, had left me bruised of ego and cock robin. But I hadn't got the time or the will, let alone the nerve, to examine myself and live with what I found, that ground-swelling, earth-moving physicality that seemed to be part of this glorious invitation that Sheila extended to me when she gave me her love.

I wanted it, but I could not afford to give in to such an unknown and potentially commanding passion. I would back off, putting down the wand. I didn't work on the magic, and things between us would cease to be magical. This love demanded an exciting but scary journey that asked too much of a self whom I hadn't the time nor inclination to develop or know. I was in the business of "other," of others. I was empowered to move, making their earth move, showing others their potential, and, through that route, realising mine.

So I loved, feared, said goodbye, even when we wed. Unfortunately I was so attracted to Sheila's beauty, but so in awe of it, that I completely forgot to get to know her. We cannot love others, so the mystics and wizards would have it, unless we can love ourselves. At that time, infatuation with myself and my potential, and a grand faith in my ability, seemed sufficient; true love would have to come into my life later. With Sheila, doors opened, bells rung, and doors closed, all at the very same time.

CHAPTER 13

*the face - peter meaden zooms back into our lives with a who /
hitchin' a ride with the beatles down phantom v avenue / arthur
alexander and buddy holly songs - stones back in the top ten again /
fits like a glove - gene pitney takes mick and keith into the top ten as
writers / stigwood stiffs us, keith uses his own lawyer / would you
let your daughter go with a rolling stone? slogan number one*

An American visited Picasso in his Paris studio just after the end
of World War II. "Picasso," he asked, "how does it feel to be Picasso,
the master of the art?" The maestro said, "Give me a dollar bill,"
which he pinned to his easel and then painted over. Picasso then
removed the painted dollar and handed it back to the astonished
American. "There," said Picasso, "this dollar is now worth five
hundred dollars, that is how it feels to be Picasso." Now that my
two little glimmers were no longer dim on the topic, I looked
forward to them painting their first bill.

It was a pivotal moment in Regent Sound when Mick and
Keith presented their first wares for the Stones to record. They
say that writing is like opening a vein and studying the blood. I
am finding this to be true as I write - it is also akin to tearing off
scabs and watching them fester and infect your hitherto accepted
view of events, while mental termites gnaw at your very pillars
of existence. In those young days, perhaps it was like having your
zits ripped off and raw. One word out of place, one smirk, and
lesser talents would have zoomed into abort, but Mick and Keith
counted off a part of the rest of their lives with, "One, two, three,
four - Keith? De-deder-de-dum ... dhum de-de de-dhumm ...
dhummm ... I-ey wantchu back a-gaayne." Now, that's an admission that most of us would have trouble speaking, let alone
singing ...

The arranger Mike Leander knew of my problem with
Eric and suggested I try his manager, publisher Freddie Poser,
for office space. Poser was to the publishing world what Eric
Easton was to the agency world, an outsider trying to get on the
inside track. Poser let me move into his spare room on the fourth
floor of 44/46 Maddox Street and I said goodbye to Piccadilly
and hallo to an abode off Bond Street.

I loved Maddox Street; it was my first real own office, with my own entrance, my own front door. I liked being on the top floor, and sparked up my small office with a painting by Peter Meaden, who'd now left the advertising job and figured that if Andy could turn a trick and earn a penny in the music biz, then there had to be room for him too. And so there was, and for a while Peter moved into the Maddox Street digs. I was pleased to have him back in my life and workplace. But Peter and I never were the best combination in a business setting.

There was no furniture in the Maddox Street office and the carpet was worn, but the place was decorated beautifully by my girl Friday Annabelle Smith, an attractive young lady on the fringes of the music business via her recent liaison with composer John Barry. The Stones were at home in my new office and enjoyed the lack of formality, as Annabelle lay on the floor answering the phone.

Phil Spector flew into England a few days before my twentieth birthday to bask in the light of his incredible success with the Ronettes. I was there to meet him, more than happy to revisit the Spector school of thought, pick those brains, and engage him as an accomplice in the rise of the Stones. The Ronettes had closed out the year with "Be My Baby" and were now about to release "Baby, I Love You." Phil was buoyant throughout his stay in London, assuming the role of hip hobgoblin that the U.S. media, particularly Tom Wolfe, had created for him.

Phil Spector at twenty-three was the most significant person in the American recording industry. Fifteen hits in a row - and if that's not genius, well, what is? The Spector sound had sold nine million records in the last eighteen months. It wasn't hard to have the London press interested in the arrival of the American Mozart. The first interview by Maureen Cleave of the London *Evening Standard* took place in the back of a limousine that carried us from Heathrow.

"I've been told I'm a genius," he said to Cleave, "What do you think?" Cleave was a stunner, in print and in person. Phil liked her, I liked her, everyone liked her.

Phil loved London and London returned his affection. "My records are built up like a Wagner opera," the diminutive thug-tycoon of one-man teen anthems told Maureen Cleave. "They start simply and they end with dynamic force, meaning, and purpose." No one had spoken like this on pop record production, and Phil elevated the role of producer to fame in the U.K. "It's in the mind. I dreamed it up. It's like art movies. I aimed to get the record industry forward a little bit, make a sound that was universal."

Back on the road with the Ronettes, the northern leg was going well and the Stones were now as popular on the Beatles' own turf as they were in London. The Beatles had just conquered America, giving us all something to think about, but not at this moment. Our working reality was the U.K. and, if one got lucky, the cold and grey Northern tips of Europe.

The U.S. was a mind-boggling, exciting challenge to our secure womb at the top. It scared us, Johnny Britain. The Moptops had taken the States; the Moptops had taken everywhere - they were the gold rush, the tea chest, the opium beat for the masses.

Sunday, August 1, 1965, the Stones were at the London Palladium, I was up north for some reason, and the Beatles were playing one night at the ABC Theatre in Blackpool, their first gig at home since taking over the world and their only U.K. gig that summer: Rule Britannia! No need to tell you which gig this boy opted for.

I trained over to Blackpool so that I could catch the event of the year. A celebratory Lancashire rang in its own day of the locusts, proud of its native sons made good, bells and hearts ringing out and screaming for the four lads who now belonged to the world. The concert was a smile expressed in sound and song. The physical presence of the Beatles was irresistible. I remember Paul grinning from start to finish. The lads just beamed at each other over the screams, as they distilled into thirty-five minutes the story till now. They rolled over Beethoven, but could have just as easily triumphed by playing "Chopsticks."

I went back to see them after the show. "How'd you get over here?" asked Lennon.

"By train," I replied.

"Leave the Stones on their own, did you?" Lennon smiled on.

"Yes, I did," I smiled back.

"Want a lift back to town?"

"You bet," I said. And what a lift it proved to be. John had his spanking new black Rolls-Royce Phantom V limo and the seal was delivered. Somehow being able to share in that acquisition was a wonderful moment of cocksure arrival. I sat on the beige jump seat opposite John and Paul. We laughed and hooted at life as the Roller headed down the M6 and eventually purred on to the M1 for town.

The humour took a macabre turn as John and Paul started to trip on what would happen if the windows of the Phantom V zooming south suddenly shattered and splintered in their faces, turning them into unacceptably scarred and disfigured Moptops, unable to carry on as part of the Fab Four now recognised the world over.

"We'd have to put on monkey costumes. We'd be a fucking vaudeville act," whooped John.

"We'd have to have bear suits or masks ... nobody could see us," Paul harmonised.

I watched and listened to this thrust and parry between the two writers and found it a little bit chilling to realise just how much they relished the idea of anonymity - even to the point of almost welcoming a shattering shower of glass that would splinter the Beatles and force them from the spotlight. It was apparent that, for all the triumphs of that breathtaking past year, symbolised by the very Rolls-Royce that we now rode in, part of the dream was already over. The eventual end of the Beatles was even then on the agenda of their informal bored meetings. The conversation in that most exclusive emblem of British excellence felt surreal enough: It's more than possible that John and Paul may have given me my first tab of acid to raise my consciousness even further. It doesn't really matter; it certainly felt like it. I slept long, deep, and sound that night once back in the Smoke. I awoke aware more than ever of my responsibilities to the Stones, feeling very protective toward my lads, and it all appeared a little daunting, awesome, even unnerving as I played back the ride-back's acid chat. By the time I hit the phones mid-morning, I was putting it down to an apathetic hard day's night and had moved on.

As manager and producer of the now second band in the land, I knew how to have fun, but I still had my eye on the ball. The Stones had cracked the top ten with a single and an EP. So far, I had bought the records, our fan club had bought the records, and the hardcore R&B mob had bought the records. The scream machine we were revving up had bought still more records. Our next order of business remained recording an out-and-out smash, tens of thousands of plastic platters that would be bought even if you didn't like the Stones. Bought because one couldn't help but buy, bought because it was a great fuckin' record.

The first week of February '64, I returned from my daily West End jaunts and hustles to the Mapesbury and found Keith exactly where I'd left him that morning - fag in mouth, guitar on knee, singing bits of Buddy Holly's "Not Fade Away." He was injecting an acoustic Bo Diddley riff into one of our favourite songs. I heard our next record. I could actually hear the record in the room. The way he played it - you could hear the whole record. It was less pop and more rock. It was a magical moment for me.

Two days later I called engineer Bill Farley at Regent Sound, and we went into the studio to get "Not Fade Away" down. It wasn't easy. The group was tired, not getting along, showing the strain of five solid months on the road. The atmosphere was getting sour and despondent. Our hit was slipping away from us. I needed help.

The Stones now had a friendly audience - they had to perform; it's in the blood. They soon settled into a groove and within twenty-five minutes everybody was happy. The Stones nailed the A-side, glued down by Keith's acoustic guitar. Spector's maracas and Charlie's backbeat leaked nicely into everything. We had a perfect pre-mix and quickly added vocal, harp, and electric guitar on the one-to-one pass and the record was ready for the nation's living rooms: a sure-fire hit.

Once I knew we'd got it, I'd invited down Graham Nash and Allen Clarke of the Hollies and Peter Meaden. Spirits were high and flowing reasonably, but now we needed a B-side. Mick Jagger and Phil Spector headed for the staircase outside the studio reception, and in ten minutes flat they polished off the lyrics to a song they called "Little by Little." In another twenty minutes the lyrics were captured on tape, over a simple twelve-bar blues structure. So far all this had been a movie in my head, now it was real life. The Rolling Stones finally knew how to make hit records. They were self-contained.

The recording session degenerated into a hilarious, quasi-drunken free for all. The Stones, prompted by Spector, recorded a tribute to me, "Andrew's Blues," which remains one of the most bootlegged of unreleased Stones tracks. Phil joined Jagger on vocals, impersonating Decca boss, Sir Edward Lewis, singing about my "qualities." I was honoured then; I still am.

> Well now, Andrew Oldham,
> Sittin' on a hill with Jack 'n' Jill,
> He fucked all night,
> 'N' he sucked all night.
> 'N' he sucked that pussy
> Till it taste just right.
> Come and get it little Andrew,
> Before Sir Edward takes it away from you.

I may have gone to a meeting with Phil at Decca, I don't remember. If I did, not all of me attended. I do know that Decca would never have considered letting Phil have the group for America. Although "I Want to Hold Your Hand" was a smash by the Beatles for Capitol in the States, EMI had let the previous singles go to Swan and Vee Jay because they didn't think the Beatles would fly in America. So Decca wasn't going to be caught in the same trap; they were still smarting from having turned down the Beatles themselves. They were being very careful; if their doorman started whistling they'd have signed him.

Anyway, although Phil Spector was an educative influence on me as a record producer, he didn't have the wherewithal or sensibility as a record company head to deal with an act. In his world he was the act. I was reared on Irving Thalberg, Alexander Korda, and MGM and, compared to their creative collectives, Phil's record company was a one-man band. However, he did predict that we would soon outgrow what Regent Sound had to offer and suggested we think about recording in America. Easier said than done: We had to get there first.

In the meantime, "Not Fade Away" was to be released late February, then it was back on the road for the Stones, promoted by Eric's new pal, Aussie Robert Stigwood, with a lackluster assortment of Stigwood acts. Only Jet Harris and Dave Berry added any spark of life to this lame bill. Unfortunately Jet was functioning at half-spark, his hitmaking partnership with Tony Meehan having just ended.

I spent too much time enjoying Jet and raising elbows at the local. I'd ignored the fact that Jet was already signed to Decca, and when I presented the results to them as an Andes Sound production, Decca told me, "You just cannot record whom you like, not when they are already under contract to us." I thought they would be delighted at the collaboration, but my track record at guessing their reaction to my manoeuvres was 50/50 at best.

Gene Pitney and I collaborated with far more success, since Gene was master of his yard and captain of his ship. Jet, sober as of late, I'm happy to say, was at that time in no shape to set sail. Pitney had the gift of adapting his unique vocal style from producer to producer, writer to writer, a have-gun-will-travel professionalism that I greatly enjoyed. Gene had not yet decided on his follow-up to "Twenty-Four Hours ..." and I pressed his ears to Mick's and Keith's songs in hopes we'd get lucky. He was drawn to a yarn named "My Only Girl" that I'd recorded but failed to get released. Pitney felt that a rewrite would be a good way to thank his British fans for their loyal support by way of acknowledging our native talent.

Olympic was booked for the Pitney session, and duly paid for by Pitney's people. I booked the musicians as well as Charles Blackwell to arrange the musical charts. Pitney allowed me to co-produce with him, and I was happy to be his pupil. Gene Pitney, like all great vocal stylists, was successful because he knew who he was and what was good for him. For me, it was a unique experience to watch Pitney shape everything for the style of his voice. Not only did he change the melody, he also re-titled the song and chorus: "My Only Girl" became "That Girl Belongs to Yesterday."

Working with Gene remains one of the outstanding pleasures of my formative years. He hired me as his publicist, encouraged Mick and Keith as writers, attempted to help Brian Jones find his voice as a writer, and took me under his wing and gave me them as a producer. He was inspirational. He made possible my first top ten U.K. record outside of the Stones.

Sean O'Mahony says he financed Gene's recording of "That Girl Belongs to Yesterday," but he must be thinking of a different record. He may have financed the George Bean recording of "My Only Girl" and lost his investment because it went unreleased.

True, that song became "That Girl Belongs to Yesterday," but the recording we did with Gene owed nothing to the Bean record. Anyway, it doesn't make sense to have had him finance the Pitney session. Gene was signed to Musicor in the States and distributed by EMI in the U.K. He was already a hit artist, and the session costs for whomever Gene approved would have been happily paid for by the labels ... unless I really was that good.

"That Girl Belongs to Yesterday" was scheduled for a March release by EMI. It would become Mick's and Keith's first entry into the U.K. top ten as songwriters. Now that I looked to Mick and Keith to provide material for recording, the other Stones, particularly Brian, often felt somewhat redundant and unappreciated. Both Charlie Watts and Eric Easton told me that Brian had songwriting ambitions, but he was too scared to put his songs forward.

Brian Jones did not have the firm foundation I required to build a Brill Building hit machine; on one hand he was obsessed with duplicating the stardom of the Beatles, whilst on the other he remained a blues "purist" and obstructed our efforts to reach the widest possible audience. As Keith Richards would have it, Brian would have played Duane Eddy's *16 Greatest Hits* to make it, but in actual fact, no one was asking.

I was bored senseless by Brian's endless theories about "subliminal themes in search of a juxtaposition," his bleating about the potential of half-finished melodies that by no means deserved completion. How many syllables Brian employed to worm his way into and out of any given point, complicating things for his listener past all caring! God knows Linda Lawrence loved him and Brian always had his own following among the legions of Stones fans, but I could not find anybody to love in there. He resisted the symbiosis demanded by the group lifestyle, and so life was becoming a little more desperate for him day by day. None of us were looking forward to Brian totally cracking up.

In the amenable Gene Pitney, I thought I might have found a practical solution, which would help to bring Jones's ideas to the table in some kind of usable form, and provide an objective professional opinion on Brian's potential as a songwriter. He kindly agreed to spend two afternoons with Brian at his London hotel, with the aim of getting a couple of songs to the point where they could be demo'd at Regent Sound. Regrettably, the results remain best unheard, even by Stones' completists.

I realised that Brian did not love pop music, therefore he could not write it. You can't write down to anyone. He didn't respect the pop song structure and thought it involved little more than rhyming "moon" with "June." Mick and Keith knew there was more to it than that, and appreciated how hard it was to keep things simple. They were prepared to work on their craft. They knew that Fats Domino had titled his hit "Blueberry Hill" because he had to find something that rhymed with "thrill."

Writing songs means that one must pay attention to life, and Brian was loath to pay attention to anything but himself. One who is not interested in life ceases to be interesting. His condescending attitude toward pop music meant that he could never satisfy his addiction to success. You can't look up or down at fame. You just have to allow for it.

"Not Fade Away" quickly rose to top five status; another first for the Stones, who finally had, for want of a better phrase, a genuine piece of plastic. I called my shoppers off the retail run when the single reached number 38. It was obvious by then that the single had legs of its own. Now we were reaching those record buyers who weren't yet Stones fans, just fans of pop music. The Stones brought home their Silver Disc, signifying sales of 250,000.

Robert Stigwood alleged that he had gone bankrupt and couldn't pay the Stones their share of the tour profits (about £16,000). Stigwood must have known he was going bankrupt while the Stones were on the road. He could have done the right thing but he didn't; the Stones had been swindled, they were the coffee and dessert of Stigwood's first run. Stigwood returned to become rich and famous as manager for Eric Clapton (from Cream through the first solo albums of the seventies), the Bee Gees, and Andrew Lloyd Webber and Tim Rice. His fortune came together most rewardingly when he signed John Travolta to a three-movie deal and produced *Saturday Night Fever* (from a Nik Cohn story), *Urban Cowboy*, and *Grease*.

When Keith Richards finally caught up with Stigwood at the Scotch of St. James club, he made sure the bankrupt Australian got a physical, if not legal, payback. Keith instructed Mick, me, and *NME* journalist Keith Altham to block the stairs against the helpless Stigwood's retreat. Keith proceeded to pummel him in the balls and many of the other soft parts of his body to the tune of "£1000" - bang, "£2000" - wallop, until the £16,000 was paid back according to the law of Keith Richards.

Aggressive and tireless Stones fans, dozens of them day and night, now besieged Mapesbury Road, wielding scissors with which to clip a keepsake if they didn't lobotomise us first. We could afford a move up, so it was time to move on. Mapesbury had served its purpose well and should have a plaque on its wall, "Mick and Keith first wrote here."

I moved to a furnished room in Haverstock Hill between Belsize Park and Chalk Farm. At £18 a week it was one of the many new abodes subdivided and redecorated for young people with disposable income. Mick and Keith moved to a larger space on Holly Hill, just north of Haverstock Hill.

I'd also outgrown the Maddox Street office, now that my reformed Image PR business with Tony Calder required space as well. Though I was burning my candle at both ends, already managing and producing the Stones, and could have lived without another job, I needed cash. I was getting tired of knocking on Easton's inhospitable pawnbroker door for what was rightfully mine. But it was better to start another independent business than to rock the Stones' boat in a public pond. We were doing so well by all outward appearances that now was not the time for taking on muddy water.

I was promoting the idea that the Rolling Stones were "the group parents loved to hate," based on my belief that pop idols fall into one of two categories - ones you wished to share with your parents and ones you did not. The Beatles were accepted and acceptable, they were the benchmark and had set the level of competition. The Stones came to be portrayed as dangerous, dirty, and degenerate, and I encouraged my charges to be as nasty as they could wish to be. At last, we had a genuine hit and I leveraged that mileage daily to embed the Stones in the psyche of the British press, like a grain of sand irritates an oyster. I was relentless and I was right. I was like a pit bull terrier that wouldn't let go. I got a lot of permanent messages across, a lot of press, and a lot of enemies.

John was so very attuned to the notion that if the music business was bollocks, it would be his bollocks, and so you never lied to Johnny Lennon. He was very fast with an opinion, an approach I was no stranger to, and it scared a lot of those he wished to scare. I'm looking through you was what John Lennon did - he invited you to walk on eggshells. His directness always brought me back to myself and he appreciated that my life and agenda were not about Alfie.

We were all so good at publicity that when John, as he might, told Maureen Cleave in 1966 that the Beatles were "more popular than Jesus," I'm sure he meant that, should the good public wish to slander him and his way of life, they might consider that he was as close to a man of integrity as their offspring were likely to get. It's really one of the most elegant remarks anybody has ever excited the press's haemorrhoids over. In John's highly sensitive presence you knew exactly who you were, and that is quite a gift to be hauling around.

Partner Paulie came down on the side of "It's all a show, so let's show off together," and Kansas City here we come. Party boys that we were, I don't know what Paul was like behind closed doors with his joint rolled and carpet slippers on. If he doesn't get enough credit for being a well-meaning geezer, blame it on the Stones.

But John would roll the joint and watch you smoke it, wear cowboy boots to bed and carpet slippers to meet the Queen - or any of them. He watched where life and the music took you, and if you were standing in clear present time he applauded you. He dared you to have airs and to be stupid; he was always hungry for a fool. He'd ask you a question and watch you contemplate, edit, and realise the futility of a less-than-total-truth answer, and this led to a rarity in the air not often breathed - a truth-only encounter. One strike and you were down with a barrage of venom, a lewd adjectival spew that many a wit and playwright would wish upon his page. Being with Johnny Lennon was like a verbal exposition of the famous chicken race sequence between James Dean and Corey Allen in Nicholas Ray's *Rebel Without a Cause*, or the Russian roulette sequence in Michael Cimino's *The Deer Hunter*.

For my part, I was working the press harder than I was "working" the boys. I didn't have to tell the Stones how to behave, I just had to let them be - they did the rest. I may have realised that, on a subconscious level, their extra long hair and mix-and-match gear strongly hinted at rebellion and degeneracy, but the group were doing what came naturally and I was only running with it. The Stones just had to open their mouths to compound what may have begun as misdemeanors into headline-grabbing felonies.

A Hit is a Hit is a Hit. I was no longer fighting for mini-inches of press clippings, plugging upcoming Stones concert appearances or record releases. Fame was a-growing daily and, although the Stones were not yet being snapped going through the airports of the world, the high streets of England would do for now.

Melody Maker repeated word-for-word my press release: "The Stones' role in music is a powerful one. They have the anger of the parents on their side. Young fans now realise that their elders groan with horror at the Rolling Stones. So their loyalty to the Stones is unswerving."

Another *MM* headline was a great example of everlasting meaning via product placement. I had dreamt up the line, "Would you let your daughter go with a Rolling Stone?" which would be translated into "Would you let your daughter marry a Rolling Stone?" by the high priests of Fleet Street who wished to avoid the ramifications of the word "go." I'd come up with it in response to something that either Ray Coleman or Jack Hutton had said to me during an interview; it got the headline and became one of the many slogans wrapped around the Rolling Stones for life.

It wasn't that hard for the Stones; they were natural. In the long run the public doesn't buy fakes. To this day people place themselves in relation to the sixties in terms of whether they liked the Stones better than the Beatles. Your answer was your identity; it stated who you were.

CHAPTER 14

jammin' with deadwood / reg the butcher carves his way into our hearts / all in a daze work - the doris richards fan club at work / i meet my very own grace kelly - marianne faithfull / lionel bart turns up musical and financial trumps and pays for marianne / i meet my muse and soul saver - the designer sean kenny / a-side sucks, b-side lucks out and takes marianne to the top of the pops / i've got a band, an orchestra, and a singin' blond - and i'm not yet twenty years old - i must remember to get a life

Style I had a good grab on. It is not as superficial as it first appears. It does not come from an undisciplined character, and mastery of it can keep you out of harm's way much of the time. It is the public face of grace, but fame is something else certainly. Fame was going to turn into a many-headed monster, and with most of them, I was happy to grapple.

I had provided a ready definition of fame for Mick Jagger, but time and its moves were suggesting that perhaps I would be better sorting out an answer for myself. I had only grasped a little bit of it in my mitt, not enough to bow to, hardly enough to savour, not enough to call a friend, yet I was already saying, "This is good, I like it. Show me where the poison is so I can start killing myself. Show me where the window is so I can start jumping."

You have a great first run, the poison tricks you, you think it's working for you, you don't feel the drip that will eventually kill you. Drip drop ... thank you Dion. The window fools you. You are many floors higher than you thought, the drop will be long whilst you whiz by the penthouse padded by that same success. It could fill another book, and it will.

I did not realise it at the time, but I'd already started to play with the loaded gun. I thought I was just flaunting my entitlement. If you are constantly jumping into a swimming pool that has a leak, eventually you'll be belly-flopping into a pool with no water. But why worry now? We'd only just begun.

I had flash readies, meaning toy money, not the real thing. Not being interested in bricks and mortar, I preferred a statement in wheels and chrome. Never dreaming the taxman cometh, I made my statement and offed the £2000 I could lay my hands four at a time, and crashed into a previously quiet reception.

"What can I do for you ... gentlemen?" asked a startled, beehived receptionist. I was already cutting through the door, having seen Greene holding court down the hall in the entrance to his office.

The ever-polite Reg was allowing himself to be asked if he had an appointment.

"Does it look like we need one, dear?" Reg asked rhetorically in his best bemused-gangster mode.

"It's OK, Reg. He's down here, follow me," I yelled, champing at my bit. The two of us charged into Richard Greene's office, power-driving him back into the wall. Reg kept his arm pressed into the scribe's Adam's apple, waiting for the word, "Kill." I got my breath, pretended to relax, took the measure of the room, and smiled laconically.

"Reg, get his fuckin' hands on the window ledge." Reg did so, warning the now green-at-the-gills Greene that if he moved his hands from the sill, Reg would throw him out the window.

"What's all this about?" blustered the writer. His hands moved.

"Attack!" I screamed to Reg.

"Don't fucking move your hands!" commanded Reg.

He didn't. We'd already caused a commotion around the offices but nobody was brave enough to come in and find out what was going on. I was glad that Peter Jones was not in the vicinity; this would not have done and he could definitely have called the meeting to order. I moved toward Greene as Reg held his hands on the sill with one hand as the other held the window, ready to bring it suddenly down at any sign of movement from the writer. It was time to bring onstage for the first time, save mirror appearances, my Burt Lancaster as J.J. Hunsecker in *Sweet Smell of Success*. Oh, I loved it! I'd done Tony Curtis' Sydney Falco for so long I grabbed this new part and made it mine.

Face to face with the flack, I shook my head with a disappointed sigh.

"Richard," I said quietly, "What is this about? You don't know? You don't proofread your own copy? You're a good writer, your musical taste may be a different matter, but you're a good writer. Why do you have to be so vindictive? Hate me, hate my act, hate their music, but ..."

I paused. Richard still had no idea what was going on. It was time to up the ante to make this scene plausible.

"Richard, I got a call this morning from a very hurt and upset Mrs. Richards. You don't know her, but she's Keith Richards's mum. She said, 'Mr. Oldham, can you do anything to stop what this man keeps saying about my boy's acne? I know you can't stop that rubbish about how they don't wash. But Keith is a sensitive boy, even if he doesn't say so. Please, Mr. Oldham, can you do anything?'"

It was so good I believed it.

"So, Richard, this is the story. If you ever again write something about Keith that is out of line, that is hurtful to his mum, because I'm responsible to Keith's mum, your hands will be where they are now, but with one big difference."

My voice got louder. I rolled my eyes and twitched once.

"Reg here will bring that fuckin' window crashing down on your ugly hands, and you will not be writing, you malicious fat turd, for a long fucking time, and you won't be dictating either, you cunt, 'cause your jaw will be sown up from where Reg fucking broke it."

Reg and I acknowledged each other with a wink. With Reg ahead of me, we brushed past the gathered onlookers. Always with a care to his manners, Reg murmured a few "Excuse me's," and a "Good day, dear, I hope we didn't startle you" to the receptionist. I followed Reg's orders to avoid eye contact or words with anyone, and we bolted down the stairs five at a time out onto the street.

A policeman stood inspecting our car as we approached the vehicle.

"Is this your car, sir?" he asked. Reg took over - this was his job.

"No, officer, it's Mr. Oldham's car," he said looking in my direction, as did the copper. "He is the manager of a group you may have heard of, the Rolling Stones, and he was upstairs in that building attending to some business with a journalist, when the journalist collapsed on the floor. I came in and we thought that the journalist might have had a heart attack, so Mr. Oldham told me to go double-quick and get his car, this car, in case it might be needed to take the writer to the hospital. I brought the car around and left it like this, on the pavement, I thought that was safer for the other motorists, and ran upstairs. It seemed that the gentleman who had collapsed was better, he just hadn't taken his medication, and after all didn't need to go to the hospital."

"All right," said the policeman, either satisfied or bored by Reg's spontaneous and imaginative scenario. "Be on your way. Next time, call an ambulance, that's what they're for you know."

We "Yes officer"d him in unison, got in the car and left, hooting and shrieking with glee as we illegally right-turned north into Wardour Street.

****

Mick and Keith wrote "Shang a Doo Lang" to order for actress/ singer Adrienne Posta. I didn't think the record was all that dreadful. I gave it my Phil Spector best. Mick and Keith rewrote "He's Sure the Boy I Love" for the occasion, and I was able to adhere to my decree that if they wrote, their songs would be recorded and we'd eventually hit the gravy train.

We convinced Sid Posta to pay for a launch party for his daughter, because, at that time, launch parties were strictly for visiting Americans, so the label wouldn't pay. The British industry thought it had nothing of its own worth "launching."

Adrienne Posta was a pretty little girl whom I believe we met through Steve Marriott. Steve had studied with her at the Italia Conti Stage School. Her record was going to be released the end of March on Decca and the party was set at her parents' flat off Seymour Place, bang next-door to fifties crooner Dickie Valentine, which I took as a good omen for all. It was at this party that I met Marianne Faithfull.

I let the Chevy cool down after a hot week with Reg at the wheel, and drove to the Friday night party in a new car I'd taken on spec - "on spec" meaning I was scrambling about for the money to pay for it. I think it cost £800, a maroon Sunbeam Tiger convertible with a V8 engine. I didn't have Reg on the weekends because he terrified Sheila. The car fit us like a glove.

The party was in go by the time we arrived. Paul McCartney and his then girl friend, the actress Jane Asher, greeted me. Her brother Peter Asher was also present; the last time I'd seen him was when Gordon and Peter were playing at a Meaden/

Oldham-produced "R&B" evening in Hampstead.

Now, having reversed the name, the pop duo were in the charts with a Lennon/McCartney ballad, "A World Without Love." So far a star-filled night, pop was definitely enjoying its own, and here I was, a rebel without pause, smack dab in the middle of it. It would be a nice night off, or so I thought. It was not to be. Peter Asher had invited his friend John Dunbar, accompanied by his fiancée Marianne Faithfull.

The moment I caught sight of Marianne I recognised my next adventure, a true star. In another century you'd have set sail for her; in 1964 you'd record her.

I approached Marianne through her fiancé Dunbar, mumbled something along the lines of, "You have something, I want to meet you, and can you sing?" That "Shang a Doo Lang" party was on a Good Friday and a very good Friday it was: I had new maroon Tiger wheels, Sheila was happy, and we were a foursome, having fixed Keith up on a blind date with Sheila's chum Linda Keith. I thought it was time that Keith went out with something other than his guitar.

On leaving the Posta party, Keith bet me that I couldn't drive the four of us all the way back to Hampstead on the wrong side of the road. Apart from crossing Edgware Road, I did.

Two days later Marianne Faithfull turned up at the Ivor Court office with a friend and an acoustic guitar. She auditioned for me by singing a couple of Joan-Baez-type folk numbers. Technically, Faithfull couldn't sing, still can't, but she reminded me of Grace Kelly, or rather Kelly's voice in the duet she sang with Bing Crosby in the 1956 film *High Society*, "True Love." I loved the record, loved the image, and for me it was Grace Kelly's magic bridge that helped to send the record to number one in early 1957. Kelly was almost speaking her parts in a captivating and sensual monotone. It was not unlike Crosby's later "White Christmas" duet with David Bowie playing Princess Grace. The microphone fell in love with Kelly's voice, the way the camera had fallen in love with her face. I hoped they would do the same for Marianne Faithfull.

Through Lionel Bart I'd met the maverick Irish stage designer Sean Kenny. Kenny worked closely with Lionel as stage designer on many of Bart's musicals such as *Fings Ain't Wot They Used t'Be*, *Oliver!* and *Lock Up Your Daughters*. Kenny was also the resident art director at the Mermaid Theatre, whose utopian message for drama - "Let us rebel, fight, break down, invent, and reconstruct a new theatre. Let us free the theatre from the cumbersome shackle of outmoded traditions." - was an example of Kenny's position. There was no one more vociferous about the new British theatre than Sean Kenny. We got on so very well.

Sean was my man, my muse. Later I named my first son after him. As I entered the rock 'n' pop end of show business, he was like someone whom God had sent down to tap me on the shoulder and say, "By the way, there's all this as well." Sean made me realise that there's more to it and more I could bring to it. As well as the angry young man, there was the angry young musical. He showed me social responsibility in practice as a living art form and imbued me with a work ethic that cut wider than self, a making of the "you-can-do-it" emblem available to every man who could dream it. At a time when my business was about trampling myth and tradition, he reminded me to engage also in building hope and awakening spirit and vision. You'd go out for the night, solve the world's ills and wake up in the morn, as I did, in Sean's bed, with the master, a lithe British actress, and an afghan hound. And you'd still be God's children and all would be right with the world.

Sean was a great mate and education, and his ethics and talent emboldened me even as I didn't practise them. I now needed money to finance recording Marianne, so I went to Lionel and suggested a joint venture. There was no way I was going to let her be signed to Decca direct for the sake of a few hundred quid.

Lionel and I were cruising down Bayswater after a night at foot-tapper Lionel Blair's, when we chatted about our big dreams and my empty pockets. With a heart of gold, on with the dance of life, Li agreed to fund the venture. He was a gem, a real rhythm of life. We formed two companies, Forward Sound to handle recording projects and Forward Music to handle the songs, Marianne to be the first Forward artist. Lionel had this song, "I Don't Know How," that we agreed would be one of the recorded songs. The fact that Marianne wouldn't be able to sing it didn't get mentioned.

Earlier that month I'd gone into Kingsway Studios. Regent was booked to cut some demos of Mick's and Keith's latest batch of songs, and amongst the musicians was ex-Wildcat Big Jim Sullivan on guitar and former Tornado Clem Cattini on drums. I was now using session musicians on their demos. I couldn't ask Brian, Bill, and Charlie to work for nearly free on their few days off. We quickly put down two or three songs, there was really nothing special there; the main point was the exercise.

Keith, for some reason, wasn't there and the session had been a little lackluster, not the best note on which to continue the day. Whilst the musicians packed up their equipment, I asked Mick, "You didn't have anything else? I didn't hear that ballad I heard you working on."

"No, that's it." Mick wasn't pleased with the day's work either.

"Let's get it down anyway." I turned to Big Jim Sullivan: "Jim, I've got fifteen minutes more of your time, haven't I? Could Mick just sing this song to you, it's simple, and then we could knock it off with just the two of you?"

"You can have all the fifteen minutes you want, Andrew, my son," said Jim, and then to Mick, "OK, Sunshine, come over here and let's listen to this song of yours."

I think that Big Jim knew that Mick was not in a compliant mood and his relaxed tone got the song to the table. Fifteen minutes later, I had them both down with "As Time Goes By."

A couple of days after Marianne had come up and done her Joan Baez warbling, Tony Calder and I sat down when everybody had left the office and talked about songs for her to record. We both ignored Lionel's song, "I Don't Know How," neither of us owning up to the fact that it wasn't a song for Marianne, unable to insult Lionel or, perhaps more to the point, afraid of 'fessing up and losing our backer. Lionel had the readies and our moral balls were locked in a greedy vise of deceit. We crossed a Jackie DeShannon song and a few others off our short list.

"Well, there's this song of Mick's I didn't play you that I cut at the 'Sleepy City' session," I offered and then whacked the 7½" tape onto the reel-to-reel.

Tony was with me when I talked to Mick. Tony wore a matte dark grey one-buttoned blazer and Anello and Davide "slippers." I wore a blue herringbone double-breasted sports jacket, grey-blue high tab-collared broadcloth shirt, and black string tie. Mick wore a checked tab-collared shirt without a tie, with mock Prince of Wales checked John Stephen trews, a combo around on a powder-blue Chevrolet Impala, with a midnight-blue roof and matching dual-blue'd leather interior. A car that would keep me on my road - my own America. And to go with this superb king of the highway came my very own spiv, minder, driver, and bodyguard, the wonderful Reg King, named "The Butcher" by Keith. Reg was much needed as, although I drove, I had not yet got a license.

Reg hailed from the East End. He was sheer charm with a snarl, a pit bull terrier dressed as a poodle. The diamond on his pinkie reflected the permanent twinkle in his pretty, killer baby blues. High, starched, white collars; broad-shouldered, discreet, bumfreezer suits; dark silk tie, tacked by a pearl. His personality was warm; he had a heart of gold. His persona lay somewhere between the gay end of the Kray twins, and Priscilla, Queen of the Desert. I met him through Lionel Bart, who told me that Reg was just what I needed.

Reg ended up getting me into more fights than I would get myself into. I spent too much time dealing with driving offences and assault charges, and I didn't even have a driving license. For a while I didn't complain, I welcomed it, as I welcomed Reg. He'd come up and say, "Don't move, there are eight people behind you." "Reg," I'd say, "We're at a concert. We're in a crowd, there are bound to be eight people standing behind us."

One writer who loved to hate the Stones was Richard Greene at the *Record Mirror*. Rock 'n' roll has its rules of conduct, same as La Cosa Nostra or the House of Commons. Richard Greene was clearly not a man of honour. If he didn't like their sound or records, fine; or their image and look, fine and under-standable. There was much to dislike about the Stones: I had seen to it. Anyone's perception of how unkempt we were was fair game. But Keith Richards' complexion had nothing to do with it.

When Greene mouthed off for a third time about Keith, I threw down the paper in disgust and shouted for Reg to bring "Boadicea's Chariot" around pronto. The Chevy made it to the *Record Mirror*'s Shaftesbury Avenue office from Gloucester Place in twelve minutes, running a few lights, jumping a few curbs, and just missing a few people.

Reg and I leapt out of the car, leaving it parked illegally half on the pavement, half on the street, ran up the office stairs of patterns that only he would have attempted to pull off.

Tony sat on a chair, swaying back and forth, hands clasped, moving his thumbs back and forth. Mick stood in front of me, at my desk going through everything that was on it.

"Mick, that song, 'As Time Goes By,' it could be great," said I, also meaning get your hands out of my things or learn to read backwards.

"I don't think so," he replied.

"I've got someone in mind for it. I'd like to look at changing the title."

"Do what you bloody like with it; it's finished as far as I'm concerned," Jagger closed as he continued to rummage through my papers.

The musicians sighed with relief when I announced that we were dumping "I Don't Know How" and moving on to "As Tears Go By." The frustration of countless takes of poor Marianne sounding like an inbred hyena gave a great impetus to their playing on "As Tears Go By." They didn't play it like a B-side; they played it with feeling, relief, and life; they were happy to be "on structure" again and you could hear it and it glued. It was a magical moment. A few takes to sort out the loose change and we were home. I congratulated Marianne and told her she'd got herself a number six.

I didn't need Lionel now, so I carved him out of the writing picture and dumped his song. There was no doubt that "As Tears Go By" was a smash, and I wanted to be on the B-side; remember a writer receives the same money riding on the back of a hit as having written the A-side. I was greedy, in money and ego; therefore Lionel had to go.

Another practical reality was that "I Don't Know How" would have given the game away and been an insult to those who'd bought "As Tears Go By" to find this hyenic rendition on the back. This was a hit and I needed a B-side that partnered, not degraded. This round-robin move would rebound on me: Years later when I stopped to take breath and count a few figures, I found that David Platz had appropriated my B-side to one of his own crew, he just figuring I'd be too busy to notice, and I was. One part of this man definitely did not survive the holocaust; he just figured I was not entitled, and used a law I was not familiar with to appropriate the money to somebody he thought was.

Hitler played God with Platz's life, and Platz played God with my money.

If you are a moaner and can't take getting fucked and screwed the first few times out, then find another business, for the hauling over is your entry fee and part of the territory.

I got an appointment to see the legendary Sir Edward Lewis to play him the finished "As Tears Go By" and get the money for a different Faithfull B-side. This was becoming an expensive session. I had never met Sir Edward over the Stones. I was nervous and wondered if he'd heard about "Andrew's Blues." He hadn't: Life was smaller and a different shop. We had not reached the stage where everybody was a star; that would come later. Right now it was a divine right given only to a few, those few who had begun those sixties; the rest of you could seize it later.

We sat in Sir Edward's sweeping office overlooking the Thames. He was sixtyish, a fossil, neat but scruffy in a worn, well-made, double-breasted suit. His eyes were shiftier than mine, but when they did make contact with yours they were grey, all knowing, and quite kind. I'd never studied ears, but now, looking at his, I realised it wasn't just the poor and old but the rich as well who had hair growing out of their ears. It seemed very strange that day. Now I know better about fossils and hair.

Another A-side with the Andrew Oldham Orchestra, "Three Hundred and Sixty-Five Rolling Stones (One for Every Day of the Year)," that I penned with Mike Leander became the main title theme for two years' worth of Rediffusion TV's *Ready, Steady, Go!* That was a nice honour and a few pennies. The B-side was a tongue-in-cheek piece of reality called "Oh, I Do Like to See Me on the B-Side," written by Charlie Watts, Bill Wyman, and yours truly.

I'd persuaded Decca a few months before to release the Andrew Oldham Orchestra, and I set about recording *16 Hip Hits* at Regent Sound with the unflappable Bill Farley engineering, John Paul Jones playing bass and arranging, and Jim Sullivan and Jimmy Page on guitars.

When Impact Sound and the Rolling Stones signed with Decca, Eric Easton did the signing, I was a minor. This time out, I was still a minor and my mother did the signing. I was pleased. She wouldn't fuck me, even if I'd made the mistake of interpreting one of her few physical showings of affection for me when I was about twelve as a sign that she had wanted me to. There, that didn't take fifty minutes and a couch, did it?

Anyway ... How many nineteen-year-olds had their own orchestras? How many producers? None or not many. The orchestra didn't go on the road; it was in permanent workshop; I was paying my way through the Regent Sound Producer's College, and I invited all of my friends to join me. Oh, we made some huge mistakes, but one started to learn where sound sat. On "Da Doo Ron Ron," which we balladed down, Mick Jagger came in and sang, and I added a couple of cellos. My budget was tight. It was my money: Not even I had the lip to get a backer for this trip; that would have been completely over the top and not done: "Excuse me, mister, could I have some money for my orchestra?" As if I really took it seriously, which, from another point of view, I did. Anyway, we added the two cellos with the tapes going mono to mono and the track just disappeared, couldn't handle the register of the cellos. You can hear the gaffe today, but you learned from it all, you learned.

I recorded instrumental, quasi-vocal, and vocal versions of songs by Bob Dylan; Chuck Berry; John Lennon and Paul Mc-Cartney; Phil Spector; Jeff Barry and Ellie Greenwich; Burt Bacharach and Hal David; Jack Nitzsche; and Sonny Bono. "Alley Oop" creator Kim Fowley and I wrote a devastating remake of "The House of the Rising Sun." We called it "The Rise of the Brighton Surf" in homage to the recent Easter punch-ups in Brighton between raving Mods and charismatic Rockers, which had thereby given England its own *West Side Story* - real on-the-seafront street theatre. Wouldn't you have?

Marianne Faithfull at Decca, 1964

CHAPTER 15

how it worked and how it works - the first recordings / "more than just a group - a way of life" slogan number two / the co-ordinated life - primrose hills and pot on the walls of our minds / peter o'toole is going to play me in a movie ... according to keith richards / more celluloid lies and banter / a summing up - rockin' with the lords of the flies

From January to March 1964, the Stones were on the road. I promoted them, ran my shop, and recorded the Andrew Oldham Orchestra. Nearly every day they had off we recorded the first album at Regent Sound. Chuck Berry, Willie Dixon, Muddy Waters, and Holland/Dozier/Holland were amongst the writers from whom we culled the covers we recorded for this razor-sharp and earnest first LP outing. It was a first and a great pleasure for the group to have that much space to express themselves (albeit not that much time to do it in!)

Thirty-five years later this fact may be overlooked in a world where, if a talent appeals to a recording company or producer, it is usually given the long-form compact disc to display its wares to the world immediately. We were not given the world or the long-play record form - we earned them. First, a debut single; then, the follow up. Then if you were good boys, you were allowed the four-song outing of an extended 45 rpm with a picture sleeve - Wowee! - something tangible for mum to hold! Then, if your life and sales were constantly going up, you were allowed the big one: the LP. Around that time you may have some product released in France, Scandinavia, or Italy, and about two years after that you may get paid ... something.

On the first Stones' LP or our later work, I was never Mick's voice teacher or director. He found himself and got in character, out of it or lack of it, and did it. I would just help him find or remember the possibilities.

His voice is a finely tuned instrument, as is his being. I often thought that I talked to him and Keith listened; but any time we went to work it was apparent he'd heard what he needed to. He plays many parts in as many songs. He started with straight, respectful to the form, R&B interpretations. He still does that, plus so much more, from the near-Cockney on our later "Mother's Little Helper" to the glimmered street nigger of his much later "Some Girls." When Mick sang about love, sex, and the women who were under his thumb, obsolete, and out of time, he was totality personified, that moving violation that separates the men from the boys.

As a member of the public I would say, "Mick, in those first verses you got me. I believe you. On the next verse could you confuse me, give me doubt, lie to me ... then haul me back in?" And he'd do that or the appropriate equivalent.

Great stars rise above their given medium, their chosen thoroughfare. They succeed in the world at large. Such are Mick Jagger, Nureyev, Monroe, Dean, as is the head gamekeeper, Keith Richards. Keith was the trackman, bagman, wonder to behold. He was to the recording studio born. Everybody, including me, had their nervous asides, either brought with them or acquired in the anxiety of that rock 'n' roll moment when somebody asked you what you thought. With Keith, you didn't have to ask, his body told you. Sometimes he nodded, sometimes he smiled, but that was just taking time up for Keith, valuable time, between the next and last note. If you ever wanted to know if the track was done or in the bag, Keith told you and he didn't often use words. He was the seal of approval. I was later asked by Allen Klein, who was educating up on who did what, "Andrew, who makes the records?" Without hesitation, I replied, "Keith does." I lied.

The debut LP was rounded out by the first Keith and Mick composition the Stones recorded, "Tell Me (You're Coming Back)." It stood out with its echo-drenched, sloppy blues, puppy-in-love feel, and carried the space of a blues traveller resting his head in a commercial place. I loved it!

The recording completed, I next embarked on what at the time was natural and obvious to me and is now looked back on as great career strategy. I did not want the Stones LP to have some inappropriate title. My attitude was "Everyone knows who they are, that's why we don't need their name on the cover." The idea came to me one night and was a permanent must-have implant by the next morning ... The Rolling Stones LP would have no title and no name, just their moody mugs staring outatcha. Decca balked, I held the tapes; Decca balked in the press, so did I. I still held the tapes. Advance orders went up - in fact doubled - during this standoff.

The real title was embedded in my sleeve notes on the back of the cover: "The Rolling Stones are more than just a group - they are a way of life." If you stand with 18,000 Americans in Madison Square Garden in January 1998 - all trying to recover a moment to which they were not entitled in the first place, a moment the Stones lent them - you'll know that my message is still true. So I stood my ground and won. Bill Townsley at Decca relented and the group's first LP went out untitled, unrelenting, and unforgiven.

At first the Stones, away on those hysteria-swamped one-night stands all over the country, were as concerned as Decca over my album design. Mick and Keith loved the whole thing, pushing me on, the way that Chris Stamp would push Kit Lambert, "Whoa, he's off again!" Eric Easton and Bill Wyman were worried that I was going too far and my antics might deplete sales and, yes, be a career curtain closer, not a raiser. Charlie smiled in time to the pedal of his life. Brian took it hard and angst'd on it, but he was inexorably moving into his own cul-de-sac. Here I was, selling this would-be serious musician as a freak.

Yet, on April 17, 1964, the Rolling Stones' debut album was released and within a week had knocked *With the Beatles* off the top of the LP charts with advance orders of over 100,000. All complaints and concerns about my actions and screaming matches at Decca were soon forgotten. I ran around town, cock of the walk with a vengeance, gleefully crowing to all that the Stones were number one and going higher. I forgot to mention that the Beatles had held the number one spot for a year and were just taking a rest before their own next number one LP.

Melody Maker's review of this debut LP concluded, "A final word of praise to Andrew Loog Oldham, who recorded the sessions. He's living up to his boast that he'd be the top independent recording manager in Britain by November." I heard Jimmy Cagney yell from within me, "Top of the world, Ma!"

****

138/147 Ivor Court, at the northern tip of Gloucester Place, was an interesting building that was supposed to be residential until

Calder and I moved in. By early 1964, its tenants included us, Charlie and Shirley Watts on the floor below, and Who co-managers Kit Lambert and Chris Stamp a couple of floors below the Wattses. It was a small great world. 147, our first flat, was basically undecorated Ideal Home Exhibition to suit Tony Calder's taste, but 138 was "done" by the interior decorator, Malfada Hall, then wife of Tony Hall.

Mafalda was what was known as an "outrageously great lady" which she was to all of us. She was responsible for the great church lectern from which I held forth, and great wild silk wallpaper in the halls leading up to the custom-made marijuana wallpaper in my office. There was a lot of smokin' going on and the decor blended in well.

By now I was having a job remembering, not where I worked, but where I lived, so I often slept over. There was no chance of Eric Easton dropping by. His disdain of my fight with Decca over the Stones' cover had shovelled more dirt on the shallow grave of our partnership. I was now living with Sheila overlooking Primrose Hill. Sean Kenny and I had already been hauled in by the law for the misuse of fire extinguishers outside our flat, and the young man that Sheila had hired to clean had incurred my wrath and given my game away by throwing out a sacred lump of hash that I'd left atop the TV set in an ashtray. "I thought it was rubbish," he squealed as I screamed.

I had a nice morning ride from Primrose Hill into Regent's Park, sliding right onto Baker Street, gliding right and burning rubber right again onto Gloucester Place, then four blocks north in my powder-blue Chevy ridden, as opposed to driven, by the ever laughing, ever gay, and always criminal Reg. It seemed a perfect world. I had mine and seemed to be in control of it. From Primrose Hill to Regent's Park to the marijuana plants on the walls of my office, life was coordinated!

In late 1963, "I Wanna Be Your Man" had been pressed for release by London Records (Decca's American subsidiary) without my consultation. I demanded it be withdrawn because it stood no chance of being a hit and I didn't want a flop. I knew my American pop and "I Wanna Be Your Man" was not it! The subsequent American single release, "Not Fade Away" / "I Wanna Be Your Man," fared slightly better, just scraping into the top thirty. It appealed to the small movement of American kids, who, after the Beatles, were looking to seize on their own the next big thing from England before the record companies foisted it on them. Later I would find out that scraping into the top thirty meant naught, and that was where the real business began, not ended.

I made film plans in my mind and had them translated into press clippings for the Stones, dropping names like Lionel Bart and Peter Sellers. I had to: The Beatles were already filming. Keith Richards announced to the press, "Peter O'Toole is going to play our manager." Keith knew how to please me: Lionel shared office space with Peter O'Toole's manager, Jules Buck, so in those days it all could have easily happened. Eric Easton started making trips to New York to line his pockets and line up the first Stones tour of the States. I didn't pay much attention to this, we hadn't had a hit, the whole idea of America seemed so huge and far away and I had no idea of how to manipulate it.

If we were in town, Friday nights were spent at the *Ready, Steady, Go!* studios. Mick, Keith, and I could be regularly seen sipping free drinks in the Green Room, laughing at the other acts. This would set the standard for another Friday night out on the town.

Michael Aldred of *Ready, Steady, Go!* was an early tragedy. "Don't throw your love away," went the Searchers' ditty. Michael threw his heart away at every opportunity and trampled his good self way too young. None of us knew - we were all too young to know - how to give warning, to understand that Michael would wear himself and his heart out. You can't fall in love every Friday. I went out with Michael a couple of times and that was one time too many. He became emotional and demanding of my time, so I whacked him. Problem was that we were in the back seat of my powder-blue Chevy late on a Friday night as *Ready, Steady, Go!* faded and the weekend began. Poor Michael started to bleed and scream, all over the two-tone leather upholstery.

"Reg, the cunt is bleeding ... Shut up, Michael!" I rallied forth, more concerned about whether my suede jacket and two-tone upholstery would be soiled.

Reg, pinkie on the wheel, leered back and said, "Throw him out, Andrew ..."

"Could you slow down a little?" I asked.

****

I tried to keep tabs on what Peter Meaden was up to, hearing he was travelling life's highway without brakes and was now promoting a band called the High Numbers. It was not pleasant being the leader of the pack in this instance, leader in so many of the games that Peter had showed me the rules to. Peter was starting to paunch out. He'd been in the ring of leapers too many times and was pill-drunk, getting soft and emotional around the edges. I'd find out later for myself that drugs' chaser is panic. With the High Numbers, Peter played his hand off every deal, tried to stand up straight, to get that lithe boy running in the street with his national anthem. He tried so hard, so hard, that even though Peter didn't, the group made it.

They had been called the Who and they would be again, their name would be called out by millions; but in this moment, Peter was the only one screaming and they were the High Numbers. He had managed to get them a singles deal on Fontana, a Philips division; he had ripped off two blues structures, put his "mod-prose-speak" to work for them, and "I'm the Face" and "Zoot Suit" were due for release. This is early '64. Grab a hold of that image, those titles, and get Meaden's genius. A record deal was hard enough to pull off, but an imprint on the future ... that must be acknowledged.

Peter asked me out to a dance hall in Islington to see the High Numbers, they were very good, better than that - great! They did Miracles and Temptations stuff with a hard slant; Townshend and Moonie were the riveting two for me that day. So were these two characters sitting in the front of the hall: one a soft Wilde looking man with worried eyes and pursed lips, the other a good-looking wild yobbo wolf who looked like his minder. The former was Kit Lambert, the latter Chris Stamp, the other bright light in the Stamp collection.

"Peter," I grinded, for when with Peter, whether on speed or not, you started grinding. He was catchy, a straight out-to-lunch pill-popping Oscar Wilde in his own jail. Too many Wildes, and I knew then, one of them had to go. "Peter," repeat 'n' grind, "Just who are those two guys in the front?"

"Oh, them" grinded Peter back, his pupils scoring the jackpot, his teeth gnashing the remains of his nails. "They're two would-be film director wankers, they want to manage the High Numbers."

"Looks like they already do, Peter," I said.

But Peter didn't hear me. He was too busy listening to himself.

****

So here we are on the eve of the big three-chord gold rush, the eves of destruction would be a slow train coming, but it wasn't yet the evening of the day. We were all still gargling life's offerings of good fortune, trying them on for size, but never placing a final order. Life was very good to us, me and, for the most part, all who sailed with me, and we were good for life. We were singing life a different tune and it liked it, and gave us a good slice of itself with a view from an equally nice room at the top. Regardless of that bullshit about "You've never had it so good," we were having it just fine.

From my first days with the Stones, we had conspired as one against the world as we knew it. America and the rest of the world was another story. We had believed that the Stones' own musical force would break down the doors of resistance, that their strength would trample over the *Schadenfreude* hierarchy and trample the "No!"s into "Yeah!"s. We'd got that "Yeah!" from the world as we knew it; but it's still 1964 and the Stones have yet to work abroad. We'd get that "Yeah!" too. We'd win the war and take our spoils in fame and money.

When I met the Stones, they were already. I didn't fall for puppets, I fell for the real thing. They tapped power from the strength of their musical purpose. Apart from the slight false start when they wore costumes in exchange for equipment, and a change in personnel, I said, "Don't change a thing ... you've got everything. I believe in you, just let me use it." I told them who they were and they became it.

After a kindergarten beginning, we started to find our recording legs. I didn't try to force my Spector wall of sound on the group (I saved that for my own extracurricular efforts). I went with their wall of noise, the noise that had first nailed me to their wall one Sunday night nigh on a year ago in Richmond. I convinced Mick and Keith that they could write their own songs, making them dependent on no one, not even me, and showed them the way to creative freedom. Nobody, no record company, told them what to play; they arrived at it all by themselves.

Together we'd planned the look of the sound, as I tried to control what was seen, and did control what was heard. I attempted to control the image and what was said about it. We were writing our own headlines, taking no prisoners, and no outsiders ever got inside the walls. We were our own buzzword, the Stones created their own sound bites, and I'd use any event in passing this message on.

We handled our own dirty laundry at home; we didn't take it outside to the cleaners.

We went out to play and we all knew the game we were playing. Life was really nice, and "nice" was the word of the day. It wasn't brilliant, it was nice. My idea of a night off was to go over to Alan Freeman's flat and play more records, to talk more shop, or nip up the M1 in my new Mini with its Philips-made 45 rpm singles player with Dusty Springfield, playing each other the new American singles we'd copped.

Most of us were aware that we were privileged to be part of this wonderful world and just wanted more, just didn't want this good thing to stop. We were all too busy to mope, and as such we wished each other well; there was plenty of room at the top. While embracing this, I drifted apart from my mother and never developed with Sheila; but I didn't have a choice in this: It's not everybody who gets a chance to telephone the gods and have them take the call.

Later I allowed myself to go mad with vanity, spent too much attention on my own details, and concentrated on being interesting, not interested, nearly ending up a very dead lunatic, and thus almost leaving a disgusting legacy to trample on my name. I would lay down with whores and criminals and recognise my waste in the mirror, but somehow I always managed to wake with the angels until the end of a slow thirty-year train ride into madness. I got taken up with the business of dying, till I got assisted in the art of surviving.

I know my work with the Stones and the many others whose talent I cherished affected the consciousness and ethic of my time, for good and for bad. Each day I am always fortunate, though sometimes saddened, to witness that the generations who have followed us bear the effects of the causes we made. We are warned never to trust the artist, to trust only the work itself. To try to define the difference would have been imprudent of me at the time; so this story includes both warts and halos.

It may have looked as if all I wanted was to have it our way, but as long ago as that, affinity, reality, and communication were what I loved about the screams, the laughs, and the dreams, so ... on this clear note:

The view of the River Thames from the Decca Albert Embankment offices was quite brilliant that wonderful spring morning in 1964, when I met the chairman for the first time, asking for what I wanted and getting what I needed. What I wanted was for Sir Edward Lewis to acknowledge me as the future of the business as I acknowledged him as its past; what I needed was a check to complete my Marianne Faithfull record.

Sir Edward put the acetate for "As Tears Go By" on his green felt turntable and the oboe floated out of the funnel of the old man's wind-up machine. The *cor anglais* took the fade, Mr. Decca picked up the phone on his desk and got through to Dick Rowe.

"Dick, give the boy the money," was all he said.

London and the Thames looked radiantly alive, and a Polaroid stopped, snapped, and smiled at me in a way that always distinguishes those special days when you are at one with the world and you both know it.

The Who, 1964

CHAPTER 16

the summer of '64 / america lowers the bar on the stones / slagged in america / sonny bono shows us the future shrine -rca recording studios, sunset and iver / getting made in america begins / the first tour is the creepiest - apart from its sex pistol moments / miracles at chess records / murray the k paves the way to vinyl legs / getting hugged into life in the big apple / jumpcut to the dawning of aquarius in the seventies and mondo caine in the eighties

Young men grow, innocence goes, and the kids, albeit alright, start to become street-fighting men. We had this almost molecular affinity with America. Its music fed the soul of the Stones - it was the soul. American music was life-giving plasma; it was our future, the great escape as we flamed into being with fashion and rhythm. It was the explanation, the clue, the glue, and the door to the room at the top to which absolute beginners and definite winners found the key.

When one is young, summer records define your life. Later they explain it. In June 1964 the U.S. charts were topped by the Dixie Cups' rendition of the Phil Spector, Jeff Barry, and Ellie Greenwich ditty "Chapel of Love" on the Red Bird label. The Beach Boys' "I Get Around" and the Four Seasons' "Rag Doll" completed this trio of Great Popness whilst Gerry and the Pacemakers, Peter and Gordon, Billy J. Kramer, and the Dave Clark Five nipped at their heels with the best and worst of the British Invasion. Even the Bachelors got to number twelve. Throughout this magical spring and summer, the Beatles always had some half-dozen singles in the U.S. top twenty.

The Rolling Stones were running late. In Britain we were running within our breath; in America we would soon be running ahead and out of it. One single, "I Wanna Be Your Man," had been released and withdrawn. The side had then been coupled with "Not Fade Away," re-released, and, apart from a few idyllic plays in the Midwest and at a few scattered oases, would do just that. The Stones' first LP outing, dressed and sold to number one in the U.K. - via its urgent accuracy and my immaculate no-name imagery - had been re-packaged behind my back by London Records and given a title, *England's Newest Hitmakers*, putting the event lower on the graphics pole than a Freddie and the Dreamers cover. We were pissed off.

In Rockin' Britain (and somewhat in Europe) the Stones already had a track record from their two top-ten singles, a top-ten EP, and a number one album - plus an avalanche of good-cop/bad-cop press, adulation and scorn (the good cops being the Moptops). I screamed inches of ink while my erstwhile partner from the vaudeville machine, Eric Easton, booked the 'oopla. The 'oopla, the Rolling Stones, played and delivered. Game, set, match. Now Eric handed over the North American booking to a crew named GAC, who could have been CIA if appearances and attitude were anything to go on. These ten-percenters lived in a conservative, Barnumless world of staggered vents, brogued battleship shoes, broadcloth button-down shirts, and Washington power haircuts, and were more at home with Jackie Mason than with Nanker Phelge. To get as many newspaper inches for the Stones in the States as I'd been able to get at home, they'd have had to heist an atomic bomb.

America! Where presidents were knocked off, the widow in the pink pillbox hat and bloodstained Chanel mini passed as royalty, and the British Invasion was looked upon with the same disdain as the twist, hula hoops, and surfin'. I suspected my British box of tricks was not going to work here. We desperately needed a vocal following, and to get that we needed real plastic bullets, real hits, and lotsa, lotsa radio play.

On June 1, 1964, at New York's formerly-Idlewild-recently-renamed-Kennedy-International-Airport, the Stones were welcomed by a few hundred girls that London Records had managed to round up. If the Beatles' landing four months earlier had been directed by Cecil B. DeMille, our arrival was helmed by Mel Brooks. All those Yank cars that had seemed so exotic and out of reach back in Blighty were a dime a dozen in the States. In the drizzle of the Manhattan drabness, they looked strangely cumbersome and lackluster. Once we left the airport we were invisible; not a soul knew who we were. The movie was out of sync with life as I'd known it, jump-cutting between black-and-white and colour. The voices didn't match the picture. Putting reality together with the movie was a strain, and as for the soundtrack, it had become a hollow-reverbed nightmare - the audio was wrong, all wrong. I don't recall being excited; all I remember is being scared.

The Stones stayed at the Astor Hotel on Times Square. I saved some money and went looking to get myself recharged and to cadge a sleep on Phil Spector's ground-floor office couch on the East River somewhere in the sixties. Phil's office was a dull, couched, and plywooded affair - his taste was strictly reserved for vinyl. I was not invited upstairs to the penthouse residence, where, I believe, a marriage was on the rocks.

The Stones were a small cult, a collector's item, i.e., we didn't mean shit. They did Les Crane's local TV talk show, hosted by some staggered-brained, lacquered pimp with a smile and demeanor so cut-out and fake that we felt like we'd stopped off on the wrong set and were in *Hogan's Heroes* meets *The Twilight Zone*. God, suddenly old Auntie Beeb seemed great and far-seeing in comparison and we missed her so! It's OK to have your home kind question and ridicule you, but I took this vulturistic gnawing and nitpicking at the Stones' very soul as a personal violation of all that was dear to me. Brian Jones looked liked he'd been turned inside out, his heart and soul flayed and scalped before his very own eyes. He hurt and we hurt for him, though nowt was said except a curse on those stillborn Yanks. If we'd anything to declare at Ellis Island, perhaps it was that our skins were not as thick as we'd thought (the Stones' collective leathery eye had not yet formed).

But that was all about to change, and did, with Charlie in the lead, as we were stalked up 7th Avenue by some creature from the Manhattan radio lagoon named Clay Cole. Cole looked like an electroshocked Anthony Perkins on steroids. His questions never got past "Why did you grow your hair?" What a dolt! Didn't he know this kind of banter was reserved for the Moptops and Herman's Hermits? The movie snapped back into focus when the dapper Watts told this inane prick to fuck off. He did, and we moved on up to 57th suddenly feeling whole again. You might say we were spoilt brats who didn't much care for this new bashing we were getting abroad. It was the old "Christians and lions" game. It was the original *Planet of the Apes*, and I was feeling more like Roddy McDowell than like Mr. NRA.

From the *papier-mâché Day of the Locusts* New York reception we winged to Los Angeles, hovered over it, and arrived as L.A.'s surviving movieola barracudas were shit-deep in make-up and cliché. Just another day in the celluloid killing fields. Yes, I was pissed off. The plane had bad lighting, most of the colours and fabric were tired and inspired by vomit, facade, and disease, and the stewardesses looked best in long shots, evoking Sandra Dee and all of Alfred Hitchcock's best blonde apparitions.

The image on the West Coast screen momentarily moved from B-movie to VistaVision as Phil Spector's right-hand promo man, Sonny Bono, greeted us at the airport with an open heart and hand to welcome us to La-La Land. There was hope yet. Thirty-something Salvatore Bono looked as whacked as the Stones - and he worked for a living! Bono was all Sicilian L.A. heart. Clad in barber-pole striped trousers, an Italian sweater of the sort thus far only dared by Carnaby poofters, sole and heel-less Indian calf-length moccasins, and paisley neck scarf, he was a sight to see. In his car trunk were boxes of Caesar and Cleo 45s because, in those pre-"I Got You, Babe" days, he was part of a duo called Caesar and Cleopatra with his then-girlfriend, Cher.

The next day the movie went back to black-and-white as we started rehearsals for *The Hollywood Palace*, an ABC-TV show guest-hosted by Dean Martin - the first surprise being that there was no Dean to be seen. A week of rehearsals with a Dean stand-in followed. Meanwhile, Dino was out on the links, touching up his tan. He turned up for the filming, immaculate and decadent (which equaled rich), and proceeded to insult the Stones as his way of getting in and out of a commercial break and into the bowels of American's suburbs and heartlands. The insults one could handle, and the goodfella laconicity - just. It was not having thought of a stand-in for Mick that hurt to the management core.

Apart from the Dean Martin experience everybody enjoyed Los Angeles. You could see a lot more of the girls in such a climate and - L.A. being L.A. - the Summer of Love was already here. Most of the girls didn't need to undress; they already had. We got good news from England - the album was still number one! On the 5th the Stones played their first U.S. concert at the Swing Auditorium in San Bernardino. A lot of enthusiastic fans showed and placed (even if the promoter didn't). The Stones felt better for it; they were back doing what they did best.

Sonny Bono took us for a ride to the RCA studios on Sunset where it crossed with Iver. The entrance to RCA was in fact on Iver, opposite the intimate Martoni's where Sam Cooke (who also recorded at RCA) had his last supper before heading south to the motel that took him. That afternoon I met three important elements in the Stones' recording future: Jack Nitzsche, Dave Hassinger, and the studio itself. Thank you, Sonny, for being an angel in your own time and helping us find our breath.

We next flew to San Antonio on propellers. Here in God's country our East Coast education in buttoning our lips served us well. In San Antonio we weren't just freaks, we were rodents. The Stones were to play two days at the Teen Fair. Wood-paneled station wagons manned by off-duty good ol' boys greeted us with surly "What-the-hayul-kinda-freaks-we-got-here?" disdain. Some mellowed out when they realised we weren't "contagious or queer," but we didn't when we realised that we were due to play directly following a *grand mer* troop of performing seals. The menfolk chewed gum, cud, or 'baccy. Whilst scuffing their heels in the sand, they eyed us like bulls in heat at the idea of some pansy-quiffed matador for dinner. The more enthusiastic girls, well ... Whereas in L.A., girls just wanted to touch and be touched, down near the border they were a little more hands-on. They wanted to poke, squeal, and see if we were real.

The mood was tense. This was not turning out to be the America of anybody's dreams. For once the Stones and I didn't have much to say to each other. Something was awry and it wasn't us. We had a crisis on our hands and I needed a serious diversion - quick - that would save the moment and allow the band to get their druthers. We weren't scoring except for the sex, which wasn't going to put us high on the charts, either, except in a doctor's office on a "My dick stings when I piss, Doctor, and I'm due home in a week" basis.

How to keep the dream alive? Keep it moving!

Whilst the Stones Barnum 'n' Bailey'd, freaked 'n' geeked at the Teen Fair, I worked the phone in the downtown two-story San Antonio motel. The bookings were lackluster, with far too many days off for a three-week tour. New York and Detroit were somewhat promising, but the idea of Minneapolis, Omaha, and Harrisburg without a hit record did not bode well. We'd left our status behind in our faraway home isles. After one year of solid slogging through and finding our recording legs and then beating down the Beatles' braveheart wall by winning fans north of St.

Albans via performance, we'd jumped onto our first 505 transatlantic flight and kaleidoscoped into this crazy, half-baked, mid-sixties, partially Beatle-ised U.S.A. playland without the benefit of even Tom Wolfe. We'd made it through two pseudo-American wonderlands - the Brill-funky-Broadway of New York and the surreal beach-party mind-bend of L.A. - and now we'd been unceremoniously plunked down into this sawdust fiasco in San Antonio. In a normal life, one should have enjoyed the rest, the dust, the breeze, and the change, and given thanks for the opportunity to break bread and visit a piece of America in all its very own life-affirming, cattle-prodding, queer-baiting glory.

But I was up for, and we had time for, no such thing. Brian made some effort to be at one with the locals, but with him it was hard to tell what was real and what was an ongoing, insatiable cry for attention. Bill and Charlie put bullets in their respective guns, with Bill firing blanks at every Miss Motel America in sight and Charlie trying out some genuine six-shooters on the outskirts of town. Keith, I hoped, was writing about it, whilst Mick rested his self in the arms of Texas, writing about that (I also hoped). I starred in my own *Parallax View*, gnawing my quicks nigh onto the bone, wondering how to stop this reel from slipping the spool as I turned for assist to my old pal, the phone.

I called Phil Spector and asked him to get us booked just as soon as was possible into Chess Studios. Phil called back and said he'd set up two days of recording time, two days hence. So I was all beam and sheen when our driver, a *Cool Hand Luke* type, station-wagoned out to the fairgrounds for the last day of the Stones' troll. I wondered if somewhere behind the glare of his prison-guard reflectors he'd heard of the late Lt. Andrew Loog. If I told him that my father was from Texas, would that change anything? I doubted it. I bit my tongue, now as sore as my nails, and resisted. There wasn't any point in engaging in small talk or trying to explain what we were doing here.

To them we were stone freaks - or worse - but compared with what was to come in the Brit export line, we were more akin to Herman's Hermits. If they wanted to see themselves reflected in a distorted mirror they'd have to wait for the Sex Pistols, who would, at Randy's Rodeo just down the road some thirteen-and-a-half unlucky years later, play their third of only seven American gigs.

As I wondered whether I'd dressed down enough for the locale, I pondered why Texans seemed to only dress in denim and beige. Was it so they'd match the upholstery, the earth, ergot, barley, or sage? And why was it that these beer-pawed Texans always drove one-handed, leaving their right arm curled around the passenger seat as if it were their goddam God-given right to have someone curled up next to them? I felt too thin, wimpy, and wiry to have my potential Texan fatherhood taken seriously by these Big Bad Johns. After the long dust-filled ride over, I happily greeted the lads. We now had something really exciting to talk about - the mythical Chess studios.

All of them saw me beaming and knew something was up. "Pack your bags," I said. "There's a change in the itinerary; we're going to Chicago to record." From their all-at-once heartfelt smiles of wonder I knew that it was still worth playing God.

But playing God was just my sideline, actually. Getting records cut was my principal business. Chicago was a piece of heaven on earth for the Stones, for the earth was scorched on most of our mid-American concert stopovers. We hadn't set any records; we didn't have the goods. 2120 South Michigan Avenue housed the Chess Recording Corp. offices and studio. In two days the group put down some thirteen tracks - their most relaxed and inspired session to date - moved, no doubt, by our new found ability to sell coals to Newcastle. Who would have thought that a bunch of English kids could produce black R&B in the States? Here they were in the *sanctum sanctorum* of Chicago blues, playing in the lap of their gods. The ground-floor room was a gem, as was Chess engineer Ron Malo. He treated them just like ... musicians. The derision, jibes, and plain stupidity of the American deejay goblins were left out in the gutter. The Stones were to South Michigan Avenue born, and the session was a joy to behold.

Nothing sensational happened at Chess except the music. For those two days, the Stones were finally true blues artists, and legend has it that true blues artists didn't have producers - they just came in and got it done. I was producing the sessions in the greatest sense of the word: I had provided the environment in which the work could get done. The Stones' job was to fill up the available space correctly and this they did. This was not the session for pop suggestions; this was the place to let them be. Oh, I may have insisted on a sordid amount of echo on the underbelly figure to "It's All Over Now," but that was only ear candy to a part that was already there. I remember being impressed with the order of things, and how quietness and calm got things done. I remember meeting Leonard, and/or perhaps Phil Chess, and being cognizant of the fact that there was no suppressive Limey stymieing from the head office to the factory floor.

Truth was: Jews and blacks were equal in the Yankee nigger parade and this shared affinity showed and glowed in the music. There was no knighted vinyl baron, pin-striped and up in the clouds, no war-pensioned doorman with orders to separate the wheat from the chaff, no scum line below which the artist could sing, swim, tour, and sink. There was just a factory floor and a very relaxed combo of artists, musicians, engineers, and salesmen all at one with each other and getting the job done. I think it's called a democracy, for all its warts and whores.

It was all inspired, but one track, "It's All Over Now," would bring the Stones a little bit closer to our devoutly-wished-for consummation, the real deal - a genuine American hit.

Back on that first day of June 1964, as the Stones stomped the less-than-sweet, successless streets of New York radiolandia, one bright beacon of good faith had emerged in the form of Murray the K (as in "Kaufman," as in the "Fifth Beatle"). We were doing the radio stations and they were doing us with their relentless shards of glass and barbed witless jibes when Murray decided to adopt us, take us in tow, claim us for his very own by becoming the Sixth Stone (he hadn't been introduced to Stu, obviously). It was still the same lame game as we smiled all over Murray's WINS radio station. "Whadja think of the Beatles, guys - are you pals or rivals?" "How long since you had a haircut? Just kiddin', Murray luuuuvvves you." "I can assure my listeners, they are clean, the Stones are clean. They do wash - don't you, guys?"

Oh, just play the fuckin' record and announce the concert date so we can piss off. Murray was a shard above the rest. He'd decided that if we were good enough for the Beatles, we were good enough for Murray. We were getting there the hard way. These first American tours would be the Rolling Stones' Hamburg. For me there'd be no more time for the Soho sweetness of *Expresso Bongo*, or the Shetland social games of the French New Wave and

Les Cousins and *Le beau Serge*. The Stones and I were working in the coal mine. The Brill Building didn't house J.J. Hunsecker in its penthouse. Columbus found America by mistake; we found it through songs.

Murray the K done for the day, Keith and I headed for a shopping foray into the upper seventies on Madison Avenue. Most of the clobber was not for us (in dollars or sense), just an American attempt to copy the look we'd left behind where, it had to be said, it was done better. New York's Upper East Side version of that English look was bland and expensive. The waists on the tweed jackets hinted at a cut and flair that didn't deliver. The stitching screamed "machined in Michigan" and the brogues were pure day-off Dixon of Dock Green. But the walk was swell and we enjoyed our peek at the vanities on money'd Mad Avenue.

Tucked into the 68th St. corner, where in years to come Jackie Rogers would give good fashion, was an austere gold-leaf painted jewelers that discreetly allowed - via handwritten window cards - that they dealt in estate jewelry.

"Ah, dead people's stuff," said Keith as I ogled a huge crested beauty of a ring with my name all over it.

With Keith, my worthy henchman, I hastily attempted to enter the premises, to no avail. The door was locked. I'd started politely knuckling the windowed portion of the door when a chinless vino-vein'd troll in his fifties shoved his pink bulldog features though t'other side of pane, and with *faux hauteur* pointed toward the bell to be used to request entry.

I rang the bell and pointed to the ring on the velvet tray on the left. The frail bulldog pursed his leprous lips and gestured, "No." He was a creature out of E.C. Comics, a crazed boneyard dog cursed from fondling the jewelry of the deceased.

"No, what?" I wondered, "No, we're closed? No, it's not for sale? No, we just put it in the window to frustrate punters the likes of you?" Then we got the true meaning of the no. "No, we're not letting you in our shop. We are not used to high boot-heeled, jean'd, and drainpiped, button-down striped shirt'd, waistcoated topped with British Railways peaked caps and happy-gait urchins asking to come in. And there's two of you ... you might kill us." Welcome to the swingin' sixties, baby!

I wanted that ring, wanted it badly. In a state of aroused

telepathy I could read the thoughts leaking out of his filigreed mind. Little sepulchral mummies were lipsynching, "How do we know you have any money?" I pulled out about one hundred bucks and flashed it. I kept pointing at the ring whilst attempting to shovel the cash through the knee-high mailbox as a show of intent. The runt on the other side went down on his knees in an attempt to stop my cash from soiling his shop, tut-tutting, getting more flustered, more veined and pink, and with his free or drinking hand attempting to wave Keith and me away.

"Fuck him," said Keith. I agreed, but I still wanted the crested royal knuckle-duster. I let the lower half of the door have it with an instep-propelled smack of my Anello and Davide boot. Had I been Jimmy Greaves I'd have definitely scored a goal on that one. The pinstriped leech jumped back aghast, visibly shocked by this quick turn to violence, and pantomimed picking up the phone as if to call the police

"You fuckin' marzipan poof reject," I offered, or something of the sort.

Keith rebel-yelled, gave the world the finger, laughed, took me by the arm, and guided me away.

As we giggled and crossed Madison arm-in-arm in the direction of the park, Keith yelled over our shoulders to the few onlookers that had gathered to view the kick-in (and had been joined on the pavement by the newly brave, still tut-tutting salesman).

"Cunts!"

I felt better and, buoyed by Keith, less like one.

We grabbed some hasty victuals from the hot dog stand on the corner of 5th, then cabbed west across the park and back into our own Holly Golightly world to attend a Bob Crewe party in our honour. The yellow stretch cab wheeled out of the park at 72nd across Central Park West and let us out at the austere and majestic granite entrance to the Dakota. Four short sixties-filled years later, the building would become infamous for housing Roman Polanski's *Rosemary's Baby*. Sixteen-and-a-half years on, it would be the site of the killing of John Lennon. Keith and I asked for "Bob Crewe, please." The rest of the Stones were already there. Bob's apartment was a film set, all ornate mod-Roman gay splendor over the park - marbled floors, bronzed Ma Bell's, African-motif zebra and leopard throw rugs, and enough brocade, tassel, and gilt to assure you that you weren't visiting John Huston. The living room sunk down to a waist-high setting with an aqua-Nero motif, complete with statues of nubile youth that gushed water. Bob Crewe was Doris Day, if Doris Day had been all man and had stayed gorgeous. Leonard Bernstein chatted with actor/neighbour Robert Ryan, who asked Mick if he knew Terence Stamp, whom he'd worked with two years before on *Billy Budd*. Mick didn't or wouldn't. Lenny B. and Ryan turned away from Jagger and resumed discussing elevator problems at the Dakota. Bob Crewe was above it all and flying. Ahmet Ertegun looked diplomatically dapper. He didn't make a play for the Stones, but it did look as if he'd made one for Liza Minnelli. She wondered if we'd met her mother. I had.

One of Bob's guest rooms (named Africa) housed our old mate Lionel Bart, who had introduced me to Liza's mum Judy Garland a month before in London. The living room filled with more famous Yanks and friendly English faces. My host's ability to spin such a night in such sumptuous surroundings summoned none-too-flattering comparisons between Bob's situation and my own. Bob Crewe produced the Four Seasons; I produced and co-managed the Rolling Stones. Whilst I was living in a one-bedroom, rented, furnished flatlet opposite the Regent's Park Zoo and Primrose Hill, he was lording it up in a six-room complete with sunken living room overlooking Central Park. He had his offices on the sixth floor of a slate peninsula on West 60th that overlooked Columbus Circle and Central Park South. Atlantic Records had its digs in the same building, and next door was Morris Levy and his rumoured Mafia-driven Roulette Records. Meanwhile, over the ocean, my partner Tony Calder and I made an otherwise drab block of Baker Street flats our office, graced by visits from various Stones. Things were livened up by the presence of the quietly mad Roy Moseley on the floor above, and the quite mad Kit Lambert and Chris Stamp, managers of the Who, etc., who had taken over a flat on a lower floor. I mulled over the discrepancies between *chez* Crewe and *chez* yours truly, my envy well-concealed up my sleeve so as not to invade my well-being.

Sometime during the evening, Murray the K pulled me to one side and put a 45 single between my hand and his. Murray stood out in these svelte surroundings, grey-blue straw titfer atop his hair replacement and ghastly tangerine skin. He was wearing a Cadillac-upholstery-coloured Teflon sweater with winkle pickers that set off fuchsia-flamed trews that wouldn't even pass for wallpaper in Slough. Murray had no shame, but was master of his game ... pop kingmaker.

He backed me against the wall, both of us still holding the 45, his free hand gripping my beige suede-jacketed elbow.

"Andy, I love the guys; I think they are fabulous. I know the Beatles love 'em too - George told me so. I don't go out of my way for many people, y'know, but I'm promoting the hell out of them - you're gonna sell tickets. The Stones are special. I really like them."

This rotund puck of pop caught his breath and allowed me time to acknowledge this outpouring.

"Murray, they like you too," was all I could muster.

"They *do*?" He came back at me, smiling vices. "Great. I could feel it, especially Brian, real straight guy, sweetheart, really genuine. Mick too. Listen, Andy, I don't often do this, and I promise you, forget whatever you've heard - I don't want anything for it, I just love this business we're in, and that's the truth of it. Don't want no freebies, no B-sides."

He paused and grinned - this was pure pop oxymoronic air we were breathing. "All I want," he continued, "is to know that whenever the guys play New York - and you will, often, I promise - you have ol' Murray the K behind you now, you're gonna be big ..." (The wonderful thing about America, I somehow found time to think, is you have nothing to do with getting there. Other people do it for you, and you are merely beholding, beholding - left holding the bag.) Murray, meanwhile, droned on, "Anyway, all I want is that Murray here is the only disc jockey who M.C.s your New York shows, and ..." - Murray pushed me further against the Africa-motif'd wall - "... you and the guys remember Murray when those cocksuckers put me down ... and they will, just you remember."

America was turning into beads of sweat trickling from questionable hairlines, and Paul Simon was still Tom of Tom and Jerry. I felt the vinyl; now it was all in mine. "Feel what's in your hand, Andy. It's yours; it's for you and the boys. Just take it home and record it. I guarantee it. Murray guarantees it, babe. I just gave you your very first American hit." He had, and God Bless America, Land of a Thousand Dances. I'd just gone to the perfect party and gotten laid by the perfect partner, Murray the K. Bob Crewe beamed knowingly from the other side of the room and raised his glass in a welcome-to-the-good-ship-lollipop salute whilst musical guest Tiny Tim entertained guests with that and other ditties from another room. The 45 that Murray the K had left in my hand was the Bobby-and-Shirley-Womack-composed, Sam-Cooke-SAR-labeled, Valentinos-recorded, breaking-out-black-but-not-white-in-the-Midwest-and-South smasharoonie, "It's All Over Now." As recorded ten days later at Chess in Chicago, it would take the Stones into the American top thirty a couple of months hence for the very first time.

Two weeks earlier on the West Coast whilst the Stones tackled San Bernardino, I'd tackled music publisher's row south of Sunset Boulevard, searching for that perfect piece of song that would put a parachute in our recording plane. I'd listened to a lot of airbag-vomit-inducing ditties. America was in the throes of Beatle recovery, and nine out of ten songs emoted variations on feeling fine, pleasing everybody from me to you, and hey-hey-hey. Seymour Stein in New York had introduced me in the Brill Building to Jerry Leiber, who had shown his disdain for the Rolling Stones' R&B proficiency by suggesting we cover Alvin Robinson's Red Bird outing, "Down Home Girl." We did. Sonny Bono and I cruised into the parking lot of a one-story thirties hacienda on the south side of Sunset in his Caesar-and-Cleo-trunk-filled maroon convertible. We breezed and smiled our way through a reception full of friendly faces and into the offices of Liberty and Imperial Records and its publishing arm, Metric Music, which had handled the breathtaking Bono-and-Jack-Nitzsche-penned "Needles and Pins" (as sanctified by Jackie DeShannon on the Liberty label). Oh lord, don't let me be misunderstood. Film sets merged with real life, and I was home.

Please recall that, up to a month earlier, my experience of record companies had been via surly, uniformed doormen and wish-thee-nothing resentful drip-dry average-clad civil servants umbrella'd by a couple of ingenious well-clad robber barons, Sir Edward Lewis and Sir Joseph Lockwood, respectively of Decca and EMI. But the Liberty/Imperial/Metric machine was all beige, stucco, and tanned - it purred and relaxed in true Johnny Stompanato/West Coast mode. The Liberty company had been started in the late fifties when Al Bennett left his gig at Randy Wood's Dot

label and, together with the Skaff brothers (Bob and Phil) and Sy
Warnocker, formed it. They were a smash out of the box with their
first release, "Witch Doctor," by David Seville, who later gifted Liberty
and a lot of the world's children, mine included, with Alvin and
the Chipmunks. Once they had thrust and parried with pressing,
selling, and getting paid, Liberty settled into becoming one of the
major independents. Eddie Cochran, Johnny Burnette, Timi Yuro,
Martin Denny, Julie London, Jackie DeShannon, Sandy Nelson,
Gene McDaniels, the Olympics, Johnny Rivers, the Ventures, Fats
Domino, Ricky Nelson, Bobby Vee, the Teddy Bears, the Fleetwoods,
Jan and Dean, and the Chipmunks were some of the Liberty/Im-
perial acts that helped to seal the deal for a successful and diverse
independent record company. A&R was headed by the impeccable
Snuff Garrett, whose marriage of Bobby Vee with Goffin and King
and other Aldon Music/Lou Adler West-Coast-helmed writers
gave Liberty a rousing run of pop anthems in the first three years
of the sixties.

It was a great big world becoming miraculously smaller and
more accessible. The ease with which I was welcomed at Liberty
amazed me. It was a far cry from East Coast rudeness masquerad-
ing as style and flare. No one was scared; everybody shared. (I am
leaving Phil Spector out of this analogy, it having become apparent
on spending time with him in the States that he was already heading
for the hills. In addition to releasing the Teddy Bears via Imperial,
Spector produced and mixed quite a few Liberty/Imperial dar-
lings like Timi Yuro, although uncredited for doing so before he
headed east.)

In a side room I met Tommy LaPuma, who worked with the
writers signed to Metric Music. Tommy, a short, jovial man whom
a circa-*Taxi* Danny DeVito would have had no problem portraying,
played me some appalling results of Beatlemania on West Coast
songwriters - even the likes of Randy Newman wanted to hold your
hand. We fast-forwarded through more well-meaning drivel. Then,
up came a white-labeled Imperial 45 bearing the artist's name, Irma
Thomas, and her devastating recording via Jerry Ragavoy (as "Norman Meade") of "Time is on My Side." Yes, it was my good fortune
to hear God two times on this first tour: once when the Valentinos
literally jumped out of the grooves and into our path with "It's All
Over Now," and twice when Irma beamed "Time is on My Side"

my way. All that was needed in the case of those last two songs was devoted apostles to pick up the mantle. White boys' will be done, as it is on radio and in America.

That languid L.A. afternoon, Sonny Bono had some Chering to do, so Tommy LaPuma took me to meet Bob Krasnow. Bob was and always would be a great record man. At the time he worked for Syd Nathan's King Records, home of James Brown. Bob would run Blue Thumb Records with LaPuma and, later, Elektra Records on his tod, where I would pick up with him again in the eighties on my last New York run. Tommy drove me to somewhere in some valley to meet Bob, talk more about "Time is on My Side," and get stoned ... very stoned. Thus far my number one smoking pleasure had been opiated hash, very mellow and very much a body, as opposed to a mind, high. At Krasnow's we talked and talked, and suddenly I got legless and could barely walk, tell the time, or listen to "Time is on My Side" without sliding into delta-9 time. I became paranoid for the first time in my life, and for no other reason but that the jane was playing with my brain. A second unwanted movie was running in my mind. I had no control over the screenplay and the improvisations were getting out of control.

Around seven I left the jovial Krasnow and LaPuma, Bob waving goodbye like a beaming Buddha, wishing me luck on the drive back to our motel on the Strip. My last thought as I tried to follow the widening chasm in my mind's road was, "I think I've got it ... 'Time is on My Side' is the answer, if I ever get back to the Sunset Strip alive." I arrived at the Landmark Motel dazed but in one piece, my mind slowly gathering itself. A little bud called Flo, who looked more like Chris Rock than Pam Grier, had been waiting poolside for my return. Halter-topped, she slipped that off and slipped me inside her before I could say a word. The attraction was, apparently, not so much my looks as my accent: When I spoke she got excited. She was sweet and young fun that summer of '64, but by the next tour when I fell into her again she was stoned and dazed and caught in the waste of dying. She remains a sweet memory, doth Flo. I got off the plane in London mid-morning and stopped off in Harley Street before going to the flat to make sure my dick wouldn't sting Sheila when I got it home.

****

It was the winter of 1970. We'd wrung out our own versions of the
sixties and a lot of things had changed. It was as if some malign
curse had been put upon that once-unstoppable decade. Ghosts,
famous long ago, now haunted the streets. Walking south on 7th
Avenue down from Carnegie Hall in front of a most bizarre hand-
bag shop, I passed two bums, two paper carrier bags apiece, in
old and matching sneakers, twenty-dollar fifties-tweed raglan'd-
shouldered overcoats, mottled and frayed wool caps and scarves,
and not a smile between them. They both had that faraway look
that frequently comes with the shattering collision of looks-like-
meth dreams and reality. As we walked along, my companion
caught me studying their aura for signs of story, of a life. He asked
me if I knew who the two were. I didn't. He said they were James
Rado and Gerome Ragni, he said, the creators of *Hair*, a musical
once considered revolutionary and innovative but, to my taste,
recycled theatrical air with hair and nudity. The two "bums" looked
frazzled and shattered. Their eyes told of a thousand losses as
they trudged along, clutching their bags the way they had once
clasped hope to their bosoms. I mindfilmed that forlorn Age of
Aquarius moment with Messrs. Rado and Ragni and walked on.

Sometimes it was I who was the ghost. On that Aquarian-
haunted corner, as I strode my block on a perfectly cast fall day in
the early eighties, outside the Russian Tea Room I spied a well-
fed, prime-fine-looking Michael Caine. We had met a couple of
times in the sixties - Hadn't we all? - but, mindful of Caine's busier
and more people-filled itinerary the past twenty years and to save
the fellow from searching through his mind to locate my mug, I
was happy to reintroduce myself with "Hallo, Michael. Andrew
Oldham. How are you?" Given the cue, Mr. Caine did a perfect
take. He pulled himself up an unneeded extra inch by clutching
the collar of his dapper double-breasted navy-blue overcoat,
sucked in the air, rosie'd up his face for the close-up and hit his
mark. "Andrew!" he chimed, "So good to see you - keeping well?"
His eyes blinkrated to zero as he realised there was no need for
an answer. "Just fine, Michael," I said anyway. "Living here now."
"Jolly good," Caine soldiered on: "How are the lads?" The lads, I
thought, how are the fuckin' lads? My hackles bristled. Climb down,
laddie, I told myself. He's just put your mug together with its
reference and hasn't updated his mind's Filofax yet. There's no

offence here, you twit, he's just trying to be polite. "How are the lads?" "Oh, just great, Michael. Everybody's just fine." My reading of the line must have been perfect, because Caine breathed a sigh of relief. This could be a take, after all. "Oh, great, good to hear that. Say hallo to Mick for me. Good to see ya, Andrew." Michael slapped my arm in camaraderie, braced himself up the unneeded inch again, locked eyes for a reverse angle shot, turned left, and strode on up 57th. I recovered - kind of.

Those days a chance encounter with a friendly acquaintance could be most disturbing, leaving my body screaming for relief and my mind diving for the grinder, without which one could say goodbye to the rest of the day. If I hadn't been in the nick I was in, I'd have learnt a valuable, time-saving lesson that day at the school of Caine, instead of later. "How are the lads?" Hmmmm ... point made, taken later. Much later.

****

On a brisk autumn day in London in '74 I found myself dodging taxis with a good pal, the late Ron Kass. In the early seventies Ron had left Apple Records and was living a wonderful world in London, married to the actress Joan Collins and running the U.K. Warner Brothers discery. It was somewhat to Ron, and less than is thought to Colombia, that I owe my entry into the long year's night of the marching powders. Oh, I'd said hallo to the lady before, but I'd never slept over.

We were striding across the Strand heading for the Savoy for a meet with Shep Gordon, Alice Cooper's manager. Ron handed me a small brown vial with the words, "You bring it out, Andrew, it'll look better coming from you." "It," we established, was cocaine. I did indeed bring it out, and later thought what a nice way this is to do business. After his death from cancer, I was somewhat surprised to read Joan Collins's claim that she'd had no idea that hubby Ron had been partial to drugs. During her *Dynasty* run I'd taken two Colombian gentlemen (who certainly didn't look like 20th Century Fox executives) to the Century City pad shared by her and Ron. None of us ate; we all had the snivels, sweated in coke rote munchies, and eyed the bathroom as if it were going to disappear. I had visited Ron and Joan on an earlier occasion for

an English Sunday roast. This was long before Joan's *Dynasty* success had her leave Blighty, and before her sexy potboilers, *The Bitch*
and *The Stud*, based on her sister Jackie's books, allowed the grand
dame to rise forever against England's mudraking view of her. She
was not at all worried about us going AWOL in the loo, Joan being
the champion at loo decor. Both their Century City pad of the eighties
and their seventies "purple belt" Surrey cottage were stocked with
every one of Joan's magazine covers since her uncredited 1951 debut
in *Lady Godiva Rides Again* (a.k.a. *Bikini Baby*). Back at Century City
the Colombians and I continued to admire Miss Collins as we all
cut across each other's sentences, grinding funky to the bone with
the coca-plus of laughing at jokes before we'd got to the punchline.
The t-bone was served, but just got cold as we looked at it. The
salad kept it company. Perhaps Joan thought we were all dieting.

At this 1970s time Ron was attempting to restore some financial dignity to the life of chum Lionel Bart, who'd been staying
at Cap D'Antibes with friends, had broken his arm, and was in
need of a pal. It was a long way from the late fifties/early sixties
pop-hit-a-week via Tommy Steele, Cliff Richard, *Fings Aint Wot*
They Used t' Be, and Lionel's jewel in the crown, *Oliver!* This Lionel,
who had made Marianne Faithfull possible for me by financing
the session, had bet the farm (as in his *Oliver!* royalties) on a few
new shows, *Maggie May* (1964), *Twang!* (1965), and *La Strada* (1969),
and lost. With Sean Kenny there had been many attempts to catch
the wind - *Quasimodo, Gulliver's Travels* - but fame was a daft mistress to Lionel. He was down in the dumps and was probably getting the message that the body would only take so much more
abuse in search of its owner's next national anthem. So, at Ron's
behest, I'd headed, kind of gladly, for my old stomping ground,
the Cote d'Azur, perhaps to recharge my own batteries in the land
where so much had begun for me, where Lionel had once been
pearly king and queen of the Croisette catwalk in Larry-Parnes-
and-*Oliver!* days gone by. The ride from the Nice airport was
breezy and balmy. I felt invigorated by the soothing evening air,
my very being ecstatic as I looked back through the rear window
of the taxi at the same view Cary Grant had Grace Kelly'd all those
VistaVision turns ago in Hitchcock's *To Catch a Thief*, the route
where it had all begun for me.

How had I managed to turn it all into this sour stench of

success? Still clad with verve I managed to pull it off on occasion, but, had it not been for my eternal optimism, I would surely have been as worn out as the Lionel Bart I was about to meet. It was no longer about fashion. It was about fading fables, the inability to participate and produce. I'll say rather the "*near* sour stench of success," as I was still managing to stay just above the fray. "The smell of opium is more agreeable than the smell of success," Graham Greene had written on the same Antibes patch for his *Ways of Escape.*

I was very lucky to have left England in 1970 for the calm and anonymity of Connecticut, where I was able to find some respite before the self-induced storm. I had left behind two failed marriages, the first (as I saw it then) to the Stones, and the second to Sheila - a double marriage that had been borderline bigamy. I had remained a child and fled my very own, whom I could not even remember holding. The scarecrow of my soul, Dr. Luke McLoughlin (Dr. Mac), did his best to calm my beasts with a hamperful of drug mixtures, electric shock treatment, and truth serums designed to drive out the demons and stop me from stepping on any more mental landmines. In sum total all this did was allow me a reasonable tan. Underneath I was very pale, wan, and alone. I'd forgotten what an intimate hug felt like, but was too chemically blocked and cold to realise it. I made do with the comfort of pals, a joint, a brilliant idea never worked on in the morning, and a drink or four. Moving to Connecticut had been good and had soothed my well-tempered madness for a while. Until, that is, I attempted to re-enter the fray.

Just before we left England for Connecticut, I got a card in the mail from the U.K. tax office asking me to send "by return of post 600,000 pounds." Sure, I thought, in coins if I had it. We had all spent so much time, and here I include the Rolling Stones, staying on top of our game and keeping seemingly abreast of the Beatles, that we had forgot to run the store. My monthly grocery bills in Richmond were £900, let's not get into the cars, doctors, and drugs. It's as old as Michaelangelo begging for advances whilst painting the Sistine Chapel, Dean Martin selling 140% of himself to dodge the dons, and our own rock 'n' roll era where our accountants changed from suits to golf clothes and we didn't hear when they told us that 83% of what we made would be required in U.K.

tax with a further third off the top for Uncle Sam.

It has been said that it was in the interests of those who represented us to leave us without a safe harbour to return to. Doesn't really matter, we were not about safe harbours, we were sailing and on the road. To add to my personal problems, I had started Immediate Records in 1965 and, although it had a nice run of hits, most of which were more than bought into the charts, it created a run on my money and by 1970 that went bust. Woody Allen said later, "Cocaine is God's way of telling you you have too much money," With me it was Immediate Records. I packed my bags and left for Connecticut; the Stones packed theirs and left for the south of France. Twenty-six is the wrong age to leave your country under the soiled umbrella of being recast as a "tax exile." It's to this day stopped a total embrace with the island I just happened to have been born in. I was miserable, loaded, and bad company in Connecticut. I hung with ne'er-do-wells who made magnificent leather goods but bought the farm by putting their earnings into drug-running then crashing their plane into a field. I could only abide junkies and drunks, as each day I wavered between the two. I existed on Stouffer's packaged beef stew, vodka, pot, and American TV. I may have allowed conversation duing the commercials. I could not handle cinemas or restaurants; they involved people. I was in freebase behaviour well before the coming of rage of that particular drug. I hung with a 400-pound kosher American gorilla who had to sit sideways in the front seat in order to drive his very big Cadillac. It made whoever was in the passenger seat a very captive audience. Irwin had been an interrogator for the U.S. Army during the Vietnam War; he never denied the story that he'd take two Vietcong up in a helicopter and throw the first one out in the expectation of getting something out of the remaining one. In one of my many separations and legal bouts with Sheila, rather than hire a lawyer, I hired Irwin. Sheila had a boyfriend/lawyer who allowed her to feel inappropriately brave. Irwin chased the lawyer man down the street in his Caddy, waving a gun at the short-distance runner whilst asking me, "Andrew, shall I shoot?" I just giggled. I may have asked Irwin to fire off a couple of rounds in the general vicinity of running heels. Irwin was killed at the beginning of the nineties in an East Side Italian place whilst he contemplated a plate of pasta. Sheila says that by the end of Connecticut it took her ten years to recover and, by the time she returned to England alone, she could hardly speak a word.

That was in 1974. I was still getting over leaving the Stones, and attempting to deal with the thought that at thirty I might have shot my load. I had bought into and was living in my own well-heeled abyss. I spent the early seventies recording 4-F Crosby, Stills, Nash, and Anybody wanna-bes whom I'd swept off Connecticut village greens and whom, I had convinced the white guys running Motown, were the next Crosby, Stills, Nash, Young, and Joni Mitchell combined. They were not. I was drinking and detained often enough to be able to give you the floor plans of Connecticut's best jails. The most dangerous thing about money seems to have been its ability to get charges for reckless driving under the influence of drugs and/or alcohol reduced to driving in the wrong lane or failing to observe a state highway notice. Which DUI it was could not be determined; I couldn't pee. I had just started taking coke, and thought it wasn't taking me. I had settled in the rolling hills of Connecticut and caught every *ABC Movie of the Week*, *Mod Squad*, *Columbo*, and *Harry O* for nigh on four years. Nothing wrong with that. For those raised on the very frugal U.K. TV rations, American TV was cathode heaven on earth. I ventured out on occasion and partied in the Hills of Beverly. I looned in somebody's garden, lined up marching powder on a sundial in the night for Ringo and Peter Sellers. I complained about the sixties and Ringo told me off. All the grinning Goon could say was: "Oh, I do love doing drugs with you rock people!"

Back East, I sat on my tod in my 450 Merc looking down on my land, and I cried. Fuck "Hey Jude," I thought, I have to make this better. So I packed and flew to London, my time in tax exile up. I hustled a glam cry-bi guy, Brett Smiley, to Ian Ralfini's Anchor Records and sold a talented Duncan Browne to Ron Kass. Duncan I had first recorded in 1968. The result, "Give Me, Take You," is well-remembered, but did not sell well at the time. He'd garner some singles success with Mickie Most before we took another crack at it in '74. Duncan, who died very prematurely of cancer in 1993, remains one of the artists I was proudest to stand in a room with and watch evolve. Brett Smiley was a fine writer with a multi-destructive lifestyle to write about, which he did well. I had come across Brett after a Detroit trip that had me meet Russ

Gibb, entrepreneurial educator extraordinaire. Russ pointed me in the direction of Brett, who was not far from his arm. I recalled pal Jerry Brandt's adventures with Elektra/Asylum Records over Jobriath in 1972-73, and figured, "My fag's not real, I've got the real deal, I can do this better." That was pure seventies-speak and finally not true for either Herr Brandt or myself, although we'd both had fun getting it done. Jerry's problem may have been dealing with David Geffen, who'd once worked under him in the mail room at William Morris. My problem may have been that I'd never worked in the mail room.

I hired a suite in the Hotel Pierre and had the walls adorned with large Gered Mankowitz blow-ups of Brett (who, in person, was getting on my nerves). I sat there for four days on room service, hope, and blow, waiting for Ian Ralfini to call and say I'd got a deal. He did, and I was free at last to hustle London once again.

I'd met Russ Gibb at L.B.'s. I'd met L.B. because John Lennon had told me in New York, "Andrew, when you're in Detroit, stop off for some free sushi and coke at L.B.'s. He's this great old queen dealer who'll give you anything you want; all ya gotta do is have your picture taken with him." I did call and stop by, got high, and indeed a duly snapped Lennon was beaming down from up on the wall of *fua* (cocaine) and fame. I made a friendship with L.B. that continued long after they shipped him off to jail. He'd been shopped by one of his musclebound young drivers named Charles, who chauffeured the coke north from Texas in a one-headlighted Rolls with a little old grandma in *Beverly Hillbillies* dressed-up mode sitting aback as decoy. Charles decided to take over the farm and retire L.B. to jail and pasture. I communicated with L.B. at his new Terre Haute, Indiana digs and attempted to be conciliatory and Zen about his fate. "No need, Andrew," L.B. wrote back, "I go bareback riding on horses and boys at least three times a week. It's heaven. I'm in a great retirement home where finally the drugs and the boys are free."

So I turned up on the Cap d'Antibes doorstep of Lionel Bart's hosts, and hugged the man. I didn't much like what I saw. Li's hosts, his "English Pals," were treating him like the village invalid, the Jew of Pooh Corner. They were enjoying the game of "giving a helping hand to poor ol' needy Li" far too much. They were treating him as a pet, a curious mascot, which is what they saw him as. It was obvious his spirits were in need of a lift and a move. "Enough of this, Lionel," I rallied and prescribed a change of scenery. "Pack yer bag but rest the arm. What you need is some room service and a friendly hotel." Perhaps I was speaking for us both. I drove us into Cannes, the Croisette, and the Hotel Martinez. An hour or two later things were much improved. Lionel was buoyed by the "Good to see you, Meester Bart!" chorus that greeted him from the older attending farts and the eager-to-serve display of hotel trainees brimming with youth and promise.

Once ensconced, Lionel and I stood on the balcony of our double Med-facing suite, enjoying the calm and nursing two *jus de framboise*, looking down at the strolling early evening Croisette tourist fair. With my chameleon nature I found myself drifting into Lionel's play, early Jewish drawing room Noël Coward. "Here, Ang, that's not bad," sighed Lionel. "What's not bad, Li?" I enquired, enjoying the *jus de framboise* cut-glass container reflecting the evening light through the empty half - a light show of night blues sharding against a fierce Mediterranean maroon. "Them," replied Lionel, pointing downwards toward a group of boisterous, tanned, short-trousered, Aryan lads. This was all I needed - a one-armed Hebe hot to trot for Nazi fare attempting to requisition yours truly as his pimp. "No, they're not bad looking at all, Ang. While I fix my arm a bit why don't you go down and suss 'em out? See if they want some of my raspberry juice." I looked over at Lionel to see if he was serious or pulling my leg. "You gotta be kidding, Lionel, look at the size of those butch fucks. And besides, I don't even speak German." I protested, Lionel sulked, his fine black devil's-peak hairdo crouched over the forehead, a still-spoilt kid who'd had it all and wanted seconds. His expressive eyes winked and resumed play: "Go on, Ang - if Terry Stamp was here he'd do it for me," he challenged. Well, I thought, Tel wasn't here and I wasn't about to, so Lionel just brooded in his raspberry juice.

****

By July 1964, the first Rolling Stones tour of America was over. I'd checked out my errant member, post-Flo, and was about to make the huge mistake with Sheila of apologising for not being there for her by marrying her. Back at the manor of the heart, Celia remained both aloof from my early rumblings of success, first as a publicist, then as a manager/producer, and unconvinced about my ability to make my way and be happy with my good lot. She accepted my enthusiasm about the Rolling Stones and my excitement about Marianne Faithfull's potential, but hoped I would not get "stars in my eyes and end up disappointed." Unavoidable, mother dear, but I would come out the other end.

Back in the mum-fighting days of '63 Celia had no doubts about what my life should be. Her idea of what happened when you didn't stick to the straight and narrow was the fate of our upstairs neighbour at 19 Netherhall Gardens, Frank Norman, the East End con and gadabout who had breezed into show biz, cracked open the safe to the la-de-dahs of the flush 'n' flash punters, and gained his freedom with his 1958 book, *Bang to Rights*, and the Bart-tuned, Norman-written, Kenny-designed, Littlewood-assembled triumph, *Fings Aint Wot They Used t' Be*. Frank had moved up to the dry side of Hampstead Heath. It was on the other side, north of Sheila's, where the real villains lived and wet their beaks.

My mother did not have much time for Frank's nightly bird-pulling *esprit*. I, however, greatly admired the man, his leer at life, and the fact that he didn't attempt to drink, drive, and the rest. My ground-floor bedroom faced the street and I'd lain there many times, with a smile to the ceiling, listening to the familiar sequence of sounds of the night - taxi chugs up the hill, stops or stalls on the corner, Frank falls out, and bird comes tumbling after. Frank picks himself up and puts on the charm, bird laughs - sometimes it's a cackle - that is picked up in the evening echo. Frank chuckles, high heels climb the steps, key finds its way into lock, there's a thumpety-thump over my head as Frank and dolly climb to his room at the top. I'd often hear one last long-distance laugh or leer that would let me know Frank was home. "What's he really got?" my mother would harp on. "Every night he comes home drunk in a taxi. He's very pleasant, mind you, always civil. Alone or with a different girl each night; it's not a life, Andy." Oh, how she willed it so, and bit her tongue perhaps as she thought back to when she was young and footloose in her pre-Andy days as a World War II hope-and-glory wild child, when it might have been her I heard outside my bedroom wall, laughing and giddy as the Frank Norman of her day tried to fit his key into her front door.

Of the Rolling Stones, Keith was her favourite. Once when I asked her and pressed for a reason she explained, "Well, you can see that Keith has a good heart ... and he likes dogs." So does Bill, Mother, I wanted to say, but didn't. What had endeared Keith to my mother, apart from his honesty, was my recounting how Keith and I had bypassed the U.K. quarantine laws by smuggling a puppy into England via Heathrow from Los Angeles in a hatbox with holes punched into it for breathing space. The puppy stayed docile throughout the long flight as we'd shared our valium with it. I left out the details of how Keith and I had come across the dog, saying simply, "A fan gave it to us," leaving out the fact that the fan was Flo, the haltered, poolside, heaving young Negrita that Keith and I had both bedded. Alas, Flo had a screw loose and suddenly turned on us, flailing at us with a kitchen knife, catching and nicking me before Keith disarmed her. Later, after she calmed down, she felt bad about the knife wielding, good about the heaving, and just before we were to leave L.A. she stopped off at our motel and gifted Keith with the puppy.

My mother had been telling me that Keith was her favourite ever since she'd come for tea at the temporary office I'd set up at the Mayfair Hotel in mid-1966. A lot went on at the Mayfair. It was there Mick and Marianne first settled on each other and the Rolling Stones furthered their rep as the great unwashed. The Mayfair staff confused the constant reek of hashish emanating out of the three suites as our own special brand of body odor. "What about the others?" I asked my mother. "Well," she said, inspecting her hands once more for wear and tear, pursing her lips to ensure the same whilst calling to mind the others: "Brian is an odd lot. I don't think he likes you, Andrew. There's something not quite right about him. Charlie and Bill are the only normal ones amongst you, so I suppose that's why you've got no time for them. And as for you three, I think you are all a little touched. I don't know what you find so funny all the time." Well, life was (and I wasn't smoking in front of Celia yet).

She kept away from Jagger as a solo subject. He was something she'd rather forget ever since he'd stayed over one night in late December back in '63. Mick and I had spent a lot of time together - as did Mick, Keith, and I from the time I followed them to 33 Mapesbury Road in early '64. Mick was developing nicely;

he already had a grab-on instinct. Now he was about study, spit, and polish as I pressed him into the responsibilities to come, as front man to both the world and the Rolling Stones. Off the road he was as busy as on, doing phone and solo in-person interviews, calling folks to thank them for the interviews done, all to the extent that we both had one major thought and action in mind - *viz.*, to propel the Stones juggernaut. One of his major roles was simply that of being seen around, checking how effectively my image-beaming of the Stones was penetrating the clubs. I would use Mick, on his social nights out, whilst he was at his most seemingly innocent and coy, to find out how their image in the myth garden was growing - as in, were people treating him any differently as a result of what had been in the papers, and what, generally, was the Stones buzz of the moment? Mick was a poll-taker working under the guise of being one of the chaps. Mick as Best Pal - an endearing sight. He'd be out with Chrissie Shrimpton, would affect surprise about any new Stones gossip that came his way, and, if questioned about any of our more outrageous plants, would pass the buck, saying, "Oh, that Andrew!" then gleefully report back to me that the ploy had hit its mark. Our days started and ended on one subject: the Rolling Stones.

On the night in question, he had come back from some ballroom show, was more than a little blitzed, not up to much social contact, having shagged himself out on the road. Shortly after 2:00 a.m. we ended up at my mother's flat in Netherhall Gardens, taking tea and talking life through, as earnest young things are born to do, though quietly, so as not to wake mother. I'd already mastered the holding and placing of cup and saucer in sink in silence and could mime "another cuppa" clearly. We would talk ourselves into the bravura of protective armor we'd need to wear to confront those in our way. "We Can Change the World!" was the mantra of the day; the universal law and order would come later. After that other cuppa and an hour or so of gabbing over tomorrows, Mick was in no mood to get off the chair, get himself together, or go anywhere. I told him to forget about leaving and to come and sleep in my room. "You're right," Mick's Shetland-clad puma frame sighed, accepted my hand, and followed me to my room. "Just a few hours; I've really had it," Mick rationalised to the shadows on the wall, and the floor creaked in agreement. We'd both really had it; we overslept, and more. My mother went to work shortly before eight-thirty without bothering to check on me, leaving me to sleep. I had been in need of kip more than I knew, and Mick was dead to the world.

My mother came back from work just on four-thirty in the afternoon, and, not knowing whether I was there or not, she came into my room - during the day my door was usually open. I came to with a start, my mother at the head of the bed focused not on me but the sleeping Mick on the other side of the bed. "Mummy," I said in the shock of seeing her there. "We worked late ... what time is it?" It being deep winter, it was now as dark outside as it had been nearly light when we got to sleep. The verbals brought a little life to Mick, who semi-stirred, one eye open, focusing up at mum. "Hallo, Mrs. Oldham," Mick yawned, but got no further, turned over, and unfortunately all but curled into my arms. "Mrs. Oldham" hadn't said a word; she never would. She gave us both one last stern look that showed she did not like the order of her life being disturbed, backed out of the room, and shut the door.

"Will she be -"

"Alright?" I finished Mick's question and answered same. "Yes, she will be." Mick eased and dozed; I semi-snoozed until I heard the front door close.

So Mick and I got up and started the day. By that time it seemed all very funny. Before we left the flat we had coffee and Mick called Chrissie. To shatter the tense atmosphere of Celia's catching us in a compromising position, Mick went into one of his Goons-meet-Percy-Thrower imitations. "Now, listeners, what will happen in next week's episode? What will happen now that Celia has found her Andy with that singer in flagrant whatever you call it? Has her Andy been led astray by those nasty rock 'n' roll boys?" I let the shock of shocking my mother go and we both laughed ourselves silly. It must have been a funny sight, but not for my mother, who could never embrace either my life or the Rolling Stones.

I knew I'd have to leave home soon. The Mick incident was, in a way, the end of my first marriage - the one to my mum. Underneath the veneer, there's instinct. As it is, mere couples have a hard enough time of it - father-mother-child structures have to have the will to work, since three into two don't go. In many ways I had been married to my mum, even flirting with the taboo of finding her attractive. Mick, Sheila, and the Rolling Stones proved just too much for that "us" to endure.

"Look," I said, "*Les Cousins* is on for another week. Let's go and see it together," meaning just Sheila and I. Last Saturday had been a nightmare for this boy attempting to feel his way into a first date. We were pretty drunk already when Peter Meaden, his girl-friend Gina, and I arrived at the party at Marc Guebard's flat at 45 Maresfield Gardens. We'd parked Peter's motorbike and sidecar in the hedge and started talking to it. Two hours later we were drunker, cheaper, trying to sort out our lives and prevent another Saturday night fiasco. There were two late arrivals at the party, a stocky, butch-dirt-blond, Aryan mod and a girl quite his opposite in the best possible way - great body, great aura, and shiny, sexy, and happy with and about herself. Her eyes went through you, her smile lingered forever, and took you into the next day. Though just seventeen, she had that earthy motherlode. She was so at one with herself she'da made a devastating terrorist - you wouldn't have minded when her bullets ripped through you. At least you'd have been inside her and at home. That's roughly what happened to me the second time I'd laid eyes on this Sheila Klein. Face of a smiling Zen-Yid angel promising quicksand of the flesh, dangerous bliss, virtual captivity, and everything you can possibly imagine or de-sire. Neither of us at that moment could have foreseen the fate that would find us and rip us apart as I courted the demons of con-suming fame. As blue turned to grey, sorrow would replace trust with deception and the fucking over of the other's mind. And that's only what I did to her. What she did is hers.

The first time I'd seen her was a week earlier at the Every-man when I'd performed my vaudeville troll for her amusement, and there were the two times I'd bitten the bullet that Saturday night. I got her telephone number from Marc and now, on the phone, had only just got past the shrink detective, Papa-Doc Hyman Sydney Klein. "Are you a friend of Sheila's?" he'd prodded. "Not yet," I feyed, pursing my lips as my mother used to do. It was hard for Sheila to talk with shrinkstalker nearby, but she agreed to call me back later on Swiss Cottage 2017 and did, the next Saturday after-noon. Celia handed the phone to me as if it were contagious. When Sheila whispered that she could get out on Sunday night and would meet me in front of the Hampstead Tube station at eight fifteen, in time to catch the eight forty-five showing of *Les Cousins*, her "yes" put me in a total state. Twice my mother asked me what was wrong; why was I rushing around the flat, talking nonstop, ironing a selection of trousers and shirts? "Andrew, haven't you already ironed the blue gingham twice?" She did offer the occasional, "Here, let me do it, the back is all creased." Sunday came and I couldn't concentrate on anything except the sound of Sheila's breath and her shadow-dancing face. By the time seven thirty arrived, I'd already had two baths and tried on all my clothes twice. I settled on the black trousers, French New Wave rollneck, and my faded beige Clark's ankle lace-up booties. My Adams-of-Piccadilly beige camel-hair peaked-lapelled driving coat topped me off.

Celia was towelling dry her hair in her bedroom above one bar of electric fire. I quietly opened the living room bar, coughed through the squeak, and quickly grabbed a shot of Manishewitz. I listened for mother, but all was mum in her room, so I slugged at the decantered sherry just to be sweet and sure. I cleaned my teeth again, cursed a zit, tried to lower my voice from the ceiling, bade mother goodnight, and, eleven minutes later, was saying hallo to Sheila Klein.

I lost my nervousness when together we let in the Everyman screen. I could easily slip and sink myself into Jean-Claude Brialy and did. I'd retrieved me again and was back ahead of the pack, laconic and flippant, no longer afraid of the dark. I reached out for her hand; it was already there. After the film we had a change of reels and ten minutes later we were standing outside her house. "Come in," Sheila whis-purred. "My parents are asleep, so we can talk in the kitchen." This we did, drinking tea, talking, and starting that slight dance into each other's ways. She shone in the harsh kitchen lighting, and her mod freckles endeared her to me.

She told me that her parents had more or less "grounded" her, having taken no joy in the most recent young man she had been seeing. (I hoped it was the blond frogman I'd seen her with.) Sheila had it that her parents felt that dating was taking her away from her art and upcoming exams. I put the teacups silently into the kitchen sink, shivered, and let her walk me to the door. The next Wednesday Sheila again invited me to her home. On entering, I first got the once over by her redheaded brother (I'd checked him out before you could say "referral") before being greeted by her

mother, Eileen, and her father. They were all smiles, overly curious, and nervously welcoming. Eileen was a mid-forties strained
Scots beauty as adrift as Hope Lange in *Death Wish*. After this charade of hollow hallo's, Sheila told them we were going up to her
bedroom and took me by the hand. I found this a bit surprising,
in light of her parents' qualms about the effect of boys on their
daughter's education. As we sat on the bed in her first-floor room,
Sheila showed me photos, old and new, followed by some of her
sketches and paintings. "I thought your parents weren't happy 'bout
you having, um ... boys around," I ventured. "Yes," she smiled, "it
was funny; they were all curious to meet you, my brother too."
"Well," I blushed, "they were very friendly, considering." "They
were curious, all right," she giggled. Now she really had my interest. "I told them they had nothing to worry about. I told them
you were gay." Suddenly I felt not very gay at all, but bitten by the
hand that had fed me, confused, and just a bit betrayed. I looked
out the window as the sun and I sunk down over the horizon.

    We were welcomed back to England - the Stones, that is -
by close to a thousand diehard fans, and yours truly by the exu-
berant Reg King. Reg, ever tacky and immaculate, had the powder-
blue Chevolet Impala illegally parked outside Terminal Four with
that incurable twinkle in his eye that dared any rozzer to move
him on. His smile could launch a thousand straight chickens and
his hug was warm and welcome. I was exhausted from the long
flight home and the energy expended by "nothing-to-declare"-ing
my way through customs. As Reg pinky-ringed the wheel on his
way around and out of the airport and headed onto the old Heathrow Road for London town, I reclined into the midnight-blue, mock-
leather, Chevy passenger seat. Whilst I had been in the States, Reg
had fallen in love and got himself into a state. It was good to sit
back and listen to the perils attached to Reg's penchant for hetero-
sexual young men, betting the course of his race on the hope that
they might stray from their straight, and, as some would have it,
narrow path. It was an attractive, engaging bunch that gathered
around Reg, and he was a devoted master of the chase. Hearing
of his latest adventures gave me the ten minutes' space I needed
to shiv the myth into being as to how the Rolling Stones had conquered the States and were returning to their homeland triumphant. The next episode, I hoped, would be customised for the

media by the simultaneous stateside and U.K. release of the major coup of our Chess recording sessions, "It's All Over Now" backed with "Good Times, Bad Times." (What better titles to describe our first North American tour?) This last-minute triumph would fudge the truth of our minor-league stateside status and I reasoned that its success could be helped, in part, by a press that was not yet on the lookout for failure. Time was still on our side.

The ride into London remains a drag to this day - the usual depressing, grey-overcast welcome mat. The architectural suburban mundaneness that borders the ride into my old hometown was, and is, as predictable as a Manfred Mann ditty. The bleak vista is only broken, shortly before Hammersmith, by a couple of interesting sandcastle-art, industrial-turreted complexes sprayed in a radiant green-grey puke, housing either a paint or a chocolate factory - perhaps both. But I had no time to be tired of London or life. I was fired by the Yank unhappening and consumed by the notion of what could happen for the Stones. We were going to have to go back, and back, until we got it right. Meantime I had this unreal holiday on ice to overcome. My mission was to convey, via some well-designed mediaspeak, how groundbreaking our U.S. tour had been.

My partner Tony Calder wasn't fooled; he immediately spotted the snarling, cocky resilience emanating from us all. Regardless of our lackluster stateside showing, the land had left its rub on us. While America broke new musical ground weekly, Britain still accepted what little it could, and tried to sweep the rest under the rug. There were a few bright sparks: deejays Alan Freeman and Jimmy Savile, the *Ready, Steady, Go!* crew - even David Jacobs was a fully paid up non-groveller - but there was none of the flame we'd warmed to in America.

All in all, being back in Britain was a rude awakening, a Magna-Carta-stuck-in-my-throat that served to remind me that the fair isles into which I had been born were gated and padlocked, an unwelcoming playground for an entrepreneur. I chewed on this fat, spat out of the window, and shuddered at my melancholy welcome home all the way down from my dove-brown, suede hunting jacket to my deep-brown Chelsea boots. I did feel tired, if only for a long moment. Black clouds hovered over my patch of Dover, and I knew what it was to be in England and depressed again.

I didn't like it that the home fires were not burning, and I was fed up being a bad British boy. In America it was a given that bad boys moved up to and between Park and 5th and Long Island Sound daily. The machine fed on Gatsbys and mavericks, and the economy, well-being, and humour of a nation depended on it. I came back to England feeling more of a mad boy, and with Reg at the wheel I had the right to be one. I'd come back to England with a different edge, a new mission and calling. The Stones had the edge, too. It became very apparent on their first homecoming weekend - when they played the Alexandra Palace and did *Ready, Steady, Go!* and *Juke Box Jury* all in one two-day chop - that something forceful, wimp-deleting, empowering, and American had taken over. The defining movement travelled north from the hips and the wrists to the shoulders and hands and childbearing lips, and Mother Jagger started to think and resist like a man.

Chris and Terence Stamp

CHAPTER 17

america becomes the body of the band / back in britain; the bbc - boring poofs and tame wankers / the u.k. press - the stones are five lord gagas / france - our kind of snob / see more of the game with seymour / kama sutra; genius inc; 1650 and the brill / back home again ... well, blackpool / fast forward to '89 and a well-fucked faithfull ... weren't we all? / smoking lessons for life from johnny carson / all the kings men; denny cordell, and nigel thomas / i get carried away and married / "you've lost that lovin' feeling" - phil spector does it forever.

July 1964:

    London was soon to become pungent with the Stones. From their clubs, the city's masons and elders huffed at our good fortune and cursed the cut of our cloth and mouth. We had raised the ante in matters of acceptance and rejection. You better sit down kids. Those of you back from America had better not act above your pre-ordained station. The Stones as one would dismiss these warnings and grind them under a well-heeled Chelsea boot, not knowing that within three years they'd be the ones under society's brogue.

    On stage the Stones could now turn on a dime. America had invaded their very being and - *voila!* - they were now rhythm kings, champions of stress and groove who knew what it was all about. No more Limey phantasmagoria for them. They'd been knighted out of serfdom and had returned as little big men; they strutted their hour upon the stage, dueling guitars soaring, and buoyed by their coming of age at Chess unto America. Keith and Brian got glued as one for a little while longer before the latter reverted to cuntdom. Mick never missed an opportunity to dance his persona into the very souls agog before him. You could seen the transference as he sculpted them, invaded them, converted them. The Stones began to finesse that muscle, the one that, when expertly flexed, turns an audience into a faithful flock.

    The Stones on *Juke Box Jury* turned out to be excellent press fodder. The show, hosted by David Jacobs, featured guests casting their votes on the week's vinyl offerings. The Stones, with no prompting from me, proceeded to behave as complete and utter

yobbos and in twenty-five minutes had managed to confirm the
nation's worst opinions of them once and for all. They grunted,
laughed amongst themselves, were merciless toward the drivel
that was being played and hostile toward the normally unflappable Mr. Jacobs. This was no planned press move. Brian and
Bill made some effort to be polite but Mick, Keith, and Charlie
would have none of it. Eventually the two Bs had to join in, put
up, and go with the flow.

The Daily Mail had it that they had "scandalised millions of
parents." Even NME, supposedly an on-our-side young musical
rag, screamed that the Stones were "an utter disgrace." Not bad
for a Saturday afternoon's work. Then they went off on holiday.
My holiday came when "It's All Over Now" went to number one
the very next week. It was telegrams and "Fuck the world I wanna
rock on!" all round.

The group came back holiday'd out - ready, willing, and
stable. From the second week of July through the second week
of October, on an extended ballroom and cinema marathon, they
gigged nonstop the length and breadth of Britain before stopping
off in Paris. The Stones would be playing Bruno Coquatrix's famed
Olympia in Paris. Slumming, slouching, and building up a following
of Frogs was not exactly on the agenda. It was straight to the top,
Ma! Top of the Tour Eiffel! L'Olympia was no slouch gig. The
Stones would seize the hour on a stage that had held, once, Edith
Piaf, and now the likes of Johnny Hallyday, Eddy Mitchell, and
Dick Rivers. They rocked it, headed home, turned around, and
headed out again for two appearances at the Academy of Music on
East 14th in New York City to kick off the second North American
tour.

London Records had reputedly invested $85,000 in the
Stones. But what on? They were wasting it on double-page adverts
in Billboard proclaiming: "They're Great! They're Outrageous!
They're Rebels! They Sell! They're England's Hottest! ... But Hot-
test Group!" I hated the ad equally as much as the tacky title that
London Records had put over the top of the Stones' debut U.K. LP
(rush-released in the U.S. for the tour) - England's Newest Hitmakers.
I was angry, but what could I do? I couldn't even get through to
London Records on the telephone. Their H.Q. in New York was
just an address. Well, I did have one get-together: Keith and I met

London A&R veep Walt Maguire in a bar off 10th Avenue and he basically pleaded with us to give them a chance. He was a nice Irish guy, mildly in his cups, and Keith and I decided to let it be. We were both aware that we hadn't delivered the vinyl. Decca's U.S. division existed by milking maximum American profit out of middle-of-the-road, English-recorded orchestras like Mantovani and Frank Chacksfield. London Records did not even pretend to be a major contender in America; it was just a very profitable sideline for Decca CEO Sir Edward Lewis. The Stones and I were probably lucky that London was not a major in the States. They operated out of the docks on West 23rd and 10th, not a good address, but they were a company where we could at least remain a priority until the hits came along.

Seymour Stein was our main greeter in New York. He continued to perform this same service for music even long after founding Sire Records in 1966 and fostering punk in the seventies and new wave in the eighties. He was now twenty-two and had recently moved to Red Bird Records, after kicking off his career at sixteen in 1958 at *Billboard*, where he allegedly moved not only heaven and earth but also the top 100 charts. Red Bird was on the ninth floor of the Brill Building and was owned by George Goldner, Jerry Leiber, and Mike Stoller. I wandered up there with Keith Richards looking for songs. The Stones were not yet a self-contained writing/arranging/producing unit. I asked Seymour if we could meet Jerry Leiber. Jerry did not want to meet us. The Brill Building and its great writer/producers like Leiber and Stoller had not yet gotten over the "British Invasion," even though most of the writers were doing fine by us. They should have erected a statue to Mickie Most alone for the gringolandia songs he shuffled into worldwide hits. Goffin and King, Mann and Weil, Greenwich and Barry were all writing teams who were scoring off the Brits, but the undisputed guv'nors were Leiber and Stoller, followed by a close chorus by Doc Pomus and Mort Shuman (who would go on to great fame in France following his translation of *Jacques Brel is Alive and Well and Living in Paris*). Leiber, therefore, was a must-meet but a no-go. He and Mike Stoller had first scored in the fifties with the original "Hound Dog" recording by Big Mama Thornton, it would hit again with Elvis. They wrote and produced for Atlantic Records, recording the Coasters, Ben E. King, and the Drifters. They took Phil Spector

under their wing; one result was "Spanish Harlem." They developed a great stable of writers including Neil Diamond, Jeff Barry,
and Ellie Greenwich, but they weren't in the mood for Keith, so
we repaired to the Turf below at 1650 Broadway for coffee and
cheesecake. We had a copy of the Red Bird recording of "Down
Home Girl" by Alvin Robinson, which, within a few weeks, the
Stones would record.

Bob Crewe was another great host to the Stones and me in
our early days in New York. Bob had been a model at the tail end
of the forties. He was devastingly "American good looking" in
the style of celluloid beefcake teen idols Tab Hunter and Troy Dona-
hue, and he knew it. He met up with Frank Slay in the early fifties
and they started writing and performing together. Eventually they
started writing and producing records and scored a string of late
fifties hits together with Freddy Cannon, Danny and the Juniors,
and the Rays. He ran into Bob Gaudio in the halls of 1650 Broadway
and the rest is Four Seasons history. 1650 was as important as the
just-a-block-away Brill Building. It didn't have the name, the rent
was cheaper, but the music and output was just as strong. One of
the tenants was Kama Sutra Records.

Artie Ripp and Phil Steinberg were the epitome of this newfound Manhattan celebration, Jewish cowboys who had ridden in
from the plains of the Bronx and Brooklyn to feast on this half-
mile radius of melody, diming, and hustle. They reigned over it
as their own Dodge City via Kama Sutra, their indie production
company. Ripp was blessed by his name, merely having to add an
"off" to it to get misunderstood and blessed into the game. Artie
was a taller, speedy, rock 'n' poppin' version of fifties actor Richard Conte, and I liked him. His passion, balls, and smoke could
get you transfixed to whatever piece of vinyl he was promoting
or rehearsing on you and make you a believer faster than Neil
Diamond. Phil Steinberg had a heart and a physique to equal at
least five of the Magnificent Seven. He minded Artie's front, mouth,
mind, and sidewalk in the same way that Chris Stamp minded
the creations and creativity of Lambert and Townshend. Third
partner Hy Mizrahi was not seen around and was rumoured to
spend most of his time at the racetrack with TV's "Ben Casey,"
actor Vince Edwards. Phil's tight Hebrew curls locked into his
Victor MacLaglenesque skull, encasing the warmest eyes and

smile you'd wish to behold whilst a true Cisco Kid black-and-silver-studded cowboy suit gloved his massive frame. Phil and I would get even closer later: In '68 he visited me at the London nursing home where I was attempting to wring and dry out my drug-addled famepain when he was facing some parallel monsters. Meanwhile, back at the pharmacological patio, drugs reigned whilst we thought it was us. Artie Ripp would later be the coil that sprung Billy Joel on the world, even if the first outing was released at Rippspeed - Joel's pitch on this faultily mastered single came nearer Alvin and the Chipmunks than the Brooklyn Pavarotti tone he'd warbled and intended.

So, the jury was out in the world of late 1964, but the results thus far were good. I bid adieu to Kama Sutra, left Seymour Stein to decide who'd make the *Billboard* charts the next week, and walked the fifteen blocks up Broadway to Columbus Circle and the northwest-corner building on Broadway and 61st, later home to Starbucks, then home to Atlantic Records and the Bob Crewe companies, operating under a name with Bob's normal flair for understatement - Genius Inc.

Bob's digs were a far cry from the garish Rupert-Pipkin/Acid-a-Go-Go-meets-Miami-Doral-Beach-vomit-green decor that templed the Kama Sutra gang. Bob had a style and a sense of art and equation reflected in hues of orange, raw brown, and ochre that were up-to-the-minute and flattering to all. The feel of his offices was generous and devoid of panic, and that mood would inspire my decorating schemes later on.

The Stones, holiday done, kicked off their three-month "Secure the Homeland" tour on July 24, 1964 at the Empress Ballroom, Blackpool, as-good-as-real Beatles home turf. The seaside holiday resort was invaded by drunken braveheart laddies who'd stormed south of the border looking for a real good-bad time, your prototype football hooligans.

The Stones started into a tight show, acting oblivious to the bawl of "Think yer as good as the Beatles!" rebel yells, gobs, and scowls that latreened, hooted, 'n' hollered from the swaying front rows of inbred factory fodder. Mick played it close to the chest and smothered his valence into the band so as not to escalate the goading into pitchforks. Brian Jones went for the opposite. He took the moment as his to upstage the sensibly reticent Mick and started off on a preening, affected dance, taunting the drunken butch frontliners. From the semaphoric pit all flags signaled danger and rage as the occupants began a contest to see which of them could gob on a Stone. Had Brian made it to Altamont, nobody would have gotten out alive.

Keith went nuts. He gave a warning to one of the stage-front trouble makers, but a minute later Keith was spat on. Keith used his Beatle boot as a weapon and struck into the hands of the gobber who'd been hanging onto the rim of the stage with his hands. He then stepped back and delivered the other boot into the same guy's mush. The Stones were lucky they were six feet off the floor; if not, they'd have been invaded.

A thirsty evil was starting to permeate our proceedings. The wild west of America had rubbed its leg against us and had given us a license to be louts. We were beginning to abuse our attitude. Violence and anger would become permanent fixtures.

Mick would laugh it off with a condescending or nervous shrug. With a flick of his wrist, as if tossing the ash off the end of a cigarette, he would feign the irritation of a tired housewife - "Oh, you lot! At it again!" He'd moan, "Go back to the Alamo," whilst Keith and I practised our fast draws with flick knives, stilettos, and bravado. On some occasions Mick would butch up, snarl, and join the gang. The newspapers enjoyed these ballroom showdowns, putting the group on the nation's breakfast tables the following morning, extolling the bravado of Jagger and Co. I would put my two cents worth in, explaining the meaning of Mick: "He stirs up some incredibly intense feelings in many males. Sex, rage, and rebellion - he brings it all to the surface." This only served to further fan the flames.

A few weeks later I managed to create my own mayhem at *Juke Box Jury*, albeit behind the scenes. I was in London and the actress Judy Huxtable, Sean Kenny's wife at the time, had been booked to appear on the panel. Sean, who was away, asked if I'd mind escorting her there and playing manager. "Not at all, "I told Sean. "My pleasure. I'd much rather a busman's holiday than another Saturday-a-Go-Go domestic."

I hugged the last of the afternoon joint and Reg hugged the curb as we said goodbye to Holland Park and zoomed into the Bush. Two blocks west, the Chevy Impala made a right and screeched into a parking spot a few paces from the BBC studio entrance. Judy H was on the first show. The BBC covered two shows fortnightly; the first one went out live at 5:25 p.m., the other was taped immediately after and aired the following Saturday. The live show went smoothly, happily back on its track after the Stones had derailed it a couple of weeks earlier. Judy, yours truly, and the effervescent Reg repaired to the empty Green Room.

On the box was the taping of the second show (it being a few minutes past 5:55 p.m.). On the "other side," the commercial ITV channel's *Thank Your Lucky Stars* would be booming out. I changed the channel to *Lucky Stars*; we poured ourselves a drink and sat down to watch the popular rival. The door flung open and in stepped a burly, curly, beetroot-faced BBC commissioner. He looked at us, looked at the telly, back at us and snapped.

"You are not allowed to have that on in here. It's against BBC policy."

With that he marched over to the set and turned it back to the BBC channel, which for some reason wasn't even showing the *Juke Box Jury* then being taped, but some regular BBC programming.

"Hold on!" said Reg, "Switch it back, dear, we was watching the other side."

"I don't care," blustered Burly Curly. "You can't watch it in here!"

"That's ridiculous," Judy chimed in. "I've just been a guest on ..."

"That doesn't make any difference," slobbered the uniformed beetroot with disdain. I stood up, happy that I now had a new show to attend to and a fresh mark to hit.

"Do you have to be so fuckin' rude?" I enquired, engine running.

"And we don't allow that language in here, mister," the commissioner honked back as Reg headed for the TV and switched it back to ITV. The commish switched it back. By now a few people had gathered in the room, either as a result of the raised voices or the end of the *Juke Box Jury* taping. Having an audience to our regrettable behaviour was like adding fuel to the fire.

"Right. You lot will all have to vacate the premises," the commish snapped. "Now!"

"Oh, fuck off, you worn-out bit of useless shrapnel ... fuckin' leave us alone," I suggested. I knew where this take was going, understood my role, and was warming to it. Burly huffed and puffed, turned on his heels, and marched out with an "I'll be back." He returned, followed in short order by a half-dozen played-out burlies.

"Right, then," crowed Burly Number One, buoyed by the numbers. "You are hereby ordered to leave the premises. This way out," he beckoned in his best Dixon of Dock Green. "Mr. Cotton's orders. He's the head of Light Entertainment here."

I hadn't got "Yeah, very fuckin' light" out of my mouth before little Billy Cotton Jr. entered the room. His father had been a bandleading icon of the airwaves from World War II on, much-loved for his opening signature cry of "Wakey wakey! Hallo all!" What Lawrence Welk was to the immigrant American viewer, Billy Cotton Sr. was to the U.K.

"I think you had all better leave. Miss Huxtable, you were an invited guest of the show, but your friends ..." he tutted in our direction. Billy Cotton Jr. was a penpusher, a dribbler, a bedwetter, and wimp. This was my possibly addled point of view at the time - so there need be no cause for alarm amongst the next batch of Cottonettes.

"You're Andrew Oldham, aren't you? You are one of the managers of the Rolling Stones, aren't you?" Junior said, accusingly.

"Guilty as charged," I nodded.

"He swore at me, Mr. Cotton, sir." Burly got hotter and bolshier.

"I think we may as well leave, Judy," I suggested. "Just as well," sneered Burly. It was that or the police. "Troops over the Chinese line," I thought. Reg didn't bother to think and shoved Burly out into the corridor. "You and whose fuckin' army? You lame-creased piece of shit," Reg roared theatrically. I could see he was getting into his part, too. "Eyes front," he screamed and winked in my direction. "If you do not leave this instant, I'll call the police!" barked Cotton Jr.

Down the corridor we went, through the ground-floor reception and out onto the street. Following us was a semi-battalion of commissioners, and, at a safe distance, the diminutive scowling head of Light Entertainment whom I thought I heard say, "Just because he's with the Rolling Stones he thinks he can ..."

The Chevy was three cars to our left. We walked to it and

started to get in, Judy first, whilst the madding crowd spilled out onto the evening pavement and gawked at our expulsion. Standing out front was Cotton Jr., who now had more than a few punters to play to. David Jacobs, fellow deejay Pete Murray, and a dozen others had also come out to see what was happening.

David Jacobs was explaining in faultless announcer tones what had just transpired to the equally dapper, taller, blue-blazered Pete Murray. "That's pretty silly, David," said Murray.

"People like him give the business a bad name. He won't be around long," I heard Cotton Jr. leer as I opened the passenger door to let myself in. I got pissed, reached down into the glove compartment for the black, leather-bound, steel-tipped cosh and started in toward Little Big Man Billy.

"Wakey wakey, you wanker. Wait till you feel this in the side of your fuckin' head."

A sixth or theatrical sense had me keep the cosh partially hidden from view as I headed for the man. I was all out of sync, moving forward into busy traffic when I should have been on the exit ramp, fading on a fast and lasting remark. Instead, I was moving in a direction fatale.

"No, Andrew ..."

I was a yard away from whacking the git when a tall bugger grabbed me from behind in a body hold. It was yer BBC Radio2 deejay, Pete Murray. His customary laid-back RAF eloquence evaporated as Pete Murray snarled in my ear in flawless cockney, "Don't be a cunt, Andrew, there's witnesses! It's not worth it ... bugger off."

I relaxed and allowed myself to look around and see the set clearly, a little bit of *noir* Chinatown finale in Shepherd's Bush. It was a crane shot - the whirly a good twenty feet up, looking down on Pete pinning my cosh-bearing arm to my side. I'm on the wrong set, I thought to myself. My script told me to cut and run for cover.

Mr. Murray felt me relax and let me go. I walked back to the car, got in, and allowed Reg to screech us away. It was another day of the locusts, the establishment holding its line, the tea-leaf gangsters marking time, all rolled into one. I did not, however, need a reading of those tea leaves to know that however stoned I might already be, but it was still way too early in this boy's tale for him to be charged with pot possession, grievous bodily harm, or any other kind of GBH.

****

In November 1989 I was in Manhattan, as was Marianne Faithfull. It was one of those razor-sharp Kojak sunny late fall days. My elder son, Sean, now twenty-four, and I set off to see Marianne at the Episcopal Church of St. Ann and the Holy Trinity in Brooklyn (rechristened St. Ann's Warehouse in 2001) in what was to be a recorded performance of her greatest hits (for 1990's *Blazing Away*) and Kurt Weill tunes. Not my cup of tea, or *Lederhosen* either. I was raised on the ultimate "Look out ol' Mackie's back." With "Mack the Knife," Bobby Darin had stylishly made the leap from the "Splish Splash"/"Dream Lover" teen crooner into the Sinatra stakes, and, in doing so, had set the standard for future pop interpretations of Weill. (The other Weil in pop was, of course, Cynthia Weil of Mann and Weil, collaborators on such classics as "(You're My) Soul and Inspiration" and "We Gotta Get Out of This Place.")

Every other decade, it seems, a bunch of air-rarified muso exiles from mainstream revive Weill's Weimar forebodings. This newfound lust for Kurt's dark melodies and intricate arrangements by ex-junkies and vegetarians is as inviting as a summer season stuck on a pier with Matt Monro crooning "Monday, Monday." I'd rather they opted for Eddie Cochran's "Twenty Flight Rock," or my idea of Kurt Weill - the real deal: Mr. Gene Vincent.

Nevertheless, it remained a glorious fall Brooklyn day, and my son and I were enjoying stellar syntony. Faithfull, the occasion, plus the plonk and the day's freedom combined to will us together, and we liked it. We walked past Norman'd Mailerville, cobblestoned, redbricked mews with views of the murky East River. Sean and I kicked up the leaves and passed many a tree as I wondered aloud, "Which one of ye grew for Brooklyn?" Then it was time to hush up and say hallo to Marianne.

I was pleased to see her rise to the occasion. Her audience seemed to consist of Mariannettes, ash-grey faces who'd bypassed life and jumped directly from youth into rehab and spinsterville. Marianne gave them hope and soothed their despair as they rubbed their souls together within the warmth of their blackvelveted angel on tits. She looked like a deliciously poisonous gift of chocolates, all paint-boxed and absolute.

God bless her for living through hell, but, at some stage of the game, you should really stop going back there. I shuddered at the metaphorical whimsy of it all, guided Sean and myself out of the still of St. Mary's and into the still of the night.

This was the first time I'd seen her since we'd neighboured in the mid-nineteen-eighties, she above Canal on-off Greenwich, me below on Tribeca's Beach Street. Marianne had been living with some physically abusive monster who'd have failed the audition for a Kiss tribute band. My pal Tony Russo had set up a formal dinner expressly so that we could beat up the little shit. I packed a cosh and one of those dual-purpose knuckle-duster switchblades for the occasion. Tony was back-up and Magnum'd, as in Clint Eastwood. My wife Esther and sons Sean and prammed 'n' bottled Maximillian came too. When we got there the boyfriend was not to be seen - either he'd made himself scarce or was out for the count.

Tony and I decided on a line of down in the bathroom, forgot about our planned vigilantism and settled down to Marianne's brave but nervous roast beef, mash, and gravy dinner, served up with reflective laughs braised in a sauce of selective memory. Sean was told what style his father once had (just what neither of us needed to hear), and Marianne asked once too often how Esther was able to deal with such a handful as myself.

Fuck this charade of broken English, I thought, and all of us - Russo, Faithfull, and me - pretending for the night that we were all so Manhattan'd and well. Take me home to Hall and Oates and "Out of Touch," my insides screamed. The night was saved by Russo, whose take on us Brits and his adventures researching the pleasures of Her Majesty's Prisondom were fresh meat for us prisoners of Greenwich Avenue - and as funny as a move out of jail.

But any leftover joy started to run out for me when I heard Marianne say, "Did I tell you, I asked Chris [as in Blackwell, owner of Island Records, who had guided Marianne on the successful second run of her career] if I could record 'As Tears Go By' again?" It felt as if she were offering me a nightmare for dessert.

"What would you want to do that for?" I muttered, passing my silver cigarette box toward Tony, motioning him away from the Davidoffs and toward the joints at the left-hand end.

"Would you be interested in doing it with me?" she asked.

I shuddered visibly at the thought. Don't get me wrong. I still loved the song; it would always have a special place in my heart. But my bottle was almost empty, and I had dedicated its remainder to building my lot with Esther. I didn't have enough left for another go-round in the world of vinyl.

"Chris doesn't think we could do it," she went on. "Bully for fuckin' Chris," I thought. "Glorified wheelbarrow merchant, let him go remake "My Boy Lollipop" if he's so damn keen on cover versions."

By now I couldn't wait to get wasted, Hall and Oates, and home.

"Of course," Marianne continued, "When I mentioned doing it with you, he said, 'Just what I need, Oldham and Faithfull, two burnt-out people working together.'"

Ouch! Chris and Blackwell, but well-canned and very spot-on.

Later, Tony Russo and I had cause to wish we had ferreted out Marianne's live-in motherfucker and done him in. I got a call from Tony on the scrambled line from his Bleecker Street loft. He told me to meet him in the lobby of the Gramercy Park Hotel as soon as possible. Marianne was there with him and not well.

I cabbed from Beach Street with a mad Russian. I alighted, thanked and tipped my man in line with the eight-minute ride. Boris Somethingorotherivitch, my huggie-bear of a cabbie, had been very accommodating. He'd even slowed down for one corner just so I could "get my things in order," which in eighties-speak meant "Fuckin' slow down so I can do a line."

Tony stood in the lobby, trusty replica .357 Magnum ever ready and tucked into his Levi'd belt. Russo was deceptively bespectacled, ponytailed, impatient, and solicitous, a walking ad for the Paragon Sports store in fur-lined silver/beige anorak and a couple of layers of woolen sweaters, his tight five-foot-seven frame cuffed in mountain-brown Dexter's - though Tony's treks were not exactly the kind that Paragon had in mind.

After a glass of wine, cup of espresso, or bagel, Tony, a video-editing star who was going through a little burning-out (which is probably why Creature One, the photographer Mick Rock, had introduced us in the first place), would become very British, metamorphising out of his Sicilian New Yorkese roots to regale us all with brilliant, comic Britspeak. With Denmother Cocaine as our surrogate mum, Tony and I became instant family speedpals. There were less than six degrees of separation between us and more than six grams in common. That's why we were converging on the Gramercy that brittle, fateful, Faithfull, November 1985 night.

"She nearly fucking did it this time, Andrew," Tony spoke of Marianne in drip-drop, *Get Carter* rapid fire as he wound me past the bar and toward a room on the dark lower ground floor.

"That fucking little cunt whacked her so hard her jaw had to be wired up." Tony referred to the little live-in runt we should have trampled back on the eve of our dinner. He took out a room key and let us both in on another episode of nearly so-long-Marianne.

I've entered a lot of dark rooms in my time. Hotel rooms, cold and expensively dreary, or faded and repainted by the over-dosing of drugs, take on that look of a room with a view of the already dead. To check in and check out on living scours the colour from even the brightest room. The curtains, the couches, the bedspread get sheened over with a deadly pallor.

Marianne lay in bed, her upper torso twisted in pain. Her jaw was wired up. The metal holding it together blended into her steel-grey complexion, which matched the yellow/white dead fluff of the blanket on her breasts. The lights in the room somehow only served to make the room murkier. I had to think fast to stop my-self from being sucked into this madness. Here was this whacked-out, hopeless fawn hit and run over by her life, she who had cried wolf once too often and now lay twittering between life and death. I can't remember what we said; all I know is that I reached into my every last reserve. We talked about talent, joy, and fun - the very topics I'd found so painful at that recent dinner. I now turned them into visions to be cherished, embraced, and reached for, consummations devoutly to be wished. Russo had assured me that we weren't there to fill the stalls; we had to give the perfor-mances of our lives.

I shocked on. I chastised her for waste, praised her for being, looked for signs of my words gripping her very soul. She insisted on coughing and smoking. I still had my Johnny Carson phobia about smoking in bed; in her state she could easily drop a cigarette and set fire to everything. But Marianne, wire-jawed, smacked and/or morphined up as she was, could hardly be expected to follow my Carson-learnt one-foot-on-the-floor smoking-in-bed rule. I insisted on placing plastic room service buckets filled to the brim with ice all over the bed. I instructed the half-asleep Marianne that these were fucking ashtrays, and she was to use them - and don't you dare fucking nod out now. I was in the white heat of my holy rolling and she'd better not spoil one of Russo's and my finest hours.

It was the blind leading the blind. Tony and I, lecturing, rallied Marianne between bouts of lines in the bathroom. We emerged, fortified, to pounce on Marianne for rounds three, four, and five of pep talk to keep her awake and coax her back into some spark of a breathing life.

It was but a few years later, 1991, that another sweetheart of rock rage, Steve Marriott, met the end of his turn on this earth. He got 2stoned and smoked in bed. He nodded out, both he and the bed caught fire, the bed slipped into gear and carried Stevie away to his maker.

Marianne checked out of the Gramercy Park Hotel and into the Hazelden Foundation Clinic in 1985, giving out that she'd broken her jaw falling downstairs. I'm not sure if it all clicked on that round or the next - I was 2stoned and not counting - but for sure, Marianne turned the corner and reclaimed her life.

Back to 1989: I think this Marianne-doth-Kurt-Weill-in-Brooklyn outing was the first time I'd ever seen her perform live. But I would not really see her fully a-live until one Friday when she played New York's Bottom Line: She was tremendous. On stage alone save bass and guitar, she did not need saving; she was sailing. Here she would have to be better than good. She wasn't torching Berlin retreads but throwing open the pages to herself and her screenplay. She got and gave more than good; she winged, arrowed, and rose above the trinity she had lived and died for these twenty five years: "As Tears Go By," drugs and fur and Mars bars, and Michael Philip Jagger. She referred to 'em all, sung 'em, and triumphed over the lot. She rose above any critique of her vocal style. In the miracle of the night, she suddenly was.

After a polite interlude I went through to see her backstage. It was the opposite of our Brooklyn backstage hallo which had been more like "Fuck you for being here." Marianne glowed from the night's success. I glowed from seeing a performance that could play anywhere in the world and win, a world in which you didn't have to know "As Tears Go By" to place her, nor did you have to have followed her tabloid'd life. You just had to be able to experience this woman at one with her life's journey and let her explain it to you in song, let her be there just for you, and finally, thank God, there for herself.

Our eyes smiled that smile. She saw how moved I was.

"Marianne," I said, "finally I can admit to you."

It was not taken as rudeness, as dismissive, or as high-handed as it may sound. She got my heartfelt shorthand and knew exactly what I meant.

She smiled and just said, "I was good, wasn't I?"

Yes, she was.

****

"What do you think?" the early A&R man would ask.

This was a setup in which basically nobody stepped up to the plate and claimed the mantle of "producer." The arranger would select the key and arrange the song or cop the already-existing American arrangement. The engineer would record the singer vocalising to the arrangement. The A&R man would generally nod approval. If the take had some magic, it could make it, but jumping in and grappling with a song in an attempt to secure that magic was not part of the A&R job description; that sort of enthusiasm would cost too much time and money. No, the general malaise was to follow the formula - pick the song, record in a three-hour haze, bung the ingredients on a conveyer belt, and hope for a hit.

In America the guv'nor of pre-beat boom A&R was Mitch Miller, arguably the most successful A&R man in the history of the record business. He broke his musical legs playing oboe and *cor anglais* on many a renowned recording. He toured with George Gershwin and accompanied him on piano. In the late forties he started working for record companies as a recording executive, concentrating on classical and children's records. Eventually, he produced Vic Damone, Frankie Laine, Guy Mitchell, Johnny Mathis, Rosemary Clooney, Percy Faith, Johnny Horton, Mahalia Jackson, and Johnnie Ray. It was during his CBS tenure that the meaning of "country division" actually came into its own with the early recordings of Ray Price, Lefty Frizzell, and Marty Robbins. He was also an instigator in the marriage of screen and vinyl, notably with the recordings he commissioned for *High Noon* and *The Bridge on the River Kwai*.

In 1985 Mr. Miller told *Audio* magazine's Ted Fox, "The same rules apply ... taste, musicianship, balance, get the best out of the artist. Many times the artist doesn't know what his best characteristics are, and you're there to remind them. You can't put in what isn't there, but you can remind them of what they have and they're not using."

"So what do you think?" the A&R man still asked.

"Oh, twelve, eight, four (violins, violas, and celli). Three trumpets, three 'bones (trombones), two altos (saxophones), and a bari. Three girls, piano, drums, bass, percussion, and guitar. That should do it," would be an arranger's response with a lineup suited to an already-successful star. Otherwise, divide it all in two and that would be the budget for an absolute beginner.

"Sounds good," imagined the A&R man, before putting down the phone and getting back to the paperwork on his desk. "Could you call the Musicians' Union, and I'll see you on the session."

"OK. We've got that charity dinner at Bruce Forsyth's house on Friday, the one Lionel and Joyce Blair are organising for Dr. Barnardo's."

"OK, I'll see you there."

There remain three elements that make up a hit record: a hit song, a hit song, and a hit song. Quincy Jones was quoted during his Michael Jackson run as saying, "You can't shine shit," but, with all due respect to some recently accomplished recordings, I'm not sure if that's true today.

You never approached Regent Sound from the east, always from the west. You'd have bounded up or down Charing Cross Road, or bounded out of Soho underneath the arches that bridged Foyles Bookshop and officed the workshop of Sean Kenny on the second floor, between a first and third where the likes of Helene offered French lessons to the discerning business gent, who, if nabbed, could claim he was *en route* to Foyles.

As I sprinted over the Charing Cross Road and headed toward No. 4 Denmark Street with Regent Sound on its ground floor, the wooden hanging signs that denoted the five or six music publishers per square foot swayed in the afternoon breeze, eerily reminding one of shylocks and pawnbrokers, whilst the storefront windows were flooded with the sheet music of the day. The piano copies were fronted by 8x10 glossy shots of young, tousled men with eight-quid guitars and crucifixes, worried thirtyish crooners in cardigans and sucking on pipes *à la* Bing Crosby, and/or wasp-waisted, flair-skirted, peroxide-topped, smiling damsels of song, one of whom could have been Helene, but was actually, as the caption assured us, the pre-"Downtown" Petula Clark, who'd actually had seven top twenty hits pre-1962, including her versions of "Alone," "Ya Ya Twist," "The Little Shoemaker," "My Friend the Sea," and "Majorca."

That corner, and that run, for some unbeknownst reason amongst all the could-be's, reminds me of Kim Fowley, Paul Simon, and Dick James. Dick looked out from a first-floor window on the north corner of Charing Cross Road and Denmark Street, counting his blessings and royalties, happy to have hung up his wig along with his days as the voice on the theme song to TV's *Robin Hood*. One day, two years earlier, a music biz miracle had befallen him when a Northern manager named Brian Epstein had walked in off the street and said, "Please take my Beatles!" and Dick did.

Paul Simon, with his short-order cuteness, was getting laid by London, strumming his guitar on the coffee bar circuit. He and Art Garfunkel - the former Tom and Jerry - were waiting for CBS to get excited over their first LP, which they did when producer Bob Johnson overdubbed drums, guitar, and bass, after which "The Sounds of Silence" went to number one and CBS called the little boy home. Whilst strumming and bumming in London, Paul hung out on the right street to learn that there were fifty ways to sign a writer (and not too many of them good for the writer). He formed Charing Cross Music, signed himself to himself, and published happily ever after, thus becoming one of the rare examples of writing thoroughbreds who didn't get skinned alive the first time round the course.

Andy Wickham may have insisted that I meet Kim Fowley because he was very tall and American. Mr. Fowley, I would guess, came to London with P.J. Proby, maybe with Bobby Jameson, whom Keith Richards and I would produce. The important thing is he came, got laid, and carried on about "Nut Rocker" by B. Bumble and the Stingers, but it was the man himself that impressed. One did not know his background, but one could sense it. When Kim came to Regent Sound one bright afternoon while I was making my first LP with the Andrew Oldham Orchestra we created "Rise of the Brighton Surf." Kim stayed whilst Mick crooned "Da Doo Ron Ron." Quite sexy it was, too, with Mick doing a laconic slo-mo hurt reading. A couple of proleptic members of Procol Harum helped out on "My Boy Lollipop" and "I Want to Hold Your Hand." That's where I met the long and the short of it, when he and Paul Simon were two yanks, not in Oxford, but at the right time in London Town.

Kim worked for P.J. Proby, a lusty American, born James Marcus Smith, who was giving the Moptops and the Stones a run for their money in the controversy sweepstakes. Proby was everything that Tom Jones would become. He had the voice, the low-brow sex appeal, and he was great on stage. They lived Elvis-style in London, which means that they went through every penny that came in and more. Proby had been brought to England by Jack Good, who thought that Proby could be Elvis for Great Britain. Good gave him a couple of hundred dollars, a round-trip ticket, and within a week John and Paul were introducing P.J. on national television. That's how the game of enthusiasm could work. He was a national phenomenon overnight.

At one of Proby's parties in 1964 in Knightsbridge one of the visitors was Brian Jones. There was also Lulu, Graham Nash, Viv Prince of the Pretty Things, and Kim. Brian was on his social best and, after he left, the Proby court were commenting on "how nice the cat was, man," when they suddenly realised that Proby's own actual cat was missing. They raced up the Knightsbridge mews to the corner, saw a bulkier Brian hailing a cab. The cat was inside his overcoat. After a couple of futile "I thought you guys didn't need it, mistreated it," etc., he reluctantly gave the feline back.

****

It was in the spring of 1970 that I'd first met Nigel Thomas when producer Denny Cordell brought him by my Wilton, Connecticut home. I don't know what it was that drew Nigel into our game. It certainly never seemed to be a love of music, but it served very well as bed and board to Nigel's love of life. Positively jaded, challenging, witty, a smooth, lovable, villainous, black sheep, Nigel was all this and more, a totally wonderful pirate - tall, dark-haired, and mustached, pale with black-coaled eyes, seemingly blackhearted, until he let you in. He deigned to be in the music business. We became very good friends and when, in 1977, Esther and I were married, Nigel made the very best man. On the one occasion that I got him to ante up on his show biz beginnings, he alluded to "doing" nightclub bookings on the London West End cabaret circuit for the Simon Sisters, who later split, became vain, and begot Carly. At the time of our Connecticut meeting, Nigel was managing, and Denny Cordell producing, the Joe Cocker/Leon Russell "Mad Dogs and Englishmen" tour and recordings. (One evening Joe sat in front of my living room fire. Outside, it was snowing heavily and northerly cold. He sipped his hot toddy, looked into the fire, silent and miles away, but seemingly at ease and happy. He looked up, smiled and said, "I'd been wondering what was between New York and Boston. So this is it, eh? Not bad, is it? Not bad at all.")

Denny Cordell was always his own man. He produced a good life, along with the Moody Blues, Procol Harum, Joe Cocker, Freddie King, and the Move. He also uncovered Tom Petty and, with Leon Russell, formed Shelter Records. Early on, after some U.K. successes, he was rewarded by the powers that be and allowed to travel to the States to record Georgie Fame (Clive Powell) with New York's finest.

Essex Music, headed in London by Dr. Jekyll and Mr. Platz, and TRO-Essex Music Inc., its U.S. owner, had more than a fair chunk of Denny (and the Stones, it would turn out) and were doing more than well from being in the right place, right time, when Cordell scored his first national anthem with Procol Harum's "Whiter Shade of Pale" and exploded Joe Cocker into our lives with the classic reworking of Lennon/McCartney's "With a Little Help from My Friends." The TRO-Essex New York house arranger was Tony Visconti, who helped the office look young. Tony was eventually shuttled to the U.K. where he produced David Bowie, Iggy Pop, and T-Rex.

Arrangements for the Georgie Fame sessions - as in size and type of studio, number of musicians, time, and day - were made by transatlantic phone before Denny and Clive flew off to

New York. In a business loath to splurge on expensive instant communication, this was a rarity in and of itself. Airmail, cables, and telexes were the norm in a world where 45 rpm records spoke louder than phones.

The session was set for 2:00 p.m. A sharp rhythm section and New York's best brass were on hand, instruments set up, and chops ready, at two sharp. At 2:30 Tony Visconti was going a little spare, with no Denny, no Georgie, and New York's finest happily sitting about kibitzing whilst being paid by the hour.

About ten of three Denny and Georgie strolled into the studio and beamed a huge hallo all around the room, both looking as though they'd just smoked a very nice lunch.

Visconti had a lot of questions.

"Where have you been, why are you late, these guys, the studio, it's all a lot of money ..."

Denny looked Visconti over, sat down, crossed his legs, tweed coat falling as it should.

"Hold on, Tony," he began. "Cool it, man, we're here. Tell everybody we'll begin in a minute. You could have asked us how was lunch."

The relaxed producer removed his coat and Georgie tried to remove or at least contain his grin.

Visconti sighed, "Just give me the parts and I'll give them out to the musicians."

"What parts?" enquired Cordell.

"The arrangements for the musicians to read from," Visconti modulated up into stress.

"We don't have any parts, do we, Clive?" Denny shrugged.

Clive agreed - no parts.

Tony was at a loss to know how fifteen musicians were going to function without written arrangements to read and play from.

"So what do we do with no parts? How does anybody know what to play? How are we going to record three sides with no parts in under two hours?" Then he stabbed angrily, "Is this how you do it in England?"

Visconti didn't get it. He'd have to go to England to get it.

"Exactly, Tony, you've got it, dear boy," smiled a laconic Cordell. "How we do it, is ... first we put the kettle on for a cup of tea. While it's boiling, we roll a good joint. Then we put on the record we're going to copy, and then we get down to work ..."

I don't recall a lot of time spent with Denny Cordell in London in the sixties. We were all very busy working and we can all remember the hits. But, further on, in 1977, I was watching the night move by with Lou Adler at the Upper West Side Manhattan club, Trax, when, across the room, my eyes locked with the beaming Cordell - hair now grey-immaculate blanco, setting off his double-breasted, grey flannel suit, all portly and settled in. No more the lithe on-the-road black curls, black smile, jeans, and cowboy bandanna; he was at the beginning of his Squire Cordell run. He oozed over to where Lou and I sat. Glued to his side was a gaunt, intense, quiet, fairheaded young gent, introduced to us as Tom Petty.

Petty was pleased to meet us. He liked my Stones period, so I was pleased, and had he been pressed on it, probably also liked Johnny Rivers, which would have pleased Lou.

But it was more than a courtesy call - Denny was enjoying having us say hallo to his star. He'd moved out from behind the studio control room, unshackled himself from Essex Music and England, and moved up front and on to Los Angeles. Both Lou and I enjoyed the real subtext of what he was saying: "Hey Guys, it's my turn to shine in the street, say hallo to my star."

Always a pleasure and thank you, Denny - and well-done, Mr. Petty, for having the savvy to jumpstart your own good lot with the life-enhancing Denny Cordell. There are only a few "firsts," Denny, and I hope that your children know that you were one of that noble band. These "firsts" in life not only succeed and, often enough, give balance to the madness, but their work manages to rise above the medium and define it for that moment in time. "Firsts" also know when to leave the room.

Denny, as you sit down to eat upstairs with Tony Secunda and Nigel Thomas, give them my love and make sure that David Platz gets the bill. In our industry of human happiness, many have pushed, tricked, and stumbled to the front pews, but only a few became "firsts." I recall our very last chat in my Tribeca loft in the eighties when our words belonged to each other. We'd eaten with Seymour and Linda Stein in Chinatown, and later you came back to my place. We felt the need once more for a solid chat, some hash, and a cup of tea. We both wondered through the night at what was going on, agreeing that New York now belonged to someone else.

Somewhere in the night one of us recalled that duty was ours and events were God's. I walked you down the five flights onto Beach Street, you bundled up, and I pointed you toward Greenwich and a morning cab north to your hotel, Kennedy airport, and back home to Ireland. I cheer your grin and loved your shine, Cordell, you who left nothing for the cutting room floor.

****

In July 1964, as "It's All Over Now" became the Stones' first British number one, I rented the higher-floored flat, 147, of Ivor Court. A number-one group needed their own office, so Tony Calder, Andy Wickham, and the girls kept Image on track from the black-and-white, Modesty Blaise-ish 138, whilst our own letter heading could now boast 138/147 Ivor Court and look like a real business. Image now handled Marianne Faithfull for management and its main PR base was the northern agency, Kennedy Street Enterprises, which gave us Herman's Hermits, Freddie and the Dreamers, Wayne Fontana and the Mindbenders, Dave Berry, and food on the table. "The more the merrier" being Tony's and my calling card, we also somehow repped those three nice bland tubs of lard known as the Bachelors. We endured lunch at a show biz Soho eatery with their manager, Philip Solomon, telling how things were done à la Arthur Askey and Lew Grade. One of the Bachelors, Dec Closkey, joined us and we gained a new respect for them when we saw him drive off in a Merc.

Later that year, we would likewise suffer in the London Hilton breakfast room with another expert, Murray Wilson, father and manager to the Beach Boys, and would walk out repping their European press interests and, for a while, their U.K. music publishing. Calder and I still enjoyed phoning the old farts in the record companies and booking agencies, who'd all dismissed us in one way or another on our early tails and now had to take our calls, as we repped their bread and butter.

Hashish was becoming part of the daily menu as was, on extremely busy weeks, speed. I had not yet hit rotation city but that wouldn't be a long time coming. Hash was a wonderful creative tool. After a hard Sydney Falco/J.J Hunsecker split-screen schizoid *Sweet Smell of Success* day manning the phones, injecting our hustle into every moving thing, it was the perfect segue. As Reg put his foot down, I put my head back and we flew across town to an evening studio date, business date, or supper. It seemed a perk of the way of life - the Percodan would come later.

I enjoyed flaunting my new best friend, Mafalda (Mrs. Tony) Hall, the effervescent interior decorator by whim and trade, who gadded about London plying her taste whilst hubby rocked on, attempting to London/Americanise the taste buds of disposable income as far as the airwaves could get him. For my quarters in 138 I had Mafalda work from my sketches to make a one-off roll of wallpaper with a marijuana-leaf motif. Now not only the carpets were thick, but the walls too. The Stones and I tittered away on more than one occasion as I suggested to some well-meaning photographer that the "light was good against that wall and perhaps he should snap the fellas against it," and there remain a few good shots of the Stones posed mischievously against my special wall.

Peter Noone and Herman's Hermits would soon be top five with the Mickie Most production of the Goffin and King gem, "I'm into Something Good." Peter came down from Manchester to London and Ivor Court to do some press as the disc was about to be released in August. I took him up onto the Ivor Court rooftop to take a breather with me and admire the view. We made an odd couple looking over Regent's Park: Peter wiry, young, and fresh meat, peacoat-clad in cynical city. Young lad up in (the) Smoke, away from home and mum and dad, you could sell him, devour him, and protect him all at the same time. After this chat, I introduced him to my new best friend, hashish, and had him smoke a huge joint all on his ownsome. I asked him if he'd enjoyed it, whether anything in the land of his perception had changed. He said "Yes" and swayed. "Right," I said, metamorphising myself into Northern bluff. "Now that you've done it, it had better be the very last time. If I ever hear of you doing drugs, I'll kill ya." And with that, we found our way back downstairs.

The second Rolling Stones EP, *Five by Five* - somewhat of a racing certainty - would be released on the same August day as Marianne Faithfull's "As Tears Go By." The first Stones LP would stay in the U.K. album charts for fifty-one weeks, had reached number one, and had even hit number 19 in the U.K. singles charts; not bad for an outing with no title.

Five by Five was culled from the Chess sessions. " ... by way of saying 'thank you' to you, their friends and fans," I hyped in the sleeve notes, "we have included an extra track on this their latest disc outing." I should have added a thank you to Elvis Presley for being as pretty as Natalie Wood and giving me the "bonus" idea via his five-pronged 1957 *Jailhouse Rock* soundtrack EP.

Image's PR clients were also well-repped and stacking up the charts. The Beach Boys surfed into the top ten for the first of many times with "I Get Around" and were soon joined by Bob Crewe's Four Season'd "Rag Doll," the Bachelors' harmless bit of old blarney, "I Wouldn't Trade You for the World," Mr. Noone's "I'm into Something Good," and our very own Buddhist, Dave Berry, with "The Crying Game."

Outside of the studio, life was again on edge. I could feel that old whore, depression, shading every thought; I could feel the dark lady of angst invading every pore. The sensation is so all-consuming that it seems to grab a vein in your head, tie itself around yer nerves, and hold on. Every time you think, the noose around that thought squeezes the vein until you're in excruciating pain. Your eyelids are sandbagged; it hurts just to focus on anything or have anybody focus on you. The pain in your temples is boiling quicksand, but you say "Fuck that dame of genetic swill!" and manage to hide it and work. The days are once again clipped and frayed. Even your speech registers pain; it must be apparent to everyone you talk to. You are crawling across the desert on your hands and knees, the mirage recedes, even the solace of solitude is no longer available. Sometimes a joint of hash, a cuppa tea, or strong whisky drink will calm you, but it could just as easily go the other way, and find you once again gripped in the bedlam of kill.

I know it's only a fuckin' hit record, not the cure for cancer, but I'm young, privileged, and invaded. I think the success of Marianne and "As Tears Go By" is overwhelming me. I'd had a similar self-questioning episode over "I Wanna Be Your Man." Instead of patting myself on the back and saying, "Only you, you lucky bugger, would have the luck to run into John and Paul and have them hand you a potential hit," I get only mad internal chatter in my head about the what and why of it all. What if I hadn't left the

Rolling Stones rehearsal at that particular moment? Why had I turned right? What if I'd turned left toward Covent Garden? What if I hadn't run into John and Paul?

To a depressive and a busy lad, just recalling how "As Tears Go By" got made was exhausting. I'd remember the musicians' sigh of relief at not having to play the B-side, Lionel's fartstopper, anymore (which was originally to have been the A-side). That feeling of release can be heard in the very playing of "As Tears Go By," making it so magical and un-B-side-ish. The mere idea of trying to repeat that sequence was draining. And for what? For the 2000, 3000 quid a hit record made you? The girl was not going to be big on stage, and at that time she did nothing except, of course, all the essentials after the fact.

Marianne was hailed as Britain's latest pop sensation. "As Tears Go By" would enter the top ten in Britain and snuggle into the top twenty in the States, where *Billboard* magazine would name her "the greatest discovery of the year." Now that I'd sold her and had my way in the world with her, depression caused me to scorn the success itself. What had I done, after all? I'd taken an attractive, educated girl, "possibly a virgin, with big tits, sings and thinks with acoustic guitar, has hit, will probably fuck - You could be the lucky one! - please buy record at a store near you or send a s.a.e. and recent photo to 138/147 Ivor Court." I'd moved her out of the Baez/Greco Gauloise bohemian coffee bar circuit and onto my revered and sacred pop charts. I was a regular fucking Siegfried and Roy. I would make one lame effort at a follow-up with Marianne, but my heart wasn't in it, girl. I'd then call it a day and allow her to move on to Tony Calder.

This was no way to handle a hit, but once you're on the up-the-down staircase, you start looking around for the "if-nots," rent space, and live there.

Nobody knew how to help, and, if help was offered, I rejected it out of hand. I wanted something that worked now. I'd drink it off, sex it off, smoke it off, and if I woke up the next day and it was not spent and gone, I'd repeat myself again until it was.

The Rolling Stones didn't help. I wished them away on a permanent tour. Having achieved some modicum of success, they now seemed to have something to lose - or was this just something I perceived? They seemed to think that I was there to unburden themselves and moan to. I was getting very short-tempered, and my personal life with Sheila was shot. I looked into the hearts and minds of older soldiers like Lionel Bart and Sean Kenny; a drink with them would temporarily assuage my horrors. After a warm night out with the boys I'd glow a little, lighten up, and be on the mend again.

In 1964 Sheila and I were much too young to get married, and, had my mother and her parents not been so against the legaled union, I might not have forced the issue and we might not have eloped. Or perhaps Sheila had told me that she would leave me and this was the cure - marriage as a bouquet for bad behaviour. Aside from giving some title and stability to having children, I don't know why she wanted to be married to me. I could be gracious and say she loved me, which she did, and I thought I did. But she didn't know me - and neither did I.

The honeymoon took place before, not after, the marriage, and, whilst Sheila was the only thing in my life, we had a very good time. I was happy, my ambition at the time achieved. I was with her. I had met the Rolling Stones and they had become my passion and ambition, and I worked at that and stopped working at being with Sheila. We were children - I was, at least. I didn't know enough at nineteen about life to realise how I was hurting her, and I certainly had no business making her my wife.

Sheila had had enough of my overwound clock. She was fed up with the numb, spent friend she had on her hands and headed for the south of France to "cool out." I followed her, but not before I'd done more damage that I'd later have to extricate myself from. Out of my mind - what else? - I had supplied some inexcusable, embarrassingly lame tripe to *Melody Maker*.

The headline ran: "Andy Won't Be Handy for the Stones." The article stated: "The sixth Rolling Stone is retiring from show business," and went on and on in that vein.

"I don't enjoy it anymore," I told them. "There are a lot of talented people of my age in this country, but there's no room for them to move. You start out wanting to earn loot and when you get it there's nothing left." The article concluded: "Oldham has been mainly instrumental in building the Rolling Stones image. We wonder if they'll let him go?" The Rolling Stones had no say in the matter; that would come later. Then I was off again to the south of France, only confirming Eric Easton's self-satisfied, tut-tut opinion of my instability and unbusinesslike demeanor. The next week, the second week of September, *Melody Maker* ran the full interview under the banner: "Stones Man Says 'I Quit!'"

The Rolling Stones should have fired or disowned me, but they knew that this was just a stray mangled bullet. They knew that I still had quite a few live chambers to fire on their behalf.

Even in the madness, I was still copping the great moves that I'd witnessed when I was in school. I traced my bizarre behaviour back to John Osborne's famous "Damn you, England" drama of 1961. Combine that with Yves Saint Laurent's nervous breakdown on being forced into the Frog army in 1960, and you've got the weight and shape of every pained and plaintive move I made.

Melody Maker informed all its readers that I was retiring the next week with a lot of money and an ulcer. In the article I was hailed by some as a genius and by more as an exhibitionist idiot.

But I was not suffering from an ulcer - that was a stand-in for what was ailing me. I just refused to mention the word "depression." My black moods were still unfathomable to me, all the more so because the trigger of depression seemed to be success.

I had done the *Melody Maker* piece whilst at an all-time low. When I returned from the south of France with Sheila, I was back on track, my effervescent sparkle intact and apparent. I'd left one matter unsorted, the matter of getting wed.

Whilst in Juan-les-Pins, I'd had Sheila call her parents from a call box and advise them that we wished to get married. She didn't get as far as asking for their blessing. From London to Juan came a resounding parental, "No!" We decided to return to London and work on both of them and my mom as well. I was lining up Celia as a public relations ally - but I didn't need her consent. Her only words on the matter were, "I think you are both being very stupid and I hope you change your mind before you do something you will both regret." Sheila's parents' consent was needed; their daughter was underage.

Back in London, I looked around me and saw the commotion that I had caused via the *Melody Maker* piece. I hope I mumbled an apology to Keith, Mick, Bill, and Charlie about letting the side down and having spoken out of turn in public. I also hoped that Brian Jones would not sense an ally and invite me to hang. I then basically rolled over the whole event, went to sleep, got up, and went to work.

I was back in Regent Sound with engineer Bill Farley to cut some more Stones sides. The standout was the group's rendition of Willie Dixon's "Little Red Rooster." They played it with so much love and flair that you could hear the passion and ease in every groove. There was nothing to balance once they settled into it; they balanced themselves and sank into the deep blues.

Brian really shone on this back-to-the-roots occasion of joy. Mick squirreled his tab-collared frame against the wall. It was cold and he rubbed his bum on the wall in warm up, then summoned up his boy-coy blues in a masterful, relaxed, on-the-edge vocal display. Charlie slapped the rest of the sound into place and magic oozed into the room and stuck to the tape.

The group thought it would make an ideal single. I was caught between agreeing and seeing it from a different point of view. I vacillated about it daily. Some days I felt it was too un-commercial, totally the wrong can of goods to propel the Stones' U.K. ascent. The next day I'd hear it and think it was just what the good doctor ordered. It was time to hold back the momentum, to avoid having to top this, top that. Why not use the occasion to enable us to set our own pace? The idea of a comfortable top five record that reminded the Stones fans of their Delta chops and played to the bottom-line R&B faithful, instead of another booming number one, was very attractive. With that idea in mind, "Little Red Rooster" b/w "Off the Hook" was scheduled for a mid-November release.

The whole process had been an audio dream. Tony Calder and I went up to Decca's West Hampstead studio to master the tape onto disc, and the audio brilliance was so apparent that the thing basically mastered itself.

I did not need to worry. The public made my mind up for me, I didn't even have to buy singles in the chart shops this time. The Stones fans, double their weight in verve since "Not Fade Away," placed pre-orders for 180,000 copies and we were assured of our next career highlight: number one first week.

Whilst the Stones were away in the North of England, Sheila and I lay in each other's arms, checked each other's smiles, let things get physical, and did a lot of walking and talking on

Hampstead Heath and Primrose Hill.

"We could get married in Scotland, Andrew." Sheila held my hand as we looked down on the zoo. She then told me she thought she was pregnant. The fact that she was with child only sealed the deal, so getting married in Scotland was what we decided to do. I wanted to be wed anyway, muted by love, good intent, and the chorus of parental no's.

We'd decided then and there on Primrose Hill. We both felt very good, very nervous, excited, and shy with pride. The sky was white above Primrose Hill and grey beyond the zoo. As we looked the other way toward Chalk Farm, the sky also made up its mind - it was both white and grey above the railway lines that ran along and around the foot of Haverstock Hill. I asked for Sheila's hand toward the evening of the day. She put her hand in mine and we started to walk back down the lane. I squeezed that last-felt drop of innocence and held onto it as if my very life depended on it - and on that day it did, with the thought of a new life on both our minds as we held each other home. I really felt that hope of innocence, though it would be mostly gone by the day she'd say "I do." The next day would be our last in London.

"My parents think I'm going to be staying at Linda Keith's. We'll be in Glasgow before they think something's wrong," Sheila smiled as she packed her suitcase, and for the first time something felt very wrong. But I was raised on my word and without one we drove to the airport, two hearts, at least one confused, beating as one.

I would still get bored easily, elopement notwithstanding. I disobeyed the actual Scottish law regarding three weeks residence in their country by taking a few day-trips down to London and back. I figured that, as long as I slept in Scotland, who would care where I took lunch. At one such run through the Glasgow airport, I came across a Scottish-only pop magazine that featured on its cover a very striking, knowing, smart bunch of lads called the Poets. It proclaimed them as Scotland's number one band, which they were. They had glam, but they were street, not kiddie-pop. I found out where the lead singer lived and presented myself at his doorstep. George Gallacher was sleeping off a gig and an acid-tabbed night. I shared a bottle of Whyte and Mackay with George's dad, a formidable, fanatical Stalinist with that strange contradictory Calvinistic morality of the Glaswegian communist. We all got on and in two weeks I was at Pye studios recording the group. Six weeks later they'd be in the charts.

Sheila and I got back married from Glasgow and we had to do our bit for the press, which I found as uncomfortable as being married. Earlier, Sheila had brought over this young boy named Andy, who'd lived in Antrim Grove around the corner from me when I'd lived on Haverstock Hill. She seemed to be offering young Andy to me as a branched olive to make up for a fight we'd just had. I refused, thinking, but not saying, that, if I were going to visit this anomalous attraction, I'd rather pick my own. Sheila left, taking, I gathered, young Andy for her own.

Meanwhile, Mick and Keith moved into a more "reet petite" address, out of the bowels of Willsden, high atop Hampstead in the very street where William Wyler would film *The Collector* with T. Stamp and Samantha Eggar, 10a Holly Hill. They were writing with a vengence and the Lord said, "You are getting nearer to the Stones."

Friday, October 23, 1964, the Rolling Stones arrived in New York for another stint with Clay Cole and an afternoon and evening show the next day at the Academy of Music to kick off their second North American tour. These two sold-out shows were followed by the Stones' debut on the Yank equivalent of our own *Sunday Night at the London Palladium - The Ed Sullivan Show,* a make-or-break, Sunday night, eight o'clock, national event. The Stones mimed "Around and Around" and "Time is on My Side." The latter, released as a U.S.-only single in September, was hovering around the top thirty, imitating our first near-hit. Much later it would emerge as one of the first signposts of the time and prove a perennial favourite amongst North American fans, especially as they got older. The chorus would become less a well-remembered refrain and more a statement of stop-clocking and hope.

Once again Phil Spector kindly lent me his couch in the ground-floor office of the same building where he maintained has east sixties penthouse. I came back there shortly after eleven on that Sunday night of the Sullivan performance, the show done and discussed over a Broadway deli dinner with a few of the Stones and Stu. Much to my surprise, Phil was in the office, all diminutive, huddled and black, hovering over his chipper promotion man,

Danny Davis. The office was small and unspectacular, the type of ground-floor space typically tenanted by dentists and chiropractors. Spread open across the desk was a Sony-type suitcase record player and speakers, built like a huge Samsonite - a mighty machine with a mighty sound.

Phil didn't pay much attention to me. I sat down on the couch as he just managed a barely audible, "Great Sullivan show, the guys were terrific."

Then he went back to what he'd been doing. He had on the turntable a white-labeled 45 rpm test-pressing, which he put into play. The room was filled with amazing sound. I had no idea what it was, but it was the most incredible thing I'd ever heard. I slowly and numbly felt my way through the aural maze and discerned what I thought was two black guys singing a very sad, tortured, oh-so-laboured, and stated regret about things that "she" didn't do anymore when they kissed, of eyes no longer closing when they called her name ... or was it kissed her lips?

Underneath lay a bed of sustained everything - drones of echo'd majestic hurt that lasted forever, the only movement provided by a "La Bamba"-thick bass on quinalbarbitone. Come the chorus, the track, as one, started a stop-start, tymph-flayed, richochet'd beat as voices, angels, and strings strained in Wagnerian, classical ache, followed by another verse of higher pain. On the altar of middle eight the rhythm got down on its knees, pulling the symphonic sustain along to the next corner - and just "baby"s and "please"s. The two voices' gospel shrieks and wails were then propelled by a bass-end Latin suggestion of rhythm and hope through the last heaven's gate to the final, telling chorus.

That last chorus was as if Jesus had risen and Moses had come down with the Ten Commandments of Sound.

I had no idea what the record was and nobody was telling me. Phil grunted, scratched his goatee, and sighed. Danny Davis studied his hands, Phil, and the wall. The record player, on auto, started again.

Was this Phil's work? I wasn't sure. It was certainly nothing like his usual up-tempo avalanches of fulfilled and celebrated love, heavy with percussion, pianos, guitars, keyboards, stabbing horns, and wailing, nubile, black songbirds, as in the Crystals' epic "He's a Rebel" or the Ronettes' transcendent "Be My Baby."

Yet it had to be Phil's, unless we were all dreaming (and we could be). I'd never heard a recorded track so emotionally giving or empowering. There was so much sound that I would not have been surprised if I'd just heard three different recordings playing different parts of the whole. The audio fidelity was that awe-inspiring.

The record was the Righteous Brothers' "You've Lost That Lovin' Feeling."

CHAPTER 18

keith and i visit another lead singer - old blue eyes as opposed to childbearing lips (thanks, joan rivers) / jack nitzsche - a divine intervention / twenty-five years later - life through the tapebox looking glass war / a strife of brian / charlie watts - puttin' on the blitz / keith channels the sixth stone

Keith Richards and I shared a great moment together in the Los Angeles of 1965. The shared moment was Frank Sinatra.

The kicks had moved from Route 66 to the Sunset Strip. The Stones and I were on a productive run ensconced, when touring and traveling allowed, at the RCA recording studios on the corner of Sunset and Iver. We were in the middle of a nearly two-year roll, and it seemed we could do no wrong: "Satisfaction," "The Last Time," "Play with Fire," "Under My Thumb," "Get Off of My Cloud," "Lady Jane," "Out of Time," "Mother's Little Helper," "19th Nervous Breakdown," "Have You Seen Your Mother, Baby?," "Paint It, Black." Mick's and Keith's songs just kept getting stronger - on the money and of the moment.

One mid-afternoon I sidled up to Keith in the centre of Studio A. As usual, he was jeaned and slightly scarved, on stool, guitar in hand, fag in mouth, plastic cups around.

"Let's take a break around five," I said.

"OK," said Keith, not giving me much thought, not wishing to leave the moment.

Mo Ostin and Joe Smith, the two number ones at Warner/ Reprise, had invited me to attend a Frank Sinatra session at five-thirty at Universal (a recording studio, nothing to do with the Universal entertainment conglomerate), a few blocks along on the south side of Sunset.

Mo and Joe built Warner/Reprise from the early sixties into the Warner-Elektra-Atlantic/WEA giant that it became by the mid-seventies. Ostin had soldiered up through the Sinatra admin-ranks and came into the Warner's pack when Frank's Reprise Records merged with Warner Brothers Records in '63. Joe Smith had begun as a deejay at Yale spinning Nat King Cole platters in the fifties. Under their astute professional care, WEA represented the true artists' home. They remain remarkable record men whose ease with themselves, the music, and the artists was a pleasure to be around. They were never desperate.

As regards the Sinatra invite, I couldn't bring the whole group - they weren't invited. Anyway, I didn't want to. Mick, as a vocalist and true star, would have had to make light of the occasion, "Oh, shall I bring a spare toupee?"

"Can I bring Keith?" I asked Joe Smith on the phone from the RCA reception. "We may as well have two musicians there."

"Sure," said a relieved Joe, for Keith was still thought of as "the quiet one."

Keith and I whipped out smartly at five. We stood on the sidewalk outside RCA for a minute watching the Sunset Strip evening rush hour crawl begin. Then a honk from a black Caddy on the other side of the street beckoned us over to Joe Smith's car.

"So where are we going, Andrew?" asked Keith as we rolled onto Sunset.

"Joe's taking us to meet Frank Sinatra," I grinned.

"Oh, nice one," said Keith, surprised but not amazed.

Fifteen Warhols later we sat in the quiet control room of the Universal studio, the engineer fiddling with dials on the console, and me, Joe Smith, and Sagittarian Keith sitting behind him on the couch waiting for Sinatra to arrive.

A few minutes later arrive he did, though to our surprise he didn't come into the control room. The man walked straight into the studio and headed for the stool in the centre of the room, surrounded by bafflers inside which stood a mike, cans, and speakers.

He sat down, adjusted himself into the stool, put a headphone on one ear, indicated he wanted the playback via the headphones and speakers, which were positioned so as not to bleed into the microphone when played at a reasonable level. He snapped his fingers to feel the air in the room, agreed with the shine on his shoes, and signaled to the booth to roll the tape. Frank was ready to go.

We were not many years down the road from direct-to-disc, the original mode of recording that had replaced cylinders or "rolls." After direct to the monolathe came monaural tape, then two-track, thus enabling us to hear duplications in stereo. Now in these mid-sixties the biz had teched up and graduated to four-track, meaning that recordings could be made utilising four separate channels, which, upon being filled, would be paired down to stereo or mono.

The evening's song was a milestone: "Strangers in the Night." The musical tracks were already in place and Ol' Blue Eyes was crooning into the warmth of the studio. Keith and I sat a wee bit gobsmacked at the pro-eaze we were seeing and hearing. In the next forty-five minutes Frank Sinatra recorded two or three takes of "Strangers in the Night" and two other songs. When satisfied with his handling of a song after two or three takes he didn't stop, or come into the control room, or ask to listen to what he had just done. He knew what he had done and just said, "Next one," and perhaps, "please."

This was high style. We were used to listening and analyzing vocal performances on studio monitors, headphones, and even car speakers before saying yes or no. The consummate Mr. Sinatra knew, at the moment of doing, what was right or wrong.

The three songs recorded, he eased off the chair, put the headphones back into their place cradling the neck of the microphone stand, then walked through the studio and into the control room.

On entering the booth, ignoring us, he slapped the back of the engineer and asked, "Everything OK?"

The engineer said, "Yes, sir." The "sir" was both mock Bilko and of total respect.

"OK, you know which ones to use," came back Frank.

Now that's the tall order. Keith and I looked at each other on that one. Frank expected the engineer to be as tuned to Sinatra as he was to himself. No drama, no questions. You're here because you are a pro and this is how the consummate Frank gets it done.

Sinatra turned toward the couched and carpeted visitors' section and Joe Smith got up. They smiled and greeted each other, arms clasped around the other's arm and shoulder, one dignified notch away from a hug.

"Hallo, Frank," said Joe. "You sounded just great."

Frank gave out a ring-a-ding smile and said nothing. He knew, but didn't know, who we were, and now that the work was done, he checked the state of his French cuffs, approved, and wondered - two, three, four - wondered - dropped the smile in all save the eyes and wondered about us with a flick toward Joe.

Joe got the flick. "Frank," Joe's left arm allowed toward Keith and me, his right still clasping Sinatra's elbow as we both rose for the occasion. "I'd like you to meet Keith Richard and Andrew Oldham from the Rolling Stones. They're in from England. I just wanted them to be able to meet you."

Joe, too, was a pro's pro. No unnecessary detail, as in "guitarist/writer/manager/producer." Just the facts for the ring-a-ding man - don't confuse the attention span granted.

Sinatra politely, and he did indeed have searing great ol' blue eyes when he put them to you, shook hands with Keith and me, thanked us for coming to see him, and hoped we were having a good time here in his realm.

"You guys know Harold Davison?" he asked as he tugged his hand back.

"Yes, we do." I spoke for us both in reference to Frank's U.K. promoter.

"Say hallo to him for me. And to Marion." He'd ref'd the singer Marion Ryan, soon-to-be Mrs. Harold Davison. Sinatra then said goodbye to one and all and left us alone in the control room.

We were both pretty knocked aback. Keith and I knew we'd just seen an amazing example of the *modus operandi* of a master, and Joe Smith was delighted to see the pleasure in our faces as we thanked him for bringing us to this memorable occasion.

We ambled into the hall and were chatting about life in general, or slagging other acts, when I turned and looked down the long hall, through the glass studio doors out onto Sunset.

There, black-straw-hatted, black-silk or mohair-slub-suited, in a black open Lincoln Continental, waiting for the lights to be green, sat Sinatra at the wheel. There was no entourage, bodyguards, rat pack, or clan. Just a man, content, alone, the day's work done, joining the rest of the early L.A. evening traffic, going home.

It was just one of those things, just one of those fabulous things - Mr. Frank Sinatra.

Few people have the happy experience to sit and realise that they have become who they truly are, to confront the worth of the work. I have, and it is a loud encounter with a clear sound.

The Stones records could not have been done in New York in that particular time because, like London, New York has seasons. That's why we went to L.A. to record. L.A. placed a tone on the records we made there. Walking outside a studio any time of the year (and this was a year when everybody was well and everything was going well) into the L.A. sunshine was a trip.

With us on that trip, faithfully, always the consummate pro, was Jack Nitzsche. Jack ended up playing on the whole RCA Stones run - all their records of that time. After I was introduced to him by Sonny Bono, he just appeared at the sessions. I didn't ask him what he was doing there in case he asked me for money. There are three keyboard players on those mid-sixties Stones RCA sessions: If it's a blues figure, it's Ian Stewart on piano. On a few occasions when it's slightly strange it might be Brian; but the rest - all the piano, organ, harpsichord playing - the denseness, the body, the glue - is Jack Nitzsche. Later, in England, Nicky Hopkins would join our three pianoteers and make it four.

There are some tracks you can definitely hear Jack on; for example, the harpsichord on "Play with Fire" is Jack. His overall contribution is a little harder to pinpoint. If I were to try and define it, I'd say he provided the melodic bond, the undercurrent to Keith and Brian's layers of guitar brainwash.

He didn't arrange - that was the Stones' job - he led, sat in the pit, was the metronome in groove time. On some tracks, like "Satisfaction" - depending on the system you're hearing it on - you might not hear Jack's piano, but it's fucking there, and if it weren't there, you'd miss it. Whereas on "Let's Spend the Night Together," of course you can hear it.

Then there was that mythical instrument, the "Nitzschephone." I made that name up for the credits on those Stones albums. It was just a regular piano (or maybe an organ) miked differently. The idea was meant to be: "My god, they've had to invent new instruments to capture this new sound they hear in their brains!" And they were inventing fresh sounds with old toys - therefore it deserved to be highlighted. It was the read-up of creation, of imagination - getting credit for a job well-done. You wouldn't, for instance, have found a "Nitzschephone" on a Freddie and the Dreamers record.

Jack gave us an understanding of tone. Which tone fits the

universe? Which thing was hummable in the street? It was never
a tone or a key that would embarrass a member of the public and
dissuade him or her from singing along. On the up-tempo things,
that's the key he provided. Tone was key in those days, because we
were, in a way, only one step away from direct-to-disc recording.
Everything was down to placement and miking. Where somebody
sat, and what leaked into what, were critical. We were pre-separa-
tion. Jack had that knowledge of instrument levels, of placement.
The other thing that Jack had was a grasp of, and interest in, sex.
How to inject sex into the sound is a gift of understanding between
you and your third ear. That's a huge component. I suppose after
awhile it could become a little frustrating if you know how to make
perfectly recorded sex. Could leave you with frustrations in the
other world.

He would go on to be a producer himself - already was, as
a matter of fact. There were no rules then - just be it and get on with
it. With Nick Venet he produced "Love Her," the second Walker
Brothers record. It was made at that same RCA studio where the
Stones recorded. This was the Barry Mann/Cynthia Weil song that
became the Walkers' first single when they arrived in England.

Jack continued to work on Stones albums up through *Let
It Bleed* and *Sticky Fingers*. And of course he was in Neil Young's
band, Crazy Horse. He played keyboards on and wrote arrangements for a slew of Neil's projects. Boy, could he sit a track down.

Jack never developed a "style" as a producer; I don't think
he had one. Basically, he chased, caught, and defined the style of
the artist, which, for many, is what a producer is supposed to do.

Back in '64 when we first met him, Jack was robust. If he
took drugs, he didn't take them in front of me. He was sweet, shy,
polite, cooperative, and fucking talented. What else do you want?
Then he went home. He was boring on other people's time. I remember him fondly as a married man who should have stayed happily married. We don't know what goes on once somebody closes
his own oak door, but where he was at the time was a very warm
and attractive place. I know that Charlie and Shirley Watts were
very attracted to that side of him - they spent a lot of time with him
and Gracia Nitzsche whilst everybody else was out chasing pussy
and buying clothes. You can only wish that kind of thing would go
on forever for people like Jack, but, for whatever reasons, he wanted

to change his life, and, unfortunately, he was one of those people who could only do that with dire consequences to themselves.

Jack's musician-idolising-fetishising thing was a treacherous area. You're supposed to make the public fall in love with the act - but if you do, it's fatal, and Jack was sometimes guilty. It's the same thing as in the eighties when the whole of American Radioland seemed to fall in love with Emmylou Harris's hair. I find a little gross what some programme directors wanted to do with her hair. That business where Jack is supposed to have shoved a gun in Carrie Snodgress's cunt is an example of such madness and drug-driven entitlement.

We all go through periods where we're good at one thing and we think that this qualifies us to be good at other things. That's probably where Jack got his dick cut off. He couldn't play producer. In a way Jack was almost too sensitive and he played with some pretty fucking hard people. I mean, I'm sure that Willy "Mink" DeVille is probably a sweetheart, but when I met him, his opening line was: "I don't trust anybody who doesn't do opiates." I ran into Jack on the staircase of the Speakeasy in 1974 when I was producing Donovan. I hadn't seen him since '66 and his opening words to me were: "Andrew! How are you? Do I have to be bisexual to make it?" And I said, "Uh oh - you've been hanging around with Mick too long, honey." Mick has this habit of playing with people who haven't actually got the head for it, like Mick Taylor. Mick and Keith assisted him into Humpty Dumpty land inside of two years.

Aside from the odd gig, mainly from the seventies on Jack was writing, arranging, scoring, and performing film music: *The Exorcist, 9 1/2 Weeks, Stand by Me, An Officer and a Gentleman, Performance, Cutter's Way, The Crossing Guard,* and *One Flew Over the Cuckoo's Nest,* for which he was nominated for an Academy Award. He did *Hardcore* - that was a great soundtrack - and *The Hot Spot,* the Dennis Hopper movie - great use of Miles Davis and all that blues stuff. But Hollywood is also a very gothic place. Jack had to mix with a lot of sick fucks in quicksand.

The last time I saw him it was a gorgeous occasion. Phil Spector flew Jack to Phil's Rock and Roll Hall of Fame induction ceremony in 1989, and all of us were managing to behave for the evening. Jack looked just like Jack of old and it was just wonderful.

He was all apple pie, you know, American apple pie around the waist. I had a sweet time, but what's not to have a sweet time on the night Phil was being honoured? For once he wasn't behaving like a Manishewitz/Prozac driven pig - which he had on other occasions, though not of late. Phil was very sweet that night. We went over to Mick Jones of Foreigner's apartment on Central Park and Phil was telling me off about taking drugs - the pot calling the kettle beige.

The final curtain must have come very fast for Jack - it does: I know from personal experience. I was only three weeks away from my own last act when I decided that I wanted to live. Jack was robust at the Rock and Roll Hall of Fame, but then decided to crash and burn.

He became a kind of maniac toward the end. I saw a picture of him taken in the Mayflower Hotel in New York the August of his demise in 2000 and he looked absolutely terrifying. He looked like he hadn't recovered from Neil Young. It was like the usual pic of Willie Nelson wearing a cowboy hat, the old Gringo Indian, but with every fucking disease under the sun. That sounds harsh, I know. I'm not trying to be tough on Jack. I'm trying to give people storm warnings, which we know they won't take, 'cause everybody's invincible till the final curtain comes down or fluffs them on the shoulder.

But through it all, Jack Nitzsche had the ability to sit and to figure it out, to get to the square root of the sound.

I only remember two other fellas getting into the inner sanctum at the RCA sessions, Lou Adler and J.W. Alexander. Everybody else, from assorted wanna-be's, chicks, and thunder, had to cool their heels in the RCA lobby, guarded by two off-duty cops (we had to watch our backs, keeping all strays and the union away). Inside the studio there was no booze, some pot, no girls, and a lot of work. Work was still play.

Where the boys are, wherever, ever are the Stones. It was the usual tight ship at RCA - just the nine of us: five Stones, Stu, engineer Dave Hassinger, keyboardist Jack Nitzsche, and *moi*.

****

Twenty-four years later I'm holding the brown tapebox that contains the three recorded takes of "Everybody Needs Somebody to Love" (one of Atlantic Records' soul gems written by Bert Berns, Solomon Burke, and Jerry Wexler) and two more of another Bert Berns Atlantic classic," Cry to Me." It's early 1989 and all does not toll well in my head. Allen Klein has asked me to stop into his office to look over some old tapes that they are attempting to clarify. I'm out of sorts, trying to clarify mere life. Last night I'd done a cable TV interview and was in such a bad mood that, when I was asked, in all fairness, "What did I do?" referring back to the Stones, I snapped, "What did I do? I took credit for other people's work." I'm still into finding new versions of what constitutes bottom; I need a fucking life before I run out of mine.

Around twelve, I leave the Iroquois Hotel. God, I know that walk. I'm past the rewards of drinking; my shyness is not lifted, it's deepened by the Italian moonshine that is my new preference and by the lines that pitter patter in its wake. Already part of the now pathetic loop, I've got the depression that I brought to life's party, that blackhearted son of a gun that still joins me on every celebratory occasion and reminds me to shoot myself. And I've added the chemical brother and Aunt Alcohol to boot the last man inside me down. It's a gallowed walk on which I'll forever see pavement; I'm not into looking up anymore. I downwalk the 44th Street block west across 6th Avenue, pick up my stride, hit my marks for a bravado-puffed entrance into a bistro called One, Two, Three. I hail a morning espresso and grappa, run to the john for my second morning line, and then make sure I'm not sweating too much with a second grappa - though the burning in my liver would light a fire. I head toward Broadway and north ten blocks in an attempt to walk the morning's boozefest into a facade of good health, gargle in the rest room, wipe off the last rim of sweat, do a toot for longevity, and sway into Allen's office around one. The tapeboxes are put in front of me and the tapes are racked up for me to listen to - another fucking chore of duty in the twilight zone. It's not a good year for me to be listening to Stones outtakes; it just makes me feel like one.

My attention is drawn to words written on the tapebox in a different hand and ink than the take-by-take data. The two words are "Brian Wilson." Does this mean anything to me? I'm asked. Well, the work of Brian Wilson has done a lot for me, whilst doing a lot to himself. *Pet Sounds* was a land of hope and glory to me, but, in this moment, I cannot fathom the what and why of his name scrawled there in red.

Meanwhile, inside my head, I can keep secrets, and I'm grinning and recalling as the tape is slowly rewound, for I remember Brian Wilson coming to the Stones sessions. He sat in the neoned RCA reception, maybe next to a Buffalo Springfield. He didn't come into the studio - nobody "came in" when we were in. I'd left the control room to clear my head and ears. It had been another eighteen-hour stretch on a four-day watch, and the tracks for the album were more or less down. After that much time in front of the console, you are merely guessing, but fortunately, it was the year of guessing right. I stretched into the hall and whacked on my two ears with a tweak of my forefinger and thumb, one crack each. The sky opened up inside and I was back in the land of heard. (I was not familiar with my third ear yet. Well, I knew him, but I didn't always go along with him.)

Five minutes later my ears were more than clear as a result of a Hawaiian joint that rushed me back to work. As I got up from the not-even-nearly-leather studio reception couch I heard Brian Wilson say, "One day I will write songs that people will pray to."

Dear Brian nearly had it right, God only knows. He should have said, "One day I will write songs that will move people to pray for me." He already had.

Back in the studio a take was completed on "Everybody Needs Somebody to Love." It had been a good day. The music ended and I heard myself speak from the console, directing my voice at Mick. Keith had already spoken with himself.

"It's fine. If we use two, there's something to be fixed. The piano ... you know?"

Mick replied curtly, "Yeah, fine. Yooou knowww, this isn't a fuckin' Brian Wilson record you knoooow."

"I know that," I replied, "I've been with you long enough to know the difference, dear."

A snigger or twitter southwest in the studio - Stu or Bill Wyman.

"Well, what do you wanna do about it?" I said into the void.

"Nothing," said Mick.

"Nothing?" I asked him.

"Keep two and fix it?" came the pouted reply.

The answer's "Yes," I said to myself, got up, and left. It was still so in January '89.

I recalled, too, a second time that the California Boy had graced us with his presence some months later, on the day that we nailed the tracks for "My Obsession" and "All Sold Out."

****

Back to the subject of keyboards, and of the faithful. It seemed light years ago, that day in 1963 that I'd sat in my back office *chez* Eric Easton and decreed to Mick and Brian that Rollin' had to have a "g," and that the Rolling Stones could only be five - ergo, Ian Stewart would have to go. A lot would then happen to all of us on this good ship rock 'n' pop. Ten years down the pike and into the seventies all the rules would have changed. In 1963 there were, for all outward appearances, just five Rolling Stones. But, in the end, Stu would stay with the Stones a lifetime longer than I did.

A while back, in the midst of my madness, I'd have liked to have had it that it was one of my brilliant moves, and give you every twist and turn with callous delight. I'd have told you that such a cold, correct move could only have been made by a cold, astute fucker, and I was never uncomfortable about what I caused to go down in front of Stu. Some years ago I might have, but not now.

Brian had to add insult to injury by following up on my "Stu must go" dictum with a fake assurance to Ian that he would be taken care of financially and would always be a part of the band. I didn't see the other Stones giving lip service to this charade, but none of them blocked my move either.

There were some fundamental things on which I know that Ian Stewart and I agreed. Like, the more the Stones rolled on, as the hits got bigger and better, Brian Jones would deliver some of his finest music in his *second* burst of inspiration. He surprised us with his adept picking up of an instrument hitherto unknown to him and coming up with a polished gem that enhanced recordings of "Lady Jane," "Out of Time," "Paint It, Black," and so many more.

But while Brian got off on the dulcimer, sitar, marimbas,

recorders, and more, he stopped getting down on the guitar; so Keith found himself doing double duty, not only on call as himself, but also subbing for Brian. Sometimes on the road Brian would shine and summon up all the power and glory of his bottleneck anthems, "I Wanna Be Your Man" and "Little Red Rooster," while scaling the twin guitar peaks of the first three Stones LPs with Keith. But all this was slipping away, as was Brian himself. Midway through March 1966 at RCA studios came a night that I couldn't leave the room (as opposed to knowing when to and being able to). Brian had finally arrived at the studio, God only knows, after days of who knew where or when, in absolutely no condition to clock in and work.

He managed to plug his guitar into his amp, but that was as far as it got. He was bulbous and bloated; no colour was right for him that day. Everything he wore, an absurd combo of velvet, stripes, and squares, reeked of disregard for the very fabric of clothing into life, of untoward disarray. He collapsed on the not-too-comfortable, cold, wood, studio floor. He didn't notice; he was beyond feeling shame or hurt. Grey to the gills, ready to explode in mind and body, he clutched his guitar like a life preserver, as though life was hard to find. He just lay in a pathetic fetal position on the floor, draining the life out of the room.

Mick got paler. It was catching. I noticed with regret I was wearing maroon. Mick folded his arms and pursed his oracular gob. He would have been much more at home in an apron and slippers, tizzying around the kitchen, tutting at the spuds for not coming to the boil. But we were in the studio, where time was never on our side and we had work to do.

For nearly an hour we all worked on eggshells, overdubbing on already-recorded basic tracks, working around the sad centrepiece of Pisces pain that lay in the centre of the studio, oblivious to being in the centre of the very world he had dreamed of and where he was now self-destructing centre-stage. After nearly two hours of stepping around and over Brian, Dave Hassinger - following the night's unspoken flight plan of "Ignore him, we don't need to talk about it, we need to work" - set up microphones for percussion and organ, with baffles surrounding the setup to keep any Brian sound out, as we now needed optimum quiet for the overdub.

Our engineer then let us know that he could no longer ignore the hum coming from the amp in response to Brian's constantly rearranging his crashed form nearer it and the mikes.

We had been working on "What to Do," which was fitting, as we all waited on each other to sort out Dave Hassinger's immediate problem of Brian zonked out on the studio floor. We all looked around the room, the floors, the walls, and each other for a volunteer to deal with the man overboard.

I looked at Charlie, who just looked back and dared me.

I looked over at Dave Hassinger, sitting there chewing the cud, his arms around his neck, feet resting on the recording console. He'd clocked out and his body language quite clearly said, "I've told you the problem. One of you has to tell me how to deal with it."

I looked at the still-sullen, pissed-off Mick. He wasn't going anywhere, his look back at me was in anger, and he said, "Produce your way out of this one, then let me know. I've had it." Charlie surveyed his kit domain and stayed in it. Bill managed to ignore the proceedings and find something to smile on for at least five of every hour.

I locked into Keith's eyes. He took them on a trip around the room and dropped me off on top of the Jones heap - the Brian unseen - then brought us both back and squared off at me. Fuck him, I thought. Mick had picked up on Keith's call and sent out the same message to management.

This was not part of the job description I thought I'd signed on for. I could do Sydney Falco, but not Monroe Stahr. I got up off the control room chair, walked into the studio toward Brian and the humming amp. I found the on/off switch, put it in off, yanked the guitar lead out of the amp, and walked back into the control room. Nothing needed to be said. It was all part of the gig, the beginning of the last rites, my day would come. We all went back to work, knowing what to do, and doing it, even though one of our aircraft was missing in action.

Back in the control room, Dave Hassinger stirred, Jack Nitzsche eased his heart back out to the Hammond and glock, and the Stones started rolling again.

"That's what happens when you fly without radar," were Keith's last words on the night.

****

In the first few days of December 1989, I saw Charlie Watts in heaven, an appropriate pre-Christmas vision in keeping with my times. The Charlie Watts Orchestra and more than twenty jazz musicians from England, Scotland, Wales, and Ireland descended upon the States for a short tour. They kicked off in Boston, then headed for the perfect venue, the Jerry Brandt-created Ritz on West 13th Street off lower 3rd Avenue in the hub of New York.

I sat in the balcony, feeling a total glow as I watched Charlie beaming behind his drums, enjoying every moment of being exactly where he wanted to be. My beam was moved along by my companion for the night, Pete Kameron. I didn't even need to drink, life was in such order. When you are on that end of the drug run, you fight for the night when it's all smooth. That night I was lucky. It was totally perfect as Charlie, sky grizzled blue, all clear, cottoned, linened, canvas-brogued, and silk-bowed, took over the whole room and let us into a very special musical place in his life, and we loved it. The band turned, swayed on a dime, and took us back to the swing that we were weaned on. Show done, I went backstage alone, Pete K. having decided to go uptown. I knew I was backstage at the Ritz and not on a nod, but I could have been rushing past effervescent Isobel on the door of the Rediffusion *Ready, Steady, Go!* Holborn Green Room. Charlie stood by the other very special place in his life, Shirley Watts. Tony King, seeing I was on and probably into behaving, graced me a "Here we are again!" happy beam, and willed me into the room. Tony looked great and not a day older than Decca. Keith Richards and Patti Hansen rounded out the circle. Tony King wanted to continue looking as good tomorrow, so he limo'd us to Keith and Patti's lower Broadway loft. Keith said come up. Tony smiled goodnight, and happily left us tucked into the evening, a replay of more than a thousand and one Tony nights as the King wafted off uptown to a face-saving sleep.

Keith opened my first visit to one of his homes in twenty-six years with a blast on his number one topic that fall, Mick. It was that year, the year of the thirty-year itch for Mick and Keith, and Keith showed no mercy: "Cunt of the month," "She should join Aerosmith," a slew of Joan Rivers one-liners dedicated to the one we love - Michael Philip. It was fast and funny - his outburst, recorded, could have been the comedy album of the year - then, just as suddenly, it was over. We switched channels, moved from E! to A&E as I listened to Keith's joy and pleasure at his 1986 production outing for Aretha Franklin on the Stones' classic, "Jumpin' Jack Flash," the title song of the Whoopi Goldberg comedic flick of the same name.

Keith was proud of his work and deservedly so. I loved the video, the shots of Keith ruling over the control room, totally in his element and in charge. The fact that I'd stopped off at the Colony and bought the single told him more than any of my words.

"It was great, man." Keith chimed. "We just went in and cut it."

"Three days," he continued proudly. "We did the whole fucking thing in three days, start to finish, video as well. She was great, ol' Aretha. I sat the bitch down at the piano and told her if she moved or got up, I'd fucking kill her. That's how I got it done; she didn't stand up once in three days. In and out, job done."

Minutes later we'd moved to another room, switched channels again, and Keith was playing tracks. I don't know how the subject of Ian Stewart came up, but he had to have been on Keith's mind a lot following his sudden death in England in 1985.

"Stu hated you, Andrew," Keith informed me. He paused, allowed the dime to drop, and continued, "But not as much as he hated Brian; he wanted to kill Brian." Keith let us both mull on that one, and I thought I heard him add, "Maybe he did."

Stu and I had been of like mind on a few things. Much to my surprise, "Satisfaction" was one of them. Whilst Mick and Keith were having entitled qualms and debating the value of their national anthem, Stu didn't give it a second thought and joined the ranks of those who loved it from the giddy-up. We also agreed, no vote needed, that I knew nothing about "their blues," and Stu would probably have added "rhythm" as well. Looking at the big picture, I'd add that my very lack of inclination for the blues, especially that version purveyed by little rich-miss white boys, actually helped me appreciate those Rollin' Stones more clearly in the beginning. It helped me to see what might be. I'm remembering that first time I saw the sextet in April '63 at the Station Hotel, Richmond, and how I'd been overwhelmed by this power and force and my life being over as I knew it. I had happily said hallo to the rest of that life, felt the hit of totality, not blinded by an opinion of "dem dere blues."

"He never forgave you for kicking him out of the group, Andrew," was what I heard Keith say instead.

"Yeah, maybe, but I couldn't have done it without help," was how I answered, wondering what revisionist journey this trip was all about.

"Well," I sighed, trying to move it further in to close the cycle, "I'm just glad Stu captured my essence so eloquently before he died. He's gone and he did me a favour. I'll never have to wonder what he really thought of me."

"What did he say?" asked Keith

"He said he wouldn't piss on me if I was on fire," I replied. We both laughed; Stu, looking down on us from above, tied the knot and grinned.

Keith's *Murder She Wrote* scenario was way northwest of any of my realities. All of this was water under the bridge, but Stu's passing was bringing it all back for Keith.

There were now three sides out and about on the "Sixth Stone." I knew what I'd been cause to and Keith could account for his own behaviour, and slipping out around in there was the truth. Neither Keith nor I was lying. We were both the masters of convenience, the art there being to serve and protect.

A few months later I'd stopped off in England on my way to no good in Oslo and was catching up with Cynthia Dillane, Stu's widow, on the phone.

"So how was Keith toward you when you met?" Cyn had asked, cutting straight to the point in a way that reminded me of what a wonderful minder and ally she had been.

"He was fine, really nice," I said.

"Good," said Cyn, waiting for more.

I made her wait, but not long. I told her about the Charlie show, seeing Tony King, my visit to Keith's, and how Joan Rivers would have applauded his timing and dissing of Mick.

"There was only one weird moment," I remembered, piquing Cyn's interest. "What weird moment?" she asked.

"It was about Stu. We were off at a tangent, first what Stu thought of me, then how he loathed Brian. Then I realised I was listening to Keith speculate on how maybe Stu hated Brian enough to kill him. Fucking blew me away, I can tell you. I'd never heard that one before."

"Oh, I have," Cyn flatlined. "Back at the time Brian died I thought about it too, and, in fact, Andrew, I went through Stu's diary just to see if he could have, but he couldn't have. He just couldn't have been there when thingally-jibb, I mean Brian, of course, just couldn't have been there when Brian died. Anyway, what did Keith say Stu thought of you?"

Cynthia had opened the door I'd left ajar, so I could tell her.

"He said Stu hated me and never forgave me for kicking him out of the Stones."

"Hmmm," even Cyn had to mark time on that one. "He was a strange man, Andrew, was our Stu. He didn't show it, but he was always terribly hurt by what happened."

"He had to be, Cyn," I was followed by silence.

"What did Keith say about the others?"

"Nothing."

"It's so sad," said Cynthia. "You know, I never thought that Stu ever felt that it was you he should hate."

"I didn't either, but it was never spoken about."

"Couldn't be," agreed Cyn. "And what did our Keith have to say about himself?"

"Nothing," I said. "I'm not even sure if Keith thinks he was there, you know, when it got done. When I did it, he just carried on about Brian."

"Yes," sighed Cyn, we'd played this one into sadness and it was time to move on.

"I think, in the end, that's what hurt Stu the most. He thought Brian was disgusting. He despised him, the little dwarf."

"Yeah, well, Keith sounded still cut up about Stu's death."

"He would be. Stu loved him a great deal."

"I know," I heaved - now we were both drained by the whole exchange.

I'd rather have been teasing the lovely Cyn, not torturing her or me. The laughs were too long ago.

"I don't know, darlin', I just wanted everybody to stay the way I made them. I didn't want any ..."

"Disappointments?" Cynthia finished my thought.

"Yeah."

"Oh, you can be sure of one thing, Andrew, Stu knew ..."

I thought it was all pretty clear and understood what and why he thought of me. Again, no words were spoken - big boys don't cry. First, I knew nothing about music as he knew music. He saw me in there in the thick of it with his Stones, and he could not quite understand why the Stones were letting me happen. He saw where Mick was going and didn't like what I was leading him to, or what was being allowed to happen to his idea of the group. Stu also saw the handwriting on the wall for the eventual end of me and the Stones, so perhaps that knowledge removed the need to hate. He didn't gloat; he never used his position to move that ship into port, and he never made one move of payback for what had happened.

One day in the early seventies, I was staying with Cynthia at the Ealing house that she shared with Stu for a day and a half between flights. Cyn was out. I was in their kitchen, brewing coffee, when in walked Stu, back from a morning of golf with Glyn Johns.

We'd never been alone in a room and we both attempted to warm above the cutting edge. I nursed my coffee, and we small-talked. I kept thinking, Christ, if Stu ever wanted to beat the shit out of me, here was his big moment. No Reg the Butcher, no weapon, no sturdy steel-tipped shoes. My elegant, monogrammed suede slippers left me less than the tea-leaf gangster Chris Stamp had so fondly labeled me, and my paisley morning jacket probably invited a bashing from the likes of the golf-clad Stu.

Nothing happened. We chatted on and I noticed for the first time the wonderful warmth and soul that smiled through his eyes. That morning in his and Cyn's kitchen I stood and talked with a good-looking man named Ian Stewart. We closed the cycle and knew where we stood with each other. My later flippancy with Keith was protective, stoned, and not needed.

I realised that day, and forgot until I cleared up my mind, that Stu knew all along what I was about and what I had done; and finally he knew, better than anyone, and took to his grave, what everybody else had not done about it. Now, Cynthia has told me that this exchange that I've recalled as taking place between us never happened, and that I've dreamt it up. So be it; I've just given you the truth of my recall.

CHAPTER 19

heathrow highlights / two wives; one fish, one loaf, and a few poets /
you hadn't lived until you stared at both of diana dors / trouble on
the factory floor - eric easton takes umbrage / getting measured in
chicago ... and not for a suit / takin' it to the max; dr. jacobson
makes me feel too good / what might have been hendrix and jones

The very day Sheila and I were wed, we arrived back in London
with Tony Calder. I was happy to be done with Glasgow. Tony
headed for the office whilst Sheila and I posed for photographers
with our Scotch cairn terrier Genius, named not after me but
after one of Bob Crewe's publishing companies, Genius Inc.

Some time later the women's page of the *Sunday Express* ran
an article by Anne Edwards headlined, "When Your Little Girl Says
'I'm Engaged'." Under the subheading. "Too Young," we read:

> What is more natural than the disappointment of another
> set of parents whose nineteen-year-old daughter Sheila
> Klein married a while ago, without their consent, a pop
> group manager of twenty who had long, golden hair and
> used make-up, and claimed he met her when he was drunk
> in a Hampstead street.
>
> "He's not the kind of man," said the daughter, "you
> would look at and say he would make the perfect kind
> of husband, is he?"
>
> "We thought she was too young to marry," said the
> mother mildly.

Somewhat less than mildly, I agreed. I also determined and probably decreed that neither Sheila nor mum should be opening
her trap to the Sunday newspapers.

Bob gave me a wonderful wedding present, the backing
track of his Four Seasons' masterpiece, "Rag Doll." Listening to the
four-track was an epiphany. Compared to the audio clarity and
brilliance that I heard on this four-track recording, I'd just been
fumbling my way through. The separation, sonic level, and placement were masterful. I'd only had the opportunity to see Phil Spector perform in airports and on headwaiters, never in the studio.
He kept that part all to himself. Bob Crewe was more sharing, and

his "Rag Doll" four-track gave me a technical standard to aspire to. Bob wanted to record an orchestral album of his Four Seasons successes. I recommended Pye Studios as the best place to go. Bob flew arranger Charlie Calello into town from New York and got down to it. I followed the Bob Crewe Orchestra into the studio with the Poets.

****

Years later, nearer now than then, I was beating a hasty retreat from London, heading for Heathrow, British Airways, and Bogotá. I was no doubt at the end of a drug-rope after another attempt to pull it together. Safe in the back of the cab and on the way home, I breathed a sigh of relief and allowed myself some one-on-one with my cabbie. After a warm-up off-tossing of a few pleasantries through the glass that protects carrier from carried, it was clear who I was, had been, and where I was going. Once it was established that I was a decent fella, the cabbie, a chap about my age with leather-collar'd coat pulled up to meet a tweed scarf that clashed, as it should, with his Andy Capp, got down to some basic chat about South America, "The Great Train Robber" Ronnie Biggs, and life in the sun.

"Ever met up with Ronnie Biggs, then?"

"No, South America is a very big place, y'know, it's anuvver six fuckin' hours from Bogotá to Rio de Janeiro; anyway they speak Portuguese, don't they ... at 'ome in Colombia we speak Spanish, and that's enough."

As we took in the Hammersmith flyover and belted for the M4, I'd reverted to the accent my mother had not paid for, the one that Mick Jagger gets away with on stage and at press conferences, but would probably not try within a mile of Bow Bells or the brothers Stamp.

"Ever miss it, then?"

"Miss what?" I yelled.

"England! Ever miss England?" he exclaimed in a tone that nearly had me as fucking dumb for not sussing there could only be one "it," our England - not Great Britain, just the great always-be-an England.

"Not really. Bogotá's been my home for fifteen years. The

climate's kinda spring and autumn all the year. We're eight thousand feet up so we don't have to put up with air conditioning and heaters and it doesn't get dark at a quarter to four about five months a year."

"Well, then, that says it all, don't it? No point in coming back, mate, you've got it made."

I actually had. It's always the same in the back of a cab or slinging lame arrows dipped in untruths to a fellow aeroplane passenger as both of you lift glasses of cheer to that life that really only exists on journeys and ceases when you get to the end of the ride or the cloud.

"Ever see the lads?" The cabbie flew my way now that we were all equal.

I knew who the lads were.

Oh, God, that one! I had enough cocaine to smooth the ride back to Bogotá. You're not likely to get searched for blow on a flight to the mother nation; the traffic goes the other way, and on those occasions that I didn't feel lucky, I'd just miss the flight. I gauged the cabbie's take on me and selected a secure angle, from which it would seem more as if I had a cold than as if I were whoofing a line in the back of a cab.

"You mean the Stones?" I cleared my throat and nasals to make sure every last iota of the marching powder had the op to jump-start my brain into fielding the question, because, truth was, I hadn't seen the lads in years and hadn't got around to handling it.

"Yeah, the Stones. Mick 'n' 'em, do you still see 'em or what?"

I'd got Ronnie Biggs, had got "it," so why was I being so slow with the Stones, was the tone from the pure heart of the real at the wheel.

"Not really," I began. "What happens is whatever the relationship you had when you left is the one you pick up on whenever you see each other, whether it's twelve minutes later or twelve years ..." I waited for that premise to land on the front seat, then curled on, "So if I haven't seen Charlie or Keith you basically pick up on the level you left off."

This was not going over.

"What about Mick then?"

"No, we don't really have much to say to each other."

"What, stuck up is he?"

"No, kinda like a first wife."

"Oh dear," Andy Capp gave a veritable chuckle of one who'd been there before.

"Nuff said then."

The rain began to greet us as we started to whiz pass the Feltham turn-off.

"When I sussed who you were when I picked you up, I'd actually been meaning to tell you, I like the Stones, 'course I do, but do you know what it is you did that really impressed me?"

I would bet a five that it wasn't Marianne Faithfull. Humble Pie? No ... Small Faces, maybe. Amen Corner, never. Maybe he'd seen me do the line.

"It was the Poets." He nearly cackled at the thought of that one - he knew I was nowhere near. "Gotcha on that, didn't I?" he chuckled.

"You certainly did," I replied. I'd never thought of that, though at the time John Lennon had, telling me then that the Poets were good and "fuckin' weird." I allowed my cabbie to carry on. He went into a description of how he thought "Now We're Thru" was a smashing record and how it was a real shame that it hadn't gone further up the charts. By the time we said our goodbyes on the pavement outside Terminal 3, Andy Capp had given me one of those moments that made the whole nine yards very worthwhile, worth all the madness. I beamed at the pleasure of having given him such pleasure. Time stood still, wrapped around the loose ends and edits, and for a moment life was all in a very good day's work.

****

Marianne embarrassed me and for that I left her. From the moment I had caught sight of her I'd recognised my next adventure. In another century you'd have set sail for her - in 1964 you recorded her. And this I did, and I was able to enjoy the totality of it, the egg and the shell. On vinyl Marianne was my audiofile Grace Kelly, a siren slut from the top drawer to undermine a nation's hard-on. But away from my vinyl screen, on stage and alone, Marianne was not very good; she was no longer truehearted Kelly and I was no longer Bing. "True Love" flew out the window, and that was too much to bear. I found it too painful to contemplate Marianne alone on the stage with an acoustic Jimmy Page in some pop fodder treadmill. So, the eggshell broke, and I abandoned her. I lived in my world, where I expected my stars to be stars 24/7, *la vida loca* total. I expected it like the truculent Flo Zitfelt schoolboy pimpresario I was. My stars had to remain stars in my eyes, or be gone.

I should have paid her not to work or put up the dough for an orchestra. But I didn't, ma; I was still learning on the job. In 1997, in the magazine *Marie Claire*, Marianne would describe "As Tears Go By" as having been "a weight around my neck for thirty-two years." She should have learnt to swim.

Life in the U.K. was ceasing to be interesting. In America, I could breathe; while at home, I felt alien. Life was more clinical as I fought to control everything, unaware that I had hit a rotation of loops where my drug-taking was starting to control me. With the Stones, I bit my tongue and just hoped that they could not hear the scream inside on those occasions when a veritable pneumatic drill re-arranged my brain and veins.

On October 18, 1964, I joined the Rolling Stones on their first European concert, squeezed in between the British Inez and Charlie Foxx tour and flying to the U.S. for the second bout with North America. I regarded the Stones' European debut at the legendary L'Olympia as a triumphant return for yours truly to what, thus far, had been my second homeland and street alma mater. At the Paris press conference I was already *tres* tipsy and gay as I toasted Vince Taylor, Charles de Gaulle, and Johnny Hallyday. To a local *gendarme* about to nick Keith and me for having our cab park too long in an illegal zone I announced, "Je suis James Bond." Without missing a beat the cop hit me with, "Move on, 007, move on."

We did - to the Pierre Cardin boutique on rue du Faubourg Saint-Honoré. Whilst Christian Dior had dressed the drawing rooms of the world, Courrèges would edify outer-planetary, pre-Sputnik mathematical beauty. As Chanel had inspired and anointed him as her spiritual heir, Yves Saint Laurent stuttered on rue Spontini, broke down at the thought of de-designed service apparel, marched on, and found his stride, line, and glory by instigating ready-to-wear. Through it all, there was always Pierre Cardin: stable, spacy, spatial, and smart Cardin, aware of the world, but not at war with it; whereas Yves, according to partner/lover Pierre

Bergé, "was born with a nervous breakdown." The Stones took Paris, Paris took us shopping, and I arrived home in stylish breakdown clobber in time to appear as myself on the BBC-TV Saturday night extoller of what was new and available in vinyl, *Juke Box Jury*.

I did the show a little tipsy but all smiles and good manners, enjoying my fellow panelists, Carry On comedian Sid James and the crass but lovely Diana Dors. Miss Dors was indeed a legend; she was as famous offscreen as Marianne Faithfull would later become off-vinyl. Whereas Marianne's scandals would have a hippie-dippy love and free sex all-around aroma to them, Diana Dors was rumoured to take on battalions and football teams with ease. The British show biz fifties from whence Diana had sprung were rife with rumour and recall of mad drunken orgies, secret two-way mirrors, and cameras filming the U.K. big screen and little screen at their biggest and barest.

Sitting next to Miss Dors on the *Juke Box Jury* panel, I would become so taken (and panicked) by that sexy know-it-all gaze that, whilst going into raptures or slaggery over some new piece of vinyl, I gesticulated and my glass of water spilled straight into the divine Diana's lap. Neither the rest of the panel, David Jacobs, nor Great Britain's viewers heard her hit me with the quick aside, "My, my, couldn't you wait -" The camera cut to host Jacobs with BBC efficiency and the show rolled on.

Half an hour later I was rolling with laughter in the Green Room hospitality suite at Miss Dors' contagious wit. She had that art of tailoring herself just for you, which I'd witness again a few years later when I met Tony Curtis, that instinct for knowing which side of themselves to play, to endear them to you forever after that first giddy meet. I don't know what held Diana's talent back; perhaps it was her rep for having spent so much time on her back. The woman I met was a sizzling star, a warm, full-blooded, all-knowing, swell, raw-diamond talent.

Diana and I took over the room, entertaining each other and all present. Like had met like, were attracted and challenged, and sparks, wit and affection flew. Our dance was cut into by a BBC steward, who informed that I was required in reception by Bill Cotton, the head of Light Entertainment, and old Pete Murray, the don't-be-a-cunt-there-are-witnesses co-star from my earlier backstage *Juke Box Jury* stand. I wondered if I'd got on the show by mistake and "Wakey Wakey Jr." had just discovered the gaffe and wanted another op at a shout-out. I said adieu, but it was a long goodbye, to my new best friend Diana; alas, we would never really meet again.

I got to the reception determined to keep my cool. Mr. Cotton was almost a cuppa niceness. The problem, I was informed, was not me at all; in fact he'd enjoyed me on the show. The problem was this gentleman in the foyer, my partner and Rolling Stones co-manager, Eric Easton, all Northern and fit to boil.

Eric had sat in his home in Acton or Ealing - I could never tell the diff - with his pal and business associate Sean O'Mahony and, for some strange poperatic reason, had taped the audio portion of the just-televised broadcast of *Juke Box Jury*. This was no mean feat. Taping a programme was nowhere near as easy as it is today - you had to be a man with a mission to mike up and record the audio off your telly back then. But Eric knew what he was about, had made up his mind to get angry, and now, some forty minutes after show time, was waving his pathetic little reel of tape in the face of anyone who'd pay him any attention, demanding that the BBC immediately put out a retraction for David Jacobs' having introduced me as, "Ladies and Gentlemen, please welcome the manager of the Rolling Stones, Mr. Andrew Oldham."

Bill Cotton refused the request. He knew perfectly well that Eric was the Rolling Stones co-manager and agent - hadn't he booked the group onto the very same *Juke Box Jury* and made the booking through Eric? Whatever this nonsense was about, it would be better settled backstage. No retraction would be forthcoming and Eric, at a loss of ash 'n' dash and armed with O'Mahony, left in a "you'll be sorry" huff. I'd been getting laid in the brain by Britain's reigning blond bombshell till Mr. Lackluster showed up.

The day after my *Juke Box Jury* appearance, the Stones, Stu, and I - minus Easton - flew out for the group's next North American tour. I was tired, Sheila had been nagging me about my not being there for her, and, by the time the tour reached Chicago, it was my turn to misbehave. I was accosted by some young girls in the lobby and asked if I was a Stone. "Why not?" I thought, and scotchingly answered, "Yes." The girls railed at my intoxication and I headed after my original idea for a walk, Mick's and Keith's room, always a safe haven when I was feeling out. This time, however, they would

not let me in, because not only was I drunk, but also, as I had forgotten and they had not, I had a gun. Whether it was real or one
of the sawn-down Irish jobs that Keith and I had bought in Dublin
I cannot recall; they still were not letting me in. Shame, I just wanted
to sit down where it was safe. Mick and Keith phoned Charlie's
room and asked him to come and remove me. Charlie resisted, but
finally got tired of all the commotion - me - in the hall, came out,
and elegently bopped me on the head. I was out cold. He returned
to his room and continued watching television. The girls whom
I'd accosted in the lobby went on to bigger and better things. They
would later gain fame as the Cynthia Plaster Caster gang, renown
for their plaster casting of rock gods' cocks. Mine, alas, is not
amongst that collection; Mick and Keith can crow for themselves.

The sex was great. Thank you, Brian. Somehow we had
twenty-four hours to kill in New York, and I accepted Brian's
offer to spend some time together and let him guide me, play
host, take me into his form of escape and freedom, which was
yer basic sex-and-drugs with a gorgeous bevy of lithe black and
pink dames in a hotel suite overlooking Central Park. The leer of
happiness on his face was a pleasant disgrace as he watched me
dive into his world of sex games, sex roles, and oblivion.

Some twelve or fifteen hours later I woke up and knew I
still hadn't landed.

I'd been taken everywhere, been everything, welcomed the
sexual freedom, so much so that I didn't feel the need to have my
own thoughts. I was a red door and she sang paint it black. I lay
in bed with D. and S. on either side of me - so many of me - arms,
heads, neck, and sex entwined. Brian stayed on the sofa, but woke
when the two black pearls and one thin pink blond got up. I shared
a bath with the two Negritas. As Brian sat on the tiled marble
bathroom floor, tired but happy, the pink blond had her head on
his. There were five of us - and, despite what you may have been
taught, two into three will go. Five became one, a sexual androgyny
mystified in one popper-driven phallic rush, chomping at the
sexual food chain whilst worshipping and devouring oneself.

That night Brian had once again been the leader of the
pack; he'd been my manager for the night and had decided what
would be best for me. The darkness of the carnal pleasure was
nevertheless lit so bright that it was hard to go outside.

****

Again in New York, some nine months, a year - I'm not sure - later, following the sexfest ... later, and in '66 to be sure, there was another scene with Brian, an eerie, gothic one that would leave a mark forever and would mould a huge chunk of my future into a dead-end street.

It was past two-thirty in the morning at the Drake Hotel where, for some bizarre reason, Brian and I had ended up with adjoining suites. I heard him on a muffled call from his bedroom. He then re-entered the central living room and said to a wasted me, "Andrew, I have to see this doctor. I don't want to go alone ... would you go with me?"

These were the days before you could channel-switch with your cable TV - back then, you could only do it in your mind. A year earlier, Allen Klein's gofers had happily delivered or collected prescriptions to and from my suite. I was the young genius having his every crazed whim catered to. Now I was being asked to help Brian, dying twit, to hammer another nail in his coffin!

And mine, perhaps. Suddenly managing the Stones was neither mine nor fun.

"What kind of doctor, Brian?" I asked in a tone that carried the weight of, "What kind of fuckin' doctor can it be you've found who sees patients at three in the morning?" I must admit I was curious.

"Well, it's hard to describe what he does, but he's good ..." Little Brian was anxious, in no mood to discourse. He wanted to get going, but still needed Andy to hold his hand.

"So are you ready? Are you coming?" He smiled.

We both laughed at the coming fiasco of God-knows-what and elevator'd down to the lobby and the waiting limo.

We limo'd uptown on Park Avenue (we limo'd around the clock now) and crossed over to Lexington near 72nd, Brian giving the directions on a first-name basis to the driver.

"Frank, it's here. We'll be back, just stay and wait, OK?"

"Sure thing, Brian," said Frank.

"Nice guy," Brian informed me as we hit the pavement. Perhaps he was Stu-ing Frank.

We ambled to the left of an apartment's ground-floor entrance, through a door, and down a hall. At the first door on the right, Brian pressed a call button and yelled, "Lewis Jones to see the doctor." The door buzzed, we hit the click, and entered a small reception.

Doctors' receptions can be grim reminders and reapers of one's potential lot at the best of times. But through an eerie 3:00 a.m. neon haze nobody beats the scenery. The magazines were as grubby and unkempt as their readers, who looked up with a collective hostile gaze that said, "We were here first and don't forget it." Brian knew what he was about; this was his beat. He crossed the reception and a glass partition opened slightly. He leaned inside the opening and spoke to the other side.

"Hallo, dear, how are you?" Brian gushed. "The doctor's expecting me. I've brought my manager. I told the doctor I would."

"Yes, Mr. Jones," said a quiet, tired, female voice, "I'll buzz you through. You're to go right in, both of you."

We were buzzed through, Mr. Jones leading the way. The man with no neck and no future turned to give me a good-luck smile, which told me that he was just as buzzed as the door with the proceedings. We marched drug left into the general area where, on one side, there was a long line of occupied, formica/linoleum, curtained cubicles, confirming the adage that the city never sleeps. Opposite the cubicle drapes was an open door leading into a dark office, impossible to detail in the bad light. Behind an oak tank of a desk and its backdraft of papers, samples, and medical journals sat a man of medium height, aged fifty to sixty. What was left of his hair was disheveled, greying to black, and curly.

He had a sweaty, pale face with eyes orbiting behind specs and was attired in a day-old, button-down, collared shirt, old striped tie, limp and dead, and off-white doctor's trust-me overall with fading blood marks over the pockets where the good doc had perhaps wiped his hands instead of washing them.

"Hallo, doc, how are you?" scraped Brian.

"Fine." The doctor didn't sound sure. He looked my way.

"This is your ... sit here and you come on in."

I sat and Brian followed the doc. I looked around. After my eyes adjusted to the dim, I could discern a row of medical jars filled with scissors of all shapes and sizes, standing up in disinfectant water. Alongside in another jar was what seemed to be, on first look, some strange human part, but on closer examination was revealed as - again standing in water - either a trio of frankfurters or perfectly cloned pricks. The next jar was waterless and half-filled with soggy sauerkraut, and the last jar held about half a dozen pickled cucumbers. Below this shelved valley of the jars was a large steel fridge-like sterilisation container and above the shelf an array of framed diplomas, citations, and individually signed photos. I started to scan the photos. The first one I recognised was the other LBJ - Lyndon Baines Johnson, President of the United States. The photo was signed, but on a quick scan impossible to decipher besides the "To" and "Your Good Friend." Next to that was a citation from the Office of the President, same Lyndon B., recognising the good works and giving thanks for and on behalf of his country to ... Dr. Max Jacobson (a.k.a. "Dr. Feelgood").

Another photo was a long shot of three or four serious-looking suited men and Jackie Kennedy. One of the men was JFK, and, half-hidden behind him in the photo, was the doctor I had just met. The wall was clad with droves of more citations, diplomas, thank-you's from the JFK administration and Attorney General RFK. The last photo to the right on the wall was of Jackie K. in that famous Dallas Chanel and Roy Halston pill box hat, looking sad and noble. There were several somber suits of power around her, and there, again in the upper-right background, was the ominous Dr. Max.

The same Dr. Max exited his office with Brian, walked past me and down the cubicled hall, opened a curtain halfway down, and gestured to Brian to follow him in. Five or so minutes later the doctor came out, leaving Brian behind the curtain, and popped into the next cubicle. I heard conversation exchanged. Then the doc came my way, went behind his desk, wiped his hands over his blood-stained overalls, and, from jar number one, took a frankfurter, dunked it in the sauerkraut of jar number two, took a bite, chewed, looked at me, took another bite, chewed, swallowed. Frank gone.

"So tell me what is wrong with you," Dr. Jacobson prompted, smiling as he little-fingered some sauerkraut and frank out of his uneven teeth.

"Nothing, I just came to keep ... him ... Mr. Jones company. I'm his manager and ..."

"Yes, I know, but Lewis told me I should see you, said I should help you, so please tell me what is wrong."

I seized on the good old on-the-road standby.

"I do have herpes on my penis. It's not from sex, it's nerves."

"That's nothing, I'll give you some ointment before you go. Lewis tells me you lead a stressful life, you have to keep going constantly, keep on the ball; people rely on you all of the time, need your decisions, that sort of thing."

Dr. Max inspected a speck of frank on the end of his finger and flicked it with his thumbnail onto the floor.

"I know what it's like, a lot of people need you ..." He indicated the wall behind him. "Like the President. It's the same sort of thing, just a different war."

He took on a George C. Scott, Dr. Strangelove stillness whilst he let that one drop in on me. He was good - getting his bearings with me and enjoying himself. He wrapped himself around a thought and carried on.

"I used to go down to the White House two or three times a week when he was there; he needed me a lot. I travelled to Florida, went to the conventions, spent a lot of time with him on the road before he got elected. Do you know what I did for him ... for them?"

His hand surveyed the photo'd wall again. I thought about the poor fuckers in the reception, chomping that bit of insanity that must accompany syntony for these office hours and habits. It was all right if you were on the road, but not on the street where you live.

"No, I don't know what you did for them, Doctor."

He was going to tell me anyway. He zeroed in on me as if making that decision, his eyes smiled, and he continued.

"I gave everyone a specific shot designed for their individual needs, but it's mainly, the essence is a shot of concentrated highly potent vitamins that rejuvenate, along with certain combined extracts from the glands of ... a monkey."

He shuffled some papers on his desk and studied me. I was solid as a rock, giving nothing up. I was in the audience and Dr. Max was the show.

"Do you have anything against injections?"

"No," I lied. I was terrified of them.

Later I'd know that he had lied, too. His injections were nothing but speed.

"By the time the President is at the podium, he's believable, he believes in what he saying with a passion and power and awareness. The audience has confidence in their President's confidence. That's what I did for him. You could almost say I helped get him elected. All of them." His hand acknowledged the photo'd wall. "I help them all."

"Then we're all one big fuckin' happy family, aren't we," I thought. Dr. Max Jacobson gestured to the wall again.

"I took care of Mrs. Kennedy at her husband's funeral."

He grew quieter, circumspect, as if remembering the time.

"The nation needed to see their former first lady strong, with dignity, showing courage in the face of loss, an example to the grieving country in its very time of need. I helped with that."

Christ, I thought, how does he know - or does he even care - that I'm not from *News of the World*. He got my thought, the canny old fuck, shrugged his shoulders, sighed, and gestured a "whatever" into the air.

"I've been studying you while I have been talking." The accent occasionally gave off a Mittel-European burr. For the most part it was no-coastal bland American flat. "I'd like to give you a treatment, an injection. I know what you need, I can tell. See how it feels, has you feel over the next few days. It's not drugs. It's vitamins and an extract, a compound of monkey glands - your body will love it. I think you'll feel better, function better; you'll find things easier, and you'll feel more assured with people and at work."

Dr. Max had rung enough bells and all of them hit home. Feel better, find things easier to do, function better, more assured, better with people ... just like a president.

"Follow me." He got up and led the way to hell.

The cubicle opposite the office had its curtain half-open. A woman was sitting with her back to me, red hair pulled up in a blue velvet bun, legs crossed under a grey tweed pleated skirt. She sat alert by a bed, pad on lap, pen in hand. She was taking dictation from an elegant, slight, late forties man, abed. His eyes were raised in thought. He had grey-silver hair swept back off a working forehead. His hands were entwined in a choreography that rhymed with his mind. He was wearing an open-necked, blue silk shirt and cashmere cardigan of a blue/powder grey that eased into the grey of his cuffed flannels over darker grey socks. A pair of brown suede, tasseled slip-ons sat neatly on the floor. It took only a second, but I got it. His eyes caught mine as I passed and took him in. He then said something about the sets not moving fast enough.

The librettist Alan Jay Lerner waxed lyrically and continued dictating in his room, spent needles in the bedpan beside him, secretary asking, "Was that stage left?" a second time.

"Yes, lie down, roll up your sleeve." I was abed next door, wondering who was there. I looked behind me for blood on the walls.

"That's right, that was Alan Jay Lerner. He's written a lot of his new show here. People like you have to keep working. That's where I come in ... make a fist."

Like a gunslinger's fast draw he was suddenly at the ready, syringe in hand, syringe to my vein. Some of my blood spat at the wall and over Dr. Max's jacket as my balls swallowed themselves and my gills flexed in fear. The last thing I remember was my cojones saying goodbye and driving up my arse as the needle plunged into my arm.

Brian was waiting with a smile for me as I re-entered the reception, herpes cream on my dick, bottle in the palm of my hand. He smiled at our little secret. Conspiracy, that's what the smile said. He was feeling that good already; he didn't want to spend any time on how bad he'd felt before. We limo'd down to the Village, to the Electric Circus on St. Mark's Place. It was way past four, nearer to five, and the Circus was closed. Brian banged on the door and asked for the owner, Jerry Brandt, ex-William Morris agent, now trendmaking host to Manhattan. Jerry came to the door, hugs passed all round, and he welcomed us in.

Jerry left us alone. The sixties were nearly over as we made our way to the floor. There, in the middle of this psychedelic arena, lying on his back on the floor, guitar in hand, plugged into the house sound system, oblivious to us, oblivious to all, lost in his sound coming back at him from a 360-degree soundaround blast, was the purple haze himself, Jimi Hendrix.

After fifteen minutes of this, my watch said five and I left Brian huddling with Jimi. I caught a cab outside and headed uptown to the hotel. I got up the next day feeling like a president, and over the next three days made some of the worst decisions of my life.

With the Small Faces at Olympic Studios, London, left to right:
Ronnie Lane, Steve Marriott, Andrew Loog Oldham, Ian McLagan

Glyn Johns

CHAPTER 20

everybody aged nineteen should have an orchestra / judy garland checks into the rainbow / a little time off is a dangerous girl to go out with / cary grant steps into everybody's spotlight / a vomitful of socialdom

The merry-go-round of 1964 continued with the release of the Andrew Loog Oldham Orchestra's homage to Lionel Bart's new musical, *Maggie May*, which was produced after Lionel's plans to have me record an LP of tunes from the show with Judy Garland went nowhere. The legendary, fatal Miss Garland was in London tasting the end of her career whilst residing in the well-heeled, American-occupied zone of Belgravia's Chester Square. She would soon astound London by apologising to her audience for her condition and then attempt to sing her entire act prostrate from the floor of the Talk of the Town.

I was up for the possible recording of Judy Garland and *Maggie May*, in the main to give Lionel pal-support. I was scheduled to tea off with her and Lionel at four o'clock one afternoon, but the diva made us wait until dark, only making it downstairs in time for hubby number four or five to pour us into the night. She reminded me of a bottle opener; shame was, she doubled as the cork. She was past being able to meet new people, and the new hubby's endearing gift seemed to be making her feel forever onstage, even when at home. The living room was hardly that, and when our star decided we hadn't suffered enough to be funny or at one with her, she gave us a look that killed for wasting her time and took herself back upstairs.

The rehearsals for *Maggie May* had become bloody murder, due in some large part to the bloody antics of Rachel Roberts, out of the kitchen sink, up from Llanelli, Carmarthenshire, fresh from *Saturday Night and Sunday Morning* and *This Sporting Life* and now a grande panicked dame - Mrs. Rex Harrison at the time, and no fair lady.

The collapse of the Judy Garland project should have been an omen to me, but I was yet buoyed by my youth and outward armor of invincibility. In truth, I found Miss Garland a pathetic old bag, still able to field the odd *bon mot*, but hardly worth a whole inning - at least that's what I told Mick when he enquired after the state of Judy. I should have noted that she'd already had electric convulsive therapy (ECT) and that - along with an Everly Brother, Alan Jay Lerner, Eddie Fisher, Van Cliburn, Tennessee Williams, Marlene Dietrich, Truman Capote, a Kennedy brother, and so many more - she had flirted with Dr. Max Jacobson. Judy was just north of forty, but was wearing out rapidly and had notched up attempted O.D.s at all the best locations. She would later be thrown off the flick that fabric'd the very life of her, Jacqueline Susann's *Valley of the Dolls*, and two years later, after another gay London wedding, with Johnnie Ray as best man, she would pull the plug and throw herself off the lot of life. Needless to say, my plans to immortalise the tail end of Judy on vinyl came to naught, and neither did I take any warning from her life of my own peaks and valleys to come.

In America, the Stones and I were on the threshold of big-time vinyl reality. "Time is on My Side" was knocking on the top thirty stateside door in our best showing yet while also, unbeknownst to us, breaking out regionally in Vietnam. Back in England, we were cock of the walk as "Little Red Rooster" crowed its way to number one. I got home from my new home, America, and Sheila told me she was pregnant with who would become Sean.

I accepted the news of Sheila's pregnancy, examined my feelings, and kept them to myself. I had no idea of how to react - the idea of being a father held no reality for me. I had no experience by which to quantify it. I had no favourite movie on the subject into which I could immerse myself and role-play the news into reality. I was confused. The roles I was playing daily as I went about my business on behalf of the Stones bordered on skitzo-frenetic. It was too much of a stretch to contemplate finishing the work day as a doting father-to-be. I sighed, and let Sheila get on with it.

One definition of insanity, especially as it relates to alco-holism and addiction, is that one repeats the same action expecting a different result. I started to add new combos to my self-medica-tion, upped the level of my daily pot inhalation, imbibed with more frequency, in a futile effort to keep myself spirited and drugged above the malaise that was slowly invading and entrenching my ability to be. Some would say that the malaise was the drugupman-ship, but, remembering the pain of those icicled moments (and the warmth once I'd bandaged and distilled them), I'd beg to disagree.

I was unaware I was approaching heavy rotation.

Life for Sheila on the social strata was barren enough, due to my schedule and chosen agenda. I severely limited my forays into sociarama to events at which I could control the room and the players. I thus suppressed Sheila's ability to enjoy the life and windfall I'd begotten us, and encouraged her in a way that would just add another nail in the coffin of our no-hope of a future together. I as much as told her to carry on going out with others and that I'd look the other way, although I never could.

For many, Mick and I were the subject of wishful thinking. This is understandable, as, for that while, we were as close as two young men could be. But we were close over cause - and that cause remained the Rolling Stones, or Mick Jagger, and whatever that difference may be. We were all experiencing an exciting awakening into a world, the reality of which, just five years earlier, would have been an excommunicable hallucination. Imagine you are just twenty, and dreams have come true ... well, some days might be overwhelming, and you might look for shelter with a fellow dreamweaver. The effect that this closeness had on our friends and lovers didn't really bother us - we knew it for what it was.

I was as close with Keith, but the tone was more boisterous. It was also more acceptable to bash around with Keith than with the perceivedly more attractive and ambiguous Mr. Jagger. In any case, wishful thinkers didn't dream of going to bed with Keith; they dream't of staying up with him.

This business I had chosen (or become addicted to, might be a better way of putting it) had, somewhere along the line, begun to consume the majority of my waking moments. I looked around the well-intentioned guests spending their nights off in songbird Alma Cogan's drawing room and viewed a prophetic babbling madness. It would only have taken Ralph Bellamy, neck cravatted, fingers jeweled, with grey locks devilishly combed forward unto youth, and Ruth Gordon, all motherly and caringly intrusive, to have popped from next door as neighbours to have had me become John Cassavettes in *Rosemary's Baby*. Suddenly I wanted no part of London show biz desperation. I'm reminded of writer Keith Altham's recall of jazz scriber George Melly meeting Mick Jagger backstage sometime late in the eighties and remarking on how Mick had more facial lines than he. Mick is supposed to have retorted that they were laugh lines, whereupon the portly Melly remarked that surely nothing was that funny.

Only in America could I freefall and feel at home and not mind when the workday ended. Perhaps it had something to do with the fact that the race was still young for us in America and the stakes not nearly as high. But America had loads to offer, and I wanted it all. The rules of play were vinyl and airplay, and I liked the isolation amongst the sweep and grandeur of the land. The movies that had screened my youth had not let me down once I'd been allowed to follow the same steps on the same streets as my heroes. I have no idea whether I could sense the danger that would follow the fame at home - but I could feel the dangerous trait of boredom. I knew I'd have to find a part that equipped me for life in better Texas order than the emptiness of James Dean as Jett Rink in *Giant*.

In contrast, the malaise of having made it in England was starting to wear my ambition thin. You could say I was starting to lose my grip. Something was around the corner, and it was not a new boutique. Within two years, by age twenty-two, I would get my perceived comeuppance - and, to quote Leonard Cohen's "First We Take Manhattan," they would have "sentenced me to twenty years of boredom for trying to change the system from within."

On the social side, Paul McCartney, John Lennon, and myself (as opposed to Mick, Keith, and myself) liked the occasional tea-time get-together with Alma Cogan and sometimes her mum and Ad Lib owner/boyfriend Brian Morris. Alma, the U.K.'s most-loved singing bird of the fifties, gracefully allowed her old-school pro show biz demeanor to carry her into the sixties, guesting on TV and starring in the occasional summer season in Blackpool. When at home in London, Alma played grand hostess and den mother to all of us upstarts, hosting soirees attended willingly by Beatles, a couple of Stones, Epstein, and *moi*. The Lionels Bart and Blair, Sean Kenny, Stanley Baker, Sean Connery, Tommy Steele, Chris Hutchins, Maurice Kinn, Alan Freeman, and Vidal Sassoon brought up the rear guard. Alma treated us all as one, and all as equally blessed runts of the same show biz litter.

I'm told that it was at one such afternoon occasion that Paul McCartney, seated at the Cogan tiny grand, twiddled and diddled his way into "Yesterday," whilst it was still called "Scrambled Eggs" as a result of Alma's mum asking if he wanted any. At another of her quieter afternoon tea and scones get-togethers, Alma played for John Lennon and me a song that she and her arranger, Stan Foster, had composed called "Now That I've Found You." John gave her an "Alma, do it with fuckin' Andrew. It's more than an LP filler; he'll make you sound like the fuckin' Ronettes, won't you Andrew?" (Her A&R man had told her that it was filler, and she did, later, record it with me.)

Earlier in the afternoon, the debonair actor Cary Grant had strolled in as if we were on the set of *To Catch a Thief*. Mr. Grant said he was contemplating *Father Goose* and felt like it. In fact, he'd draw anchor two years later, and his next film, 1966's *Walk Don't Run*, would be his last. Perhaps he autosuggested to John the optimum movement of being able to move on.

On this trip, Mr. Grant stopped long enough for tea and an immaculate display of charmed charisma that transported itself from the very screen into the living room of life with no need of lighting and pancake. God had given him a permanent star Zen. His ease was so deliberate that I had to quash my desire to applaud. I still recall the texture of the man; he veritably Monroe Stahr'd into the room. The light-cuffed flannels, open-necked shirt and blazer blended incestuously with the perfect tan. I wish that some pages of time had been a little bit more read on the day I sat with Messrs. Leach and Lennon - we could have discussed their propensity toward LSD and had them compare notes between tabs of shortbread and cups of tea. Instead, we discussed the merits of Palm Springs as a good weekend and required behaviour at royal premieres.

In October and November 1964 the Beatles were engaged on their last full-blown British concert tour, although there would be a mini Christmas run at the end of 1965. There was no doubt that the crown was still theirs to wear. Paul McCartney found time to attend the latest James Bond, *Goldfinger*, premiere and to play tambourine on an Alma Cogan EMI session.

Other freeze-frames from 1964: The Beatles, Mick Jagger, Cilla Black, and the Ronettes spend some time at the Brian Morris-run Ad Lib. Ex-2 I's rocker Vince Taylor stands on the steps of the Ad Lib and tells everybody who will listen to fuck off and to come to France where he is God. "I Feel Fine" goes to number one on the U.K. charts, making space for "Little Red Rooster" to crow in the same space a fortnight later. Brian Epstein exchanges contracts on 24 Chapel Street on the tip of Belgravia, the house in which, just short of three years later, he would decide he'd had enough of this life and move on to the next.

That autumn, the musical charts were a curious mixture of the old and the new - the old hanging on with sleight-of-new-hand and aplomb. Holland, Dozier, and Holland; Gerry Goffin and Carole King; the Bobs Crewe and Gaudio; Jackie DeShannon; Barry Mann and Cynthia Weil plus Burt Bacharach and Hal David song-monopolied the rest of the November '64 proceedings via the latest waxings from the Supremes, Herman's Hermits, the Four Seasons, the Searchers, Gene Pitney, Sandie Shaw, and Adam Faith. The old guard were repped by Henry Mancini, Jim Reeves, Matt Monro, and the Bachelors; the indifferent and the desperate by Julie Rogers and Manfred Mann; the perennials by the ever-penumbral Cliff Richard and an operatic Roy Orbison.

Shock 'n' freak was represented by the Anglo-defiled P.J. Proby, who took no song chances by hitching his pipes to *West Side Story*'s "Somewhere" whilst his velvet trousers performed scandalous twice-nightly splits on stage for the national tabloids. Hope and opportunity were represented by the assault of the Kinks with their relentless anthem, "All Day and All of the Night." Percolating in the lower reaches of the charts via George "Shadow" Morton's declassic authorship and production were the Shangri-Las with "Remember (Walking in the Sand)." Overall, The top twenty was a mixed happy bag with a chorus and verse for a whole nation to bleat to and plenty of rhythm to dance to.

Maggie May had its opening night on September 22 at the primo West End Adelphi Theatre. The night before, I'd sat bewitched and gobsmacked as Sean Kenny had writer/critic/National-Theatre-gadfly Kenneth Tynan join our table at the Terrazza and the two of them had debated the future of cartoon as the true cinematic hope. I'd nursed an Irish coffee and mummed the word as these two dueled. Tynan and Kenny argued as one that, Walt Disney's cartoon clerical hold notwithstanding, the future of film lay in full-length cartoons - which, in theory, could deliver a level above the range that any mere actor could bring to the proceedings. Although the duo used the power of painting as the example of image over reality, Sean Kenny was already thinking in terms of the digital manipulation that enhances today's movies. Ken Tynan, for all his bravado and skill, seemed a man of the fifties who would be downed by the sixties and what lay beyond. Tynan was more than pale - he was grey in palette and grey in pallor. He could not bring himself to embrace what I and the Stones or the Beatles were about. He thought us unqualified to duel in the field of art, and said so.

Sean Kenny brushed him away with enthusiasm and a good call. "You're just scared, Ken. Why don't you just give in and join them?"

To Sean, with his engineering and draftsman-like mind, the shock of the new was never a shock. Here was a man who revolutionised the working possibility of a stage with his bare hands. So too-soon, Sean suffered a brain haemorrhage in June 1973 and died whilst at a meeting in the offices of Bernard Miles at the Mermaid Theatre. I was beside myself and could only take his death personally. I felt lost without this very great friend, and will forever miss the sense of ordered madness and worldly wear-thee-well that he brushed into the lives of all those lucky enough to have been touched by him.

Tynan would, in fact, "give in and join them" with *Oh, Calcutta!* and the primed BBC3 moment when he became the first man to say "fuck" over the national airwaves - an early sex pistol to be sure - no doubt blessed with Lenny-Bruce-recall of how a *bon mot* expletive will get attention to your cause.

But in this *bon moment* he just crossed his legs, pursed his lips, and flicked his fag ash somewhat in my direction. His eyes spoke of countless aberrations and perceived betrayals that I would not be privy to until I'd scarred my own future. We hadn't yet read his diaries - his kinky habits, mild sado, and get-away whipping weekends, and all the oxymoronic behaviour the so-called straight Englishman gets up to when cricket no longer does it for him. I always think it's a pity when one cannot somehow apply one's aberrations to one's work.

The Stones and I would run into a lot of that as we contemplated sleeping with the enemy in our attempt to enter the film world. Besides Tynan, writers Keith Waterhouse and Willis Hall and directors Nicholas Ray and Bryan Forbes would all fix us with a disdain based on fear that their moment was over. The exceptions, and "their own men" in this exchange, were Lionel Bart, Sean Kenny, and director Michael Winner.

Opening night found Sheila and me dressing up for the musical whore, which was nervous fun and took longer than the night itself. I gave Reg the Butcher the evening off, as his presence always seemed to unnerve Sheila. I wore a silk and mohair, six-button, double-breasted evening suit, elastic-sided pump-in boots, crisp white shirt with covered braided buttons and links, and black braided bow tie. You'll forgive me for forgetting what Sheila wore. It may have been Portobello, Mary Quant, or even early Ossie Clark, but all you need know is that my bride of two weeks looked beautiful. We arrived at the Adelphi Theatre and glowed under the strange changing light of the mid-sixties, where the old guard and its values held court, but allowed us in to play, due to their need of our fresh young mugs to deliver them unto the next day's morning papers.

We mingled with Lionel and his "fiancée"/mate Alma Cogan. Peter Sellers and Britt Ekland were there, as were Roy Moseley with Anthony Perkins; Noël Coward and Binkie Beaumont; and Rex Harrison and Sybil Burton, bringing up their rear. Sybil was married to the Welsh B-actor, mountain-of-fame climber, Richard Burton, who'd just been propelled into the lap of the gods and a cool million per flick assisted by his onscreen/offscreen bedding of Elizabeth Taylor. Sybil would move later that year to New York and open the best-known East Coast disco, Arthur's, where good times were had by all Brits who drank and danced in Sybil's booth and, as Brits will do when gathered together, earnestly laugh down and up at their host - the great New York City. This list of Brits did not include the Stones, who, after a half-hour at Arthur's, would beat a healthy musical retreat uptown to the Apollo in Harlem.

Far from Harlem, Rex Harrison looked embalmed and em-barrassed. He had the expression of a man who wished he'd never crossed the Strand or left the safety of his quarters in the Savoy. Rachel Roberts - wife number four in a tally of six - was *Maggie May*'s not-so-lady-like leading lady, a boisterous, boozy diva who'd been carrying on so much backstage over the past few weeks' re-hearsal that the leading man, Kenneth Haigh, would look at her with a murderous glint in his eye. Rachel had turned her actress insecurity into a Welsh tornado which grasped, squeezed, and twisted the balls of production, cast, and crew. She so darkened any light left in the show that there was good reason to wonder whether it would go on. Lionel and Alma - dressed in matching winter furs of Russian Jewish pop nobility - went from mate to mate sparking the opening-night crowd to quell the night's doomy vulnerability.

Judy Garland was swaying in the wheeze with her latest gay betrothal on one arm and the ghost of prescriptions past on the other. Kenny Lynch, with manager Jean Lincoln on a rare night out, wondered why so many whores would spend good money to see another one gone bad. Smiling in the same stalls was one of Lionel's former Artful Dodgers from better *Oliver!* days, child star Gregory Phillips, whom I'd record in a few months. Greg, managed by Roy Moseley, had played Dirk Bogarde's and Judy Garland's child in *I Could Go on Singing*. Judy looked upstage and saw Greg, remembered the klieg lights and the call to action, and waved a brave but wan hallo. It was an evening not unlike *The Brady Bunch* meets *The Wicker Man* in which we were *The Mod Squad*.

Gregory Phillips had studied at the Italia Conti Academy of Theatre Arts with pre-Faces Steve Marriott. They were both renowned brothers of the big song and schlong as they played in the same band at the Italia Conti and raved their way through "Peggy Sue" and "Cut Across Shorty." They maybe-baby'd their way into any young things that would let them, with the occasional wink of hope at the odd old gay thing who wished they could. The world was getting taller and smaller as it came together in the final push toward the downsizing of whatever sixties you call your own. Steve, Greg, and I would find a lot of time together to laugh at the prismed world through rolling papers.

My life, for all intents and purposes, probably began with the opening guitar figure of "That'll Be the Day." There may have been songs in the big band or nightclub crooner days that took a similar stance toward the *femme fatale*, but I hadn't heard them. For my school pals and me, Buddy Holly's "So if we ever part, then I'll leave you, de-dum-de-dum" spoke of an alternative. We lived in a screenplay in which it looked like all our mates were slowly going down to a quicksand of pussy, but those lyrics gave me hope. It was that dividing time in youth, when you get to see which of your friends are still standing after that first close encounter with the other. Friendship was taking on a different weight.

My professional time with both Greg and Steve - short with Greg, long with Steve - had added value, because this thing between us precluded any professional lie. We didn't have to translate, edit, or exchange any thought between us - all was understood. At the age when I'd been discovering Buddy, these two scamps were already out in the trenches of "yerz paid yer money, now yerz gets your laugh." That was additional glue.

In early 1963 I'd decided that a couple of Delfont acts would be good for my PR business. They worked regular, therefore they might be able to pay me regular. I met the young office turks - Jean Lincoln and Roy Moseley - the upstarts hired to deal with the young talent and keep them out in the reception. Jean was one of the loves of my life; she took me in and showed me what's what. Roy was a decanter full of the intoxicating fumes of show business. He gravitated toward star turns and made that energy the source of his life. I was smitten with his enthusiasm for the game - he didn't close up shop and get away from the madness for a real life in some suburban trough. He lived it, dreamt it, and worked it - so in my book he had it made. Roy was practical and romantic, a great combination.

Decca would release the first two Andrew Oldham Orchestra albums within a month of each other. The first, *16 Hip Hits*, was released on their budget label Ace of Clubs with sleeve notes by Kim "Nut Rocker" Fowley. We were all quite drunk. Mick had said he'd only sing "Da Doo Ron Ron" if I sang something too, so I bleated my way quite passably through "I Wanna Be Your Man" with Jimmy Page on guitar and John Paul Jones on bass. As the big 1964 fights between Mods and Rockers had just taken place, Kim Fowley and I wrote "The Rise of the Brighton Surf." Later the same week, with John Paul Jones I recorded the Lee Hazlewood song, "Baja," which I got released on the Pye label because my mate at Decca, Dick Rowe, had turned it down. It was originally on the Jack Nitzsche Reprise LP which I so adored, *The Lonely Surfer* (as was the tempo at which I re-recorded "Da Doo Ron Ron"), and the fact that we recorded an inferior version was neither here nor there. The point was not to get into the charts, but to have that feeling of standing next to the gods whilst you're recording. It came in moments, but it gave us life. Later still, John auditioned Nico, whom Brian Jones had introduced, and I'd record her soon thereafter with Gordon Lightfoot's "I'm Not Sayin'," the single being released on Immediate in '65 b/w "The Last

Mile," a song I wrote with Jimmy Page. I submitted for the cover of *16 Hip Hits* a photo of myself taken by Crispian Woodgate, in which I had a huge pussy zit on my chin. I informed the Decca art department that I wanted the buying public to be able to squeeze the zit and get the pus out. Decca was not impressed with this suggestion.

Kim Fowley introduced me to another young American, Bobby Jameson, and within days Keith Richards and I were recording him at Decca's West Hampstead studios. Keith and I composed a lowlife sleaze 'n' dumpster sort of homage to George "Shadow" Morton's Shangri-Las recordings crossed with Bob Crewe's "Rag Doll," titled "All I Want is My Baby." I was fascinated with the structure of "Rag Doll" and Keith was tolerant of my love of the Shangri-Las. Armed with the track of the Mick and Keith ballad, "Each and Every Day of the Year" for the B-side, we stalked Mr. Jameson into the studio. Keith handled the A-side arrangements and Jimmy Page played lead guitar. Jameson had arrived in the U.K. as part of the P.J. Proby flock. He wore one black glove and was Walker Brother pretty head to foot - he could have been a Walker Brother. All of that and being American was enough of a calling card in those days to get you recorded.

John Paul Jones was still going under his real name, John Baldwin. I gave him his new name for the solo recording of "Baja" we'd made and sold to Pye. I got the name from a 1959 poster I recalled from Swiss Cottage for a Warner Brothers flick that died, starring Robert Stack, *John Paul Jones*. I had no idea he was a real live controversial American hero; I just knew that John looked the part and could do the charts, and that I didn't want my arranger to be named after a piano.

Alma Cogan

CHAPTER 21

meeting the l.a. in l.a. - mr. lou adler / california dreams
come true / a map of our musical hollywood

I'd met Lou Adler in the autumn of '64 - theta rhythm had it be and still does. We'd said hallo at the recording of *The T.A.M.I. (Teenage Awards Music International) Show*, where his act, Jan and Dean, were hosting and mine were following James Brown. Gospel and gossip has it that Mick Jagger nearly threw up at the prospect of following James Brown onto the stage at *The T.A.M.I. Show*. This is nonsense. Mick just applied himself that night, pulled out all the stops he knew (and some he didn't), and worked harder than the hardest working man in show business. By doing so Mick started the first real Stones American roll.

321 South Beverly Drive sat down on the scrubbed 'n' shrubbed Warren Beatty side of L.A.'s Wilshire, and floor two housed Dunhill Records, about to get hot with "Eve of Destruction." Dunhill had been formed on the heat of Adler's run of hits with Johnny Rivers, for which it served as the production company. Now it was an independent record company distributed by ABC. Dunhill was eared by Adler, flanked by Andy Wickham (who'd left ALO Image, choosing L.A. sun over London gloom), and hawked by a cigar-chomping sales suit named Jay Lasker. An agent named Hal Landers and a former tap dancer named Bobby Roberts made up the rest of the company's roster. These latter two went on to give the world the Charles Bronson, life-enhancing, Michael Winner-directed *Death Wish*.

One early spring day in '65, Lou said please find the time to come on down to Dunhill and be surprised. I did. I was silver-bracelet clad and Lou was gold; he smoked Luckys whilst I Salem'd my lot, though sooner and later we ended up smoking the same leaf. He wore red and I didn't know I could. *Le bon clobber* was still by Sy Devore; the De Voss boutique had yet to come on the map. We paid neat homage to Dino, Sonny-and-Cher-manager Joe DeCarlo, and hi-rolled, button-down shirts. Our trousers were either cords, jeans, or benchmark *Ocean's Eleven*, and we could pass for well-meaning, casual, doo-wop pimps. When I got to the second-floor Dunhill abode, I greeted Lou and stopped to say hallo to Andy Wickham. He knew he'd met the beginning of the new world, as did I. Then Lou popped his head around the door, and said, "Andrew, come say hallo to the Mamas and the Papas." We walked down the hall, into a room, and saw them standing there. John Phillips wore a darker red and wanted to know what you thought before you thought it; Cass gushed that motherlode and wondered how well you knew the Beatles; Denny cleared his majestic throat of debris; and Michelle knew what she had as she kinda invited you in.

That afternoon, all the leaves modulated as John sat atop the oak exec desk and acoustic'd the four of them through all the hits. I was privileged to hear a medley of their life thus far, and, as their national anthems rounded the room, I got to hear some of their future, too. Later Michelle would come up with "Dedicated to the One I Love," Cass would call John's name with "Words of Love," and Lou would get them somewhat "Dancing in the Street." But for the most part John Boy had already written the ticket stubs, entry to the royal circle of pop, given to the golden few who manage to define the moment in the right rhythm, time, and attitude of the day.

I heard 'em all that day, "California Dreamin'," "Monday, Monday," "Go Where You Wanna Go," and more. I fell in love with the choral camaraderie, the full-blown bravado leads, the insolent oh-so-coherent trade-offs, and with Papa John Phillips, our own sixties Cole Porter/Irving Berlin, whose marvelously structured, sophisticated, and witty ditties popped under your skin and into your heart. He would stir and scribe again with "San Francisco (Be Sure to Wear Flowers in Your Hair)," "Creeque Alley," and my own favourite, "Twelve Thirty (Young Girls Are Coming to the Canyon)." But basically, privileged *moi* had heard the lot. Not bad for an afternoon off on a busman's holiday ...

Thus far, America's pop chart firefight against us Brits had been the Beach Boys and the Four Seasons. The Beach Boys had the sound and a genius in Brian Wilson, but alas - save Dennis - all looked like the Wilson's dad, Murray. And, despite the Four Seasons' matinee-idol personas in photos by Bruno of Hollywood, the group looked like they would be just as happy breaking your legs as hugging your pillow.

I left very pleased. Lou was Billy Rose, and I'd just heard the Diamond Horseshoe Revue. The Mamas and the Papas would unite world-pop traffic from Haight-Ashbury to Park Avenue. My mate had the real thing. With a heart full of smiles all 'round, I headed happily northeast back up to Sunset and mine.

CALIFORNIA DREAMIN'
the mama's and the papa's

california dreamin' by the mama's and the papa's
is more relative to today
than the general election
which can only bring more bigotry,
unfulfilled promises
and the ultimately big bringdown.
california dreamin' won't put the country
back on it's feet
but it will give you a helluva lift
for two minutes and thirty two seconds
and sometimes that can be a long time.

andrew loog oldham, a bystander

p.s., i didn't write it, john phillips did; i don't publish
it, trousdale do; i didn't produce it, lou adler did;
and i don't release it, rca do — i just like it   . . .

CHAPTER 22

*more celluloid schemes / the winner in michael winner / mick and i
meet nicholas ray of darkness - we will not be playing james dean /
crap i wish i'd never heard - "it needs a lot of work" / meeting with
the duke of words - anthony burgess / a short history of the even
shorter sixties film history of the rolling stones*

The music industry was winding down for Christmas and I was
winding up my *A Clockwork Orange* schemes - dreams for transporting the Stones to the silver screen via Anthony Burgess's 1962
book that had so fueled my life and helped me feel normal. Christmas for me was a down time. Growing up, it had been something
that other people did and my mother and I only pretended to do.
I looked for ways to fan the flames of January rather than stoke
the fires at home.

I remember finding out in short order that the cinematic
rights to *A Clockwork Orange* were not available, but this did not
stop me from getting press for the Stones on the intention and
the idea. United Artists had just released the Beatles' first film, *A
Hard Day's Night*, to hearty press, popular acclaim, and even more
Moptop mania, if such a thing were possible. The lead act was
pulling even further ahead and I did not want the Stones to be
left out in the celluloid cold.

The first mentions of a forthcoming Rolling Stones feature
film had appeared in the U.K. press shortly before the first American tour in June '64. The film, provisionally titled *Rolling Stones*,
was scheduled to go into production upon the group's return to
the U.K. in July. All that remained to be decided was where to
shoot it. Peter Sellers and Lionel Bart were to be the co-producers
and the script was being co-written by Bart and myself. The executive producer was going to be Peter O'Toole's manager, Jules
Buck; hence the quote that Keith Richards wafted abreeze on the
possibility of Mr. O'Toole's making a cameo as "the group's manager." Penny Valentine reported in *Disc* and Chris Hutchins in *NME*
that the film would deal "with a group of drifters." All of this was
waffle, but, boosted by the marquee value of Sellers and O'Toole,
I managed to get it into the press as part of my effort to not strag-
gle too far behind the Beatles and their filmic progress.

We wanted photographer David Bailey as director for *A Clockwork Orange*. Neither was to be. Bailey wanted to bring in Andy Warhol, but balked when I wanted more money for the Stones than the budget for the movie. Of course, it might have helped if I'd had the rights to *A Clockwork Orange* in the first place, but life was just a dream and dreams thus far had come true when the PR-ist in me had my dreams put into print. They either did or I regarded them as true. Not so with *A Clockwork Orange*.

The next piece of celluloid fiction on which I gained press ink for the Stones was a piece of nonsense I'd contrived called *Back, Behind, and in Front*. I didn't even bother to gild this lily with marquee value, relying on Keith's quote that he "was already working on the recording of the soundtrack" and my promise to Chris Hutchins that if he printed my latest film story I'd give him an exclusive on the tracks of the next Stones LP. *Billboard* duly reported on December 18, 1965: "Cameras Set to Roll with Rolling Stones."

Around that time I met the endearing U.K. movie maverick, Michael Winner, when John Sandilands included us as a duo in a series he was writing for *Queen* magazine in which two celebrities, well-known backroom boys, got together to discuss having "made it" in their respective diverse but similar careers. Michael had already made his mark and reputation with Brit *noir* outings *The System* (1964) and *West 11* (1963), after popping out with the Billy Fury popalong, *Play It Cool*, in 1962 and a poorly received version of *The Mikado* starring Frankie Howard a year later. With the daunting *Death Wish* (1974) and *The Mechanic* (1972), Winner would move on to the company of Charles Bronson in the early seventies and define the art of rape and mayhem in a way that had not been possible for Mr. Burgess and *A Clockwork Orange* less than a decade before. The times, they seemed to be changing, and mighty fast.

Michael Winner lived in Bryanston or Montagu Square, a short walk north of Great Cumberland Place and Seymour Street. An appointment was set for our meet and chat one 6:00 p.m. on a midweek spring of 1965 evening. I'm not sure what I was up to, but, to be sure, it was all work and no good.

I was on a showboat roller coaster, crashing here, there, and whenever, working myself and my crew everywhere. As a result I turned up for the dual-celeb interview at Michael Winner's a good day late. Winner opened the door to his flat with the sureness of somebody advertising the advantages of "making it" in his early thirties as perhaps being preferable to doing so when barely nineteen. He beamed me into his sumptuous ground-floor living room and offered me a drink, which I declined. "John Sandilands couldn't wait, dear boy," smiled Michael, "He left a little ratty about a quarter to eight." ... "Last night," he added, to make sure I got it. I did, and, though steeped in fatigue, made an effort to rise above a tired mumble, and informed my host that I was jolly well aware of what day it was - and the fact that I'd turned up a good twenty-four hours late. But, surely, I brazenly insisted, that was better than not having turned up at all. Mr. Winner huffed and took that one in, leaning against the marble fireplace opposite me as I reclined (nigh on slumbering) on his comfortable, svelte settee.

I allowed myself the same look around his abode that I'd allowed myself on my first visit to Bob Crewe's Dakota grandeur and decided again, *vis-à-vis* Sheila's and my shabby Primrose Hill quarters, that I must be doing something wrong, regardless of how well my cars were appointed.

"Quite, dear boy," sighed Winner. "If you don't mind my saying, I think you look as if what you need is a bowl of cornflakes and a good night's sleep." Whereupon one of England's rudest men took himself off to his kitchen and came back with a bowl of Kellogg's. I ate up gratefully, then followed the second part of his recommendation and fell into a nice deep slumber on his couch, waking refreshed the following day. A cup of tea, not much banter, just a smile, and I was away, well-rested and back at work.

Michael Winner remained generous and pragmatic with his advice to me over the years, whenever I was considering cutting loose into a film project. At the time he pointed out how little the Beatles had actually been paid for the privilege of entering the film arena and warned me that this was the sort of remuneration that the Stones should expect from the film industry. I think he was advising us to stay on the road and follow the money. It was not for nowt that he later reminded me that Ringo Starr had probably received more money for his roles in *The Magic Christian* and *That'll Be the Day* than the Beatles had received fourfold for *A Hard Day's Night* and *Help!*

In the same square W.1-Winner mile a year later, Mick Jagger and I would meet the veteran director, Nicholas Ray. *A*

Clockwork Orange having dissolved into a fade out, Allen Klein put forward a book that had originally come his way via the Dave Clark Five, whom he represented in the U.S. The book was *Only Lovers Left Alive* by a North of England schoolteacher, Dave Wallis. The plot, passable and an attention-getter, was thus: Our island's grown-ups are committing suicide and its teenagers are turning Britain into a fascist jungle. The *Daily Mirror* reported that I'd told them: "The book could have been written for the Stones." It wasn't *A Clockwork Orange*, but it would have to do, even though its plot was less-than-credible when one actually read it all the way through.

Allen Klein had pulled off a coup in his negotiations on behalf of the Stones and myself with the Decca Record Company. Decca would only get the rights to a film soundtrack if they coughed up an extra million and a half. Those additional dollars alone should have shamed us into doing a film. It was during our quest for film that we met a lot of old farts ... and Bryan Forbes. Writers Keith Waterhouse and Willis Hall may have been hired to write a draft screenplay and, if so, their ideas felt duller than the words already on the pages of Wallis's book. Their screenplay would prove even less believable, or exciting. The generation gap appears quickly and defines itself even faster in matters of art and workissimo, especially when that work is cast unto a generation removed, to whom the very staying power of the Beatles, Stones, and the rest was a matter of some discomfort and not much joy. If I appear to get hazy and dismissive here on recall, it's because our entry into the film establishment was a fruitless nightmare, during which a host of overpaid, undertalented dolts took umbrage at the idea of the Rolling Stones taking on their game. The Stones could not be deflected into cardboard-cutout, Keystone-Kop, pop-replicas. For one thing, they were known to be "difficult."

Nicholas Ray was flown in from Spain for a meet with a view to his directing *Only Lovers Left Alive* with the Stones. He was put up in a Montagu Square mews house. Mick Jagger and I had been recording at nearby Pye Studios off Marble Arch and one evening we bounded up Great Cumberland Place headed for Mr. Ray in his mews abode. It was raining and both Mick and I agreed, whilst dodging shoe-ruining puddles, that the scene would play more optimistically had we been driving on the Sunset Strip and turning right into the Beverly Hills Hotel, instead of slogging on foot to the tune of an endless grey London drizzle. Nevertheless, we remained encouraged by the idea that what had been good for James Dean could be equally good for Mick Jagger.

Ray, according to Ephraim Katz's *The Film Encyclopedia* (1979), was "Darling of the *auteur* theory cultists, a dynamic, socially conscious director with a keen visual sense and a gift for attaining fluid motion on the screen." Ray had scored his first hit in 1949 with *Knock on Any Door*, followed the next year by *In a Lonely Place*, starring Humphrey Bogart as a Hollywood screenwriter playing out a less than savoury relationship with starlet Gloria Grahame. Ray struck true gold in 1954 with *Johnny Guitar* and went platinum with 1955's *Rebel Without a Cause*, which starred James Dean and changed all our lives and diction.

Dean had previously portrayed the troubled Cal Trask in Elia Kazan's *East of Eden*. The layered, incestuous relationships portrayed by Dean, with Richard Davalos as his brother and Jo Van Fleet as the madam/mother, were a notch above my affinity with such family values. I was taken with the brotherly Cain and Abel pain and the early Armani-esque sand and ochre college hues that Dean wore, a mere shade away from the colours of Eden. One cannot help but wonder if the experience with Dean and Kazan did not toll for the career of Mr. Davalos the way *Performance* would for James Fox, following his bout with Jagger and Donald Cammell.

After *Rebel Without a Cause*, Ray seemed to disappear into the slopes of Europe and never was at one with the street again. It is said that, the moment your artistic meanderings leave the street and relate to room service, you'll end up writing a different song from the one the public chooses to whistle. You may get a final run from the penthouse, but the street has a beat of its own.

It was under those circumstances that I sat in a dark, cruddy mews house in late 1965 and introduced a rising Leo, Mick Jagger, to the fading mane and fellow Leo, the maverick Nick Ray. Tall and lanky, he needed to stoop as he ushered us into the teeny living room, or perhaps he stooped anyway. His short hair was grizzly grey, his skin was ruddy and gone with the wind, and his eyes were cobalt, lost somewhere between disinterest and betrayal. He looked like he had spent too much time in his middle fifties, not unlike his *Johnny Guitar* star, Sterling Hayden, playing Captain McCluskey in *The Godfather*.

The lighting of the room came from lamps set on side tables that added a conquered still to the proceedings. Ray offered us a drink from the decantered silver tray. I think we had whatever he was drinking, and whatever it was, Mick and I both drank up but didn't really feel it. The director sat himself down and curled his long, red hands around the cut glass. He wore the outfit of the American director of the forties and fifties: *de rigueur* bone-buttoned, staggered-vented, grey herringbone jacket, grey trousers, and shoes buckled and brown.

"Have you been to the United States?" he asked. Mick and I looked at each other and realised that the director was according us the lowest level of interest. No homework, and even less bullshit. We told him, yes, we had in fact been to the United States and had just got back from our third visit. Ray cleared his throat. It was obvious that he didn't care if we'd just got back from the moon. He was beyond surprise and looked upon Mick as a pup sent to amuse him. If drink or whim infused him, he might throw a few scraps of c.v. Mick's way - otherwise ...

His neck looked scorched, like worn-out bagpipes. It heaved and retreated with every breath. Was he smoking? I can't recall, but he inhaled with a smoker's wheeze as he searched for his words. On closer examination, he took on the aspect of a man who had inherited Red Ridingwood's hand-me-downs from F. Scott Fitzgerald's *The Last Tycoon*. Suddenly Eric Easton, by comparison, looked dapper. Ray embarked on a long and clearly well-worn monologue on the art of James Dean and how he'd found it. He seemed to study Mick's patience, watching to see how much of this he would take.

The one thing we shared was the inability to voice enthusiasm about working together on *Only Lovers Left Alive*. The brunt of his James Dean oration seemed to be that the actor was an unruly, undisciplined pussy who had only been worth Nicholas Ray's trouble because he could act out Ray's vision. The question seemed to be whether Jagger felt that he was any of the above. Mick deferred on the pussy angle and gave Ray a feeble, "So what do you think of the book then?" Ray rejoined with a perfunctory, "It needs a lot of work."

Ray scratched his neck and examined his glass, stooped up, and asked us if we'd join him in a refill. We both said no and knew that the meeting was over, as it had never really begun. Ray tugged at the kerchief tied around his withering neck. I have always mistrusted this affectation in America's cinemafolk. On the English, it's merely an affected mistake. On an American, it screams for attention with the fey import of, "I direct." Nick Ray was pathetic, and perhaps it was the idea of the real Stones in a real movie that was pathetic too, but nobody was putting that card to the front of the deck. The idea of Hollywood was enticing, but the reality of the Stones' being as stiff as a Cliff Richard in *Summer Holiday* was there as well. I just hoped that Mr. Ray had used the free travel to visit a tailor.

The rain had not stopped, but that did not stop us from leaving. The sound of our heels slapping smack on the wet mews cobblestones grew louder with the echo of the dull night. The ricocheting disappointment left our brainset as we turned onto Upper Berkeley Street. Mick was joining Chrissie Shrimpton for a quiet supper in Chelsea; I was going home to Sheila in Primrose Hill. I allowed him the first taxi, and, having hailed it, closed the cab door on him, but not before Mick broke the silence that had dogged us in our walk from the mews: "Andrew, don't ever put me through that again." I promised that I would not; we parted in mood and lighting reminiscent of Trevor Howard and Celia Johnson in *Brief Encounter*. I walked off in search of another cab but stopped off at a pub for a drink instead.

The reality was that nobody wanted to do a movie with the Rolling Stones. It was presumed - correctly - that the Stones' alpha wolves would not be putty in filmdom's hands. If they had been prepared to turn up, disintegrate into a willing popopera of vaudeville turns, and supply the required amount of soundtrack, then all might have been different. The rebel image that had worked for them in rock worked against them in film.

There are not many examples of music personalities who have been able to shift their creative spark over to the silver screen. Rock stars seem, for the most part, to lose the very essence of their sensual being the moment they hit their mark and attempt to act - they lose the rhythm, lose the swing, and end up contorted, un-sexed, and stiff. It would have happened to Jagger in *Performance*, but that film succeeded on the basis of drugorama over content. It was also blessed by a delay in release, which gathered it a pathetic market that had had enough of pop upstarts and warmed to a story of a burnt-out rock star unable to produce anything except mental mayhem. Mick Jagger has been praised for his role in *Performance*, but the first time I attempted to watch it, toward the end of the seventies, I still had to turn away and turn it off - Jagger was playing my biggest nightmare, and James Fox was playing me. *Performance*, apart from James Fox, was totally non-actors, just a series of pop stars (Jagger), pop-star-muses (Keith's Anita Pallenberg), drug addicts, and gangsters (too average to mention), all in the hands of the autodestructive co-director Donald Cammell. Fox freaked as a result of the mind and body games played on the set. Keith Richards is alleged to have sat in his blue Rolls-Royce outside the W.1 set, waiting to see who went home with whom. Fox would spend eight years in the North of England cleaning floors for the Salvation Army or schlepping tracts for the Navigators before he returned to acting, no doubt miffed about how his brother Edward had picked up such juicy parts as the lead in Fred Zinnemann's *Day of the Jackal*.

I had met Donald Cammell in my offices in 1965 when the business manager of the Who had brought him around to pitch himself as a director on any Stones picture. He scared me. He came from a wealthy Scottish family that had lost its money, was a very talented painter, but a less talented film maker. Both Marlon Brando and Donald Sutherland supported him, though it's hard to tell whether the actors supported their perception of Cammell's talent or his lifestyle. When he visited me, I could not wait to be rid of him. The Stones and I had just received the keys to the highway and the kingdom and this guy wanted us to turn on it and denounce it. Not in my innings! To give him his due, he waited his turn and got what he wanted via Mick in the end. To give Mick his due, the film is a good controversial listing in his credits, a nice bookend to his last very credible turn as an escort service owner in *The Man from Elysian Fields* (2001). Cammell directed only a few more films and committed suicide in 1996. His book, *Fan-Tan*, supposedly co-written with Brando, was released a year after Brando's death. His *Performance* remains a celluloid tragedy, offscreen disasters befell its participants, semi-gangsters became real gangsters, killed people, and non-actresses, like Anita Pallenberg and hashed-up French teeny co-star Michèle Breton, became actresses - all due, in part, to the false invincibility with which Cammell and the film imbued them. *Performance* remains symptomatic of late-sixties ennui. Part of its sinister appeal is that it is an ode to excess, drugs, sloth, and an inability to produce. Only Jagger went in feet first and emerged head intact.

Director Bryan Forbes was a British kettle of fish. Born in Stratford-atte-Bow in the East End of London in 1926, he was acting by the age of seventeen, maybe before. After a "below the title" B career in mainly soppy war films designed to smooth the ruffled British middle-class feathers over the penalties of supposed WWII victory, the spoils of which seemed to be being squandered on the young, Forbes graduated to screenwriting, directing, and producing. Forbes and his actor pallies, like Richard Attenborough and Harry Andrews, farted around in yawn-filled war yarns, happy to play middle-class wankers on the screen whilst imitating the upper-class same once the director had yelled "Cut!" In the mid-fifties, Forbes caught the sales of the - inherited from France - British New Wave period, rather naff looking back, apart from the acting talent it produced (Albert Finney, Tom Courteney, Richard Harris, *et al.*). Forbes screenplayed and directed *The L-Shaped Room* (1962), *Seance on a Wet Afternoon* (1964), and *King Rat* (1965), and screenplayed and co-produced *The Angry Silence* (1960). This is why he was on our shopping list. Sometime late in 1964 I met him at Shepperton Studios, when he was supposed to have what Graham Greene called the needed "chip of ice in the heart." I did not know that it had melted and Forbes would go onto a lackluster directorial career that included *The Madwoman of Chaillot* (1969) and the (un)original version of *The Stepford Wives* (1975).

In the trenches of 1964-66, I continued to do battle on behalf of the Rolling Stones movie never to be. I recall one meeting with Forbes that took place in the canteen at Shepperton Studios where I was Jaggerless but accompanied by Tony Calder who, with his wife Jenny, was Forbes's Surrey neighbour. The possibility of *A Clockwork Orange* was already a lost issue. Alas, the conversation never gained ground on the subject of a Stones movie, for which, at best, Forbes remained an also-ran and a rehearsal. He personified for us the danger of our presuming that those, such as he, who'd already made their way in in life and were a half-dozen or so years older than us, might wish us well or at least consider our ability. But later, Forbes would gush up to his neighbour, Elton John, and in 1972 they'd make a silly little film together: *Elton John and*

Bernie Taupin Say Goodbye to Norma Jean and Other Things.

At one point during the lunch, Forbes enquired whether Elvis Presley was gay. In answer I related a story Peter Noone had told me about his visit with Elvis. Peter and his Herman's Hermits had been taken to Bel Air to meet the King. Elvis had engaged in his usual childish behaviour at Peter's expense for the amusement of Elvis's Memphis buffoons. Standing on the marble steps of his Bel Air mansion, he'd positioned one of his bodyguards to kneel behind Peter so that Elvis could shake hands and then push Peter over the living stool. This, amongst tuts and titters, seemed to be interpreted by Forbes as quasi-confirmation of an aberrant sexuality in the King. The British New Wave was stillborn to this sort of inanity.

As said, most pop stars, upon opening their mouth in a movie, lose whatever charisma and aplomb they walked onto the set with. It happened to Jagger in Tony Richardson's 1970 *Ned Kelly*. It happened to Grace Jones in the 1985 James Bond flick, *From a View to a Kill*. She was as sexy as ever until she opened her mouth. On the other hand, Christopher Walken's badguy Max was the very essence of cool pop sex. It happened on occasion to David Bowie, even though he is credited as being the only poptop to rise above stiffness. I disagree. It worked in *The Man Who Fell to Earth* only because this Nick Roeg flick was another drug-pervaded effort with all the life of expired Ritalin. *The Hunger* succeeded due to the casting, which gave Bowie the opportunity to shine in a *Three Women* ensemble with Catherine Deneuve and Susan Sarandon. For this fan, Dame Bowie's best screen turn remains his stellar double performance in the extended video of "Blue Jean."

The Rolling Stones' efforts into filmdom were a comedy of errors with no standing witnesses save my own *Charlie is My Darling*, filmed in '65, released in '66. You do have Hal Ashby's *Let's Spend the Night Together* and Jean-Luc Godard's *One Plus One*. The Stones seem to have had an unwitting effect on Godard. He moved to England to make *One Plus One*, mixing the Stones' recording of "Sympathy for the Devil" with Black Power tracts to limpish affect. But the exercise seems to have further depressed him. Subsequently, he almost died in a Dylan-like motorbike crash and began to retreat from the world. He rejected his old work on "ideological grounds." His old audience rejected him and, by 1974, unfinanceable in cinemas, he was reduced to video and pathetic comedy. In effect, he vanished.

Then came the Altamont travesty, *Gimme Shelter* being the other side of the twisted celluloid coin that traffics in disaster the same way that *Performance* trades on perverse indulgence and the fetishism of decadence. Obviously I'm not a warts-and-all Stones fan; *Rock and Roll Circus* also leaves me cold. The Rolling Stones' most engaging telefilmic outings remain *The T.A.M.I. Show* and various *Top of the Pops* and *Ready, Steady, Go!* outings. Mick Jagger slowwrithing in sensual motion to "It's All Over Now" on *Top of the Pops* and his sultry student-of-Jean-Seberg delivery of "You Better Move On" on *The Arthur Haynes Show* are pop moments captured with optimum reality and magic, as opposed to the later "who-am-I?" tech and mental malaises that were allowed once the zookeepers had turned on and beaded out.

In all, I was happy to have waved *adieu* to my play with celluloid dream merchants, hustlers, hypers, and Chelsea Draculas, and to be back at Ivor Court and about real, as opposed to reel, work.

****

However, my fascination with film's transporting, creative world and those that populate it would continue. In 1974, I was negotiating with Anthony Burgess's agent over the movie rights to another of the author's great yarns, *The Wanting Seed*, when the master himself invited me to tea at the Dorchester Hotel, London. The author was attractive, engaging, and all Neroesque, his skin dyed Moroccan olive by the Mediterranean sun, and with forward-thrusting blond/ grey hair. Having just flown in from Monte Carlo or Rome to dance with his second wife Liana at the Dorchester, he enjoyed telling the story and let me pour the next cup of tea. He was as comfortably upholstered as the settees upon which we sat, sipping tea from the thinnest of porcelain cups, and generous with his time, recalling his 1961 life-defining year, *A Clockwork Orange*, and how the Stones and I would never have been able to secure the rights to it.

At the time, the producer Nigel Thomas and I were attempting to acquire the rights to Mr. Burgess's *The Wanting Seed* as a possible directorial vehicle for Nigel's mate, Ridley Scott.

Nigel hung out in the best locations life had to offer. I'd visited him above Loma Vista and below Mullholland whilst he house and career-sat with Ridley, waiting on David Putnam to fuel *The Duellists* into go. Nigel was another friend who would move on before his time, passing on in the early nineties at the tender age of not-yet-forty-four. He remains a friend forever, as does his wife Pauline. This immaculate duo is part of the small coterie of good souls who have gone the distance and put up with me in lives one, two, and three.

It was never a bad life with Nigel, and if he let you in you shared a good one. His generosity of heart would bring me, one seventies evening, to Mt. Kisco, New York, where, in the few years before *Frampton Comes Alive*, dear Peter was struggling to rise above first fame in the Herd, Jonathan King's telegraphed billing and cooing, his short stint in Humble Pie, and his pretty face and body. He had made a couple of decent solo albums but was not being taken seriously in America, whilst in England he couldn't get a mention. He toured constantly in the States, building up the base that would swell with the mythic success of *FCA*, while living on and off again up in Mt. Kisco with a tall, blonde, thin, Kate Hudson-type wastrel named Penny Brigton, who was married to one of Peter's roadies. Such were the rules on the spoils of rock 'n' roll that Frampton and Penny seized each other for their own, whilst the husband roadied on. If this reeks of scenes in Cameron Crowe's delightful *Almost Famous* (2000), in which Frampton played a roadie named Reg, you'll have got it in one, and realised that nothing is sacred on the road. Frampton would immortalise Penny by name in a song for three of her fifteen minutes. In my mind, she was the embodiment of Kate Huidson's Penny Lane in *Almost Famous*, save in real life it was a little more *The Apartment* and a little less *Terms of Endearment*.

Nigel viewed Mr. Frampton's and Mrs. Brigton's spoils-of war living arrangement as atrociously convenient. He further found it atrociously inconvenient that I had been wilting away in Connecticut, not getting laid, and insisted that I wash, shave, trim up, and meet him in Manhattan for dinner at the Plaza Hotel. I certainly needed to groom up, my appearance at the time more Dan Haggerty than Don Adams, and my girth widened by booze, junk food, and a nonstop diet of couch-ridden American TV. So, I cleaned up, tweeded up, and Volvo'd myself down the Merritt Parkway to New York City. Nigel had arranged about six for dinner and I was seated next to the more-attractive-than-Frampton Penny Brigton. Frampton was elsewhere, somewhere out in the toilets of the Midwest, stoking the fires of fandom and paying for Mt Kisco. Dinner finished, I found Penny engaging; she found me the same. Nigel beamed a "Here, kids, take my limo, go have fun." We did.

We clubbed about Manhattan a bit to make sure, then limo'd out to Mt. Kisco, where we proceeded to pass the rest of the weekend making love in every room of the house. She was very good and I felt very good inside her. Nigel's call had been correct and welcome. I had been spending too much time of late in my head; now I was out of it.

One resounding recall of the weekend with Penny is of being atop her on the floor in one of the bedrooms, elbows hurting nicely as they dug into the pine floor while I dug further into Penny, when my aplomb was diminished and my seed left wanting by her series of totally inappropriate questions about the rights of the artist, i.e. Peter Frampton, *vis-à-vis* his current contractual arrangements with A&M Records and that the fact that, according to Penny, all Peter's monies went directly to his manager, Dee Anthony. My dick, at the mere *déja vu* of it all, goes a little limp.

Yet the weekend *en lolal* was a triumphant, glowing call to arms and penis for which I thanked Nigel. I have nothing but appreciation for Penny - her laughter, beauty, sensuality, and "peter" agenda were a riot. We joked that she should have got Peter to do his own dirty work. Penny remarked that she'd like to orchestrate that one, it being an experience that might remove some of the domestic ice and have Frampton come alive.

A few years later, down the other end of the seventies, I was out to lunch on a withering summer day outside Bergdorf Goodman on the corner of 5th Avenue and 58th Street when Penny wilted out to the corner, drugged and overweight, looking like a Midwestern, blown-out Marianne Faithfull. Her shopping bags were weighed down by matching Great Danes. It could have been an outtake from the Plaza Hotel scenes in *Almost Famous*. Penny looked even more untogether than I, so I did not say hallo. I hope she stopped and came back from the madness, and I do thank her for bringing me back to life all those years ago.

Back at the Dorchester on that '74 day, Anthony Burgess continued to recall how he'd been hacking away at his scribing life in '61 when a doctor had given him grave news: He had some cancer, growth, or intrusion that would render him dead in a year and a half, two at the tops, so he'd better get his life and goodbyes in order. He threw himself into a writing frenzy, buoyed and influenced by scotch, amphetamines, and no sleep. This hazy craze of wordulition produced the Russian-Cockney configuration that bound *A Clockwork Orange, Inside Mr. Enderby,* and *The Wanting Seed* so well. Mid-chapter-and-verse on this perceived last body of work, Burgess sold the film and stage rights to the lot for a pittance, the exact amount of which he did not clarify in our tea-time meet, and I did not enquire. He let me know that he'd want a cool quarter of a million for the right to option *The Wanting Seed* and another hundred thou or so for writing the first screenplay. He quite frankly didn't care if we used a word of it, he stated, so long as he was paid. Nigel and I decided that Burgess was making up for Kubrick'd time, and so we gave up the chase. We returned to our own killing fields, happier and wiser for a day off in someone else's run, dressed for the next last supper, and debated who would be the meal.

CHAPTER 23

the battle of righteous feelings / the first pop business - fashion / good press, bad press - the stones in the house of the lords / far out, far east, and down under / vinyl magic at rca - as written by mick and keith

"You've Lost That Lovin' Feeling" was about to get a U.K. January release. That same month Bill and Bobby would jump from number five to number one in the North American charts. The record that had blown my life around the previous fall in Phil Spector's New York office was in for a hard road abroad. Its future in England did not look promising with the news that Cilla Black had covered the song for British release. Cilla was managed by Brian Epstein and recorded by George Martin. She had just come off a number one with the Burt Bacharach and Hal David-penned, and originally recorded by Dionne Warwick, "Anyone Who Had a Heart." The business of popular music was not yet the globally unified beast that it would be transported into during the 1970s.

At the end of January 1965, the LP that we called *Rolling Stones No. 2* entered the U.K. album charts at number one and stayed there for a grand thirteen weeks. The cover contained neither the name of the group nor a title, and this time, unlike the first time out, Decca did not object. In America, where I had no cause to be so commercially compulsive, the work, with the same photo but a different lineup of songs, was titled *12x5*. The recordings had been made in London, Chicago, and Hollywood, and I was proud of that. It had been engineered by Bill Farley in London, Ron Malo in Chicago, and Dave Hassinger in Hollywood.

The zitgrandised, orphanesqued cover photo of the group had been taken by Mick's new best mate, David Bailey, whom I had not seen since 1960, when I worked for Mary Quant and made deliveries from Quant to *Vogue*. This fashion world of the early sixties was the first pop business that the U.K. enjoyed. Bailey, Donovan, and Parkinson flicked the shutters whilst Jean Shrimpton made the clothes look great, Vidal Sassoon cut the hair, and Mary Quant provided the clothes and the flair. Suddenly Britain had something to say and a look to go with it.

Fashion became the export - America was not interested in tired redos of fodder that had already had its day at home, and basically British pop fell into that category until the Beatles evened the score. So David Bailey knew exactly what this brand of op was all about - he'd been one of the crew who had invented the mould and didn't need any instruction from me. Besides, if I'd turned up at his studio for the shoot, he might have reconsidered not sending me the bill. This was not cheapness on my part - I was a few cars beyond that by this stage - I just thought you couldn't put a price on David Bailey taking your picture unless he chose to name it.

I had written the sleeve notes for the Stones' second album in the bath for a laugh, seeing just how close I could skate to the land of Anthony Burgess. There was no concerted effort to be controversial - I was just doing what came naturally to me at the time - the violent rhetoric I didn't give a second thought to. I was just very busy being me. The result would be surprisingly rewarding in terms of publicity, coverage, and outrage.

Questions were being asked in the House of Lords about my sleeve notes, particularly in reference to my recommendation that Stones fans take up mugging blind people to secure the funds to purchase their records! The National Association for the Blind was in a visible uproar and Lord Conesford demanded to know "what Government action" was planned to remove the offending notes. The Home Office found "no evidence that these words had been published in circumstances constituting a criminal offence." Even Decca *jefe* Sir Edward Lewis made a rare public statement: "I am told this inscription was intended to be humourous, but I'm afraid this jargon just does not make sense to me." I was thrilled by the uproar - but it hadn't really been thought out at all; I was just lucky enough to be in the right place in the right mind. The publicity definitely helped draw attention to the second album, which, with the group's next step into casual brilliance, won over another horde of fans.

The Stones looked under the rug where white America had swept the cultural rhinestone of R&B and culled nine passionate anthems. They tipped their hat again to Chuck Berry with "You Can't Catch Me," leered and laughed their way through Alvin Robinson's "Down Home Girl," and added three originals that blended seamlessly with the classic covers.

I was about to celebrate my twenty-first birthday as the Rolling Stones stepped on and off the plane for their first tour of

Australia and New Zealand. The journey was long, boring, and economic. We cut across Europe, the Near and Far East. I remember waking up as we stopped for fuel in Bombay or Calcutta and being amazed to see the runway, a concrete maze of tufts of garden inhabited by packs of dogs, nonplussed at our landing. Twenty-four hours out of London, farther from Tulsa, I reached for the schlap, offered it around to a grumpy group of young men, and prepared for our landing Down Under. We arrived at the Sydney airport to be met by three thousand rabid fans and a press conference. Another cut from *No. 2/12x5,* the Drifters' opus "Under the Boardwalk," had been released as a single and greeted us from the number one position.

The Stones would give five shows in just two days in Sydney. The audiences were wild and woolly; the Stones loved it as they searched for their land legs after a day-and-a-half in the air. There were plenty of nubile young offers to help them; even I welcomed such an assist. The Sydney press wrote that the Stones were a national scandal, shocking and ugly, blatantly sexual, both on stage and off. They intimated that the band was up to no good with the nation's minors and virgins and were indulging in all-night orgies of the flesh. "I wish we were!" was unfortunately the only quote of mine on behalf of the group that made its way back to London. Truth was, all work and party allowed and aside, the Aussie and New Zealand summer had replaced the English winter and provided us with a well-earned holiday.

On the Stones' first gig in a Sydney tin shed, along with wishing that the Opera House had been completed in time for us, my main duty was insisting that, whilst on the revolving stage, Roy Orbison, the Newbeats, and the other acts had to turn 25% between each song and remain stationary during the song. The Stones, on the other hand, were to have the stage revolving slowly all the time. This was an early example of downsizing the competition. Outside of that, I could concentrate on enjoying the Stones by night and getting a suntan by day.

The only violence on the tour occurred when a Newbeat all but had his balls bitten off by a Maori could-it-be-a-hooker during our New Zealand stopover at a hot spring - the result of his requesting some unchivalrous, below the-belt sexual act. Even the retiring Mr. Orbison laughed at the thought of the new heights of falsetto that might have been reached that night.

In Auckland the hotel took one look at us and wouldn't let us in. We got the same deal in Wellington, so had to fly back to Christchurch to a hotel that would have us. In Invercargill, the Stones were greeted by a chorus of boo's. The audience expected a headline appearance from Roy Orbison and barraged the Stones' show with nonstop "Bring back Roy!" Mick managed to outrage the Southland farming community with post-show comments that had him quoted as saying, "Invercargill is the arsehole of the earth and the local residents are a mob of sheep-farmers." I hope Mick's not having to visit Invercargill on his next solo tour.

By the time we played Melbourne, everybody was getting used to the lazy summer pace and the will-they-or-won't-they-let-us-stay at-the-inn. In Melbourne, the John Bateman Motor Inn would. It boasted a manager who would have given Honor Black-man a run for her money. Mick and I took turns ogling and making moves, whilst other members of the group concentrated on the daughters. We waterskied and even Brian relaxed. He left his mental luggage in the room and became a hearty skipper driving the speed boat as we skied all day. It was too hot for Mick to come out in the midday sun, so Keith and I concentrated on getting our tans to last till London. We walked and talked the length of the beach and wrote "I'd Much Rather Be With the Boys."

The next leg of the tour was an uncertain trip into the Far East. A promoter associate of Harry M. Miller named Freddie Yu flew down to check us out. He had to be sure of the group's beha-viour, to see if they were suitable in the matter of saving face. The group passed the test and travelled to Japan and Singapore. Keith laughed and wondered quietly as we landed, "So, Andrew, did they teach you a new way of saying, 'Give me the fuckin' money'?"

When we arrived in Hong Kong, Freddie Yu limo'd us to his penthouse for an array of food, booze, pornographic movies, and hookers. The first bunch of ladies offered were over the hill and out of teeth; none of us wished to partake. The next batch paraded were marginally younger and prettier, full-bodied, and full-toothed. They were followed by a final parade of teens and early twenties. We decided that somebody had to do the honours - we were, after all, in the land where nobody should have to lose face. We drew straws; somehow Bill Wyman won and saved the day.

Somewhere in Hong Kong, then still under British rule though part of mainland China, the Stones arrived in the middle of the night to play, none of us having any idea where we were. We were whisked from a military airstrip, escorted by machine gun-clad jeeps to a circus tent in the middle of an eerie nowhere. It was all scary shades of the later *Apocalypse Now* in which Freddie Yu was Bill Graham and the Stones were fresh bunnies flown in for the troops. The audience was six thousand up-and-at-'em actual screaming British soldiers. The show went incredibly well. Bill Wyman made an exception on this occasion and resisted taking a fan back to his room to discuss the finer points of the show.

The next morning, we were guests of honour at the British Embassy for lunch. We figured that news of our reputation was slow to reach these parts; the taxpayers' money was being spent so that the ambassador's kiddies could ask cute, stupid questions and get autographs for themselves and their schoolmates. We were able to laze this final day away amongst the gone-with-the-Empire white marble pillars and immaculate forever lawns. On the white-linen veranda we took a four-or-more-course luncheon, waited on hand-and-foot. We were all bowled over by the tour's second pearled and tanned lookalike Honor Blackman winner, in the form and shape of the ambassador's very sexy wife.

We returned February 18th from Tokyo to London via Los Angeles, where we'd recorded the next Stones single in January, two new Mick and Keith originals, "The Last Time" and "Play with Fire." After changing clothes at the Hotel Nameless and wolfing down hamburgers, fries, and beer, the group, Ian Stewart, and I had headed down Sunset to RCA to rendezvous and grab that magic. In just one year, Mick's and Keith's songwriting had graduated from soppy ballads, to commercial ballads, to album material for the Stones, and finally - with the two songs we were about to record - had cleared that last hurdle to a real, live single for the Rolling Stones.

RCA was a great studio, huge, big recording rooms, high ceilings, and nice parquet wood floors. They had an extensive microphone collection, worthy old Neumann, Telefunken, and RCA mikes, outstanding live echo chambers, and a fine, original Neve console.

After an eleven-hour run, we'd finished "The Last Time." I was so thrilled, beside myself with the result; the audio layers were just so total, hypnotic, and forever. I called up Phil Spector and asked him to come to the studio to listen to what we'd done. Everybody had really come through; this was the first Rolling Stones totality. Brian and Keith had set up a layer of guitars that allowed Mick and Keith to just sit in the sing of it. I knew we finally had that big American hit; I just wanted Phil to tell me how big. Forty-five minutes later, Phil hobbled in off the Sunset Strip in his Chelsea boots to listen to our forty-five. We put up "The Last Time." Naturally, the little big man asked to hear it much louder. As the fade neverended, Phil chuckled, shook his head, and sighed. "Number ten, guys, number ten," he said. He'd be right.

We still had to cut the B-side, "Play with Fire." Brian, Bill, and Charlie, exhausted from the all-day onslaught to complete "The Last Time," headed for the Hotel Somewhere to crash. An elderly, well-rounded, Negro cleaner in matching grey shirt and slacks quietly swept all four corners of the cavernous RCA Studio A. As the morning light rose on the Sunset Strip, Mick sat back on his stool and sang it, Keith's acoustic gave him something to sing to, Jack Nitzsche played a worldly harpsichord, Phil Spector gave the lining by playing bass - and "Play with Fire" was cut. If you listened hard, you could hear the sweeping, and if you listened inside me, you could hear my heart beating: We were home!

CHAPTER 24

got live if you want it or not / a white '64 lincoln continental - i move in, it's nicer than my home / man in the mirror - jagger on guns and cravats / driving offences are driving me nuts - reg the butcher gets the chop / going clear in clearwater - keith snores his way into "satisfaction" / a sean is born

"The Last Time" b/w "Play with Fire" was released on Decca in the U.K. on February 26, 1965. Its U.S. release would be three weeks later and its European and rest-of-the-world release would be in dribs and drabs over the coming spring into summer months.

Keith and I took a couple of days off in Paris; Charlie and Shirley Watts joined us for one of them. The highlight was a swoop 'n' shop at our favourite boutique, Pierre Cardin on rue du Faubourg Saint-Honoré. Keith and I both bought indoor riding boots in a butter glove leather that rippled down around the ankles the way actual butter glove leather does around the wrists. I remember hoping my skin would wrinkle, age, and hold as elegantly. Keith must have hoped for the same. He bought black, I brown. The price shocked us both - £46 each! That was an almost disgusting amount of money for anything, let alone a pair of boots that could not be worn in the street except at your own scuff and peril. Later in the day we went Left Bank and practical over in Saint-Germain and picked up more reasonable, short, double-breasted, navy pea coats with matching, braided, discreet, peaked sailor's caps that had us, on a later Irish tour, mistaken for railway workers and asked for directions for the train going to Cork. I'm sure by now that some of you are wishing I'd been born a guitar techno as opposed to a slut for a shop window, but I was not. And, when the going gets rich, the rich go shopping.

Back in the U.K., the Stones nonstop work 'n' tour agenda continued as they headed out on March 5 for yet another package tour presented by Eric Easton Ltd. The Stones were joined by the Hollies, Dave Berry and the Cruisers, the original Checkmates, and an American all-girl group, Goldie and the Gingerbreads, whom Keith and I had first heard at a Bob Crewe Dakota party where the group entertained along with falsetto minstrel Tiny Tim. Goldie and her Gingerbreads had come to London to record with Mickie Most for Decca and to try their hand at reversing the Brit invasion of the Americas. I would later record Goldie with the Goffin/King potboiler, "Going Back." Dusty Springfield, as it happened, had also recorded the tune. There was no point in entering the ring on that one, so I withdrew my version from release. Goldie Zelkowitz would return to the States, reinvent herself as Genya Ravan, and become known for her work with Ten Wheel Drive and her subsequent solo career.

The Righteous Brothers had been booked for the tour, but single success had caused the duo to split up, not for the first or last time, and they dropped out at the last moment. The two of them had a certified smash with "Lovin' Feeling," and that's what broke them up. Story goes that, as Bill Medley, the tall one, got to sing the verse and first chorus by himself, little Bobby Hatfield's ego was miffed and he asked Phil Spector - ego and TV appearances in mind - "What do I do?" (whilst the tall one sang alone). Phil is supposed to have replied, "Start counting the money."

It was the first total *Day of the Triffids* tour. At last, the Stones played to a never-ending drone of madness. There now no longer existed a "Beatles Only" territory north of Manchester; it was a shared prize, and, in the taking of the Moptops' home turf, we must have come on like crazed angels. No more derision on the division of England's North and South. No more bottles thrown on the stage, no more jeers, rumbles, or menace. We finally stood on the stages of the North and the sound and bleat of the male and female hordes was ours for the asking. The game had been played, sung, and now won - and oh, what a feeling!

I recorded my sun gods that night in Liverpool for the EP *Got Live If You Want It*. The band sounded magnificent on that night, and they all knew it. "I tried to get an effect on the record that, as you are listening to it, it's as if you are sitting in the cinema watching the Stones." This, at any rate, is what I told *Melody Maker* at the time. Naturally I went on to gild the lily and lower the flat data into pomp and overdo: "The overall effect is a standard I always aim for in every recording, a ball of sound in which none of the ingredients in the record are more important than the other. One must remember that one is not selling, in most cases, a melody that will go down in history, one is selling a ball of sound which attempts to hit the audience on first or second impact, because if it does not you can forget it."

The waffle I gave *Melody Maker* on the *Got Live If You Want It* sessions now gives me cause to cringe and probably gave the Stones cause to do so at the time - even given the excuse of youth - for we were all that and in our topsy-turvy *Lord of the Flies* world; no quarter was given or asked for on this score. Above and beyond the width of lip and dearth of modesty that I was allowed in that time by the media, the facts remain simple: My job was to provide the Rolling Stones with the environment in which they could create, and to make sure that their efforts had the technical support to guarantee that their work was recorded and delivered as given. Anything else was a wall of noise. The press would invite me to highwire with no net and fuck-up, and I would often oblige. To quote once more the master of dealing with the exalted, Graham Greene, from his second autobi, *Ways of Escape*: "Success is more dangerous than failure (the ripples break over a wider coastline)."

The tour continued through the end of March. The Stones made time for two valuable *Top of the Pops* TV appearances. When the security guard on duty at the Odeon in Rochester, Kent, would not let the Stones into the theatre, Keith, no doubt pissed off at being spurned in his own county, knocked the offending guard to the ground.

In addition to the Liverpool concert recording, we taped the Manchester shows. On the EP sleeve notes I added the Royal Albert Hall in London as the other venue at which we'd taped, but that was bull - I couldn't get permission to record at the Albert Hall. The sound you hear is the true call of the North, recorded superbly on this audio reunion by Glyn Johns, the engineer who had been the first to sound the Stones. Glyn still worked at the IBC studios in London and we took their three-track gear north for the recordings. There was one track for the band, one for Mick, and one for the audience via a mike dangled over the front of the circle.

The recording done and assembled by Glyn back at the Great Portland Street headquarters of IBC, I was left to deal with a slight matter of fairness *vis-à-vis* publishing royalties. On side one of the EP I'd placed two R&B evergreens from the Atlantic/Stax vaults, "Everybody Needs Somebody to Love" and "Pain in My Heart." I called the U.K. publishers of these tunes and "requested" 15% in return for keeping them on the EP. I was refused. I felt abused, so I indulged in a loogistic move by claiming the ten-second prosodic audience screaming, "We want the Stones," as a composition credited to the five Stones via the *nom-de-comp* Nanker Phelge, so that the publishing and composital equation was broken down between three songs as opposed to two. Money for new hope.

Press opposition to the group reached a new level when, on the final night of this tour, March 18, the Stones became embroiled in what would become known as the "pissing incident." I'd like to take credit for engineering this event, but that would not be true - I merely recognised the moment and transferred the credit from the bassline to the lead vocal as piss-artist. Some would call me clairvoyant, some might not be so kind. The Stones, led by Bill, were caught with their flies down addressing the wall of a Romford service station, the actual loo locked and not an offered option. The fellows were reported to the police and arrested for urinating on the service station wall. Fleet Street went ballistic over the story, so I moved Mick into the headline; the band's image as long-haired monsters of the drip was enhanced. I say "I moved" - but it probably involved nothing more than my lying in the affirmative when some optimistic scribe asked whether Mick was in the front line.

It doesn't matter how much you do; it's whether you do the right thing at the right time. If you do that one thing, make that one call, hold that one sacred meeting with the someone who can change your world for that moment, and however long it lasts, then, to paraphrase William Burroughs, you have created that frozen moment when everyone sees what is on the end of the fork, and, I must add, wants to eat it. The matter of "Would You Let Your Daughter Go With a Rolling Stone?" Did I first say it? No, but I heard someone say it and I repeated it and made it work. It had just been a part of someone else's conversation. I heard it and pushed it into a headline. I had no idea that it would be a byline for life. Some might say that it and the pissing incident were the cornerstones of the early Stones image. If they were, then I'd add "The Rolling Stones are more than just a group - they are a way of life," my closing line on their first untitled album. I pushed the pissing incident into the national papers - it didn't matter that it was Bill Wyman who did the pissing, or the fact that no one knew that Mick, to whom the role was given, wasn't even there. You make it and you sell out simultaneously. It's the inevitable for both the artist and the promoter. There are no accidents and it always takes two.

Amidst all this piss-pop publicity and furor, "The Last Time" went straight into the charts at number eight and to number one in the U.K. by its second week, becoming the group's second consecutive number one single. We didn't have to be about buying records in the stores anymore. "The Last Time" had svelte and cunning and a forever underbelly of layers that leaked fresh audio delights unto the listener, depending on the room and box it was played from. The group now knew who they were, sounded like it, and were relaxed and unfrenetic in their musical explanation of themselves.

I bought a new car - more than a car, a total celebration of automerit applause for the road so far - priced at a fitting £4000. A white, four-door, left-hand-drive, '64 Lincoln Continental, its bright white sheen resting in a bed of red leather - it looked like a swimming pool on wheels. Reg was thrilled at being let loose on the street in this new toy, and I had him look into the possibility of us "Boadicea-ing-up" by having attached to the wheels, knives (rubber-tipped of course) which, at the press of a 007 button on the dash, would extend to threaten the legs of the pedestrian enemy. I could not get any car firm to take my money to develop this idea. On a short Irish tour at the start of the year, Keith and I had purchased pistols and shoulder holsters in Dublin, the continuing beginnance of Keith's love of a good weapon. We were both well pleased with ourselves as we descended the aeroplane steps on our London arrival, smirking at each other, breathing on the weight of our new best friends. "Anything to declare, lads?" took on a cinematic aspect of its own as we shrugged our shoulders and holsters and replied with a smile.

The Beatles were busy doing airports. This same March they filmed *Help!* in the Bahamas and changed planes in London to continue on to Salzburg for more filming. They flew back at the end of April for a month's indoor shooting at Twickenham Studios, which would wrap up their visual input for their second motion picture.

The Stones continued on their British greytrek. At the Palace Theatre, a Manchester girl fell fifteen or twenty feet from the circle into the stalls - the luck of hysteric immunity and the fall being broken by the fans below allowed her no more than the need to replace a few broken teeth. That same night we were not allowed into the hotel dining room because we were not attired in ties. Those first few months of swinging 1965 were rife with acts of attritious inconsistency, wherein we could enter the hotel dining room with guns and shoulder holsters but not without ties.

Mick Jagger told the *Daily Mirror*: "The trouble with a tie is that it could dangle in the soup. It is also something that a fan can hang onto when you are trying to get in and out of a theatre." "The trouble with a gun is that it could go off," he chided Keith and I away from the press. Keith told a northern rag, "I reckon there are three reasons why American R&B stars don't click with British teenage fans. One, they're old; two, they're black; and three, they're ugly." Brian Jones told *Melody Maker* and thereby the rest of the band, "I play a lot of lead guitar and I am not really interested in rhythm guitar."

The second week of April, the Stones joined the Beatles and the rest of Brit popdom at the *NME* Annual Poll Winners Concert at the Empire Pool, Wembley. This was the last but one occasion at which both acts appeared, another early goodbye to the hurrah of the sixties. It was a quick gig, a show of hands, a few tunes, and a quick hallo. The Beatles seemed to be walking backwards, saying it's yours and welcome to it. Reg burned more rubber than called for in his attempts to protect the Stones and my Lincoln from the crazed fans. These serial-fan nutcases were made all the more chaotic and dangerous by a frivolous disregard of security, the benign "Who-do-you-think-you-are?" stupidity from the old bill.

Reg miscalculated his control over reverse and hit a few fans, as in, they wouldn't get out of the way. The court case a few months later would result in Reg's losing his driving license for five years, leaving me with deep regret and the need to find another driver, minder, and friend. Reg would have to change his position in life and find one in which he could afford a chauffeur. He had taken up with speed in an effort to work my hours and pursue his own. Our rock 'n' pop existence had the dynamic of stress as a daily given. The chuckle was starting to fade, and Reg was oft of that too-stressed lot. A great deal of his violence was only held in check by his success in the chicken department, yet my hours did not allow him the ones to pursue that most needed commodity - the young, pretty, straight boy who would bend just for him. When the magistrate banned Reg

from the road, Mick, Keith, and I gifted him with one of the
dimmer of the Glimmer Twins' songwriting output thus far, a
Costa del Sol, sun-'n'-sugar-wrenched ballad, "Each and Every
Day," which Reg was able to record with his newfound pretty
boy band, Thee, and Decca agreed to release in May 1965. As
"Each and Every Day of the Year," the song had also made it to
the B-side of Bobby Jameson's "All I Want is My Baby" in '64 and
ended up on the Stones' mix 'n' match 1975 *Metamorphosis* LP.

I didn't see much of Reg over the next few years. You spend
an insanely intense amount of time with people, as Reg did with
me and I with the Stones - a time that repels all boarders and in
which every emotion, ripple, and nuance of the day is shared and
nothing is hidden. Then that time is gone, it moves on, and there
is absolutely nothing left to say as you too move on to fresh and
separate playing fields alone. His life as pop manager did not last
long and he returned to the relative security of dealing in cars.
Years later, down in the eighties, he met his death in Bangkok,
where he holiday'd yearly to fulfill his penchant for young fellas.
He had picked two for supper and was riding them home on his
motorbike when something must have diverted his attention and
he forgot to take a corner. Reg King and two young men on a
bike cruised over the cliff, and death did them part.

Reg was master of his universe, save in the matter of his
heart and predilection of his libido, which was aberrated paedo-
philia. Whilst the age difference was still within the same decade,
he could pass his choice off as an early call, but as his age stretched
to forty and his boy choice did not keep pace, life must have taken
on a permanent tension that played a not unkind part in his death.
For me he'll be forever young, ticking and flicking his well-bred,
well-padded shoulders into gear, tossing his blond mane and
batting his sheer blue eyes in pursuit of the straight, well-hung
lad of today and tomorrow. He attended to me as a grand butch
seductress, determined to refine my day into pleasure, regardless
of how I'd arrived to it. Reg, with his love of life, is a constant
reminder of the good who have died young.

The band and I flew out for the next North American
tour shortly after *The Rolling Stones, Now!* LP was released. Our
final U.S. single of 1964, "Heart of Stone," had failed to follow up
on the first real dent made by "Time is on My Side." "Heart of

Stone" had been stupidly released one week before Christmas in the States, and, by the time the world had rejoined itself from the holiday break, American radio had forgotten us, was working from fresh playlists, and "Heart of Stone" had stopped breaking at a miserable number nineteen. "The Last Time" b/w "Play with Fire" would make top ten amends for this imbecilic *faux pas*.

The Stones were still very much in a holding pattern, in the queue for actual American success on the terms by which America defines it. We were in the wings, waiting for God's lighting to pan down on us and klieg that moment when a nation would claim us as its own. At that point of majesty there is no separating Van Cliburn, Andy Warhol, or the Rolling Stones. All are clutched to America's tit and invited to partake of its milk and money.

The American top ten countdown in May '65 ran thus: the Righteous Brothers, Sam the Sham and the Pharaohs, the Beach Boys, Wayne Fontana and the Mindbenders, Petula Clark, Herman's Hermits, the Seekers, the Beatles, Gary Lewis and the Playboys, and, at number one, Herman's Hermits. Many a month in '65 Herman's Hermits had two or three whacks in the U.S. top twenty, and very much at centre-stage stood Peter Noone. Armed with the Midas audio touch of Mickie Most and with his own professionalism, cute good looks, and winning personality, Peter would, in a two-and-a-half-year stretch, score eleven U.S. top ten singles.

We were coming back from Australia via Honolulu when Mick got entrapped in a case of mistaken identity by a half-dozen or so giggling Hawaiian braided and pigtailed schoolgirls. Pigtails were unusual for Mick; he normally got city slickers, next runt of the Sid Vicious litter, or Park Avenue minidamettes. The girls' squeals and jumps of joy immediately *Hawaii Five-O*'d into confused silence when they studied the signature on their autographed pages and realised it that spelt "Mick" instead of "Herman." The squeals were taken up with equal zeal by Keith, and, hiding managerily behind him, me.

The Stones were with the wrong U.S. agents. GAC just didn't get us. Herman's Hermits and the rest of the already-succeeding British Invasion (less the Beatles) were with the bouncy Premier Talent Agency, helmed by ex-GAC man Frank Barsalona. Frank would become and remain the major agent representing rock acts in America for the next two decades through to the new century.

In '65 he repped Freddie and the Dreamers and Wayne Fontana and the Mindbenders, plus the stateside action of the Ronettes, the Shangri-Las, and Mitch Ryder and the Detroit Wheels.

Frank Barsalona had another English connection. He would marry U.K. music journalist June Harris, who, with Judith Simons, had been two of the first journalists to "let me in" in my earlier days as a press agent. I recall standing on the side of the stage of the Granada, Slough, during the few days I repped the Little Richard/ Sam Cooke/Jet Harris Don Arden-promoted tour. I watched in awe and amazement the magic being woven oh-so-gracefully by Sam Cooke as his soul took over the basic ready-to-rip, Little Richard teddy boy audience and made them his own for his nightly moment in style. In the Cooke-induced trance, you kind of left your body and got taken up there for that while. I looked around and there was the elegant Miss Harris, her petite figure adorned in black could-be evening dress, black pumps, and white pearls. Her eyes twinkled opal and we acknowledged that we were two of the lucky ones, witnessing something wickedly cookin' and fabulous. Perhaps this astral visitation and somewhat earthly removal happens when the giver will not be with you for long. I got it with Eddie Cochran, Lenny Bruce, and, of course, with Sam.

The Stones continued to storm North America, dived and thrived in and out of Canada, freeway'd down to Albany, and shummed across the state line to Massachusetts. There were further concerts at the Academy of Music in New York, Convention Hall in Philadelphia, and another appearance on *The Ed Sullivan Show* to promote "The Last Time." We wound down south to Statesboro, Georgia; Birmingham, Alabama; and Clearwater, Florida.

I was in Clearwater, Florida, in the late summer of 1999. We stayed at the Tropicana Sky Motel, one block off the beachfront ebbing onto the Gulf of Mexico looking toward Cartagena and the coast of Colombia. You drive into what passes for the centre of beachfront Clearwater, turn right, and cross over the bridge toward downtown Clearwater and the causeway and freeway into Tampa. It's all very pleasant and Aryan Andy García. You cross the bridge, wheel left, and turn right two blocks later onto Fort Harrison Avenue. On the right, taking up the whole block, is the Church of Scientology Flag Service Organisation. The Rolling Stones stayed there at the front of the second week of May '65. It was then known as the Fort Harrison Hotel, still is. Keith Richards stayed on the sixth floor overlooking the avenue, and that's where he changed life as we knew it and all our summers by writing the structure to "(I Can't Get No) Satisfaction."

He'd gone to bed, but something woke him in the middle of the morn that would change all our lives. "Satisfaction" was what woke him. There was a cassette player next to the bed and an acoustic guitar. He hit "record" and played the riff that became the world's for a couple of minutes, then he nodded out. Keith woke up mid-morning, checked the tape; the riff was intact followed by the applause of snores.

Mick Jagger told *Rolling Stone* magazine that the lyric in the chorus was lifted off the Chuck Berry song, "Thirty Days," which features the line, "If I don't get no satisfaction from the judge." Keith suggested it to Mick, who wrote the song's verse by the hotel pool the next day.

There is an order to the events that started on the sixth floor of the Fort Harrison Hotel and ended up with the Rolling Stones getting their very first international anthem. The first order remains that they were given the opportunity to record in America. This removed the intimidation and homage factor that belaboured bands chugging out U.S. covers from cold, mortuaric studios in West Hampstead and other grey slabs north and south of the Thames. The Stones were allowed to find themselves in America - the landscape was right there in front of them. All they had to do was write it up and embrace it onto tape. Recording at Chess Studios in Chicago and RCA in Los Angeles allowed them to be at one with their original inspiration.

Brian Jones broke two ribs in a fight either with or over a woman on a tour stopover in Florida. The Stones would often keep from me the times a member was not holding his weight with the oars, unless the member, Brian, was displaying his other side in the studio. We may have been number one in the hit parade, but we were certainly not number one in the life parade , and I can only imagine the dismality for the rest of the band when Brian barked out of turn. The two-rib incident was also rumoured to have occurred when the band picked up an extra roadie, Mike Dorsey. I do not know; I was not on that leg of the tour; I missed the gigs and Keith snoring our way into "Satisfaction." Dorsey is supposed to have set upon Brian after Brian set upon some girl, at least that was his story. I disliked Mike, and I think he disliked me. He was slick and vain and so was I; he had been employed by Eric Easton - I had not. He was an oily, car-salesman type who would have made the "failed Bond," George Lazenby, look successful. Had I been there, and had Dorsey punched out Brian, I would have fired him. You do not punch out the boss. You clean his mess up - the boss will get his.

Roadies were becoming a strange new brew, mostly bird-droppings. Take your pick - Dorsey, Tom Keylock, whomever. None of them held a candle to Stu. This new mob, for starters, were not remotely about the music; they were about themselves. Nothing wrong with that in real life, but the Rolling Stones were not real life. Mike Dorsey left the moment that Allen Klein appeared. Tom Keylock used his time with the Stones, and in particular Brian, to paper his birdcage until the day he died. He would not dare soil Keith; Keith was alive and ... well, he'd have whacked him. But Brian and the whole charade of "Was-he-murdered-or-did-he-drown?" even had normally sensible filmmakers like producer Stephen Woolley foaming at the silly bin. The Stones lucked out with Bob Bonis, but Ian Stewart was part of the plan - the others all got gigs, methinks, because the meteor that carried the Stones was flying faster and faster, and so they hired " normal blokes " to help them feel normal. Obviously, it did not work. Ian Stewart was not a "normal bloke"; he was a special bloke. He kept a boring job at ICI so that he could keep his Stones afloat and on the road. And please do not confuse that statement about Stu with guilt - he was as much a part of the plan as I was.

We explained the broken ribs away as having happened during a karate class being taken poolside - a double-edged press release with a "Fuck with the lad at your peril!" subliminal undertone, whilst emphasising his healthiness. It was, in fact, Keith and I who were butching up and having the karate lessons, although that may be placing too noble a tone on our friendly persuasion - our agenda being a basic "Hold the art, honey ... a few 'kill' positions will do."

On May 9 the group played the Arie Crown Theater, Mc-Cormick Place, Chicago. The next day it was back to Chess. We recorded eighteen hours off and on the trot for two days, cutting four or five tracks. One of them was a harmonica-laden version of "Satisfaction" that would just not do. It was acoustic-driven, wayward, and the hook registered as marginal to nowt. The only thing that rose above the scumline was Brian Jones blubbering like a sitcom outtake in search of a perennial residual. He was too enthusiastic about this version of "Satisfaction" for it or him to be taken seriously. I'm sorry, dear Brian, if in my book you think I've been giving you an unfair grilling *in absentia*, but, truth be told, by now you were becoming a daily liability and an hourly pain-in-the-arse.

So, back to "Satisfaction." We were not getting what I wanted or needed. The real deal it was not; rather, it was a step backward in the strides that the band had been making with Mick's and Keith's material. The track chugged and heaved in quicksand, delayed by an echo all of its own. It had nothing to do with anything, let alone us. It sounded as if the Stones had done a version of the 1963 "Walk Right In" by the Rooftop Singers. This version called for striped shirts, Brylcreem, basketball slacks, and a time-out. I was not happy. I heard a lot more, but was not getting it. I said nothing, because, in those ol' days, you didn't talk it out - you did it.

We flew to Los Angeles and headed straight for RCA. "Satisfaction" was recorded again and nailed. It was unusual for a song to be allowed longer than thirty minutes to find its way, let alone be given a second chance, but there was something about "Satisfaction" that had the whole group happy to whack it out once more in Hollywood.

"Satisfaction" was a house of cards in which no one player held the winning hand - the house did. Recording live offers the advantage of audio sensuality, which layered-and-divided tech just cannot give you. A stab at the piano will leak over the room and connect with a certain smile of the high-hat or bass. They'll embrace and create a new harmonic, and you'll have that on tape, even though no one person played it. It's the voodoo of space and tone.

Keith overdubbed the magical fuzz - his call - the bullets were now in the gun. He then laid down a bed of acoustic guitars in order for Mick to have something to ballad the verses to, and to avoid falling into the spaces and making opposites attract. He set up the spot for seduction, sleaze, and ease. Jack Nitzsche played a stellar non-intrusive piano that glued the elements into that comfortable place. Jagger got it in one take, at his most pro and very best as he laid down one of the verses of the century. The acoustics were put back into their pocket and the group's first national anthem was mixed and ready to wreak havoc on the world. There's no drama to tell of - it snapped into place and got itself done in a day. The Rolling Stones and I belonged together for that wonderwhile, when we could do no wrong, and in that time came perfect recorded moments like these. With "Satisfaction," maybe the weather helped; maybe Hollywood added that laconic, easy, successful feel.

I've read that Mick and Keith had doubts as to whether "Satisfaction" should be a single, but I recall no doubt on anybody's part, including none from where we'd expected it - Ian Stewart, who just shook his head in quiet amazement at what his "little three-chord wonders" had just accomplished.

Everybody breathed a little easier as another sly side of fame was looked at via "The Under Assistant West Coast Promotion Man," a fitting encore to the power of the day. It's an offhand tip of the hat to George Sherlock, our actual London Records West Coast promo man. George was all tan, B-movie houndstooth suits, Dane-Clark-meets-Kramer in *Seinfeld*. He had a lot of questionables (i.e., a promo man's Rolodex of "wants and needs" so that he could cut to the chase and please), teased grey hair which we teased him about, and enough nerves to undermine the San Andreas Fault. Our homage was a good call. The last time the Stones had mocked one up was to me via Nanker Phelge's, Phil Spector's, and Gene Pitney's "Andrew's Blues," cut out of hysterical relief at having nailed "Not Fade Away" in London's Regent Sound, Denmark Street, in February '64. This time there were no hysterics. We are what we repeatedly do, and that's what this wonderful game gave us the opportunity to become - art. Excellence, a field in which the Stones were replacing dreams with reality, is not an act, but a habit. My boys were becoming hit-cutting men.

Two days later the group continued on with the West Coast leg of the tour while I flew to New York to master the two sides with Big Dom at Bell Sound. "(I Can't Get No) Satisfaction" b/w "The Under Assistant West Coast Promotion Man" was released in the U.S. on D-Day, Sixth of June, and would ripple-release around the rest of the world in the coming summer months. "Satisfaction" would chart number one in thirty-eight countries. As Anthony DeCurtis put it in his 1998 *Rolling Stone* piece, "The Making of '(I Can't Get No) Satisfaction'": "In the summer of '65 - on the radio, in the streets, in the car, at the beach - it sometimes seemed that there was only one song, and that was 'Satisfaction'."

We all got a few days off. Mick and Keith drove through Arizona and Civil War buff Charlie went to Gettysburg. Bill and Brian stayed in L.A. to make sure they left no stone unturned, and make sure that they, too, felt like kings. With the success of Mick's and Keith's songwriting came an inevitable split in the group - and resentments.

On the morning of May 24, I was back in California, but by that afternoon I was on the transatlantic flight to London. Sheila had gone into labour. Reg collected me at the airport in the Lincoln Continental then braked and raced me to the Haverstock Hill Hospital well over the speed limit and in just under a half-hour. I was nervous, tired, and excited - mostly nervous. The doctors informed me that all was in order with Sheila and bairn, and that "nothing much would be happening for an hour or so ..." I was relieved; this allowed me to repair to the car for a joint. When I ambled calmly back into the hospital my son had been born to share the same birthday as Bob Dylan. In honour of our mate, Sean Kenny, our boy would be named Sean.

CHAPTER 25

the beatles: honoured, bothered, and bewildered / play money enters the game and vain stops play / alan o'krime - or maid marian (the jury has left the building) / goodbye to audio only life with danny and the juniors, hallo to "the prisoner" and "the avengers" / emma peel and number 6 - who can tell the difference? / the sixties takes on a twist of lemon - it stings, like john on point and on occasion / vashti - everybody deserves to fall for an act with one same (and that includes liberace)

"Don't waste your time on jealousy. Sometimes you're ahead, sometimes you're behind. The race is long and, in the end, it's only with yourself."

- Mary Schmich

The Beatles recorded their last-ever live BBC radio session for broadcast on June 7, 1965. That same week Buckingham Palace announced the Fab Four were to be honoured with MBEs. Some old medal holders did not approve and returned their medals to Buckingham Palace in disgust.

The contract between the Decca Record Company and Impact Sound had now run its course and the matter could no longer be ignored. Whilst I had been in the U.S. with the Stones, Eric Easton had been negotiating with the powers that be at Decca, and on my return he presented the results of his efforts to me as a *fait accompli*. The new deal boasted an advance of £600,000 which, once investigated, turned out to be, not an advance, but a figure based on an "if earned" basis. The value of the deal was double whammy'd by the fact that, due to the way record companies paid foreign earnings (a year to eighteen months later than the sale date), Decca was only offering up money that we had already earned. I raided the shortcomings of the deal with Eric in my most diplomatic tone, but managed to infuriate him anyway. He told me to "stick to the creative side" and leave the business to him.

The Stones took their place in the wings and placed bets on the result of this contest of wills and ego as Eric and I circled each other centre-stage. The deal smelt - Eric was pushing for it far too hard. It would turn out to have golden parachute factors in it for him, a capital gain made possible by the fact that he had already moved the rights into Eric Easton Ltd. I now owned nowt of the work I had done and, further, was beholden to Eric for every penny. This was not a partnership - it was an employment contract without the contract. Eric was pissed and, to him, this deal was his entitlement. He had had enough of me and, deal done, would be saying goodbye to us all. So he was really pushing for broke - and the Stones and I were the ones that would be. I was nervous. This was a game I hadn't played or studied; the Stones watched for some inkling of an outcome. Mick and Keith were natch concerned about my ability to combat Easton on this huge issue; they knew what was and was not the area of my expertise.

Bill Wyman and Brian Jones sided with Eric. They still believed in the man who had worked hard and well for their career, and they regarded him as more for "the group," as opposed to my being glued to the Glimmer Brothers. They perceived Eric to be the steady balance required against my media-driven madness, Bill because that had been his experience, and Brian because Eric had no great affection for Mick, Keith, or me. As for Charlie, he shrugged his well-tailored shoulders, smiled at Ian Stewart, and then went home to Shirley, leaving us to sort the mess out. I attempted to get on with my day-for-night business, unaware that the next day's movie would change the state of our nation and all the rules of play.

I had set a breakfast meet at the London Hilton with J.W. Alexander, who was Sam Cooke's publishing partner in both Kags Music and Cooke's independent record label, SAR. Kags Music published the Bobby Womack-composed "It's All Over Now," the Valentinos' song that Murray the K had given us and that we had recorded at Chess. It had gone top ten in the U.K., top thirty in the States, and moved us on up around the rest of the world. Now, though a trifle late, I was looking for a piece of the publishing - never missing an opportunity to polish my craft and seize another Johnny Jackson/Sydney Falco moment, one foot gliding through Soho, t'other steppin' out on Broadway.

I crossed the Hilton lobby shortly before 9:00 a.m., averting my eyes from the goodies calling my name in the watch and jewelry store to the right of the hotel entrance's swinging glass doors. I strode past the reception, enjoying my heels click on the marble with a gratifying echo, timing my steps. I wore the choco-brown, Pierre Cardin butter leather boots; a rich brown and dull gold-striped, double-breasted suit with inverted pleat, covered buttons, flared sleeve and trouser cuffs, and slash pockets on the trews and jacket. This much yellow had me looking like a pink-zitted albino canary who should have stayed in bed. No matter - I went for joke with a roll-collared yellow linen shirt.

I glided toward the lobby's breakfast and coffee shop nest-led in the far right-hand corner. I had become a regular here, loved the no-nonsense, no-menu, seven-pound eggs. There was a pre-Kojak moment of "Who loves you, baby?" as the actor, Telly Savalas, held centre court, ordering breakfast with his engaging seductive rasp as his eyes ogled anything and everything and counted, as an actor will, how many sets of eyes were ogling his. He was in London filming his part as one of Robert Aldrich's *The Dirty Dozen*.

In the corner, I spied my breakfast date as he casually re-cognised me and parted the seas with a welcoming wave. J.W. Alexander was a cheerfully robust black gentleman with com-fortable crinkly eyes and smile, gospel in his heart and soul, and greyblack hair that seemed to recede into a halo. There's a kind of relaxed that God giveth out, and God gave it unto J.W. It's the kind of relaxed I'll never be, even at the height of calm. J.W. Alex-ander looked like Don King all gone to heaven and all forgiven. He wore a camel hair blazer, brown sports shirt, slacks and loafers. The buckle on his belt emphasised his happy girth and promoted some team or other. Having made my sweeping crane-shot en-trance into the coffee shop in one Scorsese take, eyed and admired the future Kojak, greeted and been greeted by this large percus-sive dark angel, I took my bearings.

I paused to ready, sitting down with continuing one-shot aplomb, when I realised that J.W. Alexander was not alone. We stood; he paused, and turned to the man on his left. "Andrew," he smiled, "say hallo to Allen Klein." Mr. Allen Klein got up, we shook hands, and we all sat down. In that five seconds, I'd said hallo to another length of my life. For all the toughness I would, from this moment on, observe Allen displaying on behalf of him-self and his clients, he had the most petite, soft, feminine hands I'd ever skinned with this side of Vivien Leigh. Martin Sheen could play him now, but Allen owned the whole wing, not just the west one. Back then in the day only Allen could play himself as he played you and offered you a world he ruled.

He had cut his teeth on Steve Lawrence and Eydie Gorme, Bobby Darin, Bobby Vinton, Sam Cooke, and an earlier foray into the film business. Then he set his sights on the teething British Invasion and honed in first on Mickie Most, then the Stones and me, then Donovan, and finally the Beatles. Along the way he crossed swords - for and with - the Who and the Kinks. He was the modern-day music biz Yank in King Arthur's court. Allen came, saw, conquered and, some would have it, plundered. He definitely raised the stakes of the game. He was in his early thirties, casually dressed in sports shirt and slacks, and I liked him. He was not greasy. He did not have three chins. He did not swear like a trooper or a gangster. He spoke calmly, invitingly, warmly, and had eyes that pierced through you like James Caan working the first Tangerine Dream'd twelve minutes in Michael Mann's *Thief*. On meeting Mick Jagger on the towpath outside the Station Hotel in Richmond, I'd felt Jagger's eyes asking me what was I doing with the rest of his life. Allen's search seemed to be asking me: Was I in control of any part of my life, or better yet, the life of the Stones?

Allen told me of his later being interested in representing Brian Wilson and of the non-surfing *savant* agreeing to meet with him in the Warwick Hotel in New York. When Allen walked into the room, Brian was sitting down with his feet up on the coffee table. He just raised his arms up in the air and said to Allen, "OK, dazzle me." Allen certainly dazzled me and the Stones, at least in the Mick and Keith department, and that's what was driving the train. He may have been almost the same age as Eric Easton, but America and the streets deemed him younger, more agile, interested, and interesting. More us and for us. He appealed to the orphan in you and offered you a home.

In short order, we had a killer on our side who would handle Easton and Decca - and the Stones and I could then get on with our work. The cost is still being debated by those who care and do not subscribe to there being no victims (only volunteers). This was not the nowadays of CDs and video and two leisurely years between product releasement and tours. In our day we needed a single every twelve weeks. The group was on tour fifty weeks of the year and the business with Easton was making us late at the gate. Had Allen and I not found each other, Easton and Decca would have remained a liability - and would have made me one with the Rolling Stones.

Eric, of course, via his settlement, eventually made much more money than I did, just by sitting still and waiting for the pay-day that had to come his way. Half of the recording income was held in escrow for Eric - I think he got it sometime in the seventies - and half, after Klein's 20%, went to me, out of which I had to pay the rapidly rising recording costs. This, and an eventual 83% U.K. tax bill, would eventually have me not that far from comfortably broke and begin the process that would have me have to leave England. Some said I avoided business, the opposite was true, it avoided me. Eric was wiser in the fondling of funds and got a tax-free "capital gains" deal, as by crooking me, he could show original ownership in Eric Easton Ltd., and, with quite a fortune, he and his family retired to Florida, otherwise known as "The Last Stop."

The last time I saw Eric in the flesh was in 1967. He was trying to serve legal bits of paper on me. One succeeded, and I do remember being in the High Court, being very high, thinking I not only looked the part, but had played my part in front of the judge very well. I had not. I was sort of nodding out and away, when my mind was brought back into the proceedings upon hearing the words, "However, I am not prepared to believe that Mr. Oldham is as naive as he maintains." I was nearly jailed for perjury and Eric, having won a round, kept trying to press paper into my hands that would result in the inconvenience of having all my files, papers, and memory open to examination. I was already reaching the stage where I could not allow that to happen, not because I had done any-thing wrong, but because I was having a problem remembering things I had recently done. At this time I was in my New Oxford Street office and every day Eric and his warrant-servers would be waiting for me to leave it. Laurence Harvey was away from the U.K. on location and I managed to borrow his chauffeur, who, similar in build and colouring, could pass as my double once we'd decked him up in some of my more adventurous robes, ones that would draw attention to his fashionable veneer as opposed to the rewality of his face. Chauffeur Brian would leave the office and get served with the papers of the day. He'd get into my Phantom V and the car would purr around the block. I would climb out of the Immediate Records back window and into the next door offices of Dick James Music. My car would complete its troll around the block and I'd run out of the Dick James doorway and into the backseat of my Rolls. One evening Eric had got wind of this "how-Andrew-gets-home" routine and, as I snuggled into the back of my car, I turned around to see Eric, all hot and bothered, chasing my car, banging on the rear window in a most Northern, Hitchcockian state, crying out, "C'mon out, Andy, you'll have to face the music sooner or later."

Well, Eric, I managed to make it later, no thanks to you. Eric had to get paid, and paid a lot. That was clear from the beginning of the Stones' and my relationship with Allen Klein, but was also another one of the things that did not get spoken about. We did not wish to jinx the seeming collision of good fortune: worldwide acceptance on the road, the coming of age of Mick's and Keith's songs, fueling the Stones machine into a lethal, hit-making, self-contained entity capable of "The Last Time," "(I Can't Get No) Satisfaction," and more. We'd all made our first pact, not so much with the devil, but with the devils within ourselves. We wanted this good thing to last; we did not want to rock the boat or anger the hand, Allen Klein, by any show of doubt toward the hand, which seemed to be feeding us and turning us fishes into oafs. There would be pivotal moments of "mum," silence, in the Stones/Klein/Oldham period, some of them addressed by Bill Wyman in his memoirs, none of them addressed by us at the time. This meant a growth of luggage bought from Fear, which would also mean that, before too long, one of us would have to go.

I got in touch with Eric Easton shortly before he died. I was drunk and he had cancer. I was high and he was pissed, or maybe he couldn't. He would not come to the phone. I only wanted to know why he had insisted from the beginning on robbing me. I never know why you have to burn; if you are going to fuck the talent, open a shoe store. Then again don't; someone has to design the shoes. The first big sin of denial between me and the Stones was the denial that Eric Easton had to get paid, and the first overt from Allen Klein was allowing us to go along with that. Allen knew the game better than we did. He condoned our duping ourselves by fueling the fire with Eric's stupid, but kind of minor, sins against our family, which, one could say, allowing that it takes two, became major with Allen.

The next artist I discovered and recorded was Vashti, *née* Bunyan. She was introduced to me by my shining granddame-in-armor from my press cutting days, Monte Mackay, chief rooster at the Mount Street Al Parker Agency. She had removed some of my misery by allowing me into her life and letting me press-rep would-be popster Jess Conrad for a fiver a week back in 1962. I had a huge crush on Miss Mackay; I developed an even bigger one for Vashti.

Alas, Vashti was viewed as an auburn Marianne Faithfull spin-off, which more than dented the trail I had hoped to blaze for her. She was a beautiful original with a body that Mick Jagger would have wished on his other self. A continental waif off the top Françoise Hardy shelf, she was so far from the madding crowd that I wanted to stop the day's shooting and take some time out in her world. She had a sensuality and rhythm that I wanted into. I wanted to walk with her in the hills of Tuscany, dine with her by the sea in Sicily, make her an offer she would not refuse, wake with her in the morning in a shuttered room listening to the sounds in the Piazza Navona - but I bit my tongue instead of her ear. I did not want to scare her or ask her to touch that remaining part of me that was still and dead. I never believed that I had a position which allowed me to indulge in rudeness of the heart, even though I was rude on many another occasion. I also knew that I'd turn on the two of us - this was the nature of my lame and game. So I listened to my heart, acknowledged its scream, explained to it the reality of *omertà* and its role in my life, slapped it better, and moved into song. The song was Mick's and Keith's "Some Things Just Stick in Your Mind," a fitting song and title for my vinyl excursion of the heart with Vashti. When the record was released in May '65, she suffered from the Marianne Faithfull comparison. I'd thought of keeping her recordings unreleased, for my ears only, but, in the cold light of morning, that was unrealistic. I didn't really record her successfully, by which I mean that I didn't quite capture her eyes. As you can tell, Vashti put my life in quite a flutter - and I'm glad she did. I needed that flutter as I slipped into park.

I needed that boy-meets-girl reminder; I never asked for the get. Perhaps it was already lonely at the the top - or perhaps

I already had the advantaged special life that I'd fought for, but had no idea of how to live it. She came to 138 Ivor Court one day when the record was out and over. It was raining heavily outside and she had a scruffy little dog with her on a lead made out of string. The mutt looked at me very knowingly. It wanted nothing and it didn't sing. Vashti wore an old raincoat such as French movies are made of. I looked into those eyes I had not quite recorded, said nothing, put my heart back into my pocket, and returned to the madness of my day.

The beat boom was diversifying in the late summer of 1965 and making room to share its good lot with folk rock. Bob Dylan, whose art was now bordering on the commercial, had started to make his impact in America. The Byrds had been brought to CBS and produced by Terry Melcher, and their version of Dylan's "Mr. Tambourine Man" was a big hit. America was finding its own voice. Motown still defined the way that America danced, but Dylan was starting to speak for it all. He had risen out of the coffee bars and into the trailer parks, out of the Greenwich Village cul-de-sacs and onto Highways 61 and 66, with his finger up and on the pulse of America. He opened up the space with his awesome "Like a Rolling Stone." I reviewed the recording at the time for *Disc* and *Music Week* and said, "Whether he likes it or not, this man is so commercial and has his finger on the pulse just that little bit ahead of everybody else, which makes him unique. 'Like a Rolling Stone' is the most fantastic thing he has done, a Dylan version of 'Twist and Shout' with a little Tamla Motown thrown in." Lou Adler would perfect folk rock as a top ten art by year's end with his recording of "Eve of Destruction" by Barry McGuire.

Back at home, the furore wouldn't die down over the Beatles being given MBEs. At the time of all this hoopla, I wrote about it in *Disc* and *Music Echo* as so:

The Beatles, who have had every word possible, good and bad, said about them in their meteoric rise to stardom. This group, whose talent has made them mean much more as representatives of our country than the shabby government under which we live. The whole world makes a star and the whole world helps to break one. The Beatles go on from success to success and this week release a truly fantastic record "Help!" from the film of the same name. This record is great and proves beyond doubt that the Beatles are still head and shoulders above the rest of pop music and, far from being finished, are still growing, not only financially, but as artists. It is a very hard task to grow inwardly and mature as an artist in beat music and still remain commercial. This the Beatles have done and I salute them.

Brian Epstein responded to the thoughts of Chairman O with the following: "Andrew is an incredible person. Whilst the media still plays up rivalry between the world's two top groups, this is an example of the groups' managers and their artists enjoying each other's success." We were all certainly enjoying our room at the top, with omnipotent largesse and more than a grain of *pro patria*. I was also unwittingly setting myself up for the fall. It's unsettling, as in writing this and walking the beach in Malibu and seeing the ghost of Laurence Harvey past, sitting elegantly in new faded denims, looking the twenty-six miles to Catalina Island, nursing a glass of chilled Chardonnay and the increasing pain in his gut.

LOU ADLER

Photography By

**ANDREW
OLDHAM**

ANDREW LOOG OLDHAM

Photography By

LOU
ADLER

CHAPTER 26

*the beat goes on; there's work for everyone - including the dog /
getting it right again, again, and again at rca / the joy of goin' home
with the stones / time shifts; back with the cosa tosstra ponytails
again / madness and marianne in manhattan / keeping the deer
brian out of the line of fire - keith takes on another gig*

"It's no longer funny, it's bigger than money."
- Keith Richards

In May 1965 "(I Can't Get No) Satisfaction" was recorded and released three weeks later all over the North Americas. It was the
first Stones U.S. number one and perhaps England has never forgiven its second greatest hitmakers for treating America to this
audiogem first, putting the U.K. in second place with an autumn
'65 release. The single had not been released in the U.K. due to
the Easton/Decca brouhaha and the arrival on the scene of Allen
Klein, who'd started to handle our business in June '65. Life with
Klein moved us to a new and fatter gradient.

     The Stones toured the U.K. in September and October with
the Spencer Davis Group and the Moody Blues and then headed
straight for the U.S. and their fourth tour across the North Americas,
the first with actual money in their hands. This tour would feature
at different east/west locations the Byrds, Patti LaBelle and the
Bluebelles, the Shangri-Las, the Righteous Brothers, Bo Diddley, We
Five, and Paul Revere and the Raiders. The group went away on
this tour boys, still fresh, enjoying their new toys. They came back
men. The nonstop tour continued back down under in January '66,
up through Europe, back to the States (stopping to record at every
opportunity in Los Angeles), back to Europe, and then, basically,
the first golden run was over. The spark was gone, the glimmer
was dim and from April '67 till the second run that began in late
'69, *sans* yours truly, the Rolling Stones did not step on stage and
there were no more tours.

     From May '65 to March '67 the Stones received eight U.S. gold
singles for the eight singles released and six gold album awards.
When they returned to the U.K. in November '66 the boys were tired,
wondering about the cost of money and fame, and in need of rest.

One part of their souls resided in a bizarre revisitation of Baudelairean nineteenth-century debauch and baroque, the other in a Neanderthal, pretentious, psychedelically entitled, and tripped-out world. With leisure came drugs and their aftermath, removing the need for watchclocks or moral compasses. Mistakes were made as obviously-out-of-it, velvet-clad, rock stars tripped out of Rolls-Royces into their Kings Road abodes. It was much too near both the copper shop around the bend and the real money lurking around the corner. The Stones were tolerated, even loved from afar, whilst away and on the road they could be confused with earners. But fame and familiarity bred contempt and, whilst they may have been able to purchase respectability, they were about to learn that they were considered neither worthy nor to the manor born. They'd been allowed to lay waste in the suburbs, but they were not welcome to sketch arrogant in the drawing rooms that sought to rule their world. Oh, later Mick would be allowed back in when he was harmless and had had his claws removed; but the "in" had always belonged to Keith, and Keith wasn't interested.

Back on that first '64 tour you'll recall I'd been taken by Sonny Bono to RCA's Studio B on Sunset. Jack Nitzsche, with Dave Hassinger at the controls, was producing the vocals for a Spector "Zip-a-Dee-Doo-Dah"-type version of "Yes, Sir That's My Baby" for Atlantic Records. There was no actual group, just a moniker invented for a group of session singers and friends that Jack and Sonny had pulled together. I watched and marveled at the laid-back professionalism that pervaded the room, a far cry from the shame attached to the game in Britain of late. This was an original American art form and hustle, and everybody dressed their bodies and minds in their Sunday best and came to work wailing. The chorus consisted of Sonny, Cher, Jackie DeShannon, Gracia Nitzsche, and the late Bobby Sheen (a.k.a. Bob B. Soxx of the Blue Jeans).

Everything felt fine in March '66, now that I knew I'd found the Stones a new home in which to work. Regent Sound had served its purpose, but it was a Regent's Park rowboat compared with the oceangoing liner that was RCA's Studio A. You could have fit the Stones and all of Liverpool into the studio and still have found space for most of Manchester. I didn't give out instructions or guidance - well, perhaps suggestions, for we were all learning to bounce off the recording ropes at the same time. Mick and Keith played the tune they'd composed. Sometimes it spoke for itself as to arrangement, or Mick and Keith would have an idea and direction already in mind. Sometimes they didn't, and would throw the song over to the rest of the group, no attachment, ego-less, to be kicked around for a while looking for that particular place to go.

There was no reverence, no preciousness allowed - nor mercy. How about a 3/4? A polka? A country swerve? Everything was open roadhouse and anything was possible if it would get the job done. Like what to do with "What to Do?" or what to do with "Paint It, Black"? That song was going nowhere, I thought. Another ten minutes and it'll be time to move on, change the energy, flow, and song, and perhaps come back to "Black" another day. We'd only done the second chance thing once before when, after the acoustic attempt in Chicago, we came back fuzzed to "Satisfaction" in L.A.

At the last moment, either Bill Wyman played or was listening to Jack fuck around with the pedals of the Hammond B-3 organ in a piss-take of a gypsy figure. "That's it!" I thought. I'd heard the sound and movement that we needed, the whimsy that spelt "radio." A grey-paisley-shirted, brown-velvet-trousered, at his most attractive-looking Jagger, fag in one hand, pencil in t'other, dictated lyrics to Keith like M to Miss Moneypenny, a tad annoyed at Keith's having missed a stitch on his lyric dictation and Magic-mick stream-of-consciousness flow.

"What's 'it'?" Mick sighed.

"Mick ... Bill ... Jack, do it again."

I still was not sure whether it was Bill or Jack. We'd finished one track in the past hour, and I'd been out for a joint - we didn't smoke in the control room. I had come back immersed in the texture of my Levi-type, bottle-green suede jacket and how it displayed traces of prospected gold under the neon lights of the studio control room. I'd then turned my concentration toward Keith's nigger-brown twin to see if its light held the same gold-rushed imbue. Bill looked over and said, "Do what again?" Jack looked around and would not commit. "That thing you and Jack were doing with the pedals." Bill had been down on his knees playing a bass pattern on the Hammond.

God, don't ask me for definition, or the trap of having to explain. "Oh, this?" Bill gave his churlish smirk. He knew that I held him somewhat in disdain and he had doubts that I'd ever noted his playing, except for the time I brought it dead centre as the final overdub, hurrah, and run-out on "19th Nervous Breakdown."

"I was just doodling; I didn't think anybody was listening."

He smiled on, too long. "Do it again before you forget," I commanded, not interested in the formica rationale behind the movement.

"Oh," grinned Bill, insisting on the last serf word, "I won't forget it. I was doing Eric Easton going gypsy on the Blackpool Tower pier organ."

Even Charlie looked up at that very Fellini-esque image of thought. The room was starting to get interesting and interested. Laughs all over. Bill carried the day, "You mean this, don't you, Andrew?" Bill did it, Keith had already got it, had clocked in, and was ready to work at it. Mick shrugged, got up from the studio stool, as in removing the wrinkles or a run, as if decreeing, "OK, why not? I'm here, doesn't sound too stupid," and everybody got down to work. Every song got about twenty minutes to find its legs. We averaged two to four songs a day and were in that wonderful stride where we didn't seem able to get it wrong anyway. Well, "My Girl" may have been wrong; the track may have been Ritalin-stiff, but it was a lot of fun to do.

In the previous December's sessions, the Stones were four or so minutes into "Goin' Home" and to everybody it felt like a great take - *the* take. But, as I tapped along and looked through the control room window into the studio, I knew that something was up, as Charlie looked at Keith, who didn't look back, and Bill looked at Charlie as if to say, "I don't know either." I turned to Dave Hassinger. "Dave, they don't know how to end it; they don't have a fuckin' ending." Dave, as if he could help, looked up but said nothing. A quiet, Midwest-seeming man, Dave was the epitome of our Brit view of a John-Ford-ish *Quiet Man*. In those first hallowed couple of years at the golden trough of the Americas, all of our meetings were just one reel away and a generation away from the movies, as in the American western. Sonny Bono was the town crier, your younger hippie Gabby Hayes; Jack Nitzsche was the pale pacifist who finds his courage in the last reel; Dave Hassinger was Randolph Scott, or David Janssen, minus the saddle, spurs, or Excedrin.

Dave Hassinger was tanned, tall, and well-built, with slight side tufts of oncoming grey in the temples letting you know that the middle years were but a throw of the horseshoe away. He was clad in simple, one-colour, no-nonsense, light-toned v-necks, white button-down broadcloth shirts, plainsman black trousers, black solid shoes that spoke of military grounding, haircut atop to match, with a thin gold ID bracelet as the only giveaway that he was about God's business - entertainment and the field of dreams. He would have been equally at home on the range or a rig, chewing tobacco instead of smoking it, a man happily at one with his craft. His wife was Doris Day's stand-in, and that just added to the attraction.

By this point, the Stones had taken on lives of their own in the fantasies of their fans. Like characters out of literature or the movies, their doppelgängers had escaped and were having imaginary adventures quite independent of them, out there night and day, doing outrageous things that the Stones themselves had nothing to do with. Rock 'n' roll delinquents, scourge of bourgeois society, menacing doltish adults, a long-running orgy of weed, women, and song. Even the mild-mannered Dave Hassinger wasn't immune from these flights of fantasy.

Back in Studio A, Dave turned oh-so-slowly toward me and shot me a look that said, "There ain't nothing I can do about it." Now at the five-minute line of "Goin' Home," the Rolling Stones kept rockin' along. Mick's vocal was over and he crossed his arms without missing a beat. Keith curled into his guitar, playing away any problem, not allowing anybody to catch his eye. As we crossed into six minutes, it was still the one, still *the* take, but if something didn't happen and if somebody didn't take charge and find an ending, we could be derailed. It didn't matter that the take had eclipsed the four-minutes-tops borderline; the track was holding and I wanted the Stones to make every second of this majestic piece releasable. When they'd mapped it out, they hadn't allowed that they might nail such a great one so fast, and now they were a plane looking for a safe landing. They needed a real ending; this motherfucker just would not work on fade.

Charlie couldn't catch Keith's eye; Keith would only let me have that sly underbelly of his. I locked eye 'n' grimace with Charlie and started to prance up the dance, as in "Keep the motherfucker going." His snare picked up the order and the level, the band followed suit and matched tone, and for the next four minutes the train stayed on track resolutely "Goin' Home." At seven minutes Charlie looked, I waved a circle, meaning just keep it moving. He looked at me for a few seconds, figured it in, and nodded his head. Bill heard Charlie step it up and followed him. Brian and Keith now admitted that they were playing together, stayed on the money, and got on the ride. Stu shrugged, grinned, and started to glide. Mick looked for and found the right harp, wrapped his lips around it, and sucked his way into our ears forever with a triumphant groan 'n' moan.

Charlie looked in my direction, then made the obvious suggestion by looking down at the floor. The Stones followed suit and allowed themselves to descend to a last *après* skasmic crawl. Eleven minutes-plus on the slopes and spent; thank God we'd had enough tape between reels. The group fell about, as well they should, exhilarated. They laughed, hugged each other, and collapsed on the floor. "Goin' Home" was done and so were we. I had just witnessed a wonderful musical moment of the Forever, the Rolling Stones having just broken the sound barrier with ease.

When *Aftermath* was released, "Goin' Home" was praised by fans, critics, and peers alike as a standout event on the recording. By 1965 only Dylan, the Stones, and Marty Robbins had defied the three-minute law - and kicked open the doors to the future.

At RCA the band continued that first golden recording roll. Beginning with "The Last Time," Mick and Keith mastered the art of providing compositional food for the pack. With "(I Can't Get No) Satisfaction," "Get Off of My Cloud," and "19th Nervous Breakdown" they mastered the art of the notional anthem in step with the nation. With "Mother's Little Helper," "Out of Time," "Play with Fire," and "Under My Thumb," they came off the street and into the suburban home, opened the diaries, the liquor, and the medicine cabinets, and echoed the shared hypercritical blight that suppressed and splintered American youth.

The Stones' - Fuck the other groups! - experience of America, and in particular Los Angeles, was limited to wonder, room service, a general sense of affinity (as opposed to hostility), and, overall, a climate and a hospitality that was sunny, grateful, and optimistic. One did not have to wait for Robert Towne or *Chinatown* to realise that, behind the military/industrial shrubs of Wilshire's country clubs, sat the fat, bow-tie'd men who hovered over, controlling all. Therefore, down in the valley on Sunset, Hollywood, and Vine, the musical watering holes were a magnet for the voice of youth disaffected by trailer-park squalor - as white lower-middle-class dads returned from Korea, without a bean, to find their places in the assembly lines taken by eager immigrants - and affected by the very idea of having to die in the inhospitable dikes and crannies of Cambodia and Vietnam, as the arrogant military would have them do.

I say "Fuck the other groups!" because, in '65 and '66, the Stones, in their lyrics and attitude, were the only U.K. import that seemed to be at one with what ailed America. The Rolling Stones went straight from the airport to the studio, the radio, and Beverly Hills. Inspired by what they had in fact said and stood for, American hope and fungi started to congregate, compose, and rail against the system via music. This movement was just as middle-class, until Hendrix, as the pony R&B movement that had first attracted Jagger and Jones.

The confidence of the Rolling Stones grew in this time of recording in America, an experience that was, then, unique in and of itself for a British band. We cocked our guns and guitars and took aim at convention, violated musicians' unions' petty rules, and went for it. The Stones were not intimidated. They got America down in America. The Beatles took over America, but the Stones belonged to it.

Opposite RCA stood Martoni's, an Italian eatery where we'd stand behind Frank Sinatra to get in and nobody was refused admission. Dean Martin, Tony Martin, and Cyd Charisse were always already seated. Richard Conte drummed his dice hand at the bar. Sonny Bono watched us eat with glee, whilst the rest of the star-studded ensemble paid us no mind in the way the old guard would have back home. They just figured, if we had the good sense to be there - enjoy it. We were in the entertainment capital of the world and we'd started to create pop entertainment for the world. The Rolling Stones and I were in the midst of our finest recording hours together.

I told *Disc* magazine by phone: "The whole set up is terrific. We completely insulated ourselves from the outside. The boys recorded for fifteen hours nonstop, from 11:00 a.m. till 4:00 a.m. the next morning. Then we spent the next day overdubbing onto the results, Mick and Keith doing the vocals and editing the masters. As their producer, I can honestly say these sessions have produced a new Rolling Stones sound, and certainly brought out the best of Keith, whose guitar playing has been magnificent. The only outsider is Jack Nitzsche, playing the Nitzschephone. This is actually a child's toy piano, which is projected through two separate amplifiers. Jack is able to make it sound like any instrument you like; on some tracks it even sounds like a trombone."

This was rubbish, as we know. I was just getting more ink on the Stones by summoning up that mythical instrument. As my Sydney Falco rolled onto the page, the British press managed to daub it with the post-Epstein spin of the day-highfalutin upper-class manager talking down when talking about "his boys," a damning I hardly qualified for, as I spent so much of my time, perhaps too much of my time, being one of the boys.

Looking back on that *Disc* item and other write-ups and headlines of the day, I am amazed at how the very words and subheadings used to describe me are a blueprint of the ups and downs of the bipolar depression that I constantly strived to keep in check by accomplishment. "Accomplishment" - i.e., production - required daily, constant travel outside the body and inside the head, a constant movement of ideas and people, time and space. These were the only ways I knew of to keep my depression in check.

It always worked in southern California; somehow that lady never let me down. Perhaps we were as shallow as each other, but if so, then deliciously so. Perhaps we bonded out of collusion, at the fact of both living above the faultline. It has been said by me and others that it sometimes does not pay to meet your heroes. Hollywood had been my hero from the moment - at around nine years of age - that I'd first been allowed to set foot by myself in that wonderful dream tunnel of London known as the Underground. It took me from the Mother-protected-and-edited life of Hampstead and Swiss Cottage to Piccadilly and Soho, but *en route* (and on return), the film posters that adorned the curved walls glued me to my calling. The powerful Saul Bass posters that described the Otto Preminger flicks of the fifties and early sixties - *Carmen Jones, Saint Joan, The Man with the Golden Arm, Bonjour Tristesse, Anatomy of a Murder,* and *Exodus* - epitomised the world that I fell in love with.

On one level, I was provided with an escape, as the posters took me out of Baker Street and the mundaned Metropolitan Line straphangers too concerned about their daily lot to escape with me into the Hollywood that pulled and beckoned me with every poster, credit, and slogan. I allowed myself to be sucked into that teeming world; I could feel the gun in my hand on a slow boat to Israel, the gun in my holster at the OK Corral. On another level, I was getting an education, as I studied the Woolf Brothers' Romulus Films and Jimmy Woolf's managerial promotion of Laurence Harvey and absorbed the idea that Otto Preminger was a breed apart, one who produced and directed and controlled his canvas. I marveled at how Mr. P. allowed designer Saul Bass his head to explain the work in those groundbreaking canvasses that separated the Preminger films from the competition, sometimes more ably than the films did themselves. I would later apply to the Rolling Stones the myriad of flickering poster images that I took in as my Piccadilly Line sped me south into Soho, by paralleling that experience, flicking through a rack of records, with an eye toward those whose cover images stood out from and above the fray. Message was everything; content came later and was deemed redundant if your homing pigeon didn't home.

As life became polar with flights from London to L.A., mine became more bipolar and I upped my self-medication to cushion those days when I knew I'd snap and crash as a result of the highs. I tried to clutch those days to my chest and disappear. Sometimes I couldn't, and whoever I was with would catch the black silent swell which I became. My mouth would grip my mind in anguish and it was all I could do to mumble in taut pain, betrayed that I had not anticipated the descending wall of darkness, and, having done so, given a witty aside and dived behind the descending curtain to the sound of applause.

Sometimes I'd be *The Manchurian Candidate*, others a rabid *Raging Bull*. I saw *The Man with the Golden Arm* again on a Film&Arts channel pumped down to Colombia from Mexico. Frank Sinatra remains amazing (especially on a one-take basis), Eleanor Parker demonstrates that concern is a dangerous lady, and Kim Novak moves like heroin itself. She is the translucent horse that I saw abound in slow motion from the hotels Royalton to Algonquin. The Elmer Bernstein score is balletic and almost the edit itself. The withdrawal sequences are, of course, condensed highlights, but, given the 1955 occasion, are still quite restimulative to someone who has been there. Sometimes I still think I hear mummy; I look up and it's Angela Lansbury barking orders in *The Manchurian Candidate*.

****

Before I could shake *The Man with the Golden Arm* image from my screen and separate myself from stalking Frank in matching Paul-Smith-retro, dark-grey-flannel suit, I recalled the late eighties, in my own downtrodden Manhattan hell, when I started to realise that the city now belonged to somebody else and I had better move on. But long before I did, I nearly fell off the gay, gaudy, cocaine railings of the time and developed a near fatal attraction for a leggy Texas blonde who played guitar and heroin.

The manners I adhered to in matters of the heart and hearth had me walk the line. So, rather than take the physical fall, I did the next logical thing and shot up with it. That was just another one of the days I nearly died. I remember sitting on the toilet, hanging on for dear life, as it did its damnedest to suck me in and flush me out, with the anxious Farrah-Texan pulling me out of the abyss, smacking the life back into me that I'd nearly smacked out, and walking me around the room, cold-towelling, and talking to me until all the different parts of my mind and body made their connection again and informed us all that we'd decided to live.

Two blocks south of the east fifties apartment in which this sordid slagmire occurred, was the workplace of Tony Russo, the brilliantly mad and talented commercial editor, fueled by life in all its naughtiness, the same Tony (owner of the same .357 Magnum) who had joined me for dinner at Marianne Faithfull's north-of-Canal mewsy abode to set her battering-prone, poor excuse of a boyfriend straight. Tony's enthusiasm for drugs as a *de rigueur* social state was endearing at the time - a time when his career was on hold and his life on burn-out. I felt comfortable in his company. Tony and I managed to hoist our now oft-degrading drug dependencies to the level of swashbuckling pirates warding off any invaders representing reality. The sun had set on that first line long ago and, like worn-out French Foreign Legionnaires in search of a decent movie, we paraded over the dunes of marching powder in search of the Holy Grail (the one entwined in our brain cells), always remembering the wonder and hope attached to that very first line.

When I had overshot my manageable daily load and found myself out of sorts, spirits, and wherewithal, I would avail myself of Tony's hospitality whilst I waited a few hours for the excess to wear itself out, exorcising all real and imagined pain and actualities from my system with a couple of hot lemon teas and a soft scrambled egg and mayonnaise sandwich on even softer white bread. I'd then be ready to converse with Uncle Tony, my barometer for a return to the world, and after a to-and-fro banter to make sure I really was OK, we'd Jack Daniels and Juan Toot ourselves back into the front line of life.

Tony Russo's office topped a brownstone on East 49th Street overlooking 2nd Avenue. Time could stand still in the view from its bay windows. Tony Russo was Tim Roth before Roth existed - a small, tight, ponytailed schnauzer of a man, rimmed to the eyeballs in coke and hope, the eye of an eagle, the caustic wit of a dangerous nation under siege, the cut of a priest defrocked. The rubber band that held his hair was matched by the rubber strap on his "director's" sports watch. Everything about Russo was ready to snap and made you want to hug him all the more. On his other hand, Tony wore a coloured, braided fabric, hippie bracelet - but Tony was too hip to be hippie - and he used this muse as an asset, for communication. His ability to kick at life was belied by a casual demeanor, worn tennis shoes, and on-location attire.

Tony and I would make occasional forays into health with visits to an Upper East Side acupuncture guru, the late great Dr. Robert Maynard Giller, introduced into all our lives by Pete Kameron. Once needled by Dr. G., we'd gain a 48-hour spurt that would allow us, in a state of well-being and street decorum, to pass as normal and join the throngs at some eatery of the now without a cocaine panic taking over and ruining our splurge into other people's reality. Dr. G. had another number to glue one to the wall of whatever - a forearm-sized, dildo-shaped syringe that served as an eighties "homoeopathic" sub for whatever Dr. Max Jacobson had been about in the sixties.

Once out and about, though, one wrong word, one rude waiter (perceived or real), could end the meal on wheels and we'd be back out on our well-worn pavements, teeth grinding, angry at the world, and happy to be so. Once ensconced on a bar stool, coke-fueled, and brandy-fumed, we'd flirt with anybody: Uma Thurman wanna-bes, David Bowies, Gary Oldmans. Bring out the spiv on a cocaine platter - anybody was fair game, until they presumed. Then we'd pounce, strike, and withdraw. You might wonder why communication with an outside world filled with ambitious, self-centered twits, though it might have assuaged our loneliness, was not our party of choice. Far from it; we both preferred the days when God had given the gift of gab to only a chosen few.

Our stop-offs into the Jay McInerney eighties were unsettling. The only amusingness was Tony and me and the way we were and saw all. We'd chat up the barman, star - or his or her loafer or chauffeur. I was sockless and overly influenced that eighties year by Don Johnson in *Miami Vice*. I'd thought, via "Heartbeat," that he was Sony's brightest recording star.

I'd sit clad in tight, worn 'n' frayed jeans; tasseled, woven-weaved, beige loafers; a blazer or velvet-pile casual evening jacket that draped the waist that this good/bad life was giving me; a crisp, white shirt to give me colour; and a lot of gold to dim the schlap into *La Cage*-less contour. A bemused and beaming Tony was my Manhattan Peter Meaden, seated next to me, enjoying our exchanges with the aliens whilst letting me have a peak at his accessory - that . 357 resting on his hip - the way a girl may let you have a peek between her legs.

It was all good fun as we both saved what was left of the best of us for when we were at home with our respective advantages. My stop-ups at Tony's had wisdom, within their reason. In those hours of overloaded, O.D.d madness, as I waited to become whole once more, I would take care not to be seen or heard. Outside I might react, not always to what another had said, but to the way I had read it, and risk clocking up another irretrievable error on the trail of manners. Tony's room was a womb that kept me immune from such errors or the pain of being correct whilst not being so myself. This day I collapsed on the couch at the back of his workspace and Tony asked me if I had any blow.

"You've got to be kidding, Tony," I said, as in, "The state I'm in, you think I've got some blow on me?" I managed this from the inside of a locked mouth that would have been a challenge to an anaesthetist.

"Well, I just thought I'd ask. If you had, you certainly wouldn't be needing it, the state you're in. That's all."

Tony would sit hour after hour re-editing existing commercials copied from the television that he thought left room for improvement. The fact that the commercial was already being aired and had nothing to do with him did not deter him from trying to improve on it. It was this act of devotion to a craft that had temporarily abandoned him that endeared his very soul to me.

An hour or so had passed, Manhattan was nearly home, and so was I. I'd managed the soft egg 'n' bread spread and it sounded like a munitions factory whilst I chewed. Gone was the taut and noisy silence. The visuals were no longer punctuated by black spots, my ears were no longer ringing or screaming whenever a thought threatened to get out of hand, and the sound effects were in order, normal and not peaking or shrieking.

Then Tony, who'd gone out for a spill at O'Lunney's on 45th, where he could assimilate his Italian into Irish faster than you could pour a leprechaun, returned. He tiptoed into his own space, finger on his lips, as in "hope I don't disturb," entered his well-appointed bathroom, and carefully closed the door. I let it be and allowed myself back to the calm that was at last enveloping me. A few minutes later, I was drawn back into the room by the sound of a hoof in a stable. Can't be back to zero, I thought. I wandered off again, but was called back by another resonant sound of a hoof. This time I could place its origin - it was the sound of a shoed hoof kicking against the paneling of a horse carriage, the type with wood slats on the side that one passes on the freeway or motorway on the road to Newmarket or Saratoga Springs.

I got up and moved to the front of the wood-floored office past the bathroom, having forgotten that Tony was there. Night had now fallen and East 49th Street outside was quiet with only occasional crosstown traffic, none of it urgent or loud. I switched on a couple of lamps and dimmed the overheads into slight. I walked back to the rear of the floor, took a last slug of the deli lemon tea and heard the sound of hoofs kicking again. I tried to focus on where this sound was coming from, as it was becoming increasingly clear that it was real, and not in my mind.

With no reason for doing so, I called out, "Tony?" Whilst I did that, my body was moving ahead of my mind and I strode toward the bathroom door. I gripped it and tried to open it; it was locked.

"Tony, are you in there?" I heard another would-be hoof-beat, and knew that he was. I have no idea of what providence I was granted that allowed me my next fortunate move.

"Tony," I barked in my best controlled military fashion, "I want you to get up. I want you to stand up. I want you to hear me. I want you to focus on the door."

I listened for more hoofs, but heard only the sound of Tony's sighing and my own heart pounding.

"Tony, I want you to slowly put your hand around the door handle."

The outside knob slowly turned; when I saw that, I gave a sigh of relief.

"Tony, I want you to unlock the door."

Nothing.

"Tony, hold the door handle and unlock it. You must do this."

I could now identify the hoofs-against-trailer sound as that of Tony reeling and falling down again. I then heard him mumble and curse his stumble, work himself slowly to his knees, and attempt to stand up again.

"Tony, you must stand up, you must concentrate, you must open the door!"

The door unlocked, slowly opened, and in the crack I saw with horror what had happened to my mate. He had a huge bloody gash on his forehead from falling to the floor. He looked like Hervé Villechaize doing the Jack Nicholson "Here's Johnny!" routine from *The Shining* - and, beneath the revulsion, he just looked like a little boy who knew he'd done wrong. I looked over his shoulder and saw blood on the side of the bath where he'd fallen and cracked his head. To his right, above the towel rail, the wall was smeared with more blood, and over his left shoulder were his shooting works, spoon, and syringe footcrushed into the marble floor. Tony started to shock out and fall again. I grabbed him, slapped him, shook his shoulders, shouted in his ear, and started marching him wet-toweled around the room. When I ran out of things to say and had got fed up calling him a cunt, I just left-right-left-right-lefted him until I felt some life in him. I cursed him for his selfishness and bad manners. I admonished him for having the gall to nearly die on me.

"This is all I fuckin' need, you cunt, if you'd fuckin' died they wouldn't have even mentioned your fuckin' name. It just would have been 'Ex-Stones Man Involved in Overdose.' You cunt, you fuckin'-lame-Wop-fuckin'-whore."

Tony moaned and groaned, and then he laughed. I slapped his face with affection, hugged him, and marched him around the room again. Just two weeks later Texas would be doing the same for me.

****

Back in the sixties, things were going my way - and it was a disturbing feeling. I recall the pleasure of stepping out of the RCA studios into a glorious Sunset Strip day, into the land of "What Are You Doing?" as opposed to the London that stated, "How Dare You!" I managed to keep the hounds at bay in Los Angeles, where the sun always gave me a shadow I could talk to.

The endless socialising at parties had started to take its toll on Brian Jones. He was now partying with professionals and this raised his normal plethora of drugarettes to a whole new plateau of madness. Girls in London might have sat in awe of the slovenly sexual guru, agog at his inner ability to consume and transport them. Some he may have just bashed about. But the American groupie animal now led the event, taking no prisoners, and Brian was starting to get very frayed around the edges. He could still triumph in the hotels of Manhattan, L.A., and major stopovers, but this cost him concerts and commitments throughout the Midwest and caused Keith to go it alone in Wisconsin, Kentucky, Kansas, and Ohio. Mick and Keith didn't even bother to tell me, until Brian started to nod out in the studio.

CHAPTER 27

ivor court - there is a block in regent's park harlem / tony k. - king
of the reet petite / getting launched and lynched in america / money
never sleeps - it nags you to death / heads you lose, tails you don't
win / but i thought my name was michael philip jagger, keith
richard, brian jones, william wyman, and charles watts (not in
america, it would seem) / day of the locust - the rock version / s.w.3
and 6 again, a currency i understand - david niven, conway twitty,
father christmas, and tony king all in one day / maureen cleave
shivs us good and looks good doing it / a short escape down under

Tony King had left Decca to work for Roy Orbison in Nashville, an adventurous move for a young man in the music business in the U.K. around the time the Beatles had invented America. Tony was always good at working couples, and, when Roy and his wife Claudette split up, Tony worked as a bartender in Spain, where he caught hepatitis. "The Last Time" had just been released, Tony was back in England, where I located him in a hospital bed south of the Old Brompton Road. I sent him a note asking him to come to work for me when he was better. He did so just as "(I Can't Get No) Satisfaction" was about to be released and Immediate Records launched. Tony became Immediate's head of promotion, his first task working the McCoys record "Hang On Sloopy," a 45 rpm that Tony Calder and I had bought from Bert Berns in New York for $500. He wouldn't give us Europe, he was smart. He knew that he could score off the work that we would do in England and get advances direct for himself from the Continental shelf. But we had a number one, due in no small part to Tony King stuffing the envelopes, sending out the 45s, and doing what he does best, bleating on the phones until the record came home.

My partner, Tony Calder, lived in Ivor Court with his girl-friend Josie. The girl he'd marry, Jenny, was at that time stepping out with Eric Clapton. Keith often stayed over in the spare bed. Charlie Watts and his wife Shirley had a flat at the end of the same floor. Kit Lambert (or Kitty, as Tony King knew him) and Chris Stamp moved in, to manage the Who from a lower floor. I didn't socialise with Kit and Chris, or, for that matter Brian Epstein. We were all much too busy and much too scared. Not scared about stepping out every day and doing our job. We didn't want to think or analyse, quite sensibly we just wanted to do. The few times we found ourselves in the same clubs together we'd all be stoned in our different ways and that fact would rule the evening into social acceptence. Now there were a lot of drugs in a previously naff middle-class residential building, and a lot of people working. I'd go down to the workman's cafe on the corner and have a cup of tea, egg, and chips whilst Tony King further down the block visited two hookers, who supplied us with our various grades of pot. Top of the drawer for us and grade two for the journalists and deejays who'd have got high on wood shavings.

Ivor Court was a great time. Perhaps you've seen the pictures of the Rolling Stones in their French navy peacoats lounging against my marijuana wallpaper, which we all laughed about when it went unnoticed in the national and musical press. Donovan took over the flat when we left. Thirty years later he wrote to me from Ireland to tell me I'd left some tapes behind.

Tony Calder was supposed to be my bad guy, the man who did my dirty work. He was not. He was the man who helped me realise a dream, even though, at the same time, Immediate Records would be God's way of telling me that I had too much money ... but in the end not enough business savvy and just enough spending money to make our records, advertise, promote them, and get them into history and into the charts. Still, when all is said, scolded, and told, Immediate Records seems to have served as a model and treasure for many. Sadly, its body of work has been depleted by bitter artists, awful remastering, average marketing, and all the elements that go into squandering a legacy, but, at the end of the day, Immediate recorded and released the Small Faces, the Nice, Chris Farlowe, Humble Pie, Jimmy Page, Rod Stewart, Nico, Duncan Browne, Vashti, John Mayall, Jeff Beck, Fleetwood Mac, Keith Richards's Aranbee Pop Symphony Orchestra, and a whole lot more, some of it great and successful, some of it too late or too soon.

At the end of October '65, we flew to New York for the group's fourth American tour in eighteen months. They would play thirty-five cities in six weeks. At the end of September "Get Off of My Cloud" had been released in the States and gone to number one faster than "Satisfaction." The work was getting harder.

Allen Klein orchestrated everything. This was the first time the group entered the States as stars, as more than workers. We arrived in New York for a fast press conference and headed off in a private plane for the first date in Montréal. Allen announced the tour would gross $1.5 million and for the first time the group and I would be returning to the U.K. from a U.S. tour with some real money.

Allen arranged for GAC to be replaced with the more rock 'n' pop-orientated William Morris Agency. This move from Eric Easton's choice would cost the group $50,000 in an out-of-court settlement, but it would pay dividends as the William Morris Agency, under the drive of Jerry Brandt, whacked up the Stones' touring fees into the big league. Of course, "Satisfaction" helped.

Launched in 1898 as an agency for vaudevillians, William Morris had booked Charlie Chaplin and Al Jolson and was now the leading booking agency in the world, with offices in all the major playing countries and cities. The agency had forty departments and 150 agents, and derived 60% of its income from the monster growth of television. In 1965, David Geffen and Barry Diller were in the mailroom and Jerry Brandt was running the "new" wing, repping the Beach Boys, Sam Cooke, and Sonny and Cher.

Jerry Brandt was the American dream. He stepped off the celluloid screen of my mind, landed on the streets of Broadway and survived the leap into reality. Jerry had a European air to wrap around his American drive, bathed and born in Brooklyn of a Jewish/Puerto Rican cage; he was a Sydney Falco mind-like-a-platinum-trap who had travelled and succeeded at getting out of Brooklyn and more. He knew how to buy a pair of shoes in Paris and how to order food in Rome. He was devastatingly good looking, dark, fine-featured and boned; a fine man in the heart department whose eyes could open yours. He was someone who cared, and yet, he was an agent.

The William Morris Agency now functioned as if the Beatles had not landed in America the year before. Connie Francis was their everyday hope; the old-time agents frowned on Brandt and his new order. They frowned even more when Jerry told them they were going to sign the Rolling Stones. However, they saw the money when they heard "Satisfaction." The first tour with Jerry and Allen was insane and I liked insanity. The police in Rhode Island wanted to keep the kids from barging on stage, so they shoved a hundred or so kids in wheelchairs up front. It didn't stop anything; the cripples just got trampled. The local police chief was prancing at the front of the stage in Boston. They always did. Mick took his hat off and started tapping him on his head as if he were a tambourine. This caused another riot. The police all over most of America just did not get it. The Rolling Stones were going out into the boonies and the second cities, the afterthoughts. The Beatles had played the crown jewels, we played some of them, and all the toilets. The promoters who did what we told them to do did fine; the shows ran smoothly. It was the ones who listened to the cops and not to us who had the trouble, the riots and the shows called off before the group was done. What was so great about the tour was that, regardless of our finally having found our vinyl legs in America, we were oblivious to the minutiae, which would come back to haunt some of us, but omniscient to present time and what was changing. Absolute fidelity to the fourth and fifth of the seven arts was obeyed daily; we were the dynamic. Better than that, we were still innocent.

There were not five bands or managers or agents who'd been down this road before. We were young, capable of partying, enjoying, and staying on top of our game. We had a plane to get us around America. Perhaps that sounds lush and safe. It was not. We had a four-propeller job that John Wayne would have known his way around in a WWII flick. We were playing cards when the window broke and the plane started dropping. Brian was sitting next to the window that had broke and Keith was watching to see if Brian would get sucked out. On another night flight, when the plane was veering all over the place, Jerry went up to the cockpit to see what was going on. Brian was there, breaking amyl nitrate capsules under the pilot's nose. I guess we were also invincible for that incredible while.

Before we'd even got started, the plane had hit a storm and dropped a hundred feet in seconds; I still have the bump on my roof. One moment I was sitting, resting on the armrest, talking to Charlie; the next my head was part of the ceiling.

The collapse of the stage in Montréal was awesome: kind of construction in slo-mo reverse. I will never forget it. There was a riot brewing, you could smell it in the Frenglish air. The stage was a sandpit and we were the Christians. It was a snakepit and

the venom of chaos and death was in the very air. We had the
audience in front, at the sides, and behind. We just could not contain it. It was not actually the stage that collapsed, it was the tiers
of seats that wrapped around the side and back of the stage that
fell onto it and on top of us. One moment we were standing on the
side of the stage, the next moment we were lying on the ground
with an ever-rising amount of bodies landing and lying on top of
us as the whole back and side audience followed the collapse of
the seating structure and plummeted down onto the stage. It felt
like being underwater, except that the water was bodies, and we
were fighting to be able to swim to the surface and find air and
room to breathe, pinned down by an octopusation of dead weight,
panic weight in slow motion of flaying arms, bodies, and legs.
You'd find a gap and stick your arm up, but your body could
not follow; a set of arms, a trunk, a chest is atop you and you are
five bodies down, you cannot breathe, and your chest has had
enough of the pressure and the heaving; it wants to rest and go
to sleep. You know that you cannot give in to it, you must fight,
strive, and kick - or die.

I'd managed to climb above the sea of maddened bodies
the only way I could, by pushing another layer of them closer to
the floor. I was having somewhat of a confessional in my mind,
no actual sins, no actual fact or data. I was too physically busy
for the detail, but cleaning the slate was my intent as I worked at
and around the bodies, like Clint Eastwood's determination in
The Eiger Sanction, working the granite and stone.

It's another day of the locusts, the klieg lights scream from
writhing hell. One boy lifts his arm for help and I use it to move
myself another body up above the swarm. I hold his hand, stand
on a chest, get the room to jump, and I'm outta there in the air, in
the alley, and in the limousine. As I bolt down the alley I catch
sight of Bill and Charlie disappearing into doors on my left and
right, slamming them shut. The limo is in a tunnel; inside it are
Jerry, Mick, Keith, and Brian. We are all accounted for. But, in
another moment, we will not be able to move as the fans swarm
in from all directions, surrounding the car and getting up on the
roof. The roof will not handle it and is starting to buckle and cave
in. The limo driver is frozen; he cannot - will not - move. Keith and
Brian are in the front. Brian leans over, shoves the limo driver

into his door and puts the thing into drive. Keith leans over and shoves his foot on the pedal, and we move, with Brian holding the limo driver into the glass. We are moving, just slamming and hurtling kids out of the way, the dueling guitars playing as one again. Finally, we are nearly out of the tunnel, but the roof is still caving in with the weight of the kids hanging on top. Brian and Keith stop and start the car in rapid jerks between reverse and forward, the kids fall away, and we are nearly alright.

Keith and I took our next day off in the Miami sun. The flight back to New York coincided with the big power failure of '65. We circled New York for what seemed a year, then headed for and landed in Virginia.

With our Max Jacobson visit, Brian had taken me to a new high, one that I would not care to repeat. I had also brought myself to a new low, one with lifelong repercussions that I still account to, as, during those few days, I'd signed quite a few documents that have haunted my well-being and with which I am still dealing. Brian continued to visit Dr. Feelgood, having by now gone far down the road that the rest of us had not even requested a permit for. With Anita Pallenberg by his side after September '65, his I-am-invincible factor went up as he consumed bottles of anything and pills of everything. Although I was no babe in arms, I was nevertheless in a slightly slower lane. Brian was becoming daily more unreliable. The bags under his eyes told the full story of his unhappiness and addiction to drugs, booze, and sex. The year '65 had seen a serious debilitation in his contribution to the group. This was not yet a problem on a management level; the Stones kept it hidden and the group kept on going.

The fourth American tour continued down the Pacific coast until the final show on December 5 in the Sports Arena, Los Angeles. Anita joined Brian in L.A., but not in the studio. The duo would fly for Christmas to the Virgin Islands, where Brian would be laid low by a tropical virus. A few days prior, Keith had been knocked unconscious by an electric shock on stage in Sacramento. This was not the first or last time. The group attended a party at acid-guru Ken Kesey's house to celebrate the end of the tour. I didn't have time for the party; I wanted to get the group into the recording nest. We entered RCA and in four days recorded the tracks for "Mother's Little Helper," "Sittin' on a Fence," "Take It or Leave It," "Think," "Sad Day," "Ride on Baby," "Lookin' Tired," "19th Nervous Breakdown," and "Goin' Home."

Back to England. British life was cold and losing its glow. The tour had been an incredible success, the recording another drop-dead accomplishment. My body wanted to know why I had stopped, why I had shifted gears. We had been having fun, my body and me, and it was bewildered at the change to the non-road and non-studio life that had been thrust upon us. It didn't like Christmas and neither did I; we both felt better on the move, handling the decisions of the road and the studio in a luggage-free zone. My body screamed, "Daddy, I want to go back on the road."

Between Christmas and the New Year, Sheila and I moved to Hurlingham Road off Parsons Green, to a house rented from the light and sprightly Noel Harrison, the actor son of Rex. Noel and his wife Sara's style of living was in perfect Aquarian mood with our own, and they were off to Los Angeles, where Noel would star in *The Girl From U.N.C.L.E.* with Stephanie Powers. The Harrisons' comfortable, yellow, plush, orange settees were joined by our Chinese theatrical masks on the wall, leather rhinos in the hearth, a chair carved into a peacock, and a cage in the kitchen that housed Conway Twitty, a yellow canary gifted to us by Marianne Faithfull, who had been bemused and bewildered by the bevy of stuffed hummingbirds encased in a glass dome in the hall. Noel and Sara packed; Sheila and I unpacked.

Tony King arrived with fresh-cut flowers and put the kettle on for tea. David Niven stopped by with a list of Hollywood don't-forgets and must-calls for Noel. Mr. Niven was another who seemed to bring his own lighting; he looked, and was, the most pleasant star - thin, elegant, open white shirt topped by v-neck black cashmere, dark *noir*-cuffed flannels, yellow socks, and chocolate suede slip-on brogues. He discussed his world, made it ours, and sparkled magnanimously as he held court in the kitchen and asked for a second cup of tea. He asked after Mick as he did after Rex; we were all beholden to the same trough - work. The actor's enjoyment that we were doing well made a cold London evening glow. Niven stood in the kitchen, stretched his toes, ankles, and smile-lines as if inspecting his lads in *The Guns of Navarone*, happy at this exchange of residential flurry, the result of employment, movement, and good fortune. I thought he was Father Christmas and I made my

Christmas wish, asking if I could keep this magic moment and repeat it at will. It was so wonderfully normal and special; I wanted
some of it on more than only the days around Christmas, just as
the lump in my throat said, "Andrew, you're getting pathetic ..."

Mick, Keith, and particularly Brian were blatantly flaunting
their new whimsical riches around London. I had not realised
that I was doing the same. You could sense the backlash coming.
It was OK to be "rebel poor," but "defiantly rich" was viewed as
arrogance. Secretly, we were all equally living beyond our means,
but supposed wealth gained from business might have merited
a modicum more of tolerance than that derived from posturing
with maracas and strumming a guitar.

As the Kings Road took back the fashion crown from
Carnaby Street with clothes that allowed for the glowing combo
of money and tripping, Brian Jones was out there sometimes just
shopping for company. Now that we were back home and there
was time to consider, concern became homely. Charlie Watts
told me that he had persuaded Brian to see a doctor who had
told him that, if he kept on drinking and drugging at the rate he
was, he would have not much more than two years to live. Ian
Stewart would show no such concern, later telling journalists,
"Brian set out to be as stupid as he could be. As soon as he got
any real taste of money or success, he just went mad."

The Scotch of St. James had replaced the Ad Lib as the top
night spot. The Ad Lib, which had been above the Prince Charles
Cinema off Leicester Square, had burnt down in 1965. Owner
Brian Morris had tried to make a go of it from new premises in
Covent Garden, but the fickle elite had already moved on to the
Scotch. The Scotch was at the end of a cobbled yard off Mason's
Yard in the belly of St. James, a stone's throw from Buckingham
Palace. Gered Mankowitz's studio was around the corner, as was
the Indica Gallery, run by Marianne Faithfull's now-husband
John Dunbar, Peter Asher, and Barry Miles.

You'd knock at the door and be auditioned through a peep-
hole. Once in, you'd travel downstairs via the twisting staircase - the
same one upon which Keith Richards extracted payment of Robert
Stigwood with a pummelling in lieu of unpaid tour fees. The Beatles,
the Stones, the Yardbirds, Eric Clapton, Long John Baldry, Keith
Moon, and the Searchers all starred in the main room on their nights

off. Vicki Wickham would arrive fresh from *Ready, Steady, Go!* accompanied by the latest American group passing through town.

Tom Jones was often centre-stage, a little out of place or ignored by rock royalty, making a spectacle of his recent success. Sonny and Cher would share fame with the Hollies whilst Lennon and McCartney, Jagger and Richards, I, and our ladies would sit back in a dark corner and smoke and gloat. Brian Epstein was beginning to withdraw and remove himself from the window of fun. He still worked just as passionately from behind the scenes, but was not yet outing his private hours, whereas the rest of the gang rocked on with nothing to hide.

The ubiquitous Jonathan King would be there, still celebrating his number one, "Everyone's Gone to the Moon," and Eric Burdon would celebrate anything. It was a nightly theatrical event, a celebration of being part of what was happening in the most exciting business in the world, a place to celebrate and rest your status amongst your peers and flaunt it above those whom you perceived as the also-rans. Entrances and exits were perfectly timed, every word counted and measured, every glide across the dance floor posed and lighted. It was the swinging sixties leisure hour ... who could ask for anything more?

Sheila was getting on my fucking nerves, starting to act as if she'd invented me and now wanted to redesign my mind and change my clothes. Tony Calder would join her in this illusion, and later I'd be gone and they'd have each other. The advent of drugs in the streets and minds of the public was a reality that could no longer be ignored, and brewed as one bitch of a potential nightmare. The protection of a private club would soon be gone, its members' privileges rendered obsolete and its uniqueness grounded. I saw no advantage in the public's turning on, except on the occasion that it assisted getting laid. I was wrong, of course. It would be the bonanza that transformed 45 vinyl into 33 long play big pay. The record companies now had a manacle on middle-class income, and the product of the day would be an acid-faced reflection that I could not relate to. One of my lives was gone. With this knowledge, I upped my drugs intake in an effort to stop myself from getting stoned.

"As Tears Go By" was released in the U.S. as the Stones' Christmas single, something I would not have attempted in the pull-the-other-one land of England, where it became the B-side to the February '66 release, "19th Nervous Breakdown," a number one. The American B-side of "19th Nervous Breakdown" was "Sad Day," but it was another bright day on the farm as the disc went to number two. I had no idea that this would be nearly the last number one in my run and the beginning of the end of it all.

1966 would bring many changes in the lives of the two biggest bands in the land. The Beatles would give up concert performances forever. They just couldn't stand doing them any longer; there was no more need for Pierre Cardin-inspired, Dougie Millings-tailored monkey suits. For the Beatles, the war was over and the charade came to an end.

Maureen Cleave of the *Evening Standard*, who had been so instrumental in getting me next to Phil Spector in my press agent days and been so good to the Stones first time out, had stopped looking at pop through the glasses we'd prescribed and was now much more into putting pop into its place. She would give me a nervous breakdown - and the desire to break her legs, had she been a "Monty" Cleave - when she took the shine off our number one glow with the following revealing column, printed on the day of the British release of "19th Nervous Breakdown":

For some unaccountable reason Mick Jagger is considered the most fashionable, modish man in London, the voice of today. Cecil Beaton paints him and says he reminds him of Nijinsky. Mick is also reported to be a friend of Princess Margaret. He has said nothing - apart from a few words on the new single - to suggest he is of today, yesterday or any other day. He remains uncommunicative, unforthcoming, uncooperative. He is twenty-two, lives in a three-bedroom rented flat near Baker Street. As a boy he appeared regularly with his P.E. teacher father on a television programme called *Seeing Sport*, often seen canoeing, rock climbing, or camping in a tent. He has seven "O" levels, two "A" levels and left the London School of Economics after two years of training to be an accountant. He hasn't many close friends, naming David Bailey (for whom he was best man in August 1965), Andrew and Keith amongst them. His favourite song is "Satisfaction."

- Maureen Cleave, *Evening Standard*

I got two "O" levels, no "A"s, my favourite tune at the time was also "Satisfaction," and hell hath no fury like a journalist on the rag. When I read this Cleave savaging of my client I called Mick to ask him what on earth he had done, what had happened to set this woman against him this much, and against the day-in-the-sun control we enjoyed. The bitch was foaming at the nib, enjoying the idea of sticking pins in every part left of him, the very idea of Jagger.

I hoped Mick had been rude, spilt tea or champagne down Miss Cleave's front or on her lap. I hoped he'd been a sexist pig; I hoped he'd been that Mick. I hoped he'd tried to pull her, cor-blimy'd, ogled her tits, and tugged at his dick. He assured me that he'd done none of the above; he'd been on his cucumber-sandwich best. This just made matters worse. Clearly the worm had started to turn, the vicious quill had drilled a hole in our wall. Perhaps Miss Cleave just thought how dare you, you little classless bastard. I know the barrio you bled in and I weaned you off the back page into an acceptable feature and now you are trying to pass yourself off as art. I have no idea why she called the truth marker in so damn early. Maybe Mick just forgot she knew him when, and she decided to remind us. It's probably some of that, and he probably tried to pull her as well. I would very shortly be reaching out again to press maestro Leslie Perrin for an assist - this time, to attend to our uncovered flanks and run damage control over our daily lives. Leslie would continue this task after I departed.

Meanwhile we got away from the rising cold winter of discontent by repairing down under for another bout of Australia and New Zealand.

I bumped into Mark Wynter in Sydney. Running into him was like running into the ghost of hope and ambition abused. A lot of us were crawling along that ledge. On that second tour of Australia I remember the Searchers' drummer Chris Curtis being escorted by military police off of the navy dockyards and mess quarter area. Childless Chris lived behind Harrod's in London and was renowned for having a voluptuous *au pair* girl who serviced pals in need, with Chris probably watching, finding his pals voluptuous too. He'd gone out at night after a show, a Gladstone doctor's bag in hand, trying to pass himself off as a doctor to all the young conscripts. On medical advice, he was flown back to the U.K. and a substitute drummer was flown in. I was also getting more than a little out of hand on one too many occasions. I was escorted by police and ambulance back to the John Bateman Motor Inn in Melbourne upon getting catatonic and violently weepy after being greedy with absinthe and having a quasi-breakdown at the house of a local poet. Australia was getting "don't-take-care packages" - self-mailed drugs from Vietnam - and I was later told that the poet had added acid to the absinthe. That remains no excuse for cracking up on the job. The cost of ambition would soon have me cashing in some of my chips, upping the ante, and raising the level and voltage of my game - via the insanity of ECT.

Four Liverpool lads in the loo with Maureen Cleave.

CHAPTER 28

nick o'teene, a league of gentleman, sums up thus far / after the
clubs are closed the glimmettes do motown / driving lessons with
john and paul - dreams on wheels do come true / celluloid dreams
do too - "charlie is my darling" opens in our minds

Nick O'Teene, President, Aweful Records: After you've been in the music business for while, you realise there's nothing really new. Except for the hype. Hype springs eternal. Back in '64 I was reading this story in the trades about Kit Lambert's big plans for the Who. The story came about as close to the truth as music papers usually come - about as close as parsley is to pussy. There was a clever write-up. It tossed about the notion that these boys were geniuses and these geniuses had just made a big breakthrough. It wasn't just a big breakthrough in popular music they'd got planned. It was gonna change the world as we know it. Made your head spin. And it was all this guy Kit Lambert's idea. Sort of. Kit was the manager of the Who, along with a barrow boy name of Chris Stamp. Together they were a diabolical pair. Kit was a brilliant nut case. He had plans. Big plans. He was straight out of grand opera. He loved disasters. In Kit's book the whole point of building something up was to watch it all crash down later on.

Big news of the day - For Immediate Release - Kit Lambert, Esq. was gonna get his lad Pete Townshend to write actual songs. I had to set down my teacup for this one. No more R&B covers for the Who, it said. None of that. Pete was gonna write 'em all from now on. All by hisself. The way it was written up you'd've thought he'd invented a cure for bad rugs. Never mind that the Stones had done it, the John Lennon-Paul McCartney bit, a while back - this was *news!* The Big New Fing! It wasn't all that big and it wasn't new at all, but in the land of hype, that doesn't matter. As long as you yell it loud enough and long enough people are gonna swallow it. And not only that, this Kit Lambert was gonna produce those mini-operas himself, the very ones written by his own art-school dropout Puccini-Rossini - Pete Townshend. It was a bloody renaissance, he was telling us, happening before our very eyes. Where, you might ask, did maestro Kit get these grandiose notions? From that other nutter, Andrew, of course. "Andrew seems to be getting away with it," is what the quote said.

He didn't have that far to go to find it, neither. Two floors above him were the offices of Lord Loog Whimsy and his own personal Igor, Tony Calder. All these lunatics, see, inhabited the same building: Ivor Court, a royal house of freaks, it was. In the basement you had the Euro-dyke Gaby Sturmer, the broad who did press for Philips Records. On the fifth floor was the very grand, very gay Roy Moseley, dropping names like ninepins - "As Larry Olivier said to me when I was pinning up Judy Garland's gown on our way to Lord Delfont's ..." Going up! Eleventh floor: Poncey poofs and bolshy barrow boys (the offices of Kit Lambert and Chris Stamp). Twelfth floor: Charlie and Shirley Watts. Thirteenth and fourteenth floors: *outré* fashion and mad schemes. In other words, the offices of Oldham and Calder, teeming with assorted maniacs, rogues, Rolling Stones, press flacks, rock molls, cheeky buggers, and, to top it off with a bang, the psychopathic Reg the Butcher. All you needed were bars on the windows and men in white coats and you coulda started your own asylum.

The whole city was in turmoil, for that matter. That was London in the sixties - they were here with a vengeance, but as soon as you tested them they evaporated. It was like a benign virus spreading south from Liverpool and, in London, northwest from Ivor Court. It was an unlikely revolution. Leading this army of freaks, fret-wizards, and talented layabouts were two highfalutin pooftahs: Brian Epstein and Kit Lambert; a butch East-End yob: Chris Stamp; and one Mad Hatter from Hampstead, a wide boy with public school weapons: Sir Fuckin'Andrew. Hendrix was managed by a gangster and a bass player, poor guy; one of the Kinks' managers had originally been the group's lead singer, fer chrissake; and Dylan was hondled, as they say in Yiddish, by a splenetic, ponytailed, ex-hardware store owner. Pity the poor muso with that lot to lead 'em.

Folly is contagious, and, once the wild thing hit the streets, everyone wanted to be quite mad. They held festivals of madness and everybody came. After you'd had the three Mad Hatter's balls - Monterey, Woodstock, and Altamont - the days of the high-flying, eccentric managers were gone - and some of them along with it. One way or another they all exploded or imploded. That's the way it is with crazies - they burn out. In the mid-sixties, the flamboyant (and flaming) manager gave an act street cred. By decade's end, that was all done and on came the Zen bruisers, actual bouncers, and focused percenters - Elliot Roberts, Peter Grant, and Shep Gordon - doing the absurd balancing act of accounting, GBH, and artistry.

You had managers who managed the managers - Allen Klein (Andrew) and Pete Kameron (Kit Lambert and Chris Stamp). Offstage the Who were outrageous, violent, and on the ledge. They brought all that fury on stage - just like the Stones usta do. But fame quenches anger. By 1966 the Stones were no longer street punks. They were gentry, buying manor houses in the country and cottages in the suburbs. Their songs were lyric-driven. They were playing for the man and the money. They had found the Hollywood Hills and were resting. The Who, Hendrix, the Doors, Janis Joplin and the whole San Francisco scene were outside the gate, ready to kick the door in and don the mantle until the Stones woke up twice and got back to the street for the Stones Mach II.

****

At the end of July and beginning of August 1965, the Stones played some U.K. concert dates with the Moody Blues, the Fourmost, the Steam Packet, and Julie Grant. Also on the bill were the next greatest thing since sliced bread - from California, following the P.J. Proby trail to United Kingdom come: Scott Engel, John Maus, and Gary Leeds - the Walker Brothers. They had arrived in London with a Mercury-via-Philips release produced by Jack Nitzsche, "Love Her." Love them the U.K. did, and a version of the Bacharach/David warbler, "Make It Easy on Yourself," set them up for the big one.

Scott Walker was attractive, but I made sure that I never really spoke to him, because I knew, up close and personal, that he'd bore me. He was Neurotic Boy Blue one sigh away from being a wanker. The idea of him was better than the reality. Jonathan King had told me I'd like him and encouraged me to get together with himself and Scott "for a chat" and told me how much we'd have in common - and that scared me, for starters. I didn't like the place from which Jonathan King looked at pop music - down on it - and I feared that Walker number one was the same. As Elia Kazan, I was concerned that Scott was really Richard Davalos and that John Walker would turn out to be James Dean. Scott had great pipes, emoted well, but I didn't need another social Brian-Jones-drain in my life. Besides, like Brian, he didn't write. He's safer hiding, which is the best career move he could have made. I couldn't have done anything for him; we'd have got on each other's nerves. Jonathan called me and Tony Calder once and said, "You must get up to Regent's Park. Scott is having a breakdown; he's snapped, he's talking to the hedges." I thought, "Yeah, all on half a bottle of Mateus." Gered Mankowitz and I went around to Scott's, banged on the door, shouted through his mailbox, and told him to stop acting like an old poof, do the decent thing, and put his head in the oven.

Amongst the better kind of snaps forever facsimile'd into my mind-smile is the look of amazement and utter disbelief on Paul McCartney's face as he sat in Sheila's favourite peacock chair, watching Mick, Keith, and me alternate between the Supremes and the Four Tops as Tony King pumped up the lead volume and we mimed it out to the very best of Motown. McCartney's expression was not unlike that of the straight Bill Hunter character in *The Adventures of Priscilla, Queen of the Desert*, the first time he lays eyes on Terence Stamp. Total disbelief. I mean, you know he wasn't going around to Brian Epstein's, where Brian and the NEMS gang were getting up in drag and miming to Cilla Black. The few London clubs that were worth going to - the Ad Lib, the Cromwellian, and the Scotch of St. James - all closed at two o'clock. So, on evenings when night was not done with, I would open up at home, and such was this night, as Tony King, the Glimmer Twins, and I provided the cabaret.

The road was fun. When I'd decided to head over to Blackpool for that busman's holiday with the Beatles, and when, after their wall-to-wall, screamatic, sound-drowned concert at the ABC Theatre, I'd joined John and Paul for an M6 to M1 cruise back to London in John's amazing new matte black (later psychedelic yellow), black-windowed Rolls-Royce Phantom V, I fell in love with the car and wanted one of my own.

I had acquired my new man, Eddie Reed, after meeting him driving Freddy Bienstock's grey Silver Shadow, trainspotting Allen Klein around London. Eddie was a good-looking Fulham lad who loved a pleated skirt as much as Reg had loved the charge of the short-trouser brigade. He and I spent more time with each other over the next five years than we did at our respective homes. We got on very well and were very good for and to each other. When I eventually got my own Roller, I had Eddie in constant touch with John Lennon's driver over the details in John's, wanting the exact extra embellishments that he had, as it all worked so well. I kept insisting on the same two sets of windows, one black and the other clear. After a lengthy conference, the two chauffeurs worked out the problem. There was only one set of windows on the Lennon Phantom V; I had been sufficiently stoned not to realise that the second "clear" set were just "open."

On the first day of Eddie's employ, he had to drive me to court where I was fined £20 for driving without due care and for having no current driving license. I had already failed my driving test; it was a demoralising little moment that I had no wish to re-peat. I think it was the botched three-point turn, the accompanying expletive, and some crunching through the gearbox that did it. An acquaintance of Eddie's, whom I'll name "Paul," was hired to take my driving test in a remote village in Gloucester, it being the time of no picture requirement for driving licenses. "I" passed my test - I'm told my three-point turn was immaculate - and, for a short while, our friend had a busy little sideline, reputedly taking tests for the likes of Keith Richards, Steve Marriott, and many other too-busy-to-steer pop 'n' rollers. "Paul" finished this little detour in his career by taking and passing, for a bet and a dare, his wife's test in drag.

The black Phantom V was immaculate. It had blacked-out windows, beige interior, and a completely impractical telephone system at a pound/thirty-seven per minute, per call. It boasted two stereo systems; one high-end and true, the other "spatial" or, as we dubbed it, "sound-in-stonederama." A bar hidden under an office desk rounded out the extras, which priced the immaculate glider at £19,000, as opposed to the in-the-shop tag of a mere £12,000.

Back on the Stones roll, I was on the last legs of being eager to get any Stones film made as soon as possible. I arranged for a film crew to shoot a documentary during a short Irish tour of Dublin, Cork, and Belfast at the start of September '65. In Dublin, forty or so young men got on the stage and a riot ensued. They swarmed all over the stage, pushing Mick Jagger to the floor, grabbing his microphone, taking turns at yelping and playing

Mick. Brian Jones was attacked and punched by a half-dozen of this out-of-their-heads, would-be band on the run. Oh, Mother, if you give a name to it, it surely will appear! Bill Wyman was forced to hide behind Ian Stewart and the grand piano on stage, Keith managed to make a run for it, and Charlie Watts just kept on playing. The film was to be a sort of trial run, get-your-celluloid-legs together for any forthcoming feature film, and an effort on my part to keep the Stones interested in the idea of film. It would be titled *Charlie is My Darling*, based on the fact that he indeed was - and it would be photographed, edited, and directed by Peter Whitehead.

I found Peter through my mate, Sean Kenny, who alerted me to Whitehead's *Wholly Communion*, where Peter had filmed Allen Ginsberg and a whole lot of poets at the Royal Albert Hall. I didn't even bother to see it. Sean's word was good enough for me. I met Whitehead in Soho and wondered why technically brilliant people seemed to fall short in the cleanliness department. Peter's body odor was as bad as Glyn Johns's mouth, but both these laddies remained in front in the ladies sweepstakes. In any event, I met Peter in his Soho pad and asked him if he could do the film for two grand and whether he could start on Friday. He said yes to both, I gave him the bread, and we were on. It's funny how no "actual" Stones movie got made after all, and the dry run, the few-days movie that was supposed to get the group into the mood, is the only document of that wonderful time.

CHAPTER 29

on the road again / brian jones stops playing the guitar and starts to play charles laughton / wasted on god's hash wafers on the earls court road / summer holiday - courtesy of air acido / the times they are a-changin' - america takes back the beat on the street / the doors of perception - for what it's worth

"Life is short and so is money."

- Macheath in Bertolt
Brecht's *Threepenny Opera*

I had the pick of the litter with the Rolling Stones. My life was not complicated by having to manage over-entitled dykes in distress or gutter scumline, inbred, ungrateful midgets, although the Small Faces would come under my vomit-watch a while down the Immediate line. I say vomit-watch as Ian MacLagan and Ronnie Lane made my Small Faces experience much ado about all-or-nothing, whilst the calm and manners of Kenney Jones and the loving madness of Steve Marriott made the journey worthwhile. My Immediate adventures and those with its artists, the wonderful and the wankers, are best left for another set of pages, of which time, passion, and circumstances will determine the need.

The Rolling Stones and I were still having fun getting it done and the shit to come was holding its breath. Within a year I would be unable to distinguish whether I was driving the plane or a passenger who had lost control of the ride. You'll recall that I had not learnt my job. I had no actual management skills; that was not what had attracted the Stones to me or vice versa. I was the front man, the shill, the barker, and therefore, regardless of any third-party agenda, day-to-day just had to be run and I was a traveling Stone with a free pass for a remaining while.

The fifth American tour took place in a land deeply divided by the Vietnam War and disturbed by the first run of drug culture. The unrest in America seemed to permeate everything. For this and many reasons, it was the most harrowing of tours. The bounce was still there, but a lot of the slap was flat. Even with a slew of hits, the lilt was wilting under the pressure of life getting posed

and jaded - never mind the Doors, Joplin, and the underbelly of
American music waiting in the wings. Down the Delta road, Brian
was an increasing problem. He disliked having to play Jagger/
Richards songs on principle, the principle being that he'd been unable to come up with the goods and write commercial art himself,
as opposed to miming to it or mocking the songs that fed us. He
told friends that "The Last Time" and "It's All Over Now" (although
not a Mick-and-Keithette) were probably about him and that, on
occasion, no doubt dependent on the match of drug and paranoia,
Mick, when singing the pivotal words in the chorus, would turn
to Brian and sing "because I used to love you, but it's all over now"
and "this could be the last time." Brian was now hospitalised more
often and started to miss a number of live dates. I was not aware
of this at the time. The Stones ran a very tight ship and were not
prone to moaning; they just punched in and got on with the gig.
Fortunately, these Brianless occasions took place in the sticks -
Brian was still inamorato with the big city, and would not "get
ill" in a major market.

We were somewhere in the Southwest, in limousines going
from one town to another for another show. We liked to keep moving;
we didn't make many stops. The locals thought that limos were
just for the governor or major movie stars going to a Hollywood
opening, so we kept moving. The South was still kind of backward
and rough. Pete Bennett was with us; he worked for Allen Klein
as U.S. promotion man and kept us on the radio.

We found a quiet-looking diner on an interstate lay-off and
decided to stop and eat. Everybody got out of the cars except
Brian. He wasn't hungry; he was going to stay in the car. We all
came back to the limos and no Brian; he'd changed his mind and
gone off to eat. I was annoyed. We didn't like hanging around in
the open and we were running late. We turned and saw Brian
inside the diner at a table against a far wall; he waved at us.

I said, "Pete, go in and get him now." He went into the
restaurant and picked him up by the neck and dragged him out
to the car. We were falling over laughing. Brian got in the back
of the car as white as a sheet.

Keith and I told Pete Bennett that he should have let him
finish eating. He said, "But, boss, you told me to get him now."

A date in the Northeast was stopped after just one minute

when fans broke through the inadequate barriers and police and invaded the stage. The police used tear gas to break up the riot, thus blurring the line between a Rolling Stones concert and student unrest, but the cops don't care - they were into rehearsal. This was all starting to get less than show business. We had similar experiences of ineptitude and violence in Connecticut, Pennsylvania, and Washington - the authorities seemed to be using us as a dry run for the-times-they-don't-want-changing.

Whilst the Stones played around upstate New York and the eastern seaboard, I dealt with the world from the more pristine confines of the Drake Hotel. My tailor, Roland Meledandri, was located opposite the Drake. He was a miracle worker, able to combine the tradition of yesterday with the breath and flair of the day and a sensual sense of fabric. Roland cut a fine suit for many, including the dapper threads that Steve McQueen touted in the original *Thomas Crown Affair*.

Sheila was in England minding Sean. Linda Keith, who was still seeing Keith Richards, called me up and told me to take her to dinner. I was wary of Linda because I found her attractive, *very* attractive. Back when Sheila had been frumpy, uncomfortable with herself, and pregnant, I had fairly lusted after Linda's bones when I perceived them as offered over the Christmas break. My mind had been prevented from the physical by the fact that Linda's parents were in the next room, which rather dimmed the view of a hard-on, and by the fact that I was sure that Linda was the type of gal who would give and tell.

After dinner, Linda hauled me out to Steve Paul's club, The Scene, which sat under the 59th Street Bridge. In its previous incarnation, this had been the jazz club location where, in *Sweet Smell of Success*, Tony Curtis as my man Sydney Falco planted pot on jazzman Martin Milner on the orders of Burt Lancaster's J.J. Hunsecker. I'm not sure if I recalled that at the time, but I did feel like I was about to be busted.

Linda said she wanted me to meet her latest discovery, Jimi Hendrix. Actually, she was dating him, and I was being used as the beard. One of you bright young things may wonder why this bright young thing did not change the course of history, make a beeline for Jimi Hendrix, and attempt to make him mine. Panic wove the threads of the evening. I knew that Linda was trouble,

but could not work out what part would be mine. I could hardly refuse to take Keith's lady out to eat (she might complain to my lead
guitarist), and my mind had no time to zone in and notice Jimi Hendrix, as it was in a wee bit of a tizzy and domestic haze. On getting
back to my rooms in the Drake, having left Linda entwined with
the thin black duke, I received a message which confirmed that I
had every reason to be on my domestic para-toes. Sheila had called
from London to say ... that Linda had called from New York to say
... that I had asked her out and was it all right with Sheila for her
to go out with me for a meal? The message ended with a request
that I call home, which I did, to a blazing transatlantic row. Ah!
Girls on the road.

Other freeze-frames from 1966: In L.A. the Stones are booked
to play their biggest concert yet at the Hollywood Bowl, with 17,500
tickets sold within a few hours. But even in the freewheeling atmosphere of Hollywood the mood is sour. The *Los Angeles Times* an-
nounces by headline that the Stones are a "Long-Haired Nightmare."
Suddenly the jibes of the U.K. press seem quaint. There's a feeling
of being in the beginning of a real war. The Sunset Strip will turn
into the battleground. A 10:00 p.m. curfew is put in place and
rigorously enforced; the police use optimum force to drive kids
indiscriminately off the streets. The prevalent mood all over
America is disturbing. The sixties are about to change owners and
the stage will be passing its crown to the crowd. The quote that
John Lennon had allowed Maureen Cleave in March about the
Beatles being more popular than Jesus gets America wired as the
Beatles start their last-ever Americas tour in August. Beatles
records are burnt and destroyed throughout the Bible-and-Elvis
Belt. Lenny Bruce dies in horrific circumstances, hounded by his
own drugged demons, aided and abetted by the law. This brings
Phil Spector to a new low. Lenny Bruce was a mate and idol, and
Bruce's passing, coupled with the U.S. lack of success and/or
recognition for his "River Deep - Mountain High," causes Spector
to announce his retirement. The fact that the Ike and Tina Turner
outing was lauded by nearly all and went to number three in the
U.K. is of no consolation to the master; number eighty-eight in the
U.S. stuns him, he hangs up his cloak and shades, and calls it a
night. The King of Teen Anthems is in Beverly Hills seclusion - for
two years. I try to reach him but he's taking no calls.

The American evangelist Billy Graham arrived in London
to play Earl's Court. Cliff Richard would be appearing with Mr.
Graham, so this was a must-see. Cliff had survived the Beatles,
the Stones, a lot of slagging, and much gossip about his sleeping
with more than the Lord. He was already the grand survivor of
the pop game, a master of behaviour, and the thought of Cliff in
celestial volumic surroundings had me flying back from Stock-
holm to catch the last night of the Graham event.

Eddie and I got off the plane in London, picked up the black
Mini Cooper that we'd left in the parking lot, and headed for Hurlingham Road. Sheila was out or away. Eddie rolled a joint and
made a cup of tea. I was hungry. There was a bag of biscuits on
the kitchen table with a card pinned to the top stating, "Try these!"
We were late for our date with the Lord, so I grabbed the biscuits,
we headed for the car, and I started trying them. We arrived at
Earl's Court and joined the flock entering the Exhibition Hall. My
only experience of crowds in recent years had been of only sheer
bedlam, panic, and pandemonium, but this crowd was orderly,
at ease, and friendly. I felt the same way and nibbled on another
biscuit. Eddie and I found our seats and waited for Cliff. It was a
long wait, so we had a cup of tea and I had another biscuit. The
arena started to come and go in waves, the crowd's reaction to
whatever was happening on the stage went out of sync, and the
laughter and applause went on forever. The hands were clapping
out of time with the sound of the same hands clapping behind
the sound I was about to hear. Eddie saw me reach for another
cookie and asked me for the bag. He nibbled at a corner, mulled
on it, played with it in his mouth and saliva, took another little
bite, confirmed the whatever, cleared his throat, and spoke.

"How many have you eaten of these biscuits, Andrew?"

I was annoyed at this invasion of my concentration, as I
was sure the moment was nearly Cliff. I answered and heard a
tired voice follow my answer three beats after the words that
mine had just spoken.

"Five or six, Eddie, I don't know. Why?" I sighed, hearing
the totality of the breath echo inside and outside through the
whole hall. I was surprised that nobody else heard.

"They're hash cookies, Andrew, that's why," said Eddie. He
studied me, then asked, "How are you feeling?" I didn't answer.

"Perhaps we ought to take you home," said Eddie, getting us both up and out of our chairs.

I didn't see Cliff, but I certainly saw God. Well, I saw Cliff, but from a hashish-in-surround point of view. I saw him through a telescope in reverse and heard him from the sinking flotsam that was me, my brain, and I, and I saw him sing, but all my brain fed through was the sound of trampled gargling.

I take it that Eddie took me home. I remember a lot of "Excuse me!"s as we shuffled past and stepped on the toes of a row of young Ena Sharpleses and assorted Rosemary's Babies. The faces that I passed morphed chillingly into what they would become. The movie wasn't even out, but I could see their future and they could see me now. I don't remember my body leaving, but my mind recalls a *Hiroshima mon Amour* fairly reckless, legless evening saved by the bell that was Eddie.

My next memory is of sitting up in bed at about ten o'clock the following morning, feeling as if a sledgehammer had whacked my brain, a steamroller had rolled over my body - a body my mind could not find. There were plenty of parched men in my head, panicked eunuchs trying to find a way out and into my body, which was still buried beneath the sands. Cynthia sat at the edge of the bed, a concerned look on her face as I came to.

"What the fuck happened?" was all I could muster. I was still in pre-rigor mortis.

"The cookies, dear, absolutely loaded with hash, my dear. Do you have any idea of how many you had?"

That's our Cyn, I mused, the caring dart, straight to the heart of the matter, fuck the shorthand - the lady has wavelength, and has mine. I managed a wry smile at her, which she took as meaning I was probably about to lie to her.

"Half a dozen ..."

"What, before you went out, or after you went out?"

"Probably a dozen ..."

"That's more like it."

I was getting some body feeling back. I looked around to be sure of my bearings and noted that I was still in bed. I attempted to raise my arms; I did so, but they were very sluggish as if carrying invisible weights. I don't remember eating; I was still very parched out. It was either by that evening or the following one that I could get up and get back into life. Eddie reappeared in my bedroom and flung £40 in old-fashioned white fivers onto the bed.

"What's that for?" I asked.

"That's the money you put into the collection plate that I thought it better to take back," he smiled, as he got up off the bed and took himself and an empty teacup downstairs for another cuppa.

Toward the end of the summer of '66 I rented a house in the south of France with theatrical agent Donald Langdon and his most recent wife. Donald, a comfortable soul, slightly portly and slightly bearded, represented comedians John Bird, Dudley Moore, and Peter Cook. I was flying from Los Angeles to Nice to meet up with Sheila and son Sean, who had been ensconced on the French Riviera all summer long whilst I'd toured, recorded, and officed on behalf of the Stones. I had not indulged in LSD on the same frontline level as had the Stones, having neither the time nor the inclination. I was too busy working, and, regardless of what you may have read elsewhere, was attempting to keep a roof over my head and my mind intact with a reasonable lid on the madness. By the end of 1966, the Stones, however, had fame, money, and some time off - an incrementally dangerous amount.

I indulged myself on the near fifteen-hour flight from L.A. to Nice by taking acid. I bought the first two seats in the front row of first class, ordered vegetarian food, loaded myself up with Mickey Mouse colouring books, crayons, and the little gadget that rotated Disney slides, and let the acid take over. Donald Langdon picked me up at the Nice airport in his Jaguar and, when told of my flying *modus operandi*, asked me if I had not been scared, as in "freaked out, man." The opposite, I was able to tell him. I was at one with the sky, felt I'd touched and walked on God's circle, and would forever remember the feel of the clouds - besides, I added, I didn't know how to fly a plane. I arrived in Nice very tired from the acid and the summer workload. I collapsed and rested, then threw myself into the visiting celebrity agenda that was part of summer holidaying *chez* Langdon, as Donald ran his office overlooking the Mediterranean. So I disappointed myself, Sheila, and no doubt Sean, as there was no real rest and no real family time.

I never had the honour of singing on a Rolling Stones record, although Mick was kind enough to sing "Da Doo Ron Ron" on one of mine. But I did get the pleasure, at RCA in Hollywood, during the second week of September 1966, of joining Mick and Keith as the "singing guitars" needed to chorale the start-me-up to "Have You Seen Your Mother, Baby, Standing in the Shadow?" Brian and Bill had flown back to England, Brian nursing a broken left wrist that he'd gained after another set-to with himself or Anita. Charlie had stuck around to shop and to be on hand to lend his percussive hand as Mick, Keith, and I mopped up with Dave Hassinger. The tracks were complete. We'd already bounced the four-track recording to another reel, opening up two tracks to allow us to overdub Keith and Mick and complete what we all felt had the hum of being our next single. There was a degree of urgency to the proceedings, as we were due in New York in a few days to make another *Ed Sullivan* TV show appearance, where the Stones were to mime to their last platter, "Paint It, Black," and their next, the soon-to-be-finished "Have You Seen Your Mother?" We were mixing down to mono and Dave ran the four-track down to us another time. Each time we heard it, the intro sounded just that little bit lamer.

"There's just no balls on the front," I said to everyone in particular. "Right up to the brass and guitar figure, it just dies."

"Bring up the guitars," said Keith.

"I can't," said Dave, "It'll just bring up the room noise. Listen, I can't give you enough of the guitars without the room. I don't think it'll work." He thought right.

"Then try doubling the guitars," Keith offered, guitars having worked out most of his life.

"Won't work," sighed Dave. "All in the same frequency."

In other words, we had fucked up recording the guitars, under-recorded them, and could not bring up the level without giving you a room full of noise and air-distort.

"You could try a harmony, do something up the octave," said Dave.

"Yeah, and sound like the fuckin' Byrds," snarled Mick.

"On speed," I added.

"Yeah," grunted Mick, not thinking much of my contribution.

"Well, I don't know," said Keith. "We can't leave it like this. The front sucks."

Mick and Keith wandered out into the hall and back again. Charlie and I wandered around each other.

We were all stumped. Then I had an idea, a mad one, but nonetheless an idea.

"Why don't we try it with voices?"

"What the fuck are you on about?" chided Mick. "You want me to call Phil Spector and ask for his fuckin' choir?"

Fuck you, too. "No dear, I mean like this." I squeezed my nose with thumb and finger. "Why can't we go na-na-nanana-nana with our voices, throat up, no body, noses on hold, in unison with the guitars?"

The room went quiet, everybody waiting for everybody else to say something, hear it, or lose it. Finally Dave, his eyes on his shoes, his shoes on the console, broke the silence.

"It could work."

Keith agreed, "Who's going to do it, Andrew?"

"You, me, and Mick - and Charlie can tell us how it feels." We went into the studio. Dave cued the track up for himself, found some noise cue; there was no count-off. Mick and Keith practised sounding ridiculous. I already had that down.

"Listen for the guitar clicking on - that's your cue." Dave ran the tape, and we pulled it together in two. We looked at each other, then toward the control room.

Charlie shook his head, then looked up with a grin. "I dunno, you guys. You're all mad, but it works."

"Have You Seen Your Mother, Baby, Standing in the Shadow?" was released within a day of simultaneously stateside and in the U.K. It was our last single release of 1966. While we were in New York for *The Ed Sullivan Show*, Jerry Schatzberg took the classic Stones-in-military-drag photos that confirm the English propensity for "any excuse and it's into drag." I found time to attend a Cilla Black cabaret opening at the Plaza Hotel with Brian Epstein and his U.S. attorney, Nat Weiss; it's one of the few social occasions I remember ever having taken with Brian.

"Have You Seen Your Mother?" peaked at number five in the U.K. and, in the U.S., number nine. Keith did a Richard the First and aired our laundry in the *New York Times*, protesting that I'd used the wrong mix on the top ten single and that the original was "fat and fantastic." Quite possible, dear, but if so, it's the horns that did it. The single was perhaps too spiked and hippie for our core base fans, and the single sleeve with the group in WWII drag came off a little frivolous in those frowning American times. To the emerging, opinionated underground movement, it was the Stones in commercial gear and not a real deal. The resultant shaving of our potential sales base earned us our first non-number-one in a long while.

The Stones both captured the street and missed it. In 1966, while Buffalo Springfield gave voice to a generation gripped by the horrible certainty that was Vietnam, the Doors rose from the pavement's disaffected blue jean squalor and really spoke for the times, led, almost predictably, by a military brat, Jim Morrison. In L.A., while riots festered and burned, shadows took up our space on the street, unbeknownst to us, and new life was born.

We had enjoyed three years of mutually-agreed-upon mayhem, as presented to the public in tandem with our willing partners, the press. But you could sense the change and chaos on the horizon. There was a backlash coming. The Stones spending more time at home - framed by the perception of wealth with a nonstop life of chauffeurs, loafers, Rolls-Royces, Aston Martins, shopping, clubs, clothes, mates, hangers-on, and dolly birds - was going to get on the proverbial English tit, and it would only be a matter of deadlines before the U.K. press would suss the mood of a nation and reflect it. I could not put myself out front in an effort to quell the rising storm, because I was perceived as one of the gang, another nouveau rich yobbo in need of a day of reckoning. So I went back to Fleet Street and asked the grand majordomo of the press corps, the honourable Leslie Perrin, to step back into our life and become our Dr. No, and this time out, instead of saying "Yes" and getting us into the press, to be his wily taciturn goodself and deal out an acceptable roadblock of "No."

Leslie Perrin's first gig was our "Thank You!" tour, the fall '66 U.K. tour which featured the Stones, the Ike and Tina Turner Revue, Long John Baldry, and the Yardbirds. This brought 1966's concerts to around sixty, down from 1965's 150-plus. In the upcoming year the Stones would play a lot, but only about twenty times on stage. The grand "Thank You!" was a way of saying, "Please don't get down on us because we are enjoying the fruits of four years hard work. This is a talent-packed tour on which we are losing bread in order to say thanks and bring you the very best" - as in, it's costing us our own money to entertain you. I was attempting to turn off the up-gushing resentment faucet.

The auntie of the blues, Long John Baldry, signed on as a well-paid and very camp compère. The Yardbirds were squeezed in between the Stones and the Turner Revue. Mick, Keith, and I had decided that they were cocky little upstarts, had had one more hit than they deserved, and this sandwiching between the headliners should put pay to their career.

As the Stones wound down and touring became a local social pastime, I found time to circulate on the town. Keith and I greeted Bobby Darin at the Dorchester and saw Jimi Hendrix at the Speakeasy. Jimi had arrived in England and Linda Keith had fixed him up with Chas Chandler, the Animals' bass player, as a manager. This was a great move, save for the fact that Chas came saddled with his manager, a scumbag rogue, Mike Jeffries. We marveled at Mr. Stand-By-Me, Ben E. King, at the jumping and humping Scotch club. London was now fulfilling *Time* magazine's proclamation as being the number one city of the sixties. San Francisco would have to wait its turn before it could blot its copybook.

The Stones and I, John Lennon, George Harrison, Eric Burdon, and Donovan trippily attended the opening of Brian Epstein's new pride and joy, the newly renovated in rock 'n' pop splendor, Saville Theatre, on November 13 to catch the wonders of Motown via the Four Tops. Sheila was able to get out and about and busy herself in her social scene, made up, in the main, of George Harrison's wife, Pattie Boyd, the designer Ossie Clark and his partner Celia Birtwell, and the always-present Tony King. In terms of my estrangement from the inquisitive and the caring, my mother was now firmly on the list of people I avoided seeing. It seemed much easier, and the polite thing to do at the time, to walk away rather than appear a mess in front of my mother.

August 1967, London Meditation Centre, Kensington, left to right: Mal Evans, Neil Aspinall, Paul, unknown, Jane Asher, Pattie Boyd, unknown, Mike McGear, Ringo, John, Maureen Starkey, George, Maharishi Mahesh Yogi

Paul McCartney and Pattie Boyd grin while Jane Asher looks away.

CHAPTER 30

socially out of control - according to late britain / fear and loathing in park lane, dartford, and n.w.3 / allen takes over ... everything / who, here, and everywhere - another summing up

"I'd rather the Mafia than Decca."

- Keith Richards

"Nothing happened in the sixties except that we all dressed up."

- John Lennon

"The pop groups are winning the battle against those who would promote the arts as a means of teaching people what are the worthwhile things in life."

- Lord Goodman, Chairman
of the Arts Council, 1966

"Sex and rock 'n' roll could be tolerated, but drugs could not."

- Robert Hewison, *Too Much: Art and
Society in the Sixties, 1960-1975*

We spent a lot of nights up at Whitehead's editing *Charlie is My Darling*. Good company helps to secure the mission and we'd be joined by, in the daytime, Mick, Keith, and Charlie, and at night, Tony King, Georgie Fame, and his lady, Carmen. The credits and the slo-mo were costing as much as the shoot had, but I did not have much choice if I wanted the film done. We had filmed in Belfast, Dublin, and Cork, but not recorded any sound except a guide operated by Glyn Johns on a small portable Grundig. I then took the three-track IBC live recordings that Glyn had done in Liverpool and Manchester and matched them to the Irish visuals. A few days later, after we'd been up a few days, I took Tony King to the south of France for a break. By afternoon, we were getting stoned in Cannes on the beach in front of the Martinez, where I had once spotted Picasso having a spliff. I didn't realise it at the time, but Tony was about to leave us. He couldn't stand my new personal assistant, Cynthia Dillane, who could stand Ian Stewart and would soon be married to him.

We gave parts of *Charlie is My Darling* to TV companies to use to promote our singles - a little pre-video-age action in production - we had to. The fame had made it impossible for the Stones to whip around and do quite so much in a twenty-four hour day. Now we had logistics, security, hired help. You couldn't just say, "OK, boys, meet you at the BBC at eleven o'clock in Bond Street" anymore; chauffeurs wanted to know which car to bring. High passion was getting sublimated to suburban detail. Immediately after finishing the Irish tour and the basic filming of *Charlie* we were off to RCA in Los Angeles to nail another single. You still needed another new single every twelve weeks. Success in the sixties did not take the pressure away from product requirement; it just re-emphasised it. The Stones stood up to it very well, rose to the challenge in sound and song, though none of us at the time realised how exhausting it was. We were strong, we were invincible, and they delivered.

They were raised on the responsibility of having to come up with a single every three months. Once Mick and Keith had got the writing groove down, thus eliminating that masochistic search for someone else's song to fit the bill, we just got on with the first golden run. The song business would have killed us if Mick and Keith had not pulled it off. You cannot rely on "It's All Over Now" or "Time is on My Side" falling into your lap each time out; it's just not going to happen. Had my Dimmer Twins not got it right, it could have been a life of searching the bin for records not covered by the Searchers or the Swinging Blue Jeans. For me a final bell had tolled one summer of '63 day when Freddie and the Dreamers released their cover of James Ray's "If You Gotta Make a Fool of Somebody." Mick, Keith, and I all liked the James Ray original - I more than liked it; I thought it was royalty, an amazing recording and song. Full marks to Freddie or his A&R man John Burgess for unearthing this gem, but for me it meant that Mick and Keith had better get a-writin'. Even the rare gems were being unearthed and moved to the high street. Nobody gave me any moody about pressure; they, except Brian, were workers. Brian was still a different story, the tormented peninsula cutting himself off from the main land mass. Fortunately, I could ignore Brian, because the Stones were already doing just that.

At the end of September, it was back on the U.K. road for a hectic, two-shows-a-day, three-week trek ending at the Granada in London on October 17. The Beatles had the month off. At the Odeon Theatre in Manchester, fans smashed three rows of seats trying to get to the stage and the police had to form a human barricade to stop fans from trampling those sitting in wheelchairs on top of the orchestra pit. Keith was hit in the face by a flying missile and knocked out, and another thrown object cut Mick above the eye - the fans were no longer just calling their name. In Berlin, I suggested to Mick that it might be a good idea to goose-step a little around the stage to "Satisfaction," both for the fans and as a good laugh for me and Keith. This wasn't a big stretch for feudal, British, war babies who, in 2000, could still come up with slogans like, "So many Germans - so few Concordes." Mick took the suggestion one goose-step führther and *Sieg Heil*-ed his way around the stage to the kick and riff of "Satisfaction." The stadium erupted in celebratory memoric violence. Forty-three rows of seats were trampled and destroyed and one hundred and twenty-three cars were smashed and wrecked outside.

Mick remains a moving effigy, but the effigy he was mocking - the goose-stepping *Führer* - was getting taken at face value by these young German audiences. His put-on, instead of being seen as a kind of Nazi camp like "Springtime for Hitler," turned inadvertently into an impromptu Nazi rally, more like the embodiment of Hitler (in Jaggersprechen) - The Picture of Dorian Gray. He was turning on the German audiences, but on a terrifyingly comedic - and real - level. Once all of *die Halbstarken* got out of the tin-shed stadium and away from the police, the violence really began - first the nearby parked cars fell victim to the mayhem stirred, then they wrecked every train taking them back to the sticks.

"Get Off of My Cloud," the result of our most recent recording trip to L.A., entered the U.S. charts in the second week of October. It would stay there for twelve weeks, taking two at the number one position in November, six weeks after Barry McGuire's number one, the P.F. Sloan/Steve Barri-composed "Eve of Destruction," the first major record on Lou Adler's new label, Dunhill Records, and the defining moment in folk rock until Lou and the Mamas and the Papas nailed that movement.

Out of Our Heads was released and became the Stones' first number one U.S. album. It entered the U.K charts at number three and stayed in the top ten for eighteen weeks, peaking at two. The photo for the English cover was shot by Gered Mankowitz, whose main qualifications were some nice snaps of Marianne Faithfull, being a nice guy, and being the son of Wolf Mankowitz. David Bailey was globetrotting for *Vogue* and Gered became our man.

****

The *Evening Standard* reported that the Rolling Stones had a new agent, Tito Burns, who also represented Bob Dylan in the U.K.; that they had a new co-manager, Allen Klein; and that they had signed a new five-year contract with Decca. Judith Simons reported in the *Daily Express* that the Stones would stay with London Records in the States. She quoted me as saying, "Under the terms of the deal concluded with our American business manager, Mr. Allen Klein, the Stones are guaranteed three million dollars over the next five years." Miss Simons continued, "Expenses are high. Each guitarist owns about eight instruments, and the total cost of the present equipment is about £4000. When the Stones are on tour, hotel bills are about £700 a week. Salaries for secretarial and other staff account for £200 a week." Brian Jones announced that it was not true the group would be moving to the States: "I think this got started because I've just bought a house in Los Angeles. It's purely a business investment and neither I nor any of the others have plans to settle out there." This was desperate bullshit. I felt sick. Judith Simons recalls the story being leaked to her by "someone in the Stones' office."

The *Daily Express* piece was a story about money and how we'd given up the ghost and finally the Stones were in show business. This was a puff article worthy of Colonel Parker, reeking of American "doing-well" nonsense, out of place whilst, at the same time, an ironic hint of the future life that Mick would step up to, all on his ownsome without any assist from Allen Klein. At that time, however, you didn't originate a story on how well you had done out of the working man whilst he was on the job. I found it counterproductive and rude to tell a public, who had forked out hard-earned dosh for vinyl and shows, just how much money we

were earning - or worth. It's OK if the press originates such a specu-
lation, but from the horse's mouth it's just not on. For the Beatles,
OK - the whole world wanted to see them do well. But for the
Stones? I don't think so. The jury was out on them until they got
busted - which was just around the corner. It was not a dissimilar
situation to the Krays. The public may have admired them from a
distance, but if the Kray twins had taken to poncing around Mayfair in Rolls-Royces with personalised number plates, the tide of
public tolerance would have surely turned. That's press rules
according to Loog.

I said nothing about Klein taking the press reins on my
turf, but my territory had been invaded by him and the Stones
knew it. My days were getting done in a third-party scenario
where Allen was Andrew, Andrew was Stu, and the Stones remained the same.

Our new agent, Tito Burns, had also once managed Cliff
Richard and the Shadows and was the U.K. agent for Dusty
Springfield; the Searchers; Peter, Paul, and Mary; Otis Redding;
and the Lovin' Spoonful. He's one of the great, old, borderline,
rumoured rogues.

The Summer of Love was still around the corner.

Allen Klein told me sometime in the 2000s that I had ended
Stoned with 1964 because I had not worked out how to handle him.
That's pretty arrogant, an understandable call from Allen, and the
natural entitlement of the barracuda keeping the shine on his ivory
tower. The history of any art form can never be kind to the Allen
Kleins of this world - and I say "of this world," even though Allen
was a unique artist in his own world - the art of making money and
taking control. My life is very simple when viewed on this canvas,
whereas, on that of another morality play, say the world of Gordon
Gekko in *Wall Street*, I'd be out of here by the end of the first reel.
Not so Allen, who'd be riding off into the sunset in the back of a
limo in a tickertape parade with dollar bills raining from every
Wall Street window. My life is simpler in this scenario because I
created. I was able to take somebody else's vision of themselves, a
group of people who had an idea and love of a music form and a
way of life that might go with that music, and I was able to work
that concept into making sense for the artist, and communicate it
to the music business and to a greater section of the public. Under

that lens, the pop pharisees of our world never created anything, never had a vision (beyond their own coffers), never heard a sound, never took an idea from someone's mind and moved it onto tape, onto the radio, into a video, or into the hearts and minds of the "all of us" who are out there with a need for "this thing." Oh, they heard a sound all right - the sound of money.

Allen was an acrimonist. An acrimonist is only required when something is wrong, or something can be perceived or presented as wrong, and by that standard he's a required part of the chain. Almost famous doesn't enter that equation; you have to be actually famous for a Klein to brew - he is only able to play mummy and daddy when the art is in question, in decline, or in chaos, and the kids are fighting over the toy of fame. Allen comes in when your harvest is not as plentiful as your expectations on the sow, but part of the price is that he gets the farm. The next thing you know, you are causing havoc wherever you go, because, for some inexplicable reason, life doesn't add up to any more than it did before.

The irony is that the sixties are not over and may never be. It's a fruit with so many peels of wrath, and one of those skins involves the what-are-we-worth call. It's part of life's agenda, and I wish you your Allen Klein in that time of your climb. Gross is the number and nature of the artbeast, the skin on the bone. Allen didn't change the game; he enjoyed it. There was a price to be paid for being made to feel that you were as big as you were, and in Mick's and Keith's case that price was their songs.

****

The Beatles made only two U.K. appearances in 1966, at the Empire Pool in Wembley on January 5 and a fleeting, fifteen-minute set at the May 1 NME Annual Poll Winners Concert, which would be their last homeground gig until the famous 1969 rooftop sing. There was some disagreement over the joint appearance of the Beatles and the Stones in the NME show.

John Lennon in disguise had come into the NME to see Derek Johnson. He'd got a false beard and he was dressed in the most ragged clothes you've ever seen. He said, "I don't want to be recognised by anybody. Let's go and have a cup of tea." They went to Julie's and sat talking about the concert. After a while another cafe door opened and another altogether disreputable figure with ragged trousers, beard, and lanky, dirty hair shambled up to the counter to pick up a cup of tea. As he passed their table he said, "Hallo, John," and John said, "Hallo, George." The next week there was one hell of a battle backstage between Epstein and myself about who was going to close the show and finally it was worked out that the Beatles would close it. But in fact they didn't. There was the awards and then the Beatles did their act. They'd insisted on one of the lesser acts playing after them to finish the show so that they could nip off in their limos before the audience came streaming around the stage door and trapped them.

The Stones weren't due to play that year. About ten days before the show, I called Maurice Kinn, founder of *NME*, and said that the Stones would like to appear at the Poll concert but that they wanted to be a complete surprise, they did not want any announcement made in the papers. They just wanted to walk up on stage and that would be that, the first anybody knew about it. The Stones didn't want any money; even the Beatles only got £70; it was a prestige show. I made one stipulation on behalf of the Stones - that they would not appear immediately before the Beatles. Kinn said, no problem, the Beatles'll close the show after the awards. The Stones walked on and the place erupted; their appearance, totally unexpected, what an extra bloody bonus, one of the major attractions in the world, what an unexpected surprise. They'd done a couple of numbers, then John and the Beatles appeared at the bottom of the stage. Kinn said to Lennon, "John, you're much too early; the Stones have got another ten minutes, then it's the awards. Go away, you're not on for another thirty minutes." He said, "We're not waiting. We're going on now." Kinn got hold of Brian Epstein, who said, "Maurice, I can't do anything with them. John's insisting they go on now and that's it, that or nothing." But Kinn had a contract with the Stones, so what was he going to do?

Kinn said to Brian, "Let me tell you the position. The Beatles are not going on next. I'm going to tell Jimmy Savile to tell the audience that the Beatles are here but they refuse to appear. There will be a riot, this place will be smashed up, and not only will you, Brian, be responsible for the thousands of pounds worth of damage, but you'll be sued by *NME* for the irreparable harm you've done to the reputation of my paper." Epstein gave him a balling out, "We'll never appear here again as long as we live. You can't do this to us." Kinn said, "I don't care if it's the King and Jesus Christ together. I can't change it. I gave it in writing to Andrew; that's it." So the Beatles waited.

You could say that Brian Epstein was losing his grip. I'd prefer to think that it was just I who'd had a better day and perhaps confirmed for Brian that the decision to stop playing the Beatles was correct. The decision had to be both logical and not so. After all, you got to the top to have the world in your hand, and then your answered prayers bit it. The price was being unable to continue with the very joy that propelled your mission in the first place. You had no barometer save perhaps Hitler or Jesus. Stop touring, stop invading, stop preaching. Same choice. That's a lot of adjusting to do.

****

La Trattoria Terrazza was like a shrine to me, a sign that I'd arrived and that I enjoyed. It was where I relaxed into the comfort of deep superficiality, good company, and great food. It was the favoured eating place of the celluloid aristocracy: Frank Sinatra and Laurence Harvey made it their London home. I preferred it to Alvaro's in the Kings Road. The Trat reverberated work and action, Alvaro's the oncoming Chelsea sloth. When Nik Cohn arrived to interview me at the Trat, I was very taken aback and shocked when, after our meal, he passed on espresso, took out a grimy bag of cocaine, and offered me some on the end of a used nail file.

Eddie arrived at the Terrazza with the Phantom V and I offered to drive Nik to his evening appointment. The Phantom V now sported an orange light on the rooftop, replicating Her Majesty's blue light on top of her matching Phantom V (although I know that hers was without the dark windows and will presume that it did not have the telephone or record player either). I'd decided *en route* to give King Cohn a rock 'n' roll shock for his highness and nerve at bringing out a mound of off-white powder onto the Terrazza table. I discussed with Eddie what I wanted in rapid code on the Soho pavement as I girls-and-Nik-first'd us into the back of the car.

The Phantom V did a smart right onto Pall Mall, headed for Buckingham Palace. We approached the gates and kept on going. Cohn was in disbelief about what was obviously about to happen; he jumped off the back seat onto all fours on the floor, having forgotten that the dark windows rendered this move redundant, let alone cowardly. The policeman on duty at the gates saluted and waved us through, and we drove toward the palace, through the arches, and circled the inside at a leisurely pace. This was all possible in the days before the pursuit of me-ism had driven the populace to a position of aberrated entitlement that would let a gent appear in Ma'am's bedroom in the wee small hours of the morning. The later pursuit of drugs and terrorism by the populace in general would call for security in all the monied homes of the land.

We then exited the palace. As we did so, Cohn screamed bejesus as Eddie nonchalantly electric'd his window down and informed the saluting bimbo on the gates that we had forgotten something over at Princess Margaret's and would be back. I was pleased to squawk at Cohn about how we'd pulled that off without the need of MBEs and instructed Eddie to carry on the drive and take Nik to Kit Lambert's where he'd be meeting with Kit, Chris, and Pete Kameron. I was invited to lull for the evening, but fortunately refused, as that might have involved dropping Nik off home at the end of the night. When Cohn did exit a few hours later, he was so visibly the better and worse for wear and tear that he was detained by Her Majesty's finest, a fitting end to a royal evening.

Nik was the first to get it and write it up. He had an Elmore Leonard, dissolute, on-the-street understanding of us all - with all warts and halos allowed and counted on. He got pop's purity of purpose, celebrated it for and with us, and left it before the needle slipped off the vinyl and into the arm. There are not many of us self-inventors inventive enough to cover more than one decade with aplomb - but young King Cohn did just that when he met and created Tony Manero and left us with the best quick-take on the seventies, *Saturday Night Fever*. In the mid-eighties, I had occasion to run into him on Broadway and he joined me in a trot up to Allen Klein's office, where I was about yet another advance to handle my drug-addled ways. We entered Allen's space and I got surprised when we ran into Tony Calder. I went into a combine of kill minus will - the shakes, a familiar drug tone. I was much too high too much of the time to have anything but sickened, mixed emotions about my former partner's having been a recent partner of my first wife. I was glad when Nik took me by the arm, led me to the fire exit, out on the landing, and gave me a good whack of smack. The idea of Tony didn't look quite so frightening when Nik and I nodded back into the room, and I had enough narco-composure reinstalled to recall the fact that it still takes two of you to do it - and a third party to start a war.

****

Regarding the Who, I never intended to become their producer; it would have been an unrealistic scenario. First, from the point of view of the Stones, it was OK to have a record company, but a bit much to have another actual band. I had to think how they might feel about it and the incredibly all-consuming timetable and agenda that we maintained already. The second reason was that I was not qualified, and I knew it at the time. I liked the idea of the Who. I particularly liked Pete Townshend and Keith Moon and the wham-bam-thank-you-ma'am management combo of Chris Stamp and Kit Lambert - Chris being the wham-bam and Kit the very grand thank-you-ma'am.

Daltrey and John Entwistle were to me the Who's version of Brian Jones and Bill Wyman - very essential parts of the engine, but not part of the passionate roar offstage that propelled and created momentum, as I could with Mick and Keith, and as Kit and Chris so obviously did with Mr. T. I liked the whole idea and end result of the Who - the manifestos and the potential for international anthems - but I didn't have a passion for the spare parts, the detail, or the ingredients that manufactured the fury. Therefore, I would not qualify to hold the producing reins.

I was at one with my own amiable, laconic louts, with their trivial pursuits of fame, wealth, and position. This newly arrived sense of, and/or actual, wealth was driving a certain coldness into matters and manners of the Stones' day. Only because of this, I decided that, perhaps, I'd better get involved with something that was just business, something to which my heart was not attached, and thus was not a moving target that could bleed. My Who agenda was very simple. Pick up the mantra of "Fuck Shel Talmy," for whom, from my snob-driven lack of an ethical position, I had no feelings one way or the other. Insert Lambert and Stamp as producers, myself as executive producer on the art and hustle, and Allen as the financial manager over the whole lot of us. I knew that this was not going to happen on Allen's yacht with Chris, so I stayed away and concentrated on my tan. Kit and Chris could not accept my intentions as not including wishing to be rid of them. If anybody did have that revolving, tortured intention at the time, it was Pete Townshend; and Chris was just picking up the right vibe from the wrong party. Lambert and Stamp, it was apparent, would never take to Allen. They had Pete Kameron and nobody counted that factor in at the time. So it all just ended up as a nice try on a nice boat, whosoever's it was.

The Who had come a long way. We'd all come a long way since my mate and founding father, Peter Meaden, showed me what was to become of my life and a group he called the High Numbers. But by 1978 Peter had had enough and, living back at mum's and dad's, he toppled down the stairs and died. This was just a few weeks short of Keith Moon's overdosing on the very pill that was designed to stop one's boozing.

****

Aftermath was released and "Paint It, Black" zoomed to number one on the same day in the U.S. and the U.K. Appallingly late - this was, after all, 1966 - *Time* magazine got the picture and heralded London as the world's most happening city. It decreed a decade dominated by youth and tells of London's having burst into bloom. London swings - it is the scene. The London summer is as never before, London is switched on. *Time* just foamed at the nib as to the city being alive with mini cars and skirts, Beatles, and telly stars, and how, in a once sedate world of faded splendor, everything new, uninhibited, and kinky is blooming at the top of London life. With this *Time* issue began the continuing cycle of announcements and issues devoted to telling us what had already passed and averaged out.

The Rolling Stones didn't really get a mention, their lack of uniform and loutish reputation preventing them from joining the rest of the swinging sixties into *Time*-speak. Just as *Time* was promoting London, the British Invasion of America was waning and stalled on the beach. England had dominated the stateside charts for almost three years and now America was back with a vengeance. The *Billboard* top ten had been retaken by the Mamas and the Papas, the Lovin' Spoonful, Bob Dylan, the Young Rascals, the Beach Boys, Paul Revere and the Raiders, a lot of Motown, and Percy Sledge. By the end of 1966, top twenty one-offs and inroads were being enjoyed by the Mindbenders, Dusty Springfield, Donovan, Crispian St. Peters, and the invincible Petula Clark; but only the Beatles, Herman's Hermits, and the Rolling Stones managed to really hold their own.

Some of our sixties are over, whilst for a whole world it's only just begun.

CHAPTER 31

the new bel air - goodbye nelson eddy, hallo papa john / the hills are alive with the sound of our music, money, and s.t.p. / sheila and the drive along a six-lane freak avenue / the dream is more than over - who wants to be busted? i don't / as ella fitzgerald sang, "get out of town before it's too late my love" / "monterey pop" - the first festival - a three-day miracle / as kissinger would go to china, lou adler and i go to san francisco / dennis hopper, nico, brian jones - owsley's list

I sat in the everyday thunder of the late eighties and early nineties while fifty-fifty narco-generic combos stopped any four daze becoming a total rain-stopped play. But it so easily could have been so, very much of the time. One slip of the hand and the body follows, one mistake in the memory of what's been took and the next taking could be the last. My depression was evolving into a never-ending hyperactive narcoleptic downshift into the very brakepads of my mind. I couldn't even cry over spilt milk - that's all it was. If it had been more, had it had some Absolut spirit to it, I'd have lapped it up and poured it over my cornflakes.

The body was willing but my engine was shot. Pads so low that when my scuffed shoes hit the high road of my mind, the heels would smoulder to a stop, screaming, "Don't leave me on this alien standby!" Awful, just awful. I'd fuck with my body, fool it with some food; it would roar back with the sound of life but it was just not game anymore. A Chapter 11 body should stay at home, not run the gauntlet against younger cars without thought or overdraft and with a whole reserve of real staying power. Confirmation that I was truly whacked would come when booze didn't do it, coke cut right through it, and Percodan was just making me sicker. You reach the stage when you're taking the painkillers to get rid of the pain that signals the Percos stopped working and it's time to go flirting with brown sugar again. Then I'd feel the quicksand in my temples dissolve into liquid glass and I knew I'd be OK for the next few ...

When Crosby, Stills, Nash, and sometimes Young member David Crosby finally got the bill for twenty-five years of excess, with its minimum down payment of a replacement liver, he didn't get much sympathy from me. For in the L.A. Monterey Pop Summer of Love, love had nothing to do with it when Crosby conned me into an unnecessarily evil, mind-destroying roller coaster ride, just as I was finally relaxing and away from the pressures of the Stones' drug busts and newspaper lynchings in London.

Sheila and I drove the hallowed half-mile from Lou Adler's Stone Canyon Road abode down to the intersection occupied by the mock Tudor where once Tony Curtis, now Sonny and Cher, and later house *Hustler* publisher Larry Flynt would reside in their turn as if to the manor born. We turned left, up Bellagio Road's hilly twists and turns, toward another McTudor mansion at 783 Bel Air Road, home to Papa John and Mama Michelle Phillips, though "lair" might have described it more accurately. The Phillips Deux lived the highest of high lives, all you could smoke, snort, eat, and drink. Their guest, Crosby, formerly of the Hollywood Byrds, was doing his best to keep up with his hosts and seemed determined that I should swallow whatever pill he himself was on. A suedette version of Robin Hood who looked like he'd been living too long off the land, Crosby fit in perfectly with the fake beams of the Phillips's living room. In that Summer of Love his mission was apparently to raid the medicine cabinets of the rich in order to "elevate" the poor.

"It's fine, Andrew. I wouldn't put you wrong. You'll just groove for a few hours, then go to sleep," Crosby slurred like a young rascal on cough syrup. I didn't trust him, or myself.

"Yeah, but David," I slurred back, "Tell me exactly what it is. I like to know where I'm going and if I want to go there ..."

"It's nothing, man, mild ... sort of like an English Mandrax. No side trips. You'll just groove for a while ... then sleep."

I was yet just enough in possession of myself to notice that behind the groovy, far-out smiles of the party people lay scars and agendas, more Hollywood than Haight. Life seemed so easy that they took a false security from the luxuriously opiated foliage that canopied Papa John and Mama Michelle's latter day garden of Eden. Life might be a karma-free kaleidoscope on these lofty top ten heights, but there were already a couple of colours missing, some bulbs already burned out amidst the neon. It has ever been my weakness that, whatever warnings the losers around me might be unconsciously giving off, I can often find it in myself to ignore them. We birds of the canyon, eight miles high and climbing, were all too ready to follow the likes of Crosby, shabby pied piper though he might have been.

As Dylan, who largely had the sense to stay away from gatherings such as this, said at the time, which Crosby of all people should have appreciated, "I was so much older then, I'm younger than that now." As years have gone by, while David and I cycled through our respective serial addictions, I have a bit more empathy for our common plight. As the hard-boiled master of pulp fiction Mickey Spillane once noted, "Nobody goes into a bar to get sober." In the sixties, nobody visited John and Michelle Phillips to stay straight.

Not to be denied, Crosby held his hand out and asked me to take it, while Sheila was, as usual, enough drinks and drugs behind my pace to show some concerned common sense.

"What's wrong, Andrew?" Sheila always seemed especially beautiful when she was on my side.

"That's no fuckin' Mandrax and I'm not staying here so that cunt Crosby can watch it work ..."

But I swallowed Crosby's shit anyway.

Like a fool I'd decided to believe Dr. Crosby and allowed myself to fiddle with fate. I accepted the off-white tablet, but thank god only half a fool - I only took half. Half an hour later I was not feeling half funny, nor groovy, nor well. I looked for Sheila, found her, took her hand, and told her we were leaving.

Ah, there'll always be an Empire that dictates decorum, even if it's just inside my mind. Sheila and I nervously made our way out of the funhouse and drove ourselves away from the wandering peacocks and valet-parked Rollers, escaping a slightmare where Nelson Eddy and Jeanette MacDonald met Kenneth Anger in yet another remake of *Hollywood Babylon*.

In control of the car and somewhat more of myself, I felt a whole lot better and allowed myself to breathe the relatively smog-free air of the hills above the Strip. We were quiet for a few. We had not been having too many good evenings together.

Sheila was relieved to have escaped the madness disemboweling our swinging London while I was in a state of denial that did not benefit from the consciousness-expanding drugs that I was taking in excess. I longed for the mettle to return to London and stand with Keith and Mick during their legal ordeal, yet I reluctantly admitted that both of them had retained an emotional and mental stamina whilst I had surrendered mine to shock treatment and psychiatric drugs. I was similarly ambivalent toward Allen Klein, increasingly the Stones' anchor in a stormy sea. Was he simply rising to the occasion by taking on the duties that I had abandoned, or had this been his agenda all along and now the time was ripe?

There are those who were close to me at the time, as well as those who only admired or envied my early career from afar, who have it that "I never got over leaving the Stones." By the time the split was made public, however, I was almost (not quite) over it. The harsh reality, no doubt difficult for the Stones as well, if a great deal more difficult for me, could be spun as due to "musical differences," as two mighty forces in pop music going "our separate ways." But in truth, it was our Willie-Dixon-marries-the-Ronettes odd-coupling that often lent brilliance to the music.

The real chasm between me and the band had opened long before the *Satanic Majesties'* sessions drove me 'round the bend. Certainly my surrender to Allen Klein of much of my business portfolio weakened me somehow in their estimation, made me less deserving of the generous terms upon which they had originally signed with me. My imperial ambitions, which led to side-projects such as Marianne Faithfull and Immediate Records, might have made them seem less of a priority in their version of my eyes. Not to mention my ongoing love affair with America and its tycoons of teen. My man-crushes on Phil Spector, Lou Adler, and Brian Wilson were not something that the Stones totally shared - or could. If truth be told, they probably knew before I did that, at the height of our success, I was no longer taking the drugs, they were taking me. With the exception of Brian Jones, who was tarred by the same addicted brush as I, the Stones viewed drugs much the way they did the many other perks of their lifestyle - the homes, the cars, the clothes, the chicks, the money, were all things they could more or less take or leave as long as they felt that they were keeping up with the Beatles.

Meanwhile, back on the short but winding road back to Lou Adler's, where we were staying, my worst suspicions about Crosby's gift were overwhelmingly confirmed. As streets in the hills above Hollywood will, Stone Canyon Road suddenly presented me with at least six different choices, and I hadn't a clue which one led back to a bathroom that I could lock myself into. So while the sky painted itself black and all the leaves were no longer brown but a shade of evil itself, I bounced the car over various curbs and wondered if an earthquake had overtaken us. "This is a fuckin' nightmare!" I screamed into the night. "I'll kill that cunt." Peace and love were not around my corner. Sheila looked as if she didn't dare care; that just made my desire to murder her even stronger than her fear that she might not live through my latest experiment. In fact, it was Sheila's gift for keeping her fear to herself while taunting me for my folly that revved my rage that much more.

You ask why young stars and starlets insist on driving themselves when they could easily afford to hire sober chauffeurs? It's because it's nobody's fucking business how fucked up we get, until the police pull us over and make it theirs. After an eternity, Sheila and I managed to arrive at 800 Stone Canyon, alive, even if not well.

I made straight for the bathroom and threw up more than my body weight in bile. For an hour I kept vomiting, then crawled into bed. Inside the blankets I tripped beyond reason. I felt I was in a cylinder circling the earth, out of control, the horrors never ending, a roller coaster tearing my body and mind apart. Then I made another mistake. After hurling another several gallons of vomitus, I took a couple of sleeping pills to try to slow down the hellish journey and somehow return to earth. The acid-soaked synapses of my brain greeted the sleepers like long-lost brothers and got down to the serious work of potentiating each other. Against their powerful chemistry I was helpless; any other physical substance left in my stomach had long since been evacuated.

Curled in fetal position, I screamed and cursed within the grey, coffin-like cylinder which, I hallucinated, had entrapped me, spinning now fast, now slower, but always at a dizzying pace, throwing me sideways and back as it occasionally reversed itself. Though nothing any longer came up, I continued to gag and vomit until, finally sometime around dawn, I fell into an exhausted if troubled sleep in Sheila's arms.

Ironically, Sheila was wonderful; she always was when I needed her - a doyen of support. Naturally on my recovery I interpreted that as meaning she could only handle me helpless. When I awoke everything was better and I gently tripped the next twenty-four hours. But what wouldn't have seemed better after that vomit-ridden nightmare in the aphasic abyss?

I found out later that what I'd been given by Byrd-brained Crosby was STP, a powerful hallucinogenic that had driven more than a few good men out of their minds. If I was going to get fucked up, which I would continue to do, it would have to be by my own choosing. I could not afford to accept candy from strangers; purity of intention and purity of formula were seldom on offer.

A couple of years later I stood in New York's Kennedy TWA terminal, in line behind a demented David Crosby who, with a seemingly sedated ex-Hollie Graham Nash, had been allowed to teach our children well. He and Graham had left their passports and their marbles in L.A. Crosby was outraged as to why "they" would need credentials to board their flight to London, when by appearance and disposition, the only thing they didn't need was a plane. I still say, "Fuck you, David Crosby!" though I'm glad you finally got your new liver. There are no accidents and I have to put you down as part of my experience. But I would have been the first one to laugh if the liver you got had been one that Keith Richards had thrown away ...

The third summer of this century found my second wife Esther and me in Vancouver B.C. (Esther had allowed me to marry her in 1977.) Our son Max was matriculating at Santa Monica College in Los Angeles, living away from our home in Bogotá, Colombia for the first time, and we were already missing our boy. Vancouver was far enough away for Max to enjoy his independence yet close enough for him to fly up and drop in on ma and pa, were he so inclined.

While strolling on Burrard one lovely shopaholic Saturday who should we spy in our path but David Crosby. Though I had not seen him in thirty-five-some-odd years, and in many of those years he had not seen himself either, my mother's upbringing won out over my reluctance to renew our acquaintance. I got into mode and set upon him.

"David," I beamed, pretty sure that he might not recognise me. "Andrew Oldham," I added helpfully.

"Andrew," he beamed back without missing the beat that

sometimes eludes him on stage. "How are you?"

Esther and Mrs. Crosby were duly introduced along with the Crosbys' companion, Mrs. Robin Williams. For so many of us escapees from the leper colony of drugs, wives provided a mast to which we tied ourselves while the storm threatened to sweep us off the deck into the sea. It helped to have someone to bring what was left of us home. Of course this service could work in reverse, co-dependency being the flip side of addiction.

David looked as clean as a whistle and buttonholed me into his fold. I remembered having described him as a "cunt" in *2Stoned*, and while, come to think of it, I had been one too, I rather hoped he hadn't read my books. Or at least, if he had read them, had forgotten them.

No, of course, he hadn't read them; he was too busy being David Crosby.

What had the memoirs of a fellow survivor of the sixties to do with the life he now got up to live every morning. Survivors prey upon; they are not prey. "Will it serve my day?" they ask themselves, consciously or not. "Can I sponge from it, will it give me energy, is it what I am about? If yes, then OK. If not, then fuck it."

Crosby broke into my reverie by asking, "Are you coming to the show tonight?"

Crosby, Stills, and Nash were performing for 7000 that evening, although David later confided that with Young onstage with them, they doubled their score.

"Let me arrange some tickets," he offered.

He put me on the spot: I'd remarked to a friend earlier that day over tea "that there was no fucking way I was going to spend a night listening to that dreck." Now good manners required me to take the tickets, more than appreciative of the fact that they were offered *gratis*, in contrast to Stones' concerts, for which I was expected to pay.

Opening my mind to the entertainment at hand, we had a really good time. The skunk weed from the cheap seats mingled with the chronic that those in the front rows were smoking. The music was a joyous celebration of old hippies who had moved on. I set my cynical prejudices aside and enjoyed the lady bank officers, automat waitresses, and soccer mums as they hauled their middle-aged butts onto folding chairs to sing "Teach Your Children."

The females were the rowdy ones - while the males nodded quietly in the corners of their aging minds. The mothers, God love 'em, could celebrate this night out as just another part of the journey.

Backstage after the show Crosby guffawed and patted himself on the back - he had had a good one. We too had enjoyed an edutaining good time. I told him so.

"Hey, if you are over fifty and can stand up and remember the words there's work for everyone," he crowed. Still a musical co-op - nice one, David.

Graham Nash and I caught up. We knew each other well from the days before he became one of the richest immigrants in America. His Hollies provided the very best vocal sound the U.K. had to offer in a very competitive field.

The Stones and the Hollies had toured the U.K. together in early 1964. Keith and I often got bored between shows, especially when the tour trudged its way through the vast, cold, empty spaces of the Midlands and North. Our imaginations had nowhere to flow, so we decided to wind up the Hollies by suggesting that they could do with better management. We weren't serious, but we were in our *Clockwork Orange* period and loved a bit of trouble. That night in Vancouver I asked Graham what had become of the hapless manager whom we'd made our foil. Nash, as discreet as I was not, described his former manager's demise with a mimed gesture which let me know that the fellow had drunk himself to death.

Just before Esther and I headed out, having gotten ourselves back to the garden as it were, Crosby asked me if I knew anyone still doing cocaine. Sober myself for a number of years, I was taken aback; I thought he'd also quit. And he had. But Stephen Stills, at that time, still had a cocaine lump across his forehead as thick as the Pennine Chain. I saw him more recently on the box and it looked as if he had made it to the safer flatlands. I hope so.

Altogether a nice Vancooler occasion *chez* Crosby and Nash where, once again, I came, I sang, I learnt. Still, I was glad not to have been offered any refreshment by himself of the walrus mustache.

****

Despite my occasional poor choices in recreational drugs, spending the spring and summer of 1967 in L.A. brought relief from the pressures that the Stones, the law, and Allen Klein were visiting upon me. An exciting time it was on America's West Coast, as much as or more so than in the clubs of London, where Cream and Jimi Hendrix were momentarily "underground." Lou Adler and John Phillips were busy organising the Monterey International Pop Festival, which would be a prototype for the much larger Woodstock Music and Art Fair in 1969. BMW defined the future of popular music: BMW = Beatles, Monterey, Woodstock. Lou and John created a board of directors to steer the festival, scheduled for June 16th through 18th, and to advise on talent and policy. Along with Mick Jagger and Paul McCartney, whose roles were more or less symbolic since neither attended, I was appointed to head "International Affairs." The Beatles' favourite flack, Derek Taylor, handled PR. We commissioned D.A. Pennebaker, who had done such a stunning job on Dylan's *Don't Look Back*, to direct a documentary cum concert film. The recording would be done by Wally Heider and Bones Howe via Heider's state-of-the-art mobile studio.

The first generation raised on TV and rock 'n' roll came of age that summer and there was much for them to be negative about. When I think back on that 1967 Summer of Love, it's amazing it was ever called that. John F. Kennedy had been assassinated only three and a half years before; a huge U.S. military buildup was underway in Vietnam, topping the half-million mark in '67; and the antiwar movement was raging. Martin Luther King Jr. was urging massive civil disobedience and Stokely Carmichael was calling for a black revolution. Race riots had been savaging U.S. cities since Watts in '65. The Summer of Love obviously got its name from something else, and, from that something else, Monterey Pop came about. By the summer of 1968 student riots had gone global and Richard Nixon, whom we had thought we wouldn't have to kick around anymore, was looking likely to become the next U.S. president.

In early 1967, promoters Alan Pariser and Ben Shapiro had originally proposed a two-day rock event at the Monterey County Fairgrounds, home of the Monterey Jazz Festival. They booked Ravi Shankar for a $3500 fee and approached John and Michelle Phillips of the Mamas and the Papas to have the group assist and get the good word spread. Because Lou Adler was the group's manager and producer, John Phillips came to him. John had had a conversation with Paul McCartney at Mama Cass Elliot's house about how rock music, for all its growing sophistication and creativity, was still not regarded as an art form like jazz. John realised two things: one, that the festival ought to have an international bill of pop performers from every genre; and two, that no one could afford to pay them. The answer was to have all the participants donate all their performances to charity. Shapiro was not interested in a non-profit event, so Phillips and Adler, Paul Simon, Johnny Rivers, and Terry Melcher bought him out.

To validate what they were doing, they put together a board that included Paul Simon, Paul McCartney, Brian Wilson, Donovan, Mick Jagger, Smokey Robinson, and myself. Although it never met, the board served its purpose. They wanted not only to present the most amazing rock show the audience had ever seen, but also to have the best of everything for the performers as well. They started by contacting artists in our own backyard on the Sunset Strip. In late '66 you could hear innovative L.A. bands on the Strip at nightclubs like the Whisky-a-Go-Go, The Trip, and London Fog. From L.A. they enlisted Buffalo Springfield as well as the Byrds. Simon and Garfunkel came on board, as did the Beach Boys, but, when they dropped out, I suggested Otis Redding.

John and Lou knew that in order to have a successful as well as meaningful festival we needed groundbreaking San Francisco groups like the Jefferson Airplane and Big Brother and the Holding Company. The scene in San Francisco was marked by the colourful LSD commune of Ken Kesey and the Merry Pranksters. San Francisco's bands had learned their trade at psychedelic street festivals and gigging in the Fillmore Auditorium and the Avalon Ballroom. They were suspicious of anything from L.A., and it didn't help that John and Lou had recently produced Scott McKenzie's hit "San Francisco."

Lou and I flew up to San Francisco to meet with the journo patron saint of the West Coast movement, Ralph Gleason. By our having the courtesy to explain the festival's intentions, we hoped to return to L.A. with Gleason's approval. By stamping our festival kosher, Gleason could help us to overcome the social and aesthetic snobbery of Baghdad-by-the-Bay's new musical aristocracy. Mr. Gleason graciously consented to endorse us. We left his home in the waiting limo and on the way to the airport I asked Lou if he'd think me crazy for wondering whether the writer had spiked our afternoon tea.

"Feels the same way to me," said Lou, with his typical economy of expression.

"How is it?"

"Not bad, Andrew."

"Not bad for me too, Lou."

My appointment to the Monterey gang was a busman's holiday that blessed my sky with diamonds. Lou was familiar with and supported my self-imposed remove to L.A. He understood that my limbo here was preferable to incarceration in London.

Mick and Keith had been busted at Keith's Redlands home on February 12. Waiting on whether Mick and Keith would be detained at Her Majesty's Pleasure was not conducive to productivity. There were no shows set and none of the Stones could deal with recording. Time booked at Olympic was basically wasted. Charlie, Bill, and Ian Stewart were ready to clock in and Glyn Johns was always clocked in and on the factory floor, but Mick, Keith, and Brian were three different stories. Only at the "We Love You" session in late July, when the apparitional John and Paul appeared again as one live one, did anything get done.

You have to know this about the twin Moptops. They never let love and peace bring or slow them down. A feast of velvet, silks, hustle, and speed hovered into Olympic like knights of the real table. Genghis can and do. Prior to their arrival the atmosphere in the studio had been akin to a bunch of relatives waiting graveside for a priest to do the honours and give life some order and shine. Not too much different from the rehearsal in '63 that give birth to "I Wanna Be Your Man" and the Stones' first real hit. Those four years, full as they were with so much action and accomplishment, seemed like a lifetime.

The two Beatles didn't listen to the "We Love You" track for much longer than they'd spent running down "I Wanna Be Your Man" to my songless Stones just three and a half years before. They picked up the cans and sniffed each other out like two dogs in heat for the right part. The Stones' own attempts to harmonise were, for the most part, either "interesting" or the result of hard work, and often neither worked. As one who held that

Pet Sounds was the greatest album of all time, you can imagine how much that pained me.

John and Paul just glided in and transformed a runway into a launch pad. Their voices smiled at each other like brothers, while disarray and fractured arrangements fell away to reveal ... a hit. Once again the disorganised and discouraged Stones had been taken to school by their betters and were better for it. After all the bad karma we'd all endured, I'd just seen and heard a fuckin' miracle.

Perhaps my immersion in that other miracle at Monterey a month before had helped a bit to even the karmic score. I'd asked Lou Adler and John Phillips, "So what do I have to do?"

"Just don't get busted," cracked John - a friendly way of saying take care, brother. "Don't go back to England, just call and tell 'em where you are and where you'd better not be. Let Allen Krime go," he Shirley Ellis'd, and grinned.

Monterey Pop was moving fast and Lou was talking slowly.

"We've got Derek Taylor here, Paul McCartney there, you here. All we need to know is which acts do we need from England."

Only in L.A. I smiled.

"Easy. The Who and Jimi Hendrix."

Lou to John, "That's exactly what McCartney said."

And to me, "Who do we call?"

"I'll do the Who, Kit, and Chris."

I picked up the phone, "Kit, Andrew - remember that America that didn't want you? It's changed its mind. I'm calling from the Monterey Pop Festival offices, and we want the Who."

I had had trouble raising more than a few days' enthusiasm for the new San Francisco acts - all they meant to me was another reason to buy a new wardrobe. As the San Francisco sound took off on its trip, the once-again-late *Time* magazine called the city "a caldron of creative activity," hipper even than London. I didn't like the bands; to me they weren't stars. They were dirtier-than-thou, unoriginal, and totally fueled by drugs and liquor. I couldn't understand the attraction. I like my stars to behave like stars. Again the pot was calling the kettle beige. The reality was, I was out of touch, living in my 45 rpm world.

CHAPTER 32

let's spend some time together - dead on ed sullivan / sunday fright
at the london palladium - mick turns on the world, i am that world /
let the drug busts begin / blues of the world follow madame cleave
into the let's cleaver the stones brigade / the stones tour europe -
chaos be thy name / the revolution is not far behind, lads / chalk
stripes in chalk farm - a timely meeting with the remarkable mr.
harvey / slumfight at the olympic corral / last words on the life of
brian from pete t. and sheila / and so the sixties start to leave us in
their twenties / it feels like the evening of every day / there'll always
be an england but it's colombia i call home / faithfull to the road /
saying hallo to the rest of my life whilst saying goodbye to mother /
last tango in oxford and once again park lane removes the pain

The first Stones single of 1967, "Let's Spend the Night Together,"
was released simultaneously in the U.K. and U.S. on January 13.
Although the lyric was as fervently sexual as you could hope for
from the Stones, the sound was a real departure - no more of that
over-the-edge sonic onslaught, nothing spiky, just a real, heavily
blended, perfectly balanced mix of piano and guitar, with Charlie's drums leading the charge. Even the backing harmonies were
reasonably smooth.

The Stones flew to New York to promote the single on *The
Ed Sullivan Show*. Controversy flared over the sexual demands
laid down in the lyrics and the show's producers were insistent
that the chorus line of "Let's Spend the Night Together" be deleted,
even though the Stones had previously sung "I Just Wanna Make
Love to You" on the Sullivan show. Now, though, they were inviting the world to spend the night together from a much higher
profile and would suffer the consequences. Eighteen months
earlier we would have told Ed to go fuck himself and walked off
the show. But now it's show bizness and in this moment we're at
the top, we all have something to lose. A decision had to be made
on the spot - in public. I asked the band, "Do you wanna stay or
walk?" The next thing I knew, Mick was rolling his eyes and singing, "Let's spend some time together." Years later Jagger would
claim he didn't do it, that he'd mumbled his way through the line,
but it's clear from the tape that he sang the alterations.

To promote both the single and the album in the U.K., I agreed that for the first time the Stones would appear on *Sunday Night at the London Palladium* just one week later on January 22. Previously I had noisily refused to allow the Stones to appear on the show (even though the Beatles were regulars), considering this bastion of all-round entertainment, televised to ten million viewers, too "family-oriented and showbizzy." But the U.K. papers had picked up the Ed Sullivan story - the Stones had backed down, toeing the line of authority and bowing to the establishment who ruled the American TV networks.

Now Mick was a rebel with a pause. He had lost face in the Sullivan incident, perhaps as much with the other Stones as with the public. But now no one was asking him to change the lyrics to "Let's Spend the Night Together." Even the drug-addled "Connection" got the green light for national TV in Britain. So, huffing and puffing, our favourite little wolf cub looked around for another house to blow down and foolishly decided to insult millions of his fellow countrymen for whom *Sunday Night at the London Palladium* was akin to and more important than Sunday mass. In the twelve years the show had been on air, no one had ever refused to hop up on the huge revolving stage and wave to the audience, in a kind of acknowledgment that it was that audience who made them possible. That is, until Michael Philip Jagger got his nose up. I would have preferred he just kick me in the balls. With this act of defiance, Mick once again established himself as the bad boy of rock 'n' roll, but, unlike a drug bust or a sex scandal, the British public took this snub *personally*. Thus was created a backlash that still works against him today: Even though he is a Knight of the Realm, he is not the same as Sir Paul; his knighthood is a bit ratty, but what do you expect if you turn up at the palace in tennis shoes with lifts? Then again, that's all subjective hindsight; it's just as likely to have been part of a plan to test me where I would hurt, with the kill to come later, or do something divine and immaculate for the Rolling Stones.

At the end of January '67 I turned twenty-three. I had been the Rolling Stones' boy wonder manager and producer for a little less than four years, just about the same amount of time and at the same age that other public school alumni would have earned a baccalaureate degree. Just two weeks later, on February 12, Mick and Keith were busted and the honeymoon was well and truly

over for all of us. Now the bad boy pop star who until then would
not even wave to a nation of his fans was holding back tears as he
waved, still handcuffed, to cameramen outside the police station,
having been thrown into the back of a Black Maria instead of his
customary Rolls-Royce.

The first major pop star drug bust of many to follow happened - where else - at a Stones party. Keith Richards had been
designated Jesse James to Mick's Billy the Kid, so, tipped off by
the *News of the World*, the Sussex police swept down upon Keith's
Redlands country retreat in West Wittering. There they found
Mick, Marianne Faithfull, Robert Fraser, Michael Cooper, and
"Acid King" David Schneiderman (a.k.a. David Britton, perhaps
a *News of the World* mole) all present and in alleged possession of
heroin, amphetamines, and marijuana, although which illegal
drugs belonged to which partygoer would be sorted out later. It
was not lost on me that this disaster was yet another example of
Mick's taking himself far too seriously. When a Fleet Street muck-
raker mistook Brian Jones for Mick Jagger in a London bar and
published a gossipy item about the rocker's taste for underage
girls, Mick publicly threatened to sue. Apparently he had never
heard the adage, "Never sue anyone who buys printer's ink by
the barrel." Not to be fucked with, *News of the World* used their
long standing connections with law enforcement to teach the lad
a lesson he wouldn't soon forget.

"Drug Squad Raids Pop Stars' Party," sang the *News of the
World* merrily. I went missing in California as soon as I heard the
news, a block above the exclusive Bel Air hotel on Stone Canyon
Road, enjoying Lou Adler's hospitality.

Mick, Keith, and Robert Fraser were arrested and charged,
with a court date set for May 10. Against the Rolling Stones in
attendance, the charges were flimsy at best. Mick had gallantly
told the cops that Marianne's pep pills, legally obtained while in
Italy but technically illegal to bring into the U.K., were his own.
The evidence against Keith consisted of hashish residue stuck to
the bottom of an ashtray in his living room. The fuzz had allowed
George Harrison to drive away from Keith's house before they
went about the bust.

Anyway, rock opera lovers, you still don't shit where you
eat, and this childish gesture - "I'll sing but I refuse to wave" -

translated into "Who Do You Think You Are, Mick Jagger?" More than any drug bust, this set the mould for the triangle of Mick, the press, and the public that exists today.

They say that bad news comes in threes. On this same May 10 that Allen Klein and Les Perrin arranged for Mick, Keith, and Fraser to be remanded on £100 bail for a trial on June 22, Brian Jones got his. By tea-time that afternoon, Brian and his pal, Pretty Things percussionist Prince Stanislaus Klossowski de Rowla, had been hauled from Brian's Courtfield Road flat into Chelsea Police Station and charged with possession of hashish. The arresting officer was Detective Sergeant Norman Pilcher, who had dedicated his career of late to setting up every rock star foolish enough still to reside in London. In most of his cases, it was never entirely clear if the drugs allegedly found were in the musicians' possession before Pilcher arrived on the scene. Nevertheless, Pilcher ordered a large amount of Brian's property held for analysis on the assumption that a Rolling Stone had to have something to hide. After being released, the pair headed straight for Allen Klein at the Hilton. The night before, after his appearance in court, Keith Richards had left in his Bentley for Paris with Anita Pallenberg. The next day, May 11, Brian and the Prince, known as "Stash" to his intimates, were remanded on £250 bail at the Magistrates' Court on Great Marlborough Street for a June 2 trial.

A day later, several shoppers at the Chelsea Antique Market were somewhat surprised to spot Brian fingering the merchandise in an attempt to forget his troubles. He would have been either shopping or shoplifting.

After a while I returned to England quietly and remained silent over the bust. On the one hand, I was terrified that I would be busted myself, and on the other, I felt that the Stones had asked for it by their behaviour both on and off stage in the past few months. Allen Klein flew into London with none of the trepidation that I felt. He told the *Daily Mirror*, "Their problems are mine. I'm working my ass off to get them the best lawyers and will be in the front row of the trial every day." To escape the media glare that the drug bust had brought upon their lifestyle, Mick, Keith, and Brian were keen to get out of the country. They had fled to Morocco, via France and Spain, in late February and early March. It was on this trip that Anita Pallenberg had famously changed partners, dropping Brian, taking up Keith. Stigmatised by the drug bust and uncertain as to whether they were facing prison sentences, the Stones were still forced to uphold contractual agreements. On March 24 they had set off on a European tour, their last live gigs for the "foreseeable future." I had stayed behind, in the nursing home or in L.A. (I can't remember which - they were both home.)

At every airport they flew through, customs officials took great delight in haranguing the "drug group," methodically searching every last piece of luggage. The group stormed Sweden, Germany, Austria, Italy, and France, continuing on to Poland and Russia, where shortages of tickets led to huge riots and police with machine guns and tear gas were brought in to disperse the crowds. The Stones provoked displays of mass vandalism in Switzerland, Holland, and Greece. The group were relieved when the tour was finally complete; Mick informed the press he was "done with touring and would never tour America again."

I continued to find ways to kill the domestic and professional pain and escape the hell that seemed to be around every corner. ECT was considered effective treatment for severe clinical depression in the sixties. The side effects include devastating brain damage, in which memory, personality, intellect, ambition, persistence in life, and vigor could all be impaired. For a while the treatment seems to work, but only because the brain is so injured that the patient is too confused to know or remember what was troubling him. When the brain begins to recover, the problems usually return, and ECT is more likely to destroy than cure a person. The patient may become "docile and quiet" - manageable - but the treatment does not address the source or cause of problems. For the next thirty years, I would display classic after-effects of ECT.

Not content to zap my brain into submission, Dr. Mac experimented with an equally dangerous variety of pharmaceuticals. I'd spent many nights at Dr. Mac's house surrounded by antique tables overflowing with the latest anti-depressants, tranqs, and mood elevators - there seemed a new one every week. I had come to rely on McLoughlin. If the pills did not knock me out and there was nothing on TV, Eddie would drive doctor and patient in the Phantom V up the M1 to some Northern "fish and chips" nightclub where we laughed darkly at comics like Bob Monkhouse and Frankie Howard. Rumours about my mental condition spread fast, but in my mind I had nowhere to go save Mac's.

The sessions at Olympic Studios sounded the death knell. The Stones came in one night when they were out on bail. They were doing "We Love You" and it was a dog. My only contribution would be to invite John and Paul down to sing and to add prison doors clanking shut at the beginning and end of the record. Lennon said, "Set the mike up," and they put the falsetto voices on. It was magic, that, absolute magic. It rescued the record - no, it *made* the record. It was phenomenal. The single was scheduled for release after Mick and Keith had been sentenced. All were hoping they'd get off the drug charges but, if they didn't - prison doors clanking shut were simulated and pre-recorded in the studio. I organised a short film for "We Love You," ready for *Top of the Pops* just in case Mick, Keith, and/or Brian were behind bars. Filmed by Peter Whitehead, it was shot in a church in Essex and featured Marianne Faithfull, Keith, Brian, and Mick acting out the trial of Oscar Wilde. It was like a predecessor to that George Michael video that was shot in a toilet.

Now the winds of forever changes roared with satanic majesty. Calder and I had finished an early supper at the Terrazza. Eddie had arrived about 8:30, called Olympic, and come downstairs to give me word that no Stones were expected at Olympic before ten o'clock. We stood on the sidewalk outside La Trattoria Terrazza as Eddie cruised my Phantom V around and Tony's new driver Brian followed suit with Tony's brand new six-door chocolate-brown Mercedes, waiting on two pop tycoons who had no particular place to go. In a few years Tony's Merc would end up *chez* Pete Townshend and my Phantom V would first go to Lou Adler and was last seen with Sammy Davis Jr. Perhaps we should have bought the film rights and remade *The Yellow Rolls-Royce*. Brian was a pal of Eddie's and had joined Tony on a temp basis, not having completely left his globetrotting permanent employer, Laurence Harvey.

"Brian sez that Harvey's filming nights in Chalk Farm and would love for us to 'op by. How ' bout it?" sez Eddie.

How about it? Given the confused existence I'd been prescribed and subscribed to, along with the station in life I still presumed I assumed, I didn't react outwardly to Eddie's suggestion. But the boy who had thrilled to Harvey's performance as Johnny

Jackson in *Expresso Bongo* was as excited as a kid on Christmas Eve and hoped Larry wouldn't look askance at the troubled young adult who came to pay his respects.

"Tony, how about it?" said I.

"Sounds good to me. At least somebody's working," said a not-in-the-least-bit-bitter Calder.

"OK lads, back to show business." I managed a smile. We got into our cars and convoyed off to Chalk Farm and Mr. Harvey.

Our man was starring with Mia Farrow, at the time Mrs. Frank Sinatra, in the spy thriller *A Dandy in Aspic*, directed by Anthony Mann, with the yards behind the Chalk Farm Roundhouse passing for Berlin at night. Our cars passed Checkpoint Camden and cruised onto the set. Suddenly I felt a whole lot better. Action was in the very air. Lights, trailers, wind machines, crew, cameras, a few old Mercs with left-hand drives and German plates; all evidence of a bustling production but no Laurence Harvey in sight. In the movies of my mind, I'd been Laurence Harvey many times and would be again - from *Expresso Bongo* to *Room at the Top*, *The Manchurian Candidate*, even the bleached and bearded Lt. Crabb in *The Silent Enemy* - but the thought of us occupying the same set together made me nervous. Very nervous - and, as we've seen, those nerves of mine were not serving me very well at the time.

Brian filled us in on what was going down on the set.

"Anthony Mann is not at all well and it's rumoured that Mr. H. may take over. He's already directed some scenes when Mann was too sick to turn up for work." (Anthony Mann died a week later in Berlin and Laurence Harvey picked up the directing reins and completed the picture.)

Half an hour later Brian led us into Harvey's trailer. Brian's knock at the door was answered by the man himself. David Bowie has said how disappointing it is to meet one's idols, for they are always smaller in real life. Not a bit of it this time 'round. He was not taller than I'd thought, but as tall as he should be. His black shiny hair was long, elegantly disheveled, and fell into his face as he beckoned us into his trailer. His bright green eyes pulled you into his life. He wore a thin beige rollneck jumper, dark brown drainpipe trousers, uncuffed jeans-style, matching brown suede Chelsea boots, and a wafer-thin gold watch, perhaps Audemars Piguet. A heavy gold ID bracelet hung from a thin wrist as we shook hands and sat down.

"Welcome to a quiet mess. I do wish it were more organised here and there was something for you to see, but for the
moment we won't be doing a thing until eleven. How about a
little wine? Some Pouilly-Fuisse Louis Latour perhaps? Brian,
you know where everything is."

Brian did. We poured up and wished each other a nervous "Cheers!" as Larry Harvey picked up the flow.

"And all that trouble you've been having with the police ...
it's all a bit Oscar Wilde revisited to me. I've never had a problem
with the police or drugs. I'm my own drug, dear hearts ..."

I was right. Laurence Harvey was Britain's first pop star.
He smiled and segued into, "So you've got a Phantom V? Just be
careful how you use it. Too much parading up and down with
dolly birds, and jolly old Britain will soon stop wishing you well.
I should know; I had my first Roller in '54. Couldn't afford it, but
that's half the pleasure, isn't it?"

I laughed so hard, Harvey laughed back. He laughed so
well at himself.

"You mean you can't afford yours either? Good for you.
Back when I got mine everybody said that nobody under sixty
should have a Rolls, so I just had to have one. Now I'm running
around in a Mini Cooper and working nights." He checked his
watch and sighed, "Brian, please go out and find out what's
going on."

"Andrew, you come with me for a minute." He got up and
addressed himself to Eddie and Tony: "Have some more wine.
I'm just going to show Andrew my new toy."

With that Harvey patted me on the shoulder and guided me
out of the trailer. He wasn't all Mini Coopers yet. He led me to a
gleaming grey Roller, Ward-Mulliner model as I recall, opened
the back door, and we got in. He'd brought an opened bottle of
Pouilly-Fuisse, and two glasses emerged as if by magic from his
brown corduroy trench coat. He poured, lit a cigarette and placed
it in a holder, and continued from where he thought we'd left off.

"Andrew, I'm never one for putting my opinion where it
might not be wanted, except with an audience, of course. But I do
know a little about you and I do know that if there's something
you might admire about me it's mostly my dear departed Jimmy

Woolf. An actor doesn't usually give credit where it's due; in fact he usually tries to disown it and claim he was responsible for himself. Brian has told me of your interest and knowledge about Jimmy, and I'm happy to tell you that everything you could have thought about him is true. The man opened up his life to me and taught me everything I know, and were he still alive I can assure you he would not put up with me being stuck out here in Chalk Farm waiting to work. He showed me what I could be and how to accomplish being exactly that."

He paused, looked away, and let the rain sliding down the window in glistening drops catch its breath and his meaning.

"He gave me all this unselfishly and unsparingly, more than any woman could or has, because his love for what I could be was beyond all barriers. Jimmy died; he left me, which sort of makes my life simpler and harder at the very same time. I have his box of tricks, I know how to use them, and I'll never have the curse of thinking I can do without him. It sounds by all accounts as if you have given some of the same to your Mr. Jagger and his Rolling Stones."

I stumbled and muttered in the dark, "Yes, of course you are right. I gave ..."

I was losing it. Mr. Harvey did not mind.

"Of course you did. If you don't mind me saying so, the boy couldn't have learnt to be that camp on his own."

We laughed. Christ, the man did not fuck about. His voice was warm and honed.

"Look, Jimmy loved control, he loved the game and not much more. You'll get hurt. You can't fight a witch hunt. Sean Kenny has told me what's going on, and I've read the papers. Your lads are turning from boys into men; they're leaving home and there's nothing you'll be able to do about it. It's the nature of the beast. The artist has to rise and shine and dismiss his maker - it's as true as Adam and Eve ..."

We talked on for quite a while. I can't remember what I said. I think for a change I mostly listened. Finally, I'd got to the end of *Expresso Bongo* and had the ending, that the public was never meant to see, revealed by the master himself.

We got into our cars outside the set. Tony and I made plans for tomorrow as I prepared to go to Olympic.

"What did you two talk about?" Tony asked.

"I didn't talk too much, Tony. I listened."

Tony looked surprised.

"He gave me a message from Jimmy Woolf," I added.

"I hope it helped. See you tomorrow." And with that we were gone.

The nightly Olympic sessions had fallen into a pattern, and they were not recording sessions as I had known them. Charlie, Bill, Stu, and Glyn Johns would be the first to arrive and when Brian, Mick, and Keith *avec entourage* eventually drifted in and deigned to play, they didn't sound so much like a group as a waste of life force. Something had gotten hold of their hearts and Andrew's rallying cry to volume and commerce was not inviting anymore. The camaraderie of the road and of making it had been replaced by the been-there-done-that jaded air of courtiers plotting to usurp the throne. They communicated in ways I did not comprehend. Everybody was very clever, laughing at every laugh and nuance of left-unsaid conversation. Sentences seemed to be unnecessary - everybody was very cool, uncalm, and hardly collected, very detached and, with the exception of Stu, Bill, and Charlie, stoned.

Brian was now showing signs of his nightly abuses; Charles Laughton could have donned a blond wig and played him in drag. The costumes had gotten out of hand and, on any street he walked or stumbled, there was no need for a bolisha beacon, traffic light, or zebra. Keith was bringing up the rear, waiting for something to happen on Mick's front. Mick was all front, stoned as a matter of convenience and in control of the ball and hence, the game.

Whether they were playing everything badly, or just blues badly, it was all Ravi Shankar to me. When they experimented with mellotrons and keyboards and astounded themselves, I listened for and longed for your actual beefy, solid track. I listened for riffs and figures and got none. I don't even know if they knew they were torturing me by not coming up with any songs. For this while they were invincible, above and beyond songs. Occasionally they merged and got it together, but it would invariably fade into a false alarm. They appeared to be rejecting everything that they had become masters at, making recordings out of songs. They wanted, it would turn out, to be masters of their own art, and of course they would become it. But they -we - had not mastered communication. The drug busts, the nights in jail, the near misses, the every night of watching for the law - this was some "Welcome Home to England!" Checking our cars and houses to make sure we were clean was a hardship when we were not. The press had turned on them - us - since the Palladium fiasco in January, the busts had tripled in a few weeks. The world had turned on the Stones for making it and daring to come home for some time off. Fleet Street smiled that smile and raised its sodden elbows - "You've Had Your Time, Boys, Now Read Us and Weep." Mick Jagger, Keith Richards, Brian Jones, and the Rolling Stones were spelt the same, took the same headlines, but as of '67 we had no control over the copy, and that, regardless of who's been driving their car, has remained the same, with press reaction to Mick's various solo and sexual escapades as proof. In 1967 the Metropolitan Police took over our PR and Fleet Street lapped it up and pounced on the big beat *verbatim*, just as only a year before they had lapped up our PR whims and outrages. The Rolling Stones, and to a lesser extent the busted among the Beatles, were being taught a lesson in public - you can't get away with it anymore; we've decided who you are and the public agrees.

I looked at Glyn Johns sitting at the console saying nothing. Whether they played something or not, it didn't matter to Glyn - he was still getting his fifteen quid per hour. Glyn's meter was running, so he didn't mind. I did. They stayed away from the studio for five days on the trot. Later I found out that Mick and Keith had flown to New York to see Klein, to get his OK on what they had in mind for me.

One night Mick told me that Michael Cooper was doing the next sleeve, which meant that Gered Mankowitz was not. This meant that Mick was not listening to me anymore, perhaps a small blow in the scheme of things but a mortal one. Gered would have to fend for himself; Mick had found the most efficient way to stick the boot in. We'd recorded nothing in three weeks. The studio bill was £18,000 and here we were discussing the fucking sleeve. Cooper stood on one foot, hand on hip, watching Mick bring his pictures into the picture. I knew that Keith loved Michael Cooper and I knew that Mick needed him for the next chapter. Michael Cooper was not an extraordinary photographer. He was in the right place at the right time with a second-rate talent that sought to capture the Stones' next big run.

The youth run was over. Soon they would be street fightin' men. Brian hovered behind the Hammond organ, a blonde, wigged-out, acid-junkie version of Marlon Brando in *Apocalypse Now* - a bizarre, pale, grey deformity of candy-striped, Granny Takes a Trip, box-jacketed, double-breasted suit and off-white shirt. He picked his cold cobalt marble eyes off the ivory Hammond keyboard and seemed to marvel that it was my turn, too. Stu shrugged, buried his head in his arms at the grand, and let his "little three-chord wonders" start to nip at the heels of the kill. Bill chatted with an embarrassed Charlie and pretended neither he nor I was there. Keith studied his guitar, gnawed his fingers, and ignored me, in that order. Michael Cooper hovered like an angel of death, a smackstenched gargoyle of doom channelling Jagger over my moribundity, not daring to go for the kill or the body but eager for a wing to chew on. No matter. Knowing how little I cared for Cooper, Mick's insistence on his presence made his point all too clear. Cooper was Mick's weapon of choice - his Uzi. Talent had nowt to do with it; he wielded the photographer like a gun. Gered bit his lip and got paler by the ex-change. Even with all this going down I had time to notice Mick's attempt at middle-class fey hippiedom trying to pass for the real thing, all sixes and sevens in a mismatch of pale blues and greys that just made him paler as he envenomed. And here we were, nothing actually recorded, discussing the fucking sleeve.

After Redlands, Keith had started to get noticed. Before that it had been all Mick and Brian. Keith's turn started in the witness box, that rebel yell, that defiance, that's what started the folk hero ... the legend. And Keith was no dummy; he got the picture fast and liked it. It gave him that first real sense of self. He turned the drawbacks of the busts to his own advantage. The demonic bit, the knocking-at-death's-door charade - in the end he actually became all that - but thankfully also, so much more.

The police wanted me as well, of course. I was petrified of getting busted and basically stayed out of the country until it was all over, which in the end was what became the unmendable break between me and the Stones. Mick and Keith felt I'd abandoned them and decided I had.

In July we were three weeks into recording *Satanic Majesties*.

It had been a non-productive party, one that I had not organised, did not want to go to, and was getting disinvited from. I felt redundant. "2000 Light Years from Home" and "She's a Rainbow" would be all that would emerge from this psychedelic effort in trying to top the Beatles. The Stones may have got the clothes to go with the material but they did not have the material itself.

Ian Stewart, as usual, took matters down to the essential when he told *Melody Maker*: "There must have been some sort of bust up with Andrew because all of a sudden they really wanted to get rid of him. Before they started *Satanic Majesties* a lot of time had been booked at Olympic. Andrew was supposed to be there as a producer. And he was there only in a literal sense. We went in and played a lot of blues just as badly as we could. Andrew just walked out. At the time I didn't understand what was going on."

I left the studio one night in September, another night of nothing recorded, just a lot of drugfoolery and clever asides. I walked out of Olympic's front door. Nobody noticed, nobody said goodbye. I got into the Rolls and Eddie drove me away into the night. We stopped. Suddenly I had had it, and I got out of the car to make a call. What was I doing? It was as clear as day. I felt finally that I did not belong and was not wanted. I dialed Olympic and asked for Mick.

"Yes, Andrew."

"Mick, I'm not coming back. I think it's time we called it a day."

"Well, Andrew, if that is how you feel ..."

There, I thought, that didn't take long.

"Yes, Mick, that is how I feel," I said, feeling like that and shit.

"Well, Andrew." Was that Andrew to me? No, it was thrown by a pro to the control room stalls. "If you've made up your mind."

"Yes, I have. We don't need to do our laundry in public, so if you agree ..."

"I agree."

"We can sort it out between ourselves and Allen. Hopefully, Allen can work it out."

"Sounds good to me," said Mick. "So that's it then?"

"Yep, that's it, Mick."

"OK, Andrew, goodnight."

"Goodbye, Mick, have a good life."

I left the phone booth. I somehow felt better when it seemed things couldn't be worse. The silence had stopped and I heard the creak and sigh of relief from the phone booth door's hinges. I cringed, shrugged a don't-know-why, sort of sighed and got back in the car.

Vinny Fusco said it best: "The ultimate destiny of the manager who breaks the act is to get blown off; it's almost irrevocable. Unless the artist is going to continue to grow and needs a grower, now anyone can do the job for a lot less money. Get a fucking bookkeeper." Our friend Mick Jagger remains one of the greatest performers of any century and has also proven himself to be more than a great bookkeeper. Looking back, I don't think in that time, that situation, that it could have been handled any other way.

PR doyen Les Perrin would deliver the official statement: "The Stones have parted from their recording manager because the band have taken over more and more of the production of their own music. Andrew Oldham no longer has any connection whatsoever with the Rolling Stones."

Just in case that wasn't clear or dismissive enough, Mick Jagger added this in NME: "I felt we were doing practically everything ourselves anyway. And we just didn't think along the same lines. But I don't want to have a go at Andrew. Allen Klein is just a financial scene. We'll really be managing ourselves. We'll be producing our own records too."

In what was the most agonising moment of my life to date, I tried to appear strong and fair. I told NME: "Everything the Stones have done has been natural. They were not puppets, they were people. Whatever else is said about them they were as close to professional as any five artists can get. We split because we had no need of each other anymore. As people we went in different directions. There was no definite decision. It was just over. We just weren't on the same wavelength anymore. We'd gone as far as we could together. It was time to move on."

Who the fuck was I kidding? I can still feel the shame that twisted my mouth into a grimace as my brain throbbed with pain. I was killing myself, the Stones were helping me along, and Allen Klein was banking the dominoes as he watched them fall. The Rolling Stones had become a game I could not win under any circumstances. Had I not left and thus endured a psychological pain akin to death, I might have carried on and literally died. In the end, they were all, save Brian, stronger than I: Bill, Charlie, and Ian because the Rolling Stones was their job and it did not consume them. Mick and Keith because, for a while, despite the temporary musical lapses and the very expensive mistake they make in trusting Allen Klein, all the excesses, all the egotism, all the cruelty that they inflicted upon me and Brian, just made them stronger. The life blood they drained from others gave them powers no other rock stars had ever known. No one should be surprised that as the "World's Greatest Rock 'n' Roll Band," they have outlived everyone. The Beatles, Led Zeppelin, and the Who are now history. The Stones, although no one much cares except those who pay exorbitant amounts to hear them perform, continue to make history.

For decades to come the Stones would retain their gift for performance and be richly rewarded therefrom. For a while Jimmy Miller was able to steer them in the studio toward some great singles and arguably better albums, until, he too, became another burnt offering on the altar of the band's self-importance. By the mid-seventies they had lost their ability to communicate in any meaningful way with the huge global audience that they and the Beatles had created. They were universally knocked by a new generation of musicians, born in the fifties, who spared no pains to imitate the Stones but went out of their way to put them down.

As years went passing by, Mick would go out of his way to find opportunities to perform without the Stones. He memorialised the group's great influence, Solomon Burke, in a solo turn at the 2011 Grammy Awards and turned in a rather forgettable appearance at the fortieth anniversary of *Rolling Stone* magazine at Madison Square Garden. He takes his knighthood seriously and without a hint of irony.

Meanwhile, back in September 1967, with both of my marriages on the rocks, Eddie Reed was looking very good. Though nominally only my driver, he was proving to be a lifesaving friend, whose steady hand on the wheel helped me hold the road.

"Where to, Andrew?" said Eddie.

"I don't know, Eddie ... just drive around."

"What happened in there, if you don't mind me asking?"

Eddie enquired as he squired the Rolls toward the Hammersmith Bridge.

"Is it over?" He helped me along.

"Yes, Eddie, it's over."

"Well, it may not feel so at this very moment, but in my opinion it's for the best."

"Yes, Eddie."

"C'mon, Andrew, you're better out of that mess."

We drove across the bridge around Hammersmith and back over, down past Olympic, and headed for Barnes. The eerily quiet roads gave our equally dark thoughts all the space they needed. When we came off the M4, turned left, and passed the Station Hotel in Richmond, I had to laugh as we flew by where it had all started. Eddie heard only the laughter but not the pain.

"That's better, Andrew ... so what happens now?"

"How do you mean?" I replied, feeling all too much like a Roy Orbison ballad.

"You know, you and the Stones ..."

"I told Mick I'd ask Allen to sort it out."

"Well, Allen'll be happy. He's been waiting for that from the start." Eddie's street smarts were often sharper than mine.

"We don't know that, Eddie, maybe, maybe not. It doesn't matter now, it's easier for me if Allen sorts it out."

We wandered around Richmond and cruised the M4 for a while with no particular place to go.

"You ready to go home, Andrew?" asked Eddie as in he was.

"Not really, but it's close to three and I really have nowhere else to go."

"What are you going to tell Sheila?"

"That's a problem - I don't know, maybe nothing."

"You've got to let her know."

"I wouldn't know what to tell her. 'Hallo, dear! I'm home and, oh, by the way, I just left the Stones - how was your day?'"

"Yeah, I see what you mean," concurred Eddie as he twisted the wheel another degree closer to home.

I dreaded facing Sheila. There was no one with whom I would rather have spent my first few hours "after the Stones" than Eddie. In the privacy and solitude of "our" Rolls, we shared a peace I wasn't likely to find at home. But at the moment, swathed in its leather and mahogany luxury, my prized possession felt very much like a hearse.

****

The Stones, or rather Mick and Keith, may have felt they had solved their "Andrew problem," but Brian presented a much trickier challenge. In Brian's drug-addled mind he not only continued to be a Rolling Stone, he was the *original* Rolling Stone. Although Brian somehow knew that Mick wouldn't mind at all if he stepped in front of a bus, and had never gotten over Keith's purported theft of Anita, without the Stones he was truly a nowhere man. Yet Brian was too dangerous for Mick and Keith to simply ignore or torture. As long as he was a target for every narc in the British police force, all five Rolling Stones were vulnerable.

There was a more philosophical void that some felt was deepened by my departure. Pete Townshend, for whom rock 'n' roll was a religion before he discovered Meher Baba, observed: "Andrew understood that there was a spiritual potential to pop music that had no relevance whatsoever to someone like Keith. I always believed the Stones were one of the few bands that could aspire to something greater and more inspiring than a number one record but at the end of the day, they were all journeymen, brilliant at their craft in their own way, but still just journeymen."

Townshend witnessed the slow deterioration of Brian Jones with a heavy heart:

> We did the *Rock and Roll Circus* with the Stones and it seemed to me that Brian was dying before our eyes. I hoped he'd already decided to leave the band because by then I could see that soon he wouldn't have a choice. I'd spent time with Brian and Anita, whom I'd always thought of as Brian's girlfriend, and now suddenly she was with Keith. Brian was just a wreck. He couldn't play and was terrible when he tried. I took his pain very personally; he'd always been incredibly nice to me, much nicer than any of the other Stones, and he was in just such bad shape. They kept taking him out and when he returned he'd be a little better because maybe he'd had a shot of cortisone or something.

And what made it worse was that Mick was just spec-
tacular; even though the band overall weren't up to their
normal standard, Mick never lost concentration for a second.
Of course, he was the complete opposite of Brian and you
got a sense that if Brian were dying the rest of them weren't
going to lift a finger to help him. I know it's a terrible thing
to say, but they were so cold, they made me feel responsible because Brian was my friend and he was so alone.

Though Sheila suffered from her own deficit of compassion, particularly at that time when she was so exasperated by our change
of circumstances, she, too, was touched by Brian's disintegration:
"Brian came around to the house toward the end, shortly before
he died," she recalls. "He was trying to smoke a cigarette and
couldn't find his face. I think Allen had sent him round hoping
that Andrew could find some way of helping him but we didn't
know what to do with him. What he needed was good professional
care. Interventions and clinics were unknown then. There weren't
that many people taking drugs in those days that were in the
public eye."
     To hear Sheila tell it, I was giving Brian a run for his money:
"Andrew would go into these psychotic rages. He'd injured himself; there was blood all over the house," she said with her customary flare for the melodramatic:

> He tried to kill me with hammers and anything else he
> could lay his hands on. Of course, he was manic depres-
> sive and the shock treatments were making him much
> much worse. One day I looked through the window and
> saw him keep getting into the Rolls and then getting out
> of it again. He had a towel wrapped around his arm and
> then he ran away and jumped on a bus.
>   I didn't hear from him for a couple of days and then I
> finally got it out of Eddie that he had gone to a nursing
> home in Highgate where nuns were tending to him. But
> the psychological problems had been going on for a long
> time; they just got worse after the split with the Stones. Like
> most performers he didn't know what to do with himself
> when he wasn't in the studio or on the road, so he'd sink

into depression. Of course he wasn't eating or sleeping well, so a lot of the suffering he brought on himself.

You can't be in character 24/7, and I think it got harder and harder for him to switch it on and off. The off bit was probably the real Andrew. He can be quite sentimental and that was a very private, vulnerable, and tender part of him. It scared him that others might see that and take advantage. And of course, nobody knew Andrew better than Mick, so once things went bad between them, Mick knew just how to get to Andrew. All of his closest relationships fell apart at the same time.

In the aftermath of my departure from the Stones, I busied myself with my own independent label, Immediate Records, found some solace in the Small Faces, whom I'd taken over from Don Arden, and tried to regain a sanity that those close to me weren't sure I'd ever entirely had to begin with. Knowing well ahead of the event how Brian's stretch with the Stones would end, I left the details to time and fate, and appreciated that one benefit of my estrangement was that, when the end came, it would not be my hands dripping with Brian's spiritual and mental blood.

Finally, on June 9, 1969, professional bearer of ill tidings Leslie Perrin issued a joint press release from Mick Jagger and Brian Jones formally announcing that Brian was no longer a Rolling Stone. The day before, Mick, Keith, and Charlie had visited Brian to inform him that, since he would be unable to obtain a work permit to perform in the U.S., due to his drug busts, the band had no choice but to replace him. Apparently even the other "original" Rolling Stone, Brian's closest friend in the band, Ian Stewart, supported dropping Brian. So, it's fair to say that, however much Mick and Keith helped Brian's self-destruction along, it was by his own hand, so to speak, that his life as a Stone was taken.

The Glimmer Twins, now fully back in control of their organisation, at least musically, could afford to be generous and allowed Brian the opportunity to save what was left of his face in Les's statement: "I no longer see eye-to-eye with the others over the discs we are cutting. The work of Mick and Keith has progressed at a tangent at least to my way of thinking." Jagger added, both truthfully and ironically: "Brian wants to play music that is more his own rather than always playing ours. We have parted on the best of terms."

The remaining Stones were confident that their new guitarist, twenty-year-old Mick Taylor, would do as he was told and let them get on with it. That Taylor was both an ingenue and prodigiously talented would enable the Stones to make up for the time they'd lost waiting for Brian to go away. So it was that "Honky Tonk Women," the first track that Taylor played on, became the Stones' first number one in America since "Ruby Tuesday," almost three years earlier.

Though a physical wreck, overweight and bloated as he was, Brian seemed to have gotten a second wind emotionally after his fate was finally sealed. He had seemed to handle his break from the Stones in a remarkably sober and practical manner, at least on the surface. Even I had to admit that he seemed to have taken a turn for the better and had admired his newfound aplomb from my distance. I hoped that this surface had some substance and that he intended to use the split for positive change and not abuse himself, or others, any further.

In the first few weeks after the split, Brian's plans were extensively discussed in both the music and popular press, usually expressing the hope that he would somehow pull it out. The iconic British bluesman, Alexis Korner, had taken Brian under his caring wing and Creedence Clearwater Revival, the American blues-based band enjoying much chart success at the time, was declared a model for the future. Brian presumably longed for chart hits of his own; both his standard of living and his ego required them. There would be no going back to clubs and pubs.

Brian may well have been having a mental revival of sorts that helped buoy him against the trauma of "deciding to leave the Stones," but a physical revival had been out of the question for a long time. Then, one balmy summer night, less than a month after the Stones' visit of gloom, he was dead at the bottom of his swimming pool, though whether by drowning, overdose, or murder has never been fully settled. At the coroner's inquest, his asthma, the possibility of an epileptic fit, and his drug and alcohol intake were each examined as to the part they may have played in his death. The verdict was "death by misadventure," a term of art that seems both accurate and poetic in these circumstances. The autopsy revealed pleurisy, an enlarged heart, and a diseased liver, enough to have proven fatal - the lot of a much older man.

A mere two days after his death the Stones and their new protégé performed at a free concert in London's Hyde Park. The event had been planned weeks before. Mick had been feeling a bit behind the "love-in" curve and wanted to prove that the Stones were just as relevant as newer bands like the Jefferson Airplane and the Grateful Dead, who routinely gave free concerts in the States. But the timing of the show helped to make the Stones bigger than ever. Rather disingenuously dedicating the concert to Brian's memory, Jagger was simultaneously at his sexiest and his most pretentious, a template that he hasn't seen fit to revise in nearly fifty years.

The swimming pool was an incidental, thrown in for Brian's closing night, as Brian had, for a fatal length of time, been drowning under the influence of life. One of the sad ironies of entertainment and life in the public eye is that so many who are highly esteemed in the fields of artistic endeavour suffer from and are cripplingly motivated by low self-esteem.

In the final analysis, Brian could not live without stardom, yet he was so ill-equipped to handle it. Without Keith's true passion for the music or Mick's outsized self-confidence, Brian remained a brat whose neediness could never be satisfied. Brian always had an agenda; yet he was unwilling or unable to support the alternate agendas of those he depended upon. Mick, Keith, and I quickly tired of taking Brian the least bit seriously, and one hopes that Ian Stewart, the pianist and road manager who was famously attributed to me as my first casualty, did not believe Brian when he was told he would be "taken care of."

The truth is I had no emotional reaction at all to the news of Brian's death. In life it had been useless to empathise with Brian's many problems; he was animal enough to take empathy for weakness and use it against one. Whatever there was behind those glassy brown eyes could have provided a model for Anne Rice, a confirmation of evil for David Mamet, or a warning for Truman Capote. Having been granted nine lives, Brian had made the mistake of assuming he had ten.

The film director Peter Whitehead conducted a series of one-on-one interviews with the individual Rolling Stones whilst shooting the "documentary" that I had commissioned for the Ireland tour in September 1965, *Charlie is My Darling*. The Charlie referred to is, of course, not the Bonnie Prince but Mr. Watts. The film had revealed Charlie Watts to be the only one of the five with any degree of naturalness, that is, authenticity, before the camera. As the *vérité* style demanded, Charlie alone was un-self-conscious and true to himself. Then again he never thought as much of himself as he did the great jazz drummer, Art Blakey.

In the naturalness sweeps, Bill Wyman came in second, much to the surprise of my effete elitism, with Mick, Keith, and Brian tying and dying in last place. Bill managed to come across as human if predictable. I had spent months worrying and wondering how I could get the Stones onto the next level that the Beatles had risen to with *A Hard Day's Night* and *Help!* Now I had my answer and it wasn't what I had hoped for. (Yet, a half-century later, Keith landed on the red carpet as part of the franchise headed by the actor whom, when they first met, Keith had assumed was his son's drug dealer.) However secure the Rolling Stones might be as the world's second most popular music group, they were never going to be movie stars. I accepted this with a heavy heart in 1965; it's something Mick refuses to accept all these decades later. Well, I guess he's earned the right to his delusions.

Brian never.

One of Brian's less fortunate delusions was that he fancied himself an intellectual. In *Charlie is My Darling*, Brian was in full intellectual mode, spinning his claim to be not only the vision but the brains behind the Stones. He didn't communicate with his interviewer, nor did he listen. In the editing room, Brian's footage kept Peter and me in hysterics as we kept rewinding and playing back the film, hardly believing with our own ears the nonsense that Brian was piously pitching.

"Peter," I'd said, "it's just words; he's not actually saying anything."

Peter thought for a moment and then replied, "Whilst the rest beg off from being asked to take themselves seriously, that's all poor Brian does."

The saddest part was Brian's premonition that he'd not live to see his twenty-eighth birthday. On the screen at age twenty-three, he was for once on the road to being right.

A year later, in 1966, the Stones had recorded a Christmas spot for Radio London, much in the same vein that the Beatles had done for their fan club several years running. Though lacking the knack for comedy and warmth of the Fab Four, for the most part the spot was hilarious with a lot of giggling that sounded more like schoolchildren than the world's most disgraceful rock stars. Many years later, in the eighties, I was working with the outtakes from that spot to create a commercial for ABKCO's CD re-release of *Big Hits (High Tide and Green Grass)*. Then it struck me when I once again heard Brian's voice from beyond the grave how dark and disconnected it was in contrast to the joy and mirth of his bandmates. I didn't want to mix it into the voices of Mick, Keith, Charlie, and Bill, and I found I couldn't. It didn't belong.

We'll let one of Brian's last and only friends, Pete Townshend, have the last word. The day he heard the news (oh boy) Pete felt compelled to write a song. He called it "A Normal Day for Brian, a Man Who Died Every Day."

> "I used to play my guitar as a kid
> wishing that I could be like him
> But today I changed my mind
> I decided that I don't want to die
> But it was a normal day for Brian
> Rock and Roll's that way
> It was a normal day for Brian
> A man who died every day"

****

In the spring of 1995, I took back my life and began to clear my mind, my body, and my universe. After some sixteen years of this effort, I have made my life anew and often find it dazzling despite, or perhaps because of, its sobriety. Being straight in and of itself does not plug all the holes in my soul, and occasionally, like all those who were once in love, I miss the honeymoon that is long gone. But my life and my environment are generally in harmony, and I don't miss the clashes with reality that once passed for thrills.

For some time now my daily existence has followed a pattern of routine that I would scarcely have recognised or desired in my youth, at least when I am not travelling and at home in Bogotá.

I arise at 5:00 a.m. and walk our two dogs around the quiet dark streets, from which they came before they found us. Upon returning home, I descend to my second-floor office and begin to sort through the day's e-mails, tweets, and blogs. The Internet and my keyboard skills, such as they are, have greatly mitigated the isolation I felt when I first moved to Colombia in the late eighties, or should I say, would have felt had I not been so stoned for the first few years.

The walls of my study are lined with books and music, often in duplicate, since at one time I was paranoid about the survival of the printed word and so acquired extra copies of my favourites. Were Graham Greene here in 3D glasses he would feel right at home. The view to the south is inviting: The green mountains that hold Bogotá in their embrace contrast with red brick apartment blocks, long and winding highways throbbing with life in the fast lane, university campuses, and even farther south, the densely industrial and steepled downtown of the city. From my perch it is easy to forget how dangerous Bogotá below can be, but I have only to turn on CNN to appreciate that the rest of the world is catching up.

One day in 2000 I was enjoying the view while waiting for inspiration to return when our maid called me to the phone. "Don Andrew ... un Engleesh," she informed me, neglecting to tell me who was calling either out of respect for my privacy or simple indifference. These days, household help are not so much servants as associates whose self-respect one must take pains to preserve, whatever their limitations. This particular member of our ménage does not do toilets, although performing the chore myself provides a certain Zenlike chop-wood-carry-water satisfaction.

The unbroken "Engleesh" voice on the other end of the phone belongs to Marianne Faithfull, who no doubt is as surprised to be calling me as I am to be called by her. For, in the over forty years we have known each other, we have only spoken on the phone perhaps a dozen times. I am pleased to be reminded how well her cultivated accent carries over the wire. She is hoping I will travel to New York in September to attend one of her infrequent concerts and I am happy to comply. It's been too long since we last saw each other; it is simply a matter of what to pack.

Marianne's rare Manhattan appearance is at the Sylvia and Danny Kaye Playhouse within Hunter College's midtown campus. She keeps us waiting for an interminable thirty minutes until even the Sapphic couples who had come to celebrate one of their idols begin to boo their discontent in a disconcerting alto unison. Later she rationalises her procrastination thus: Having given her very best at the previous evening's show, she worries that she might not have anything left to give tonight's audience but her love. Apparently the thought of having to return our money inspires her, so we are belatedly treated to her hit, "Broken English," albeit even more hoarsely than we remember.

For a woman of a certain age, Marianne's fashion sense is, to put it mildly, idiosyncratic. She has adopted a sort of Dale Evans cowgirl look by way of Vivienne Westwood with a knowing nod to Trigger. Her breasts remain her greatest physical asset, bringing to mind the American frat-boy slang term, "headlights." Her hair is an electrifying shade of white and she constantly calls our attention to it by running her hands through it, sometimes nervously, sometimes lovingly. Withal, she is attractive, glowing, vital; one understands her appeal to younger women seeking an identity that does not require a male for validation.

She is a bit silly but that is part of her charm. She retains much of what I found stunning about her as a very young girl. She wears her wounds like medals and survival shines in her eyes. She aerobicises Leonard Cohen, soothes us with Roger Waters, and, sharing her toy chest with us, pulls out a Harry Nilsson nevergreen. The audience responds most enthusiastically to the songs from her late seventies triumphant-return-from-the-abyss. "Why D'Ya Do It?" and "The Ballad of Lucy Jordan" more than make up for her dallying backstage. She casually smokes Marlboros during the solos, her sore throat apparently no longer an impediment to air pollution. While she's at it, the roadie brings her a spot of tea and she beams at him as if he were a dealer giving samples. Despite her narrow range of facial expressions, all four of them are endearing. There are "Panic," "More Panic," "God, I'm Getting Away With It," and finally, "I Am Good, Aren't I?" She is not exactly graceful on stage; sometimes we worry that she is working without a net, so clumsily does she make her way from one spot to another. Yet there are times when once fancies one would enjoy a dance with her, should the unlikely occasion arise.

She sits smartly on her summer of '65 hit, "Come and Stay with Me," and gives me the moment I came for as she sails dreamily into "As Tears Go By." Now even I have forgiven her for keeping us waiting. While Marianne's faithful share a distressing preference for sensible walking shoes, she encourages them to believe that good can come of failed suicide attempts and that recreational drugs, provided they are pharmaceutical grade, are a valuable substitute for various everyday relationships that one might be missing from one's life at the moment. They seem to think she wrote "Working Class Hero," so well does she wear Lennon's primal classic.

Unfortunately, it is not always thus. Some time later I venture out to New York's deco shrine high atop Rockefeller Center to hear her in a cabaret setting. She is joined in the Rainbow Room by Darlene "He's a Rebel" Love and Merry "Gimme Shelter" Clayton, two magnificent voices each given a few seconds on record that they can never again hope to equal. Though their performances in the distant past are transcendent, they don't amount to even the fifteen minutes that Warhol promised. Let it suffice to say that the third performer in this trio, Marianne Faithfull, is not a soul singer, though at her best she can be soulful. As it happens, tonight they would be trounced by Take That or almost any glee club worth their uniforms. Three Divas do not an evening equal to the Three Tenors make. You haven't died until you have heard these three ruin Brian Wilson's "In My Room."

When Marianne was interviewed for British TV on the significance of Brian Epstein and asserted that Brian was the only manager of the sixties that counted, I forgave her. She was only telling her audience what they wanted to hear. Many times she had done as much for me. Despite her many years' experience she is no more a musician than Mick Jagger. She tends to take young peoples' interest in her as a confirmation of her talent rather than as fascination with her life itself.

Marianne's latest recording was made in Louisiana, where most white people I have known go for no good reason. New Orleans is not a natural setting for Marianne, despite her occasional resemblance to Blanche DuBois. Known once as a notorious lover, she came into her own as a fighter, and her protégés such as Robbie Williams can learn much from her about surviving life in the public eye. But the clock is winding down on Brigitte Bardot, Juliette Greco, and indeed on "La Motocyclette" (Rebecca naked under leather!) who once looked so good riding behind Alain Delon.

Mick and Keith should do the decent thing and pension her off.

****

In 2002, Celia had had Alzheimer's for twenty years. We first spotted her condition when, in 1982, she journeyed alone from her home in Australia to New York City for her grandson Max's christening. Once in New York she became disoriented and confused. She got lost and, of course, I got impatient. We realised that we could not chance her making her New York / Los Angeles connecting flight back to Sydney, so I flew back with her as far as L.A., squeezing in a visit to a dealer I knew in Venice. My mother found him charming.

Under the circumstances, at LAX the airline allowed me to escort my mother onto the plane to see her seated safely and say goodbye. She had been happy, slightly lost in her own world when she turned around at me and looked me straight in the eyes and said, "You know I love you, I always have." That did me in. We two seemingly cold Aquarians did not speak like that to each other. If my mother had ever said that to me before I had blown it away.

A few years later, while her devoted husband, my medical stepfather Janez, was halfway around the world in Ethiopia auditioning for a job at a hospital there, Celia wandered away from her home in Brisbane on an unintentional "walkabout." Fortunately she was taken in by a local hospice, which called me in New York. A surfeit of cocaine and a deficiency of sleep combined to make this bad news even more overwhelming. I panicked with the realisation that I could not travel without cocaine nor could I risk travelling with it. Habits were high, cash-flow low.

Despite my preoccupation with my own concerns, I felt obliged to ask, "Should I come to Australia?"

"Only if it helps *you*," the hospice gentleman replied, I fancy somewhat dryly if pragmatically.

Thus I was let off the hook for the time being, knowing I would have to confront the reality of Celia's deterioration sooner or later.

So, twenty years on, and straight, I travelled from Bogotá to Celia's home in Oxford for what would likely be the last time.

Distance alone could not explain the many years that had passed between our visits. The last time we had spent any time together was in the short while that I lived at home after I left school. There was more between us than the usual rebellion of a teenage boy against parental authority; our values were proving to be diametrically opposed and Celia could never have been described as a live-and-let-live type. I was too thin-skinned to take what was worthwhile in her criticism and shrug off the rest. As the years went by and getting high became job number one, Celia remained the very definition of buzz-kill and if I could possibly avoid her, I did.

Now in her eighties and infirm beyond the ravages of Alzheimer's, Celia is no longer the iron lady I lived with as a child. The expert care she has received from her doctor husband has been a mixed blessing; while most patients are sedated to the point of coma, usually to the relief of their near and dear ones, Celia's life has been professionally prolonged. Her eyes seem to me to plead, "How much more of this do I have to take?"

I need to leave her bedside frequently for sanity breaks in the lobby where I phone Esther to boost my morale. I begin to understand the release afforded by deathbed conversions, but I know a last-minute embrace of faith is not for Celia. The three weeks I spend in Oxford are all the harder for the strain they put on my commitment to sobriety. Every wine bottle seems to have my name on it in the same small print used to designate alcohol content. Every shelf in the high street chemist offers its own cocktail of pain relief.

Whether my mother knew me or not is neither here nor there; I think she approved of whomever was in the room. Whether she recognised me as from her womb or merely a friend, who can say, Alzheimer's being so essentially mysterious. When the one little wire that allows the brain to make sense of a senseless reality has burned out, might not the mind still scream silently to be understood? If one is forced to choose, then the Buddhist concept that suffering, old age, and death are but three of the Four Sufferings that all, even Siddhartha himself, must endure, surely trumps the Christian notion that God is getting back at us for our sins. But now Celia is past philosophy. Abstractions never held much charm for her to begin with.

I lean over her bed and cradle her head. Her thinning hair reveals the scars of her facelifts on her eggshell fragile skull. Celia is past the point of being wounded by her own vanity. The compassion with which my calls to Esther have infused me overcomes my revulsion. I'm coined up and have plenty of speaking time left for my mum.

"Celia," says I, "I came here to smother you with love, but if there is any way you can tell me what you want ... if you could just wink three times, blink, or squeeze my hand, please know if you give me the sign I will happily smother you with a pillow."

My mother's eyes fixed mine with what I hoped was an expression of appreciation if not comprehension.

Then it was time to leave Oxford and return home. I made my way to the M40 in great haste. I had not driven in the U.K. for many years, could not see the signs telling me how fast or slow I could go, and had forgotten that now they had cameras above the road.

Two months later seven speeding tickets, all accumulated within a mere ninety minutes, had tracked me down in Colombia. Leaving home again ...

I got to London, ditched the car and walked down Park Lane, hoping to disinfect myself of sadness in the good day sunshine of its affluence. The bright brisk air was indeed bracing and I was feeling a bit better when I stepped into the Mini Cooper showroom to pick up a few toys for Esther's ride. Despite myself, I found myself in conversation with a friendly Yank to whom I soon confided my sorrow.

"You sound like you could do with some music," my fellow Mini fan advised. It seems our respective careers in music allow us the freedom to be lolling around a Park Lane auto showroom while most other fellows are at their desks or at least their cell phones.

Nevertheless I dreaded the invitation I knew was coming. It would take some very good music indeed for me to venture out that particular evening.

"There's a concert tonight in Hammersmith to benefit the landmine effort. I manage one of the acts appearing, John Prine. He'll be there with Elvis Costello, Emmylou Harris, and a few others. You should come on down. What's your name?"

"Andrew Loog Oldham."

"No shit!"

At the box office of the Apollo Hammersmith there is a ticket waiting for "No Shit!" left by my recent guardian angel, the thoughtful Al Bunetta. As Prine, Costello, and Harris, joined by Nanci Griffith and Steve Earle, lend their voices in a kind of prayer for peace, I curl up in the stalls and bathe in the purity of the cause, the music, and, most of all, the songs. Before the concert is over I have taken a journey through my life and found it good. Thanks to the healing power of song, I am once more time able to start anew.

I had followed the music and could breathe again ...

www.ingramcontent.com/pod-product-compliance
Lightning Source LLC
Chambersburg PA
CBHW060037100426
42742CB00014B/2616